Praise for

A TICKET TO THE CIRCUS

"In this blazingly alive memoir of her thirty-two years with the late Norman Mailer, sixth wife Norris Church Mailer proves herself every bit as fascinating as her illustrious mate. Her narrative glitters with famous faces and events, from Bob Dylan and Bill Clinton (whom she dated) to the 1975 Ali fight in the Philippines. . . . 'I'll never write about you. Nobody would believe it,' Norris often told him. You'll be glad she did."

—*People* (four stars)

"Norris Church Mailer's reminiscence, *A Ticket to the Circus,* still manages to add a fat new sheaf to the public dossier on her late husband, Norman Mailer, and tells an involving coming-of-age story to boot. . . . She shows exactly what type of woman could tolerate and at least partly subdue such a king-size corkscrew of a man. The book will be of interest to anyone who works in a university marriage lab. It also shows that Norman wasn't the only talented raconteur in the family."

—*The New York Times Book Review*

"Captivating."

—*Booklist*

"Norris Church Mailer's surprisingly honest, graceful and forthright memoir of life with Norman as his sixth and final wife."

—*The Washington Times*

"Norris offers a straightforward account of her life with her Pulitzer Prize–winning husband that is remarkably devoid of bitterness, blame, or self-aggrandizement. . . . She presents the details of her relationship with a humble but headstrong tone that somehow disassembles our preconceptions about the sort of statuesque redheaded southern girl who clamors to meet famous married authors."

—*Bookforum*

"*A Ticket to the Circus* is a remarkable memoir—blunt, funny, extraordinarily candid and self-aware, as deeply moving as it is wonderfully entertaining. Above all, it is a memorable double portrait of two very unusual people, a couple for whom the term *meant for each other* is wholly appropriate."

—Joyce Carol Oates

"*A Ticket to the Circus* is a brave memoir. Norris Church Mailer writes with grace, clarity, and verve. She achieves what a good memoirist must: believability. Norman Mailer would be proud."

—Douglas Brinkley

"Entertaining . . . *A Ticket to the Circus* is not a tell-all memoir; it's a tell-enough memoir. It's Ms. Mailer's own plucky and sometimes sentimental autobiography. . . . [A] gracious memoir."

—*The New York Times*

"If you want to be both edified and amused, you really can't do better than *A Ticket to the Circus*. The title is apt."

—*The Washington Post*

"[*A Ticket to the Circus* is] a wild ride. . . . In her entertaining, well-composed memoir, she reveals what it was like for a smart, gutsy woman to subsume herself to a legendary jerk who was as incorrigible and irresistible in life as he was in his art. . . . Lovely and inspiring."

—*The Miami Herald*

"A memoir that's candid and poignant, filled with joy and humor, sex and heartbreak."

—*USA Today*

ALSO BY NORRIS CHURCH MAILER

Windchill Summer

Cheap Diamonds

A Ticket to the Circus

10

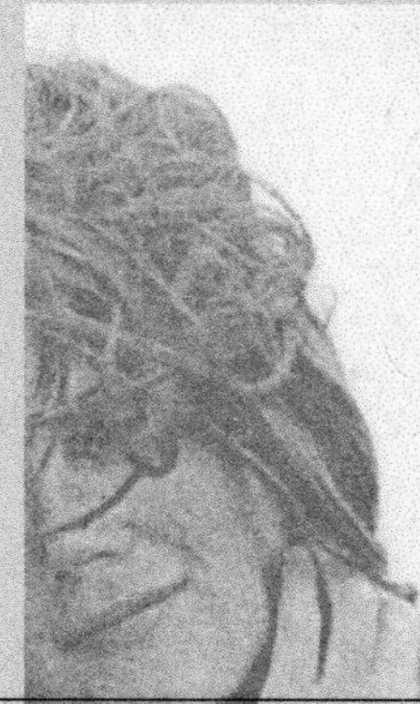

A TICKET TO THE CIRCUS

A Memoir

NORRIS CHURCH MAILER

RANDOM HOUSE TRADE PAPERBACKS
NEW YORK

A Ticket to the Circus is a work of nonfiction. Some names and identifying details have been changed.

2011 Random House Trade Paperback Edition

Published in the United States by Random House Trade Paperbacks, an imprint of The Random House Publishing Group, a division of Random House, Inc., New York.

RANDOM HOUSE TRADE PAPERBACKS and colophon are trademarks of Random House, Inc.
RANDOM HOUSE READER'S CIRCLE & Design is a registered trademark of Random House, Inc.

Originally published in hardcover in the United States by Random House, an imprint of The Random House Publishing Group, a division of Random House, Inc., in 2010.

Photo credits appear on page 415.

LIBRARY OF CONGRESS CATALOGING-IN-PUBLICATION DATA
Mailer, Norris Church.
A ticket to the circus : a memoir / Norris Church Mailer.
p. cm.
ISBN 978-0-8129-7987-9
eBook ISBN 978-1-58836-979-6
1. Mailer, Norris Church—Marriage. 2. Authors, American—20th century—Biography. 3. Authors' spouses—United States—Biography. 4. Mailer, Norman—Marriage. I. Title.
PS3563.A3824Z47 2010
813'.54—dc22
[B] 2009 033941

Printed in the United States of America

www.randomhousereaderscircle.com

9 8 7 6 5 4 3 2 1

Title page photo by Francis Delia

Book design by Barbara M. Bachman

For my grandchildren,
Mattie James Mailer and
Jackson Kingsley Mailer

Well, I bought a ticket to the circus.

I don't know why I was surprised to see elephants.

NORRIS CHURCH MAILER

A Note from the Author

Everything in this book is true. At least, it is true for me. Memory is treacherous, and we probably all have said "Glad to meet you" to people we have met before. Sometimes we have had whole conversations—or even much more than that—with them and *still* don't remember them, which gets complicated and embarrassing. (Once, my husband argued with a woman who claimed they had dated that she was mistaken, and then on the cab ride home, he slapped his forehead and said, "She's right!") But to the best of my knowledge, all of the things I've written about in this book happened to me.

There are instances where I have changed the names of people. If I say, for example, "Let's call her . . . " it means I'm not giving her real name. I have used first names for the most part, although at times I've used whole names. No real reason, I just thought some people might not like to be totally identified. A few times, no name has been used at all. Those stories are probably not good ones.

It's funny, the things that mean so much to one person and nothing to another, the small thoughtless comment that inadvertently cuts to the quick. I didn't intend to hurt anyone in the telling of my story, and if I did, I apologize now, before you read it. Please know that I went into this with a good heart, and I hope that comes through.

A Ticket to the Circus

Prologue

Every evening at six, after an afternoon of writing in our studios, Norman and I would meet in the bar next to the living room for a glass of wine. We'd look out at the sea and the boats in Provincetown Harbor, watch the gulls, and talk. After a lifetime of booze—bourbon and gin and rum, scotch and vodka—now Norman liked red wine mixed with orange juice, a mild sangria punch, while I sipped a dry Kir on ice—soda pop wines, a taste of sweet, a drop of alcohol, to help us unwind. Those were hard, slow days, the last days of summer 2007. Norman was still writing, but fighting to breathe, and I had my problems, too. Eternity was on our minds a lot of the time when we talked.

"I wonder if people will remember me when I'm gone," Norman would frequently muse. "Will they continue to read my books, do you think? Or will they just forget me?"

Most of the time, I replied, "Of course you'll be remembered, sweetie. You're one of the most famous writers in the world!" But he knew as well as I did that there were a lot of dead and forgotten writers who had once been famous.

"When I'm gone," he'd continue, "and you write about me, I want you to say—"

I would invariably interrupt him. "I'm not going to write about you. I'll never write about you. Nobody would believe it." It was almost a game we played; he never gave up telling me what to write about him, whether it was some message to the kids, or something about his work. I always brushed him off with, "Why don't you tell them yourself? Why don't you write your own memoirs?"

"It's too late," he'd answer.

"I might go before you. You never know," I'd say. We didn't want to face it, which one of us would go first, so we just kept on playing the game.

Andy Warhol had once urged me to put a tape recorder on a belt and wear it around all the time. "Norris," he said, in that soft talcum powder voice, "you live such a fascinating life. Every word that comes out of Norman's mouth is a pearl. It's so easy. All you have to do is change the tape every hour, and you'll have a complete record of your life." I laughed, but Andy was dead serious.

I don't believe that every word out of my husband's mouth was a pearl—what wife does? Although now I wish I had recorded some of those pearls Norman dropped along the way.

I truly believed I would never write about Norman. And if I ever *did* write about him, it would not be as his secretary taking dictation. Even though we'd lived together for thirty-three years, Norman wasn't my whole life; I had been married before, and had a child from that marriage. I'd had a career. Family. I once had ambitions and dreams that had nothing to do with Norman Mailer. But we met, and nothing was ever the same again.

After he was gone, I found myself haunted by our life together. It spooled across my mind at night like the reels of a movie. Vivid. Garish. Heartbreaking. Frustrating. Sexy. Comical. Too often, it had been public. I used to say I had no skeletons in my closet; they were all in the pages of the *New York Post*. Night after night, the past played out, in that space between memory and sleep, until finally I realized that Norman was going to get his way; I was going to write about him. But, as I said to his spirit, it was *my* life as well as his. I would write it on my own terms.

"Whatever you say, dear," I imagined him replying, a smile on his face, as he continued to send me notes in my dreams.

One

My grandpa was a mule skinner. My husband, Norman Mailer, thought that was a noteworthy fact, and he loved to toss it out there in conversation at New York dinner parties, watching the stiff smiles of the socialites as they imagined someone like the *Texas Chain Saw Massacre* guy skinning out a mule and nailing its bloody hide to the barn door. They'd glance at me a tad uneasily, Norman much amused, while

My mule skinner grandpa Jeames (standing), my great-grandpa Benjamin Franklin Davis, and my half-Cherokee great-grandma, Mary Davis.

I'd explain that a mule skinner was a mule *trainer* and try to change the subject. The truth was, there might have been a little flick or two of a black snake whip involved to get their attention (mules being one of God's most stubborn creatures), but they were valuable property, not to be abused, and while I'm proud of my ancestry, I don't think that particular talent dribbled down to me in any ability to skin—er, train—Norman. He loved to hear the stories of my family—he said he felt like he had married the great American novel. I guess you could look at it like that, since I have a Cherokee great-great-grandma and I can trace both sides back to the early and mid-1700s, when the first big wave of immigrants started arriving from the British Isles, looking for a better life—or maybe running from the sheriff. Nobody really knows now; it's all lost to the years.

I don't even know for sure which country they came from, the Davises and the Phillipses, but several family stories survive, some birth and death records, and a few old pictures. My great-great-great-grandpa Stephen Phillips fought in the Revolutionary War; maybe my great-great-great-grandpa Caleb Davis did, too. He was in America then, living in Maryland, but records are sketchy. Both my great-grandpas fought for the rebels in the War Between the States, as they called it then. Down the line, the assorted grandpas and uncles married women with names such as Sarah Allen, Dicey Benefield, America Dillard, Tennessee Chronister, and Lavinia Pigg and named various of their children after George Washington, and Benjamin Franklin, and Andrew Jackson. Somebody in the mix was called Seaborne Featherstone. The majority of them are now only names on a register, dates on a page, the women giving up their fathers' names to take their husbands', whole branches of family for the most part lost. They settled in Virginia or Maryland or the Carolinas, raised cotton and farmed; some had slaves. I hate that but choose to believe they were at least kind to them, because one of the slaves on record, Granny Flowers—along with her son Jasper—didn't leave the family after the Civil War but went with my great-grandpa George Washington Phillips and his wife, Sarah, to Dardanelle, Arkansas, in 1869, where they started a cotton gin. Granny helped raise their kids. It was noted that she liked to gather apples in her apron and eat them while sitting out under the apple tree.

A few stories survive, like the one about my great-great-grandpa's sister Anthroit Phillips (she called herself Ankie, as anybody with that name would), who lived in a one-room log cabin her father built in Hendersonville, North Carolina. She never married, instead staying home to take care of her mother, Violet, which is what people did back then before nursing homes were invented, and Violet, bless her heart, lived to be more than a hundred. Right across the road from Ankie and Violet's cabin was the Ebenezer Baptist Church and the graveyard, and one rainy day there was a funeral. After the funeral was over and the cemetery deserted, Ankie looked out and saw a little girl of about six sitting on the fresh grave, crying. It was getting dark, so she walked

From left, Anthroit, her sister Theresa, and her mother, Violet Phillips.

over to see why the child was still there. She was named Ellen Morgan, it was her mother who had died, and everybody probably thought someone else had taken her, but she had no place to go, so Ankie took her home and raised her as if she were her own daughter. Because that's what people did. The good ones.

Ellen Morgan,
the adopted girl.

On my father's side, my great-great-great-grandpa Caleb Davis and his wife, Catherine, moved west from North Carolina to New Madrid, Missouri, in 1808, which was just time enough to get settled in before the great earthquake of 1811 wiped out most of the town, his house included. Fortunately, nobody was killed, so he built a houseboat, loaded it down with all the furniture and livestock and goods he could salvage, floated it down the Mississippi to the Arkansas, took a right turn upriver, and settled in Gum Log Valley, Arkansas, where he claimed nine hundred acres and built the first house in the Valley. He farmed, raised livestock, and built a Methodist church and a school. He became a county judge and was the postmaster. His great-grandson was my mule skinner grandpa, Jeames, who raised cotton and corn right on the home place in Gum Log Valley. Jeames died at forty-seven during the Great Depression, leaving my grandmother Sallie with five children and a two-thousand-dollar mortgage he had taken out to buy more land to put in cotton. My beloved father, James, who was nine, never got over his father's death. In those days, two thousand dollars might as well have been two million to a widow with small children; they lost the farm and struggled along, my grandmother cleaning houses or taking in wash or whatever she could do, until my father got big enough to go to the Civilian Conservation Corps (CCC) camp and help out. Then he joined the navy right after Pearl Harbor and sent money back to support his mother and little sister, Chloe Dean.

There are so many stories that have been passed down in this family, stories that might even be true. So many characters—judges and doctors, bootleggers and drunks; sharecroppers and cotton gin owners; grocers and truck drivers and coal miners. Somebody stole a car and did time in San Quentin; somebody was the deputy warden in the McAlester prisons. Most were farmers who worked the land and did the best they could. One great-whatever-uncle got drunk one Thanksgiving and slung the turkey down the table, scattering sweet potatoes

My daddy, James; his little sister, Chloe Dean (in front); and their cousin Juanita Pigg.

and cranberry sauce, and it landed in the lap of his brother, who calmly put it back on the platter, sliced off a piece, and finished his dinner. Another great-uncle had a goat that climbed up and ate the cloth top off his brand-new Model T, so he went into the house, got his gun, and shot it. They ate barbecued goat for a week.

Some were good-hearted; some were as hard as new whiskey, like my great-great-uncle Phillips who, when accosted by the revenuers for bootlegging pear brandy, ratted out his neighbors who were doing the same thing, and took a deal that allowed him a government still. He invited the neighbors over for a barn dance, and—surprise!—they were locked in his barn for several days until the judge could get there. The neighbors were tried and sent to jail—although, unfortunately, not for long, and the great-great-uncle, who clearly hadn't thought the thing through, had to pack up his family in the dead of night and move to Indian territory, as the neighbors were out to kill him.

He was not the happiest with his lot there—the only work he could get was in a coal mine—but his son made out fine. Working with an old braided Creek named Boney Reynolds, he rounded up, broke, and sold wild Indian ponies for five dollars a head, and he excelled at a game the young men played, in which they put a cow's skull on top of a high pole and tried to knock it off with a rawhide ball flung by a hollowed-out, curved stick. The games were mayhem. More than one of the men had his own skull cracked, and a few were actually killed. A white boy who could keep up with that pack earned a lot of respect. When the government gave every Creek child on the reservation one hundred sixty acres, and oil was later discovered, my great-great-uncle's son married an Indian woman. They built a big brick house, they had black servants, and he joined the Masonic lodge. He tried to set his brother up with his wife's girlfriend, Susie Tiger, but she was too fat and ugly and his brother couldn't bring himself to marry her, even for a hundred sixty acres and oil.

Then there are the Civil War stories! My great-grandfather Benjamin Franklin Davis and his two brothers, who had spent months walking home across the country after the signing of the peace, were attacked by outlaws who snuck up on them in an old church while they slept and killed one of the brothers, just one day's walk away from home. Another story was of when one of the uncles pulled a gun on the battlefield surgeon who was about to saw off his leg, and then ran off with a nurse. (P.S. The leg healed.) There are a lot of Depression stories and World War II stories from my father. Every one of these people lived a life full of adventure and pain and love and drama and dull hard work. Any one of them is worthy of a book, but this is my story, my little link in the chain, my page in the great American novel. It starts in Washington state, where I was born, and ends, as far as it goes, in New York City with Norman Mailer, who, Lord knows, had his own story. I was his sixth wife and the mother of his eighth and ninth children. Rude people (there are way too many rude people in this world) used to ask me, "Which wife are *you*?"

"The last one," I would answer. I didn't even knock wood. I was certain it would be true.

And it was.

Two

After the war, my father, James Davis, who had learned how to operate heavy earthmoving equipment in the Seabees on Okinawa, came back to Atkins, Arkansas, and worked in his cousin Check's grocery store (called Davis Groceries). One Saturday night my father and his buddy Reece drove fifteen miles to Dardanelle to hang out and look for girls. James was cute—twenty-two, tall and lanky, with curly blond hair and blue eyes, and a big shiny smile that featured a gold cap on the bottom half of his front tooth, acquired at fourteen when he stuck a broom handle into a buzz saw and a piece of it flew back and hit him in the mouth.

My mother, Gaynell Phillips, was walking down the street with her girlfriend Mary Sue when a car with boys hanging out the windows passed them. The girls pretended not to notice them, sauntered on into the drugstore, and sat in a booth at the soda fountain. My mother was a beautiful girl, with long black curls and chocolate drop eyes. The friend was maybe not so beautiful, as she had regrettable frizzy hair, but the boys didn't care. They parked and followed the girls into the drugstore and began the age-old game of "What's your name? Can I buy you a Coke?" "No, thank you. My mama said I shouldn't talk to strangers." After they had drunk their Cokes, the girls announced they had to get back before it got dark, and set out walking the two miles home. Slowly. The boys of course followed, and by then the girls had dropped the coy act and let them drive them on home. After all, a ride's a ride.

My mother lived in the middle of a cotton patch where her mother, Annie, and stepfather, Z. T. Shepherd, were sharecroppers. Her father had died when she was three and her baby brother, George, was one. Her mother soon married Z.T., a widower with six children. My mother had two older brothers and an older sister as well, so at one time there had been eleven children and two adults living in this four-room house that was perched on rocks stacked on the ground at each of its corners. Gaynell and George were the only ones left at home to help in the fields by the time she met James. Dragging that long heavy sack up and down the dusty rows of cotton in the shadow of Nebo Mountain was hard, sweaty work, and at twenty-seven, Gaynell was more than ready to do something else. Not that she was desperate, but she was verging on becoming an old maid, as the boy she'd been engaged to had been killed in the war. James pursued her hot and heavy for a few weeks. Then one day he pulled into the yard, scattering chickens,

James and Gaynell in Washington state.

and announced he was going out to Washington state to work on the O'Sullivan Dam and if she wanted to go with him, they could get married. By then she knew he was not the owner of Davis Groceries, as he had kind of let her assume in the beginning, but she liked him anyway. He was sweet. So, two months after they met, on January 18, 1947, they got married, packed up the old car, and headed to the Northwest to

Moses Lake, Washington. They lived in a tiny homemade trailer with a bed resting on orange crates, and no fridge, but what the heck? They were newlyweds.

After a couple of years, I came along, and they were entranced by me even though I arrived with red hair, which totally threw my father for a loop. He was expecting me to be blond and blue-eyed like him. They named me Barbara Jean, after the little girl who lived next door,

OFFICIAL SCORE CARD
U. S. P. H.

Baby's Name Barbara Jean Davis
Address 4403 W 23rd
Parent's Initials J. A.
Age 3 yrs Date of Birth Jan 31 - 49
Weight at Birth 8lb 3oz Height at Birth 22"
Height 38 Weight 30 Average 30 3/4
Posture Good Muscletone Good Skin Clear
Heart NSA Lungs Neg Nose Neg
Head Neg Scalp Neg Gums Neg
Eyes Neg Ears Neg Glands Neg
Mouth Neg Teeth Good Adenoids Neg
Tonsils Neg Genitalia Normal
Back Neg Abdomen Neg
Arms, Hands, Fingers, Neg
Legs Neg Feet Neg
Deportment during Examination Poor
Shots and Vaccinations 3 in 1 shots
No Vacc.
Suggestions: Smallpox Vaccination

My health card for Little Miss Little Rock.

and when the dam was completed, we moved back to Little Rock, where Daddy got a job building roads. When I was three, my mother saw a sign in a store advertising for little girls to compete in the Little Miss Little Rock contest, so she entered me and I won. I was by all accounts an adorable handful. On the health checkup we all had to take, I got good in all the categories except deportment, which was marked "poor."

(In my defense, there was a category on the card marked "genitalia," for which I got a "normal." If indeed some strange doctor was examining my genitals, it's no wonder I pitched a fit and earned a "poor" rating in deportment. Examining a little girl's genitals should have been outlawed, but it was 1952 and nobody thought anything about things like that in those days. If it was a doctor doing it, it must have been all right.)

Me, the year I won Little Miss Little Rock.

My mother had a great time getting me all dolled up in a yellow chiffon dress with rhinestones, white patent leather Mary Jane shoes, and socks with ruffles. The mistress of ceremonies, a former beauty queen in a purple evening dress, handed me the golden trophy and put the crown on my head, and when the audience clapped and cheered, I loved it so much that I wouldn't leave the stage. The woman in the purple dress tried to take my hand to lead me off, but I ran from her, and let me tell you, it was hard work for her to catch me in those high heels.

The audience went crazy. I still have the trophy, my only beauty contest win. That gave me a taste for the spotlight, and my daddy, red-faced with embarrassment, had to drag me off the stage at church because I climbed up there to mimic the preacher. I liked the way he waved his hands around, and I wanted to get up and wave mine, too. I deservedly got my bottom tanned a few times when I was little.

A lot of memories of my third year of life are as clear as glass. My daddy worked nights, and my mother, always nervous and delicate, was terrified of staying home alone with me. She was afraid I was going to get hurt, or some man was going to kidnap me, and I unfortunately thought it was a fun game to hide from her, or to run off in department stores. Once, in Woolworth's, I was riding up and down the escalator when she found me talking to a drunk man who was trying to get me to go home with him.

Things got worse for my mother after my fingers were smashed. I was playing in the yard with my toy cooking set when the dough roller somehow rolled off the sidewalk into the sewer. My father, who was at home during the days, lifted the manhole cover and climbed down to rescue it, and I had my hands on the edge of the hole, peering in, when the iron cover slipped and crushed my two left middle fingers. My mother, who was hanging out wash, heard my shrieks and came running. She wrapped my bloody hand in a white organdy pinafore she was holding, and we rushed to the doctor, who bandaged them up and told us babies didn't have bones in their fingers, only gristle, so they didn't need to be set. Those fingers have served their purpose all my life, although they are a bit crooked and the nails a little weird.

At any rate, I think the last straw for my mother was when I escaped from home, standing on the back of a little neighbor boy's red tricycle, holding tight to his shoulders like a pint-size Ann-Margret on Elvis's Harley, red curls bobbing in the wind. I can still remember the thrill of freedom as we rode, he pedaling as fast as he could, taking me down the block to play with another friend. When I came back, I was surprised to find my mother out in the yard, screaming my name and crying, and soon after that we moved back to Atkins, out in the country near Gum Log. She just couldn't take city life anymore.

This next part is vague for me in its details. It's something that has been carefully hidden over the years, and I'm hesitant to talk about it even now, but I think it is probably central to my life in ways I can only half comprehend. After this last episode, before we moved to Atkins, my mother went into the hospital and got shock treatments. I remember it only through my three-year-old sensibilities, and I, of course, wasn't told where she was, but I believed it was my fault, that I had done something so bad that I'd made her go away. I stayed with my aunt Ella Belle and cousins Carla and Billy Darel while she was gone, I don't know how long, as time doesn't mean much to a three-year-old.

I do remember it was summer and we were out in the yard in our underwear playing with the water hose when a strange new brown and tan car drove up. I couldn't see who was in it. A woman I didn't recognize got out and held out her arms to me, but I was frightened and didn't run to her. It was my mother. She looked different; maybe she had a new haircut. After a moment I realized who she was, but how painful it must have been for her to come home from Lord knows what kind of brutal situation and find that her daughter didn't remember her.

I didn't learn until I was a teenager what had happened; even to this day at age ninety she won't talk about it, but all her life my mother would go into depressions and rages. I know she loved me more than anything in the world, and I loved her, but we never understood each other. It was hard for us to talk.

One night when I was about seventeen, I was in the car with my future first husband and some friends on our way to a party on Petit Jean Mountain. It started to snow, and my mother had a premonition we were going to get killed in a car wreck. She sent my father to chase down the car and bring me home. Of course I was humiliated and so angry at her. It was then, in the car on the way home, that my father told me the story of her breakdown and asked me to be tolerant of her. Since then, I have always felt guilty about my mother, rational or not, and have believed that my being the feisty child that I was caused her to snap.

Moving back to Atkins was much better for her. We were in the country, and since she couldn't drive, it was just the two of us in the house all day long. (My father taught me to drive when I was eight; I would sit on his lap and steer. Then, later, I sat on a cushion until my legs could reach the pedals. By the time I was twelve, I was driving my mother everywhere, hoping I wouldn't get stopped by a cop.) I would keep her company while she gardened or ironed or cooked, and she read to me until I memorized all my Little Golden Books and pretended to read them myself. Then one day when I was about five, I realized I *could* read them.

We watched *The Mickey Mouse Club* together and made chocolate chip cookies and played with Pickles the cat, who had babies as fast as she could, feral cats who lived wild under the house. One day Pickles disappeared, along with the gang of offspring, and when I asked where

Gaynell, me, and Pickles the cat on the porch of our house in the country.

she was, I was told she had run away. Along with all her children. I didn't find out until much later that my uncle George had come and taken them all off, he would never say where. I chose to believe they were adopted by a kind family who needed twenty-two cats and fed them cream every day. I've always been an optimist.

I think life in those days was good for Mother for the most part, and for me, too. My father still worked in Little Rock, which meant he had to get up early in the morning for the hour-and-a-half commute. I guess we were poor—well, no guessing about it. Although we had cold water from a pump at the kitchen sink, we didn't have hot running water in the house or an indoor toilet. (We did use toilet paper in the outhouse, however. My daddy used to tell me that when he was a boy on the farm, they used corncobs, red ones and white ones. You used a red one first, then you used a white one to see if you needed to use another red one.) But a lot of people didn't have running water or indoor bathrooms, like my grandparents in the Dardanelle cotton fields. My grandma cooked on a wood burning stove like her mother and grandmother had, and like us, they used coal for heat in a black potbellied stove in the living room. Our bedrooms were icy in winter, and the only way anybody could sleep was to be nestled in a feather bed, weighed down under a big stack of quilts my grandma had made, so heavy it was a chore to turn over.

My grandparents raised or grew everything they ate, made their own soap from rendered fat and wood ashes, and sewed some of their clothes from flour sacks, which were lovely soft cotton prints, designed by the flour companies in fifty- or hundred-pound bags for just that purpose. I still have baby clothes my grandmother made for me from flour sacks, and my own granddaughter wore them.

The infamous year I was three, we went to Grandma's house for Sunday dinner, as we often did, and I went out in the yard to watch her chase a chicken down and wring its neck. Then she sat with it between her knees, plucked off the feathers, cleaned it, and threw the insides into a bucket she gave to the hogs. Finally, she chopped off the feet and tossed them to me, saying, "Here, baby, you can play and make tracks in the dirt with these." I looked at those yellow disembodied feet lying there—I was still in shock from seeing the pigs chowing down on the entrails—and got sick and threw up. I didn't eat any chicken that day, and never touched meat of any kind again until I was around fourteen and started to date. All the kids made fun of me for ordering a hamburger without the meat. (In grade school, they liked the fact I didn't eat meat; somebody was always vying to sit next to me in the lunchroom to ask for mine, so I was popular.) After I learned to eat hamburger, all was lost. That led to hot dogs, then chicken, then bacon and everything else.

By the time I was in first grade, riding the big yellow bus every day, my parents decided they wanted to move to town so I could walk to school and have an easier life, so my father took out a loan and built a house two blocks from school with an indoor bathroom. Besides the wonder of the flush toilet and being able to take a hot bath without having to heat the water on the stove, we had a floor furnace. I used to stand on the furnace and let the hot air blow my skirts up, like Marilyn Monroe on the subway grate, while my bottom burned, toasty and warm. The whole house was warm, not just the spot right in front of the coal stove. And I became one of the town children. That made a big difference in my social life. I could ride my bike to visit my friends and play with the other kids on the block, running from yard to yard flying kites or playing tag or chasing lightning bugs, all the moms watching after us from their kitchen windows, until it got dark and they called us in to supper.

There was one dark cloud in this idyllic time. My father was working on a job building a paper mill near Atkins, and he was standing underneath a huge iron slab, directing it into place, when the chains broke and the slab fell on him, crushing his feet. It was a miracle he wasn't killed. I was in the first grade in the little white building that housed the first two grades, when Carla, my older cousin (by only two months, but a grade ahead of me) came with a teacher who took me out of class. The teacher told me my father was in the hospital and someone would come and get me. I was scared, but Carla sat with me on the steps, her arm around me, until my aunt could pick me up. It was the most terrifying thing, to see my handsome, big strong daddy lying there in the hospital bed, his feet all bandaged. He never complained, no matter how much pain he was in, and tried to make like it was nothing, but I'm sure he was frightened.

We had just built a new house, and he would be out of work for several months. I was too young to understand what that meant, but until he could walk again and go back to work, we had little money. I remember him once telling my mother all we had left was twenty-five dollars. We borrowed some, I think, and his cousin Check gave us credit at the grocery store, but for a while we weren't sure if my father was ever going to be able to walk, much less work again. I remember my mother trying to help him get in and out of bed into his wheelchair, he in his maroon bathrobe and blue pajamas, but he never let on to me that he was afraid. He had a lot of major illnesses in his life and was always stoic through them all, joking and laughing when I know he must have been in tremendous pain. I have tried to emulate him in my own life, sometimes succeeding, more often failing, but it is something I always remember.

When he was able to walk again, we went to the offices of the company where he worked, hoping to get a settlement, but all they offered him was two thousand dollars, less than his salary would have been for the same period, and he took it without question. They knew we had no money for a lawyer. He walked with a limp from then on, and couldn't run or play ball with me. His feet hurt him all the time, and over the years he had to have several operations on them, almost losing one of his feet once. The paper mill, of course, was built without him and proceeded to stink up the environment with its chemicals, and decimate all the trees in the area. And I'm quite sure the owners, if they even knew, must have congratulated themselves for saving a few thousand dollars by cheating a good man out of the money that should have come to him for their wrecking his life.

Three

While Mother and Daddy were living in Washington and I was just an infant, some friends of my father's went out one night, I never knew to do what, and got killed in a car wreck. There was alcohol involved, but my parents never told me anything about it. I only heard bits of adult conversation later, but the way my mother always said the word, *"Drinking,"* let me know it was something really bad. My daddy was supposed to go with them that night, but for some reason he decided not to. He was never a big drinker, but he would occasionally have a beer or two, and once in a while he got drunk. This near miss made him totally give it up, get saved, and join the church.

I was carried, a baby in arms, to the Freewill Baptist Church and was taught religion almost before I learned to talk. In those days, along with school, churches were the center of social life in small-town America, and for the most part it was a sweet life. Besides the three-times-a-week services, there were revivals and singings, dinner-on-the-ground picnics and summer ice cream suppers under somebody's big shade trees, vacation Bible school, and teenage get-togethers. There was summer camp, where we slept in low concrete-block dormitories (with a lot of spiders) and where we went to church several times a day in a tabernacle with sawdust floors and open sides. We played softball and Ping-Pong and did arts and crafts as well (wearing dresses, since shorts and pants for girls were not allowed). One activity I liked was Bible drill. We kids would line up shoulder to shoulder, and a teacher facing us would say, "Attention! Salute! Draw Swords!" (swords were our Bibles—the old Christian solider metaphor) and then give us a Bible verse. The first one to find it would take a step forward and get to read it. The winner at the end of camp would get an official Freewill Baptist Bible drill Bible, which I still have.

The preachers were the rock stars of the churches, and their sermons were *showtime*. Each preacher had his own style. Some spoke in a loud singsong cadence, pounded the pulpit, jumped on and off the stage, shook their fists, and perspired so profusely that the first row of the audience would be sprinkled by sweat. Some preachers were quieter, speaking sincerely to the heart, while others were a combination. Just as your mind started to drift off, the quiet preacher would suddenly shout and wake you up. The goal was for the preachers to move their congregations emotionally, and to see how many people would come up to the altar and be saved and join the church.

Another way to do that, for some preachers, was to scare the flock into being saved by describing what would happen if someone committed a sin and died unforgiven and unsaved. If you had even *one* sin on your soul when you died, they preached, you would go to hell, and it seemed like nearly everything was a sin. Drinking alcohol, of course—that was one of the worst ones—or dancing or anything sexual outside holy matrimony. (There was an old joke: Why won't Baptists make love standing up? Because someone might think they were dancing.) Going to movies was a sin. Gambling and playing cards, even if you weren't doing it for money, was a sin (the *appearance* of gambling was enough). Going fishing on Sunday, or doing anything fun or worldly on Sunday instead of going to church, was a sin. Swearing was out, of course—even something called wooden swearing, which was saying "darn" in place of "damn," or "heck" instead of "hell." My father once spanked me for saying "pooey," but it was probably the ugly way I said it, not the word itself that got me into trouble. I never heard Daddy swear even once, wooden or otherwise. When he was exasperated, sometimes he would say "Oh, me." (I guess you can't blaspheme yourself.) If my mother was feeling really angry, she would say "Oh, the devil," which my father wasn't happy about. (I never said the word "fuck" out loud until I met Norman. How's that for irony? Something in him just brought it out in me, I guess. I still have trouble swearing, and for the most part don't.)

Our church frowned on wearing shorts or spaghetti strap dresses or anything that showed too much skin. Although I was allowed to wear a bathing suit to the public pool, some of the church members wouldn't let their daughters wear them. So on the hot summer Sundays when I went home with one of the girls from church after service, if we went swimming in the creek, we had to wear old dresses, which got tangled around our legs and made it hard to kick. I was never much of a swimmer. My mother's fear of water, if not her other fears, transferred down to me. When she was a kid, her older sister and two friends were wading in the Arkansas River on a sandbar when they fell into a sinkhole, and the two friends drowned. My aunt Modene nearly drowned, too, and later she developed TB and died when she was twenty-seven, probably from ingesting that nasty river water.

When I was about eight, we got a preacher named Brother Tommy whose favorite thing was to preach about hell. "Tonight we're going to talk about . . . HELL," he would intone, his eyes smoking with brimstone under shaggy white eyebrows. At that time there was no such thing as children's church, and the kids were expected to sit quietly with the grown-ups for the whole service. For a little girl, it was terrifying. I would be as small as possible on the bench, cold and still, wishing I could get up and go out, while he preached for an hour and more about the devil with horns and cloven feet, the burning flesh and pools of liquid fire, on and on and on. He really got off on the details of what the devil was going to do to us. "No man knows when the world is going to end," he'd say, "but, brothers, it's coming, and it's coming soon. It might be tomorrow . . . or it might be *tonight* . . . at the midnight hour. The clock will chime, the moon will turn to blood, and the sky will roll away to reveal the Lord Jesus, riding on clouds of glory, coming down to take His own with Him to heaven, and all the sinners will be left behind to BURN . . . forever and ever, with no hope of redemption, in HELL . . . where the fire is not quenched and the worm dieth not." Brother Tommy dragged people up to the altar, too, telling the congregation he had seen them come out of a movie or a dance, and make them kneel down so the whole church could come up and pray for their souls. I think he used to patrol the streets after the dances and movies let out, looking for kids from his church.

By the time we got home after service, I was so scared I couldn't sleep. I would lie there and watch the clock hands, waiting for the midnight hour when the world would end. Only after the hands passed twelve could I relax and go to sleep, often to have dreams that I was standing in the middle of a beautiful meadow when the sky opened up and there was an angry God, telling me I had committed a sin and hadn't asked for forgiveness, and I was going to hell. Then the ground would open up and I would start to fall into the fire below. I woke up screaming for my daddy, who always came and held me until I could go back to sleep.

Those dreams went on for years. Finally, at one of the services, I was so overwrought that I went up when he made the altar call, and everyone came and prayed with me, asking that Jesus would save my soul. I'm not sure what it was I was asking forgiveness for at eight, probably for not liking Brother Tommy, but I prayed, "Forgive me of all my sins," thinking that should cover it. Then, a few Sundays later, we all went to the creek and I was baptized, along with several other new Christians. I wore a dress, of course, pinched my nose, and tried not to panic as a preacher named Brother Henry held me and dipped me backward under the water, saying, "In the name of the Father, and the Son, and the Holy Ghost, I baptize you, my sister." I thought the nightmares would go away, but it didn't really help.

In one way or another, either in living the Christian life or rebelling against it, religion has shaped me more than anything else. No matter how hard I try, I've never really gotten away from worrying about sin, although I've certainly left most of the harsh hell beliefs behind and have forged my own optimistic vision of God as a loving creator who would never send His children to burn forever for having a glass of wine or dancing or making love. Sex is something that God Himself created, and it was man who decided it was evil for a lot of twisted reasons. The story of Jesus is a beautiful one, if the words attributed to Him in the Bible are what He actually said, which, frankly, is unlikely given the propensity of reporters to get it all wrong and translators to screw it up, but even if the Bible didn't record His exact words, I believe His message of love is truly what God is. I don't think Jesus ever once threatened anybody with hell.

By the time I was eleven or twelve, we had a different preacher who didn't preach hell or lurk around outside dances, so I relaxed a little bit. I had a friend named Cherry, a year older than me, who had great-smelling honey-colored hair, green eyes, and tan skin. (I named the heroine Cherry in my two novels, although my fictional Cherry was nowhere as cool as the real one was.) She was the granddaughter of the town banker and had a blue parakeet named Elvis who could wolf whistle and say his name. She always had the newest clothes and enormous piles of presents under her tree at Christmas. One year, we got autograph books, and Cherry's page to me read: "On top of old Smoky, all covered with blood, I saw my (UGH) friend Bar—her head stuck in the mud. There's an axe in her stomach and a knife in her head. I jumped to the conclusion that Barbara was dead!"

That not being enough, she wrote one more: "Sitting by a stream, Barbara had a dream. She dreamed she was a fat old trout and some creep fished her out."

I laughed because I wanted her to like me, but it wasn't funny. Cherry had great legs from taking ballet lessons. I so envied her those legs and the pink satin toe shoes and net tutu, but it never occurred to me to ask to take ballet myself. At twelve, Cherry had breasts, wore white lipstick and white short shorts, and gave the best dance parties under her carport, while I was still playing with dolls. She didn't want to invite me to her parties unless I danced, so she decided to teach me, along with a chubby boy named Kenny from across the street. We were her charity project. I felt uncomfortable about it, but I really wanted to go to those parties. Cherry played the Everly Brothers' "Wake Up Little Susie" while Kenny and I tried to do the steps she showed us, and somehow we got good enough to be invited. Later that year, she told me she wouldn't continue to be my friend if I kept on playing with Barbie, and since she made me choose and I wouldn't lie about it, I chose Barbie. She called me on Christmas morning to ask if I had gotten a second Barbie, which I had, and she was as good as her word and threw me over for an older girl named Bobbye Ann, another cool girl with boobs who already went out with boys. It was my first touch of heartbreak.

The dancing was my first little foray into sin, but it was so much fun I didn't worry too much about it. It somehow didn't feel like a sin. And I didn't tell my parents. I loved them both so much, but I learned early on that I couldn't tell them what I was feeling, what I wanted or needed or feared. Once, when I was having one of my nightmares, my mother wanted to call the preacher over to pray with me. She had no idea he was the reason for the nightmare. I always wanted to be the perfect daughter, the perfect Christian, and so I learned to pretend to them that I was. I wish I could have confided in them and asked their advice sometimes, but I knew they would just say "Don't do that, it's a sin" and be disappointed in me. My father was the most perfect man I knew. He was always helping someone else, driving old ladies to the doctor, taking fatherless little boys swimming or fishing, always doing things for everyone.

But as much as my father believed in Jesus, as good as he had lived his life, religion was not a comfort to him as he was dying years later when he was seventy-eight. He lay there in the hospital for months, worrying, combing his memory, trying to remember something he had done wrong, something that he had done and hadn't been forgiven for, something he should have done and didn't do. Something that would send him to hell. He even said to me, "I'm so sorry I spanked you when you were a little girl." I couldn't hold back the tears. "Oh, Daddy," I said, "I don't even remember that. And I probably deserved it anyhow." But he wouldn't be comforted. I told him, "You've loved Jesus all your life, and He's not going to let you go to hell." I sincerely believed that. If anybody is in heaven, my father is, but I knew then that I wasn't the only one who had been affected by those hell sermons, and I wish to God it had been different.

Four

When I was twelve, my mother turned our carport into a beauty shop. A few years before that, when I could stay on my own in the afternoons after school, she had decided to go back to work. After my father's accident, we needed the income, so she tried a string of different jobs. One was picking cotton, which she at least was familiar with. Every morning before I went to school, a rattletrap pickup truck would stop outside our house. My mother—wearing faded jeans, some kind of old shirt, and one of those sunbonnets made from printed cotton that puffed out on top like a muffin—would climb up into the open back with a load of people dressed just like she was and head for some cotton patch. She worked all day in the hot sun and came back long after I got home from school. That didn't last too long. I was happy when she quit. I was embarrassed for anybody to see her dressed like that, riding in the back of a truck.

Then she got an even worse job on the pinning line at the chicken plant, but it paid more. She and several other women stood for eight hours a shift on a wet concrete floor and pulled feathers out of chickens after they had been tied, flopping and screeching, by the feet, had been hung on a moving wire, and had had their heads dipped into a pool of electrified water, which shocked them to death. Her arms ached so much from holding them up in the same position and pulling out feathers that she could hardly move at night, and she was always slightly green and sick with a runny nose from the cold plant, even though she wore sweaters under her coverall and two pairs of socks inside her rubber boots. I went with her to pick up her last check, and I nearly threw up from the smell, just in the office. I had the courage only once to peek inside the actual plant to look at the chickens drifting around the room on their conveyer wire, getting plucked here, split open there, and their innards pulled out at the next station, and then I had to get out into the fresh air.

When no other job could be found, we were driving down the street in Russellville and saw that someone was putting in a new beauty school. It was a six-month course, and my father said he would turn the carport into a beauty shop for her if she wanted. She was so happy at the school with all the other women, a lot of them her age, learning how to cut hair and do perms and color and perform the newest rage, back-combing, also known as teasing or ratting, to make all the hair fluff out into a bubble. They used real people for the students to practice on, and since beauty school treatments were, of course, cheaper than regular beauty shops, it gave women who normally couldn't afford it the luxury of having their hair and nails done. The local nursing home would bring all the old ladies in by the busload once a week, and when they left, they waved cheerfully from the bus, their bouffant hair in assorted pastel hues filling the windows like cotton candy. I used to go and hang out with Mother on Saturday, and at lunchtime we'd go across the street to the drugstore and get a pimento cheese sandwich and a Coke at the soda fountain. All day, I would watch and absorb the lessons. I practiced on my friends, and am still a pretty good haircutter, if I do say so myself. (Norman never again went to a barber after we got together, and he delighted in telling people I cut his hair. "Just think of all the money we've saved over the years!" he'd say.)

Me in the sixth grade with my cat's-eye glasses.

Of course, I was my mother's at-home practice dummy, and for a year or two after she started school, I had short perm-fried hair that embarrassed me. So when I was thirteen, I put my foot down and told her I was never letting her cut or perm my hair again. I felt bad about hurting her feelings, but that hair, along with my thick rhinestone cat's-eye glasses, made me the ugliest girl in the sixth grade. At least one of them.

Mother loved everything about her little *Steel Magnolias* shop. She had people to talk to all day, the work wasn't odious or odiferous or backbreaking, and she made decent money. The going rate in 1963 was a dollar and a quarter for a shampoo and set. (Your hair was rolled on brush rollers and you were put under a hair dryer that looked like a space helmet. It roared so loudly it made you deaf, while hot jets of air cooked your ears.) Another dollar bought you a haircut, and ten dollars got you a perm, cut included. She named the shop Gay's Beauty Shop, which was lovely until the term "gay" for homosexuals became popular, and then some kid or other was always prank-calling her, thinking they were so clever. She worked in that little shop until she was in her eighties, and then when my father passed away, she moved to Cape Cod to live with me.

Just about the time my hair grew out in seventh grade, I fell at the skating rink, my rhinestone glasses flew off and slid across the floor, and somebody skated right over them. I had to wait two weeks to get new ones, groping in a fog of nearsightedness and squinting at the blackboard. I went to a basketball game in the gym, where the concession stand was up on a high stage, and when I started back down the stairs, I missed the top step and fell about seven feet to the gym floor, flinging my popcorn and Coke out onto the court. They had to stop the game and clean it up. I was bruised from the fall, but was more humiliated as everyone clapped and cheered while I slunk out. But the strangest thing was happening: without the glasses, all of a sudden guys were taking another look at me and started asking me out.

My first real date was with a boy named Jimmy, who played cornet in the band. I had come down with hepatitis A the summer I was fourteen and had to stay in bed for six weeks. That was 1963, and Lesley Gore's "It's My Party" and a Japanese song called "Sukiyaki" played over and over and over on the radio until I thought I would lose my

Gaynell in her beauty shop.

mind. As I was contagious and could have no visitors, Jimmy used to come and stand outside my window and talk to me for hours. Then one day he slipped his silver band medal through a crack in the screen, and we were going steady. It seemed that I was forever going steady, but in that little town, after you dated someone a few times, everyone assumed you were a couple and the other boys didn't ask you out.

After I recovered from hepatitis, we double-dated with Larry Aldridge, a friend of Jimmy's who was sixteen and had his own car—a 1958 blue-and-white DeSoto with huge fins. We went to church or the movies or places like Al's snack bar for great hamburgers and curlicue french fries, or to the Freezer Fresh, which was the kids' favorite hangout owned by a couple—Winnie and Leon, who had only one arm. It was amazing how he could do everything like make milk shakes and flip burgers with that stump. Then we'd drive around the streets, and wind up the evening by parking out by the lake or up on the bluffs of Crow Mountain. That was about the only thing there was to do in Atkins, although there was a skating rink and a bowling alley and a movie theater twelve miles away in Russellville, and a drive-in movie in the summer. After a year or so, Jimmy fell in love with a friend of mine named Ann, and he broke up with me, although she was a year older than he was and only thought of him as a little brother. Of course, I was devastated, although now I really can't remember quite why I was so taken with him.

Now that I'm writing my memoir, it will be clear to those of you who have read my novels that I'm shattering a lot of my crystals. Norman had a great image he called the crystal to explain a tool for writing fiction. You take the crystal of your experience and beam the light of your imagination through it, and the story comes out in a different direction, in different colors, but the basis is the same experience. One situation might serve as the crystal for several scenes in your fiction, and I have done that throughout my work. You will probably recognize certain things in this book if you have read *Windchill Summer* and *Cheap Diamonds*.

After Jimmy, I started dating a boy I'll call Rex. Rex and I went steady as well, when all I really wanted was to be free and date a lot of guys, but he kept on putting his ring on a chain around my neck, which felt more like a dog leash. He wouldn't take no for an answer, and I finally went along because it was easier than arguing with him. Nobody else was asking me out anyhow. Rex was jealous and big and was a star football player with a reputation for being somewhat of a tough guy.

Then a boy named Jerry came to visit his aunt and uncle for the summer. He was from California and had actually surfed, which was a huge deal at the time, as the Beach Boys were at the height of their fame, and the Mamas and the Papas' monster hit "California Dreamin' " made us all long to go to, or at least *know* somebody from, California. He wasn't in the least afraid of Rex. Jerry and I went to the drive-in with another couple, where *A Summer Place* with Sandra Dee and Troy Donahue was playing. Sitting in the backseat with Jerry was such sweet torture. I wouldn't let him kiss me, as I was going steady, and I guess I thought if we didn't kiss it wasn't really cheating, but we would almost kiss, our lips getting so close we could feel the heat. It was exquisitely painful. Then we stopped at a gas station on the way home, and while the attendant was filling up the tank, Rex happened by and saw us. What bad luck. I can't remember if actual blows were exchanged or not, but there was a fight of sorts.

After that, there was no reason not to kiss Jerry, so I did and fell hard for him, as only one can at fifteen with an older boy of seventeen. After the summer, he went back to his family, who had by then moved to Kentucky, which was not nearly as glamorous as California, but he promised he was going to come back at Thanksgiving vacation and we were going to run away to California and get married. I didn't take it too seriously, and I frankly don't know what I would have done if he had pulled up in the yard and said, "Hop in. Let's go," but I did desperately want to see him again. One day, right before Thanksgiving, the letters we had been exchanging every few days just stopped. My old boyfriend Rex dropped by to give me a cryptic message. "Have you heard from Jerry?" he asked, smirking a little.

"Not in a while," I said. I never was any good at lying.

"Well, I just wondered. You might want to call him." That was weird. He seemed so happy about something.

I got Jerry's father on the phone. In those days, it would never have occurred to me to call a boy, especially long distance, but I was really worried. "Could I speak to Jerry, please?" I asked.

"He's not here."

"Where is he?"

"He's gone to get his marriage license."

"Oh," I said, when I could finally speak. "Well, can you give him a message for me? Tell him Barbara Davis called and said for him to drop dead."

What an ugly thing to say to his father! But I was so angry I didn't know what else to say. I never spoke to him again, but years later I heard that he became a professional wrestler and then a preacher (or maybe it was the other way around). He and the girl, whose name, I think, was Barbara, had four children and are probably still married, and I thanked my lucky stars it wasn't me who bought that license with him.

Five

I had known the boy who would become my first husband, Larry Norris, most of my life, but we weren't friends, as he was two classes ahead of me and had gone steady with a girl in his grade named Sharon for most of high school. He was popular, a good football player, a track star, and an all-around athlete. Sharon wore his little gold track shoe on a delicate chain around her neck, and I remember being a little envious of it. Then she fell in love with a boy named Bill and broke up with Larry, breaking his heart. She and Bill got married, and Larry went off to Arkansas Tech. The summer before my senior year, he was working for the school, going around to all the seniors in the area and trying to convince them to go to school there. I had already decided to go to Arkansas State Teachers College in Conway, and I even had an academic scholarship promised, but Larry showed up at my door early one summer morning.

I was still asleep, and looked out the window when his knock woke me up. I threw on some clothes, ran a brush through my hair, and answered the door in less than two minutes. He looked a little like Burt Reynolds, with ultramarine blue eyes and dark hair. He was funny and convincing, and I decided Tech might not be such a bad place to go after all. I said I'd think about it. Before he left, he asked me out to the movies. His family lived up on Crow Mountain and grew watermelons as a cash crop. He was paying his way through school on an ROTC scholarship, so it was a foregone conclusion that he would be joining the army when he graduated. This was 1966, and Vietnam was just beginning to get hot but wasn't yet the explosive war it became in the next couple of years.

When I started dating Larry, I was still seeing Rex off and on, and occasionally a few others as well, such as a boy named Audie Ray, who had a tiny Triumph sports car and a broken left leg. He had to drive with his cast out the window, so we worked out a routine where he would use the clutch and brake with his right foot and I would work the gas pedal. I can't believe we didn't wreck the car. One memorable afternoon, Audie Ray was at my house, Larry stopped by, and Rex showed up. We all sat in the living room trying to talk, them waiting one another out. I wanted to sneak out the back door and leave, but I was too much of a good Southern hostess, so there we sat, drinking Cokes, them talking about football like they had all come there specifically to hang out with one another. Finally, after what seemed like hours, Audie Ray left, then Rex, and Larry was the winner. That got him a lot of points.

I had promised Rex I would go with him to the homecoming dance months in advance, and he held me to the promise even though I was seeing more of Larry at that time. I don't know why I just didn't say no, but I had some weird, strong ideas about keeping my word, and Rex was emphatic that I couldn't back out on a promise. I was the homecoming maid, and since Rex was the captain of the football team and had to escort the queen, another football player named Robert Lee (whom I wasn't dating) escorted me across the field.

It was the biggest thrill of my high school years. Although I never got to be a cheerleader, which the most popular girls were, I made good grades in class, was in most of the clubs, edited the school newspaper, and sang in the glee club. I was a good kid who didn't smoke or drink, and was certainly not going to have sex until I married. At least that was the plan.

Larry wasn't happy that I was at homecoming with Rex, but he came with another girl named Janet and we spent the entire night gloomily looking at each other across the dance floor, dancing with the wrong partner. It was my last date with Rex. From then on, Larry and I were going steady.

Our dates consisted for the most part of going to his brother and sister-in-law's house to play cards. If you remember, cards were on the sin list (Larry didn't go to church, so he didn't have a sin list), but we never played for money, just for fun, so I didn't worry too much about it. My mother and father had relaxed a bit, knowing it was impossible to ask me to stay home from movies. They knew I went to parties but never asked me head-on if I was dancing, and I never said. Needless to say, Mother, Daddy, and I never once discussed sex, or even said the word out loud.

When I was thirteen, I of course knew I would start my period soon. Several of my girlfriends already had theirs, and one had gotten hers in the fourth grade. We all used to accompany her to the high school bathroom where they had a Kotex machine, and stand guard while she put in her nickel and got her pad. We felt grown-up, indeed. Finally one summer day, when my mother was outside in the garden, I found a spot of blood on my underwear. I was thrilled and frightened, and although she had never once mentioned anything about it to me, I needed her to know it had happened. I went out and said, "Mother, I think I've just started my period." She stopped hoeing the weeds for a minute and said, "Well, go take care of it," then continued chopping. I went back in and found her box of pads and some safety pins and took care of it.

My friends and I never discussed sex like friends do today, their role models being the *Sex and the City* girls, ours being Nancy Drew and Sandra Dee. We talked about girls who were sleeping with boys as being tramps, and if any of us were doing it, or anything close to it, we never admitted it to one another. I think most of our crowd in the senior class were virgins. Most of the boys were, too, in spite of what they bragged about. The furthest I had gone with anyone was kissing and wrestling in the backseat, and a little light boob petting. I was, of course, determined to save the big moment for the honeymoon. But at seventeen, hormones seemed to kick into a higher gear, and when Larry and I had been going steady for a while, the life changing experience occurred. I was wearing a pink Bobbie Brooks skirt and sweater, and the main thing I remember was worrying that it would get blood on it. I really liked that skirt. While I was worrying, the event came and went. Or went and came, as the case may be. I remember thinking, "Is that IT?" I felt like I had gotten distracted for a moment and missed it. There was a small amount of blood—a spot the size of a silver dollar—on my underwear, but my skirt was fine. I remember going to bed that night thinking, "Well, now we're married in the eyes of God." That was a popular rationalization. It meant that as long as you intended to get married at some point down the road, sex wasn't a sin. Or as much of one.

The sex got better as we learned together. I think he had been with one other girl before me (one of the bad girls we all talked about, not Sharon), which had been a disagreeable experience, so we were pretty much on the same level. From then on, along with playing cards with his brother and sister-in-law, sex was the big thing on our dates, and people began to treat us like an old married couple. Several of my friends got married right after graduation. A few had gotten married while they were still in school, with babies on the way. That, of course, was a constant worry, but for some reason I never got pregnant, even though we didn't use birth control. Perversely, I began to wonder if I could have children.

I did indeed go to Tech instead of State Teachers, rooming with Larry's twin sister, Linda, and even managed to get an academic scholarship, which I lost my second semester after getting a C in chemistry. I normally would never have gone near chemistry, but I was required to take it for my major, and I wanted to get it over with. My lab partner was inept, too, and we once set the lab on fire, which didn't endear me to my professor.

I was the center of everything in high school, but college was a whole new experience. There were more people at Tech than in the entire town of Atkins, half of them were boys—half of those were cute, and I wanted to date them. Having my boyfriend's twin sister as my roommate was a little tricky, though; even if I'd wanted to cheat, she knew where I was every minute. So I didn't cheat, but I wanted to, and even that made me feel guilty.

I started off as a home economics major, since I had loved my teacher in high school, Mary Gay, and couldn't think of anything else I wanted to do. Then, along with chemistry, one of the required courses for the home ec major was basic art, and I fell in love with it. The art teacher, Helen Marshall, convinced me I was good at painting, drawing, clay, and other studio arts. Art was so much more fun than anything else I had tried; there were no tests, just displays of our work, and so I changed my major and became part of the art crowd, which was also, de facto, the hippie crowd. In 1967, boys were just beginning to grow their hair long in Arkansas, and most of them were art majors.

I also entered my second beauty contest, for Miss Arkansas Tech, but I only got fourth runner-up, even though I did great on my song, "I Wanna Be Free" by the Monkees. After that, encouraged by my friends, I entered the Miss Russellville competition, but unhappily on the night of the pageant, I got a stomach virus and had to keep running backstage to throw up. Not too attractive, coming out onstage in a white bathing suit with a green complexion. Or singing "What Now, My Love," which was partly in French, while trying to keep from barfing. Although I worked hard on learning the lyrics by rote with a French teacher, it was a big fiasco when I switched to French on the second verse and got mixed up on the words. The audience sat there, stunned, not having a clue what I was saying or what language I was saying it in. As an added bonus, it was slightly off-key, just enough to make you grind your teeth, so that was the end of my pageant life. Still, the contests nudged me a little bit further into the limelight at school. Guys started asking me out in greater numbers, and I hated to have to tell them I was going steady, but I was.

Larry was a wildlife biology major, was in ROTC—with his hair shorn into a military buzz cut—and we were already beginning to grow apart. More than anything, he loved fishing and hunting, things I couldn't bear. (One of his favorite fishing spots was called the Snake Hole. The name pretty much said it all.) When I went over to his house, I never knew if the boiling pot on the stove contained dinner, or if it was six or eight decapitated roadkill heads he was cleaning for a skull collection in one of his classes. (Well, actually, it wasn't *that* hard to tell the difference.) Once, I was looking in the freezer for ice cream and saw, poking out of Reynolds Wrap, the feet of a mink he was going to use for taxidermy class.

I tried to take an interest in hunting and fishing. He got out the shotgun and gave me a lesson, but it had such a kick that it sent me flying backward and bruised my shoulder. I went with him once to the deer woods, getting up in the early morning dark and tracking around in the freezing snow, but I made so much noise that he sent me back to the car. He thought I did it on purpose so the deer would hear me and run away. He was a state champion archer, but when I tried it, I couldn't hold my arm properly and kept hitting it with the string until my arm was one bruise from my shoulder to my wrist. I tried to go fishing with him—I at least liked to eat fish—but he had to bait my hook. I just couldn't put that sharp thing through the eye of a minnow or thread a worm onto it, and it was so boring that I would bring a book and read. Once we went out for what I thought was going to be a romantic boat ride on the lake. We took only a flimsy rubber raft, but we weren't going far from the shore. It was a clear night with a full moon, and I quickly discovered he really had fishing on his mind, not romance. I was bored, sitting in the dark, looking up at the sky, when a dark object flew across the moon. "Oh, look, Larry! That's so weird. There's a bird flying at night!"

"That's no bird; that's a bat." He ignored it and kept throwing his line out, trying for a huge catfish, which are easier to catch at night or something. The lake, usually romantic from the front seat of the car, was creepy in the light rubber boat. Frogs croaked a lonesome song, and things splashed in the water next to our raft with slithery sounds. I looked up, and the bat flew across the moon again, this time lower. I hunkered down in the boat as the thing starting circling us, and soon it was flying close enough to make us duck. Larry swung the paddle at the bat, and I took off my shirt and wrapped it around my head so it wouldn't get hung up in my hair. I'd heard that had happened once, and the girl had gone crazy, as I suspected I would, too.

"This thing is acting strange. It might be rabid," he said, slightly out of breath. "Let's get out of here!" But getting out of there entailed paddling, and he couldn't paddle and swing at the bat at the same time. It came so close that I felt it brush my head, which really flipped me out. Larry paddled as fast as he could, taking time to flail at the bat as it passed over us. Instead of the bat going away after we got on land, it was still attacking us. We ran down the road, the bat chasing us, dive-bombing our heads, and finally, panting with fear and exhaustion, we got to the car. Larry jumped in and locked the doors before he realized I wasn't in the car, too, and there I was, without my shirt—which was wrapped around my head so I could hardly see—pounding on the windows. He quickly let me in, and I slammed the door just as the bat smacked into the window. It fell to the ground, but we didn't stop to see if it was dead or not. I'm sure it was rabid. Bats just don't attack humans unless they are. So that was one more reason for me never to go out night fishing again. As if I needed another one.

Larry, on the other hand, had absolutely no interest at all in my artwork. He said that art was just playing, it wasn't even a real college major. Still, we were together, having great sex. In God's eyes we were married, as I convinced myself, still fending off my nightmares of hell, and we did have fun. He had a great sense of humor, and he could make me laugh, which was a fine attribute.

I WORKED AS secretary to my adviser, Helen Marshall, who became my mentor. She was my inspiration as an artist and as a woman. She had lived in Puerto Rico, had traveled all around the world, and told me I had talent and could do anything I wanted to do if I just wanted it badly enough. There were two other girls, Aurora Young and Jean Jewell, who worked for Mrs. Marshall as well, and we became like the Three Musketeers. Aurora was from the Philippines but had moved here when she was three, so she was as much a hillbilly as the rest of us. Jean was from Little Rock, a gentle mother earth type who had honest blue eyes and long hair that was already beginning to gray at eighteen, and she practiced Buddhism, getting up early in the mornings to chant.

As well as being Mrs. Marshall's secretary, I posed for figure drawing class (in a bathing suit) and worked in a little art shop she owned. I didn't make much money at the shop since there was always some goodie like a handwoven poncho or a silver ring I wanted to buy instead of taking the salary. But with the money I had saved from working at the pickle plant the previous summer (I worked there three summers) it was enough to pay my tuition, although not quite enough for my room and board, so I moved back home for my second year, which wasn't nearly as much fun as living in the dorm. Larry was set to graduate at midterm to join the service as a second lieutenant and I convinced him we had to get married before he left. I was afraid he would be killed in Vietnam, and then, of course, there would be no possibility of getting married, and what we were doing in the backseat of his blue Chevy Nova would send me to hell. Larry, God knows why, went along with me, even though I really don't believe he wanted to, and we got married August 15, 1969. He was twenty-two and I was twenty.

I had nightmares about the wedding for weeks before it occurred. In every dream, I would be walking down the aisle in some bizarre, creepy setting, like an abandoned warehouse, or the train tracks late at night. Then I would step up to take his hand and discover it wasn't Larry at all but some monster. I was obviously feeling a little unsure about the whole thing, but I forged ahead anyhow. My cousin Carla Watson and my best friend since the age of five, Susan Gibson, were my bridesmaids, and when I told them I wanted yellow to be my color, neither of them felt like they looked good in yellow, so I agreed to have blue, even though it is one of my least favorite colors. I bought fabric and had a wedding gown made by Ruby Eakes, a nice lady from the

Larry and me at the altar with Brother Bob Rackley.

church who sewed for people, for twenty-five dollars. It was a satin Empire waistline dress with a lace mantilla, and I carried daisies, so at least I had a touch of yellow. A friend, Martha Bowden, made the cake, and we had punch and nuts and mints at the reception. I think the whole thing must have cost less than fifty dollars.

As my father and I were standing in the vestibule of the church, waiting to walk down the aisle, he turned to me with tears in his eyes and said, "You don't have to go through with this. You can leave right now and it will be okay." I was crying myself, but said, "No, I have to. It's too late." He knew why I was doing it, I'm pretty sure, and knew I was making a mistake, but I was saving my soul from hellfire, so down the aisle we went.

We didn't have a honeymoon. I had quit school and taken a job as a secretary in a small steel company to support us until Larry graduated in January. Then I was going back to school to finish the year while he went to basic training. I would join him after school was out in May. The job was an absolute fiasco. I had lied and told them I could take shorthand dictation, and while I was a pretty good typist, I had three male bosses who each piled so much work on me it would have been impossible for one experienced woman to do it all, much less an untrained girl. I had to make coffee for them all day, copy blueprints, and do all the billing. (They taught me to change the way I wrote numbers: eights were to be two O's stacked on top of each other like a snowman, sevens had a line across the leg, twos never had a loop on the bottom, fours came to a peak at the top and were never open. I still do them that way.) I had to answer the phone, type up the contracts and letters with four carbons (so I couldn't make any mistakes or I had to retype them), plus whatever else there was to do. I preferred to doodle portraits on the desk pad while answering the phone, which I thought were pretty good, but the bosses were unimpressed. We were located a couple of miles from town, too, and one of the bosses who was a chain-smoker kept me running into town for cigarettes for him (using my own car and gas, which I resented). I was simply overwhelmed and in way over my head.

Larry and I had gotten married on a Friday, and on Monday, as he did every week, the big boss came in and added more stuff for me to do. He was probably around thirty-five, an old man to me, but looking back, he was rather attractive in a slick diamond-pinkie-ring way—buffed nails, blinding white shirts, and bright ties. I was bending over the file cabinet (wearing a miniskirt, as was the fashion then and probably the reason I was hired in the first place) when I felt a hand placed intimately on my rear end. Without thinking or checking to see who it was, I whirled around and clocked him. His face turned purple red with anger, and while I was shocked by what I had done, I was more angry at him. Without a word, he stormed out, and later in the afternoon, the next in command called me into the office and fired me. I asked him why, and he answered, "Mistakes." I wasn't such a good secretary that I could defend my work. Maybe it was legitimately work mistakes. But I don't think so.

I had been married for three days and had lost my job. We had rent to pay, groceries to buy, and no income. So I drove directly from the steel company to the employment agency and was sent to the shoe factory, where I immediately got an office job. (I was still wearing the miniskirt.) I think it was even for more money. I had been making around fifty dollars a week at the steel company, which was minimum wage—$1.30 an hour—and I think I was making $1.35, maybe even $1.37, at the shoe factory. And the bonus was that we could get shoes at wholesale—every girl's dream!

I worked through the fall semester, then quit the minute Larry graduated in January. I hated the job, which I wasn't good at, either, as it was keeping an accounting of eyelets and shoelaces and whatever else went into the shoes, and numbers are not my friends. Still, Larry and I had fun those first few months, looking at our thick white gold rings, saying "my husband" or "my wife," playing house, and, most important of all, sleeping in a real bed instead of the backseat of the car. We rented a two-bedroom apartment in Atkins near my parents, and I learned to cook, experimenting on poor Larry, since my mother had never taught me. When I was growing up, she thought it was easier to do it herself than try to teach me, and I agreed. Her mother never taught her, either, so she probably thought that if she could figure it out, I could, too, and eventually I did.

I made a lot of Kraft macaroni and cheese dinners, spaghetti, and pizza from a Chef Boyardee mix. (There were no pizza parlors in those days, or Chinese restaurants or Italian or anything remotely ethnic. They didn't even sell garlic in some markets. Nobody knew what to do with it.) I would use the crust mix from the pizza box and make the dough, then add more tomato sauce to the small can provided and put Jimmy Dean sausage or pepperoni or mushrooms and mozzarella cheese on top. It was better than any I have had since. The rest of our meals were fried something or other. For meat we had ham or pork or bacon his parents cured themselves, beef they grew, chickens that ran around, and the fish and occasional game Larry brought home, like deer or quail or squirrel. I would eat the quail, watching for bird shot that might break a tooth, but I wouldn't touch the deer or squirrel at all. His mother cooked that.

Mrs. Norris had happily cooked game all her life—deer and squirrels (with the macabre squirrel heads on the platter, their little eyeholes and teeth peeking out of the crispy brown crust), but I couldn't bring myself to even taste it—it was too close to rat for me. Larry's mother and father gave us part of a calf they butchered every year for the freezer, and they had a huge garden. I still salivate thinking of the big ripe tomatoes, the fresh corn taken right out of the field and boiled before it lost its sweetness, and the squash and okra we picked and promptly sliced thin, dipped in flour, salt, and pepper, and then fried. We ate chicken-fried steak, cornbread and pinto beans or green beans cooked all morning with a piece of salt pork until they were a greasy wonderful mush, and baby green onions; turnip greens with hot pepper sauce and homemade pickles. My mother-in-law tried to teach me how to can and make jelly and jam, but I was not that into it. I once fell out of a mulberry tree trying to get berries for jam and landed in a prickly pear patch. Everyone thought that was hilarious except me. We picked ripe peaches and apples out of trees, and flicked wasps off juicy yellow plums. They were so drunk on the sweet juice, they didn't even sting.

I drove the tractor while they harvested huge black diamond watermelons, and we would sometimes bust one open in the field and eat the red hearts out with our hands, juice running down our elbows. When we were in high school, boys were always sneaking up on the mountain to steal watermelons at night, and sometimes a farmer kept a shotgun loaded with rock salt to shoot at them for their trouble. The doctor was always sighing and picking rock salt out of someone's behind. It was weird to know that some of my friends were helping themselves to my boyfriend's family's living, but it was the adventure as much as the watermelons they craved, and they never took too many.

Larry's midterm graduation finally came, with a ceremony where I pinned the lieutenant's bars on his new uniform and we got our picture in the paper. Then he went off to Fort Knox, Kentucky, for basic training, and I went back to college for the first half of my junior year. And that's when my troubles began.

Six

I soon discovered that being married put me into a whole new category at Tech. I was excluded from all kinds of things, like being in the Athena Troop, an elite drill team the ROTC members chose that performed at football games at halftime in short, tight uniforms and hats with gold feathers. I got my hand-embossed invitation in the mail, then they found out I was married and rescinded it. Of course, there was no question of being in the homecoming court, or being the sweetheart of any fraternity. I was married. I was twenty years old and might as well have been eighty as far as college life was concerned. The only thing I still managed to do was a little modeling. A photographer named Bill Ward had been hired to take pictures of all the contestants for the Miss Russellville pageant program the year before, and he later asked me to pose from time to time for local department store ads in the *Log Cabin Democrat*. An older man of twenty-seven, he was married and was also the choir director at church, so there was no romance, but he did have nice green eyes and longish blond hair, which was cool. He'd started a new trend of posing his subjects outdoors near brooks and in meadows of wildflowers, old barns, and woods instead of in a stiff studio, and everyone went to him for their wedding announcement pictures.

Ever since high school, I'd had the impossible dream of becoming a model, and I read *Glamour* and *Vogue* every month. Seeing myself in the *Log Cabin Democrat* ads made me believe it might be a real possibility. One of the teachers from Atkins had a daughter named Sarah Thom who was once a successful model in New York. Before the wedding, I got up my courage and wrote her a letter, included some pictures Bill Ward had taken, and asked her if she thought I had a chance. I suppose it was a secret last-ditch effort to go for a dream and not settle for life in a small town, cleaning fish and teaching school, so I didn't tell anyone else I had done it. Sarah Thom sent the pictures on to Eileen Ford, her agent, who sent me back a form letter basically saying I should forget it and seek another career. It was a harsh wake-up to reality, and I filed that dream away. But it was fun to be a *Log Cabin Democrat* girl once in a while.

I moved back home to save money after Larry went to basic training, and my parents were even tougher on me than when I was single. They thought I should be home by nine o'clock so nobody would think I was doing anything improper. "What will people think?" was their mantra. I couldn't go to a dance or party, and even going to the movies with my girlfriends was suspect. I spent a lot of evenings watching TV and writing to Larry. In those days, a long-distance phone call was an

Modeling for Bill Ward.

event worthy of mention in the social section of *The Atkins Chronicle*, as in, "Viola Higgins's daughter, Sue Ellen, called her all the way from Visalia, California, to wish her a happy birthday." Long distance was expensive, and stamps were only six cents.

Then Russellville had its centennial celebration. They hired a company out of Virginia to come and organize the show, and to get me out of the house and doing something fun, a girlfriend of mine named Toni brought me to a meeting about it. The man they sent as the director was an adorable guy I'll call Edmond who was a dancer full of graceful energy. He was small and compact and had a neat black beard, longish hair (but not offensively long for the older folks), and wore yellow aviator sunglasses. I fell madly in love (or something approximating it) with him at first sight. Of course, being married was much more restrictive than going steady, and the last thing I was ever going to do was cheat on my husband; even the thought of it was enough to make me worry about hell, but these things have a life of their own, hell or not, and I found myself alone in the house one day when he dropped by to discuss some skit he wanted me to be in. I swear nothing was going on except talk, but my parents came back while he was in the living room and knew immediately from the pheromones in the air that this guy was trouble.

I found myself making excuses to stop by his office, reasons to linger after rehearsals. He needed special meetings with me to work on a song, he needed help writing some dialogue. We kissed once, a stolen one, and then we kissed a lot. He was terrific at it. It was much more painful than the almost-kisses with Jerry in the backseat at the drive-in, because now that the cork was out of the bottle sex-wise, there was no putting it back in. I was used to a lively sex life and my husband was gone. But I didn't dare cross that line.

School was out in May, I'd completed half my junior year, and it was time for me to join Larry. He had been transferred from Fort Knox to Fort Campbell, Kentucky, and I was going to be with him there until he had to leave for Vietnam right before Christmas. Edmond had given up on getting me into bed—it was just too frustrating, he said—and we agreed we'd never see each other again. But the day before I was to leave, I couldn't stand it any longer. I got up my courage and went to his apartment early in the morning, driving around the block about ten times first.

It was a stupid thing to do, for many reasons, but one was that it never occurred to me he might have another woman there. Fortunately, he didn't, and when he saw me standing in the doorway, he grabbed me and pulled me into the bedroom. It took about one minute to get undressed, and another two or three from start to finish. It was over before I really knew what had happened. Because he was such a great kisser, I had expected the rest to be something spectacular, but it was like those pastries in the bakery case that look so delicious but taste like white paste. I got dressed and left in a flood of guilt and anxiety, and the next day I squeezed into my green Volkswagen, which was packed to the roof, to drive to Fort Campbell and move into army housing. I'm sure my parents breathed a sigh of relief when I left town. I was a ticking bomb waiting to go off at any minute. I'm sure they had no idea the bomb had already gone off, and had been a dud.

Seven

Fort Campbell is right on the border between Kentucky and Tennessee, and our house was spot on the line, our living room in Tennessee and our bedroom in Kentucky. It was small, a two-bedroom bungalow with gray linoleum floors and the walls a freshly painted chalk-white. I can't bear flat white walls or the color gray, but we weren't allowed to paint them, so I had to settle for hanging up colorful pictures and putting down rugs to make it seem less like an institution. The kitchen had old appliances from the fifties, and nestled in the

Larry at Fort Campbell.

white metal cabinets was a roll of roach killing paper packed tight with the nest of a thousand roaches. Across the street was a golf course, handy for Larry, who was good at most sports and liked golfing. The house was a two-family bungalow, the other side a mirror of ours but empty. I was so happy to see Larry, so guilty about my little escapade with Edmond, that we had a great reunion.

Larry was an armored cavalry officer, the 3rd Platoon leader for F Troop 17th Cavalry, 23rd Infantry Division (made famous by Lieutenant William Calley, who was at the center of the infamous My Lai Massacre). Larry didn't mind spending his days inside a hot tank, but I had such claustrophobia that I popped in and back out of it in ten seconds when he took me on a tour.

Life on an army base is insular, and the chain of command extends to the wives. I was an officer's wife, albeit the lowest ranking officer, and I learned I was supposed to act like it. Officers got better everything—housing, food, all kinds of things—than the enlisted men. I knew no one, of course, but we were expected to go to parties for the officers whether we wanted to or not, and I had to go to teas and luncheons and events for the wives, which was fine, but I didn't seem to meet anyone who was girlfriend material. At one of these first parties we were at the colonel's house, standing outside beside a shimmery blue swimming pool, and a waiter in a white coat was passing around a tray of pretty juice drinks with fruit and little umbrellas stuck in them. It was a warm night and I was thirsty, so I took one, and it tasted pretty good. Nervous and trying to make conversation with the older officers, I drank it down quickly, and the waiter was right there on the spot and handed me a second. I was beginning to feel pretty relaxed for some reason and didn't really want it, but took it to be gracious and sipped it.

About halfway through the second drink, I began to get dizzy and sleepy, and I remember thinking how nice it would be to lie down, just for a minute, and take a little nap on the cool tile beside the pool. The next thing I remember is Larry carrying me into our house over his shoulder. He was so humiliated, and I can't remember what he did or how he explained it, but I hope the one thing he didn't say was the truth, "My wife has never tasted alcohol in her life, and she's an idiot. Sorry." I really, truly, hadn't known there was alcohol in the drink. Isn't that sad? At the wives' teas, there was sometimes tart white wine, and I had a little, pretending to drink it but mostly just holding the glass. One of the ladies once put fresh cut peaches into the glasses, which made the wine sweeter and more palatable. I had done so many bad things, I was past the point of worrying about sin, and never even pretended to look for a church, as my father kept asking me to do, so what was the harm in having a glass of wine?

Larry had to get up at five in order to be at work by six, and I had nothing to do all day, so I slept late, had breakfast, cleaned the small house, and then either drove aimlessly around trying to get a handle on the area or walked the aisles of the PX or the mall and poked around in stores. I had made no friends; it seemed hard to find any outside the social functions. And Larry was gone all day. At night he would come home, tired and down. We would eat dinner, watch TV for a short while, and go to bed, since he had to get up so early. He was having a hard time adjusting to the job, and occasionally he got migraines. I didn't notice it as much before we got married, but at times he would seem blue for days or weeks on end, and then for no apparent reason he would snap out of it and be his old funny, chipper self again. Once, back when we were dating, we were watching *Green Acres* during one of these times, and he started laughing. Afterward he was cheery, like nothing harsher than rain had ever fallen on his head.

I'm sure his job made it worse. He had a lot of responsibility on his young shoulders as the leader of a platoon of soldiers and tanks, and he knew that he would be headed to Vietnam in a few months, where he would be responsible for the lives of his men. But while he was working things through, I was going quietly stir-crazy. We never went out to a movie or to eat. He was too tired to even talk much. We rarely had sex.

Then the phone rang one day and it was Edmond. We began to talk frequently, and the more detached Larry got, the more I began to miss home. I knew more clearly every day that I'd made a terrible mistake getting married. I began to think more and more about Edmond. He told me he was finishing up the centennial and would be going to Missouri next, and if I wanted to come back, I could go with him.

Obviously I couldn't tell Larry the truth, so I just told him I wanted to go back home for a visit. He said fine, perhaps with relief, and I got on the bus. I didn't know what would happen on the other end, but I couldn't wait to get away from where I was, the small gray and chalk-white house with roaches, TV, and the boredom of the mall.

It was a bright, sunny day, I was full of nervous anticipation, I had a good book to read—Mary Stewart's new book about Merlin, *The Crystal Cave*—and I felt like I'd been let out of a cage. Then somewhere between Clarksville, Tennessee, and Nashville the bus conked out. We sat on the side of the road for a couple of hours until somebody came and fixed it. I called Edmond and told him I was going to be late. He said not to worry, that he'd be at the Little Rock bus station, where we had arranged to meet. We made it to Memphis before the bus broke down again. It was hot and muggy, it was late, and we were still more than three hours from Little Rock.

The Memphis bus station had to have been built off the blueprints for purgatory. The lights were dim fluorescent, making everyone look wan and sick. There were people who, I assumed, lived there—unwashed, with greasy hair, nasty clothes, and rusty ankles. Several slept soundly on the benches, not moving as my fellow passengers and I shuffled in. I was wearing a yellow voile dress that had wilted and glued itself to my sweaty skin hours before. My Arrid had given out some time ago, too, and I smelled like a skunk. It didn't really matter, because everyone smelled like that, or worse. One of the drunk men kept coming over to talk to me with breath that would melt mascara, trying to get me to go out with him for a drink. I huddled on my bench, attempting to ignore him, and finally he went away.

I called Edmond again and told him it was going to be later. The clock ticked on and I had to call again. It was going to be later. And later. Until finally they said the bus was fixed and we would arrive at three in the morning.

Edmond was worn out with the waiting, but good-natured about it, and when we rolled in, he was there with his yellow glasses waiting for me. He gave me one of those great kisses, and we went to a little dump of a motel near the bus station. It was dark and I was exhausted from the trip. I don't know how he stood the smell of me, but he didn't want to wait for me to take a shower, so we went in, stripped down, and did the deed in the first five minutes we were inside the room. It was exactly like the first time. Maybe it was worse, because I was so tired and conscious of how sweaty and bad I smelled. I fell into the rough sheets, passed out, and the next morning we showered and tried again, but we both realized there was no magic there. We packed our bags, went out into the bright sunshine, and to my horror we were right across the street from the construction project my father was working on. He was running a crane, and I looked up and saw a tiny figure in the cab of the machine. I jumped into the car, terrified he had caught a glimpse of my bright red hair, and off we went.

Edmond tried hard to make a fun day out of it. We went to breakfast, and then he took me to the zoo, but the sad animals lying on concrete floors, panting in the heat behind bars, were so depressing. I knew how they felt. We had lunch, and then I asked him to drop me off at the bus station. I called my mother and told her I was coming home and would tell her all about it when I got there. She was in total shock, so I didn't linger on the phone. Edmond and I had a final (great) kiss, and I waved goodbye at the departing candy-apple-red VW bug—same year as my green one, which I had once seen as some kind of portent, now meaningless—trundling up the road toward Missouri. We had never once mentioned my going with him.

Of course, everyone in Atkins was stunned that I was back, but in spite of the circumstances, I knew more than ever that I didn't want to be married. I called Larry and told him I wasn't coming back. He got right into the car (I have no idea how he managed to get away from his duties so quickly) and drove straight to Atkins. Everyone said, "Give it a chance," "You've only been married a few months," "All newlyweds are like this in the beginning," "He loves you so much, you love him so much," and so on. But the main reason I decided to stay with him was because *he* convinced me that he loved me and wanted me back. He really did want to be married to me. He hadn't been coerced into it.

So we went back to Fort Campbell, and things were a lot better. I guess my leaving snapped him out of his funk, and we began to go out, make friends, and have fun. A couple moved into the other side of our house and I had a girlfriend to hang out with. I was so grateful that I hadn't ruined my life by running away with the wrong man, and grateful that no one ever knew about my near disaster. (Except now *everyone* knows.) I vowed to do better, to become a better wife and Christian. I rededicated my life to Jesus. (The great thing about Freewill Baptists is that you can sin and then rededicate and you are shiny clean and new, like a slightly used car that has been detailed.) I was determined to be the best wife ever. And for a while I was.

Eight

It was December and we were home. Larry was shipping out for Vietnam five days before Christmas, and we were trying to make it as festive as we could, splitting our time between my parents' house and his parents' house. He was one of nine children, and all of his siblings had come home to say goodbye to him. (His mother had had change of life babies, Larry and his twin sister, Linda, when she was forty-five, so Larry had nieces and nephews older than he was.) We had a big raucous dinner, and after we had cleaned up the kitchen and laughed and talked for a while longer, his older sister from Virginia and her husband went—without a by-your-leave—and got into our bed! It was the only spare bedroom, and we had been using it. I don't remember why we just didn't tell them it was our room, or go on down to my parents' place, but it was late and we didn't, so Larry's mother gave us quilts to make a bed on the floor in the living room, with several kids scattered around on couches.

The floor was, well, a floor, and we had only a quilt or two between us and it. I was skinny, and my bones were digging hard into the linoleum. I could feel the bruises forming. I couldn't find a place to even get comfortable, much less sleep. Then, for some insane reason, Larry decided to get amorous. I whispered, "No, the kids will hear," but he had his mind made up, and I nearly strangled myself senseless keeping quiet, normally being somewhat of a screamer. I think that was the night I conceived our son, Matthew.

The night before Larry left, we booked a room in the fanciest hotel in Little Rock, splurging more than we could afford. (It could have been that night, too, that I conceived. It was just a day or two later. Or it might have been another day around that time. He was going to Vietnam, after all.) I took him to the airport the next day, then drove back home alone to cry, watch Walter Cronkite, and write letters every night. In January, I went back to Tech to finish my junior year.

In a couple of weeks, I began to feel odd things going on. My period didn't come and my breasts were strangely tender. I waited it out for another week or so, and when the period still hadn't come, I went to the doctor. Yes, dear reader, I was pregnant. At the exact minute I walked in the door from the doctor's office, the phone rang. It was Larry, calling from Saigon to tell me he was okay. "That's wonderful, sweetheart. I have a little news myself. You're going to be a daddy!" There was a long silence, and then I heard a thud as he dropped the phone.

By good luck, my best friend Susan, who'd been my bridesmaid (and who looked good in blue), got pregnant two weeks after I did, and Aurora, my best friend at Tech, was already two months pregnant, so we all went through it together. (I gained the most weight.) I had a host of other friends from home and my art and English classes who were all there for me as well, not to mention the church.

My favorite class was creative writing with a teacher named B. C. Hall, or Clarence, as we called him. It was in his class that I learned to write. He sat cross-legged on the desk, as cool and hip as could be, hair just that little bit too long, giving us words of wisdom through clouds of cigarette smoke and squinted eyes, in a languorous drawl that held us spellbound. (Teachers were allowed to smoke in those days, I think. Or, more likely, he just said "screw the rules.") On one of my stories, he wrote, "What's an intelligent woman like you doing in a place like this?" I saved it and cherish it. We were friends until he died in 2005, and we wrote three screenplays together, two of which were optioned although not made. (Yet. I'm still an optimist.) It was in that class that I started writing stories that turned into my first novel, *Windchill Summer,* twenty-nine years later, a story about boys going to Vietnam and the toll it took on them and everyone close to them.

In class, I sat between a couple of hippie guys named Matthew and Larry, who were always under surveillance for being the typical long-haired peace-symbol-wearing dopers. Matthew had the longest hair of anybody at school, a droopy blond George Custer mustache, and little round John Lennon glasses. He walked with an odd bounce up onto his toes with every step, which reminded me of Bugs Bunny. Matthew and Larry of course smoked pot, which was still exotic to most of the kids, and owned a head shop called the Family Hand, which had a black light room with psychedelic posters of Jimi Hendrix, Janis Joplin, the Grateful Dead, and others on the walls. In the middle was a giant water bed, where you could lie and float and pass some groovy hours. They felt sorry for me, since my husband was in the hated war, and adopted me and brought me milk to drink in class so I'd be healthy. If I had a couple of hours to kill, they insisted I go over to the shop and take a nap on the cool undulating water bed. I liked it so much I later got myself one.

I was hungry all the time and nervous with the strain of the war and the pregnancy. By the end, I had gained sixty-five pounds. Once when I was in a Taco Bell, a guy who had been in one of my classes the previous year came up and asked me if I had a sister. I said no, and he said, "Are you sure? This girl looks a lot like you, except she's thin." I wanted to smear his face with my enchilada. What a moron. But it sadly brought home the fact that I was fat. As school let out and the summer hit like an open oven door, I was huge and miserable. No air conditioners back then. At least not in our house. I was obsessed with the war, and I knew that every letter I got from Larry had been written two weeks earlier, or more, so I had no idea how he was doing or where he was. They weren't allowed to say, exactly, but he named places such as the Pineapple Forest, Arizona Territory, and Da Nang. He was also near the Laotian border, and every night on the news when any of those places were mentioned, I squinted to see if he was one of the soldiers pictured.

I enrolled in summer classes in English, as I had every summer, to get a second teaching major. Then the fall semester started. I was the size of a blimp and totally miserable, waiting for my baby to arrive, sliding by my due date with no sign of labor. I had a night class in Asian art history with Mrs. Marshall, and one night I felt strange. This I announced to the class: "I feel strange."

"Go HOME!" they all yelled at me, in unison, but even though I was two weeks past my due date, I just didn't think it was labor. I didn't have any pains. So I stayed until class was over, everyone watching me out of the corners of their eyes, and soon after I got home my water broke and my mother said I had to go to the hospital. I still wasn't sure I was in labor, and when we walked through the door, I said to the nurse that I was sorry, I thought I might be in labor but wasn't sure since I wasn't in pain. I was afraid she would scold me and send me back home. She slapped me down on the table, laughed, assured me I would have some pains, and then stuck me with a big needle full of painkillers. That's what they did to ignorant twenty-two-year-old girls in 1971. They didn't even ask me if I wanted to do a natural birth. Why would anybody want to do that? That's why God invented morphine.

The labor went on for eight hours. I was groggy the whole time and don't remember much. I had brought my art history book thinking I would study for a test. Can you believe it? I do seem to remember floating penises in the pictures of the ruins at Angkor Wat—which frankly I wasn't interested in at that point—and a lot of Buddhas, but not much else.

At one point they gave me an enema, and just as I sat down on the pot beside the bed, the entire ladies' auxiliary of the church trooped in with their flowered dresses and big smiles to give me their support. I screamed at them, *"Get out of here!"* and threw toilet paper rolls at them, poor things. They scurried away, and I felt bad, but really—this Christian business of visiting the sick is just too much. The sick just want to be left alone to fart at will, or to get up in a backless johnny with their butts exposed and go to the bathroom without having to entertain somebody who is underfoot praying over them.

I had a spinal for the last big pain, and they whisked my baby boy away before I had a glimpse of him, because he had mucus in his lungs that had to be suctioned (he was probably zonked out on the painkillers, too, poor baby), and then I passed out. So I don't remember seeing him until later, when I went to the incubator, and there he was, the spitting image of Larry. At least people could stop counting on their fingers the months Larry had been away. He was so beautiful—lots of dark hair, an adorable little monkey face, and he was huge! Nine pounds, with rosy cheeks hanging like ripe peaches. My friends Matthew and Larry from creative writing class bounced in to congratulate me, totally stoned, and were like, "Cool! Awesome, man! Look at his little toesies!" when they saw him. The nurses' eyes were the size of dessert plates. Obviously, I hadn't had a husband there with me, so I'm sure they were whispering, "I wonder which one the daddy is. I wonder if she knows." I named him Matthew Davis, but not because of my friend. Larry and I had already picked out the name before I'd even met Matthew in class, but it was a nice coincidence, the Matthew and Larry thing.

By October 1971, Nixon had started to withdraw some of the troops early, and Larry got to come home two months ahead of schedule. I met him at the airport, and I truly don't think he recognized me. The look on his face still haunts me, as if he were looking at a not particularly attractive girl and then realized it was me. Matthew was six weeks old at this point, and I was still carrying around a lot of the baby weight and had cut my boob-length auburn hair into a Jane Fonda shag because it was so hot and miserable. We were happy to see each other, it goes without saying, but a little like strangers for a while, as if we were acquaintances who had bumped into each other at the airport and started a romance. Matthew was the biggest thing in my world, and Larry had seen only pictures of him. We had to remake our life together.

We moved to Perryville, about thirty miles from Atkins, where Larry got a job teaching physics in the high school. I was doing my practice teaching in the art department at Subiaco Catholic Boys' Academy, fifty or sixty miles in the opposite direction over winding country roads, and it was just too tough a commute for me, so before we had time to even hang curtains, we moved back to Atkins, which was in the middle, and we each had a commute. I dropped the baby off with my mother—bless her sweet heart—in the morning and picked him up in the afternoon. Matthew had big serious brown eyes, and he was precocious at everything. He walked at ten months, and I took him off the bottle at a year, as he was eating and drinking from a cup. I was so harried I wanted to make things happen as fast and as easily as possible. Looking back, I'm sorry I did that. Babyhood goes by so quickly that I wish I had just taken the time and let him be a baby instead of pushing him to be a big boy.

Being a working mother, I never got enough sleep. I remember rocking Matthew all night and crying, saying, "Please, Matthew, just go to sleep for an hour. Let me get just one hour's rest before I have to go to work." Sometimes we had to put him in the car in the middle of the night and drive him around so he would go to sleep. But while he wasn't a great sleeper, he was a great eater. He could eat four eggs at a time if I would give them to him. Once, though, he was taking such a long time getting the eggs down that I lost patience and, late for school, started rushing him, cramming in the spoonfuls as he slowly and carefully chewed and swallowed. After he ate the whole plate of eggs, he leaned over and spat out three paper clips. I nearly fainted, thinking of how close I had come to choking him. I tried to have more patience after that.

I finally lost the weight, my hair grew back, and life settled down a bit for us. After graduation, I got an art teaching job in Clarksville, which was about twenty miles from Atkins, and Larry decided he wanted to do something other than teach that brought in more money, so he got a job selling insurance, which put him on the road a lot.

Baby Matthew and Larry.

It was during this time, when I was all by myself, exhausted from lack of sleep and harried from working, taking care of the baby, and dealing with the minutiae of life, when a little voice whispered in my ear, telling me I had missed the parade.

Nine

In Clarksville, I was assigned to teach lower-school art in the morning, then a seventh-grade English class before lunch, and in the afternoons I drove to the high school, where I taught art. The only thing I enjoyed was the high school. English class was my least favorite. Seventh graders are at that curious age when they are still children but hormones are hijacking their bodies. Some of the boys had a crush on me, some saw me as the enemy; some of the girls were bored, some thought I was cool. Nobody had the foggiest idea what a noun or verb was, and none of them wanted to find out. I was also from time to time a surrogate mother to them. One girl was quietly crying during class, and when I asked her to stay after and talk to me, I learned she had kissed a boy, he had put his tongue into her mouth, and she was terrified she was pregnant. I gave her a quick lesson on how the body reproduces, and she was much relieved.

I was only four or five years older than some of my high school students, and it was difficult to maintain the teacher-student relationship. I have former students who became lifelong friends whom I still see today, thirty-seven years later. For most of them, art was a blast, a break from "real" classes. I would do a demonstration of, say, printmaking and pass out the supplies, then they would start their own versions, with me walking around the room making suggestions when they needed it but never actually laying hands on their work—the first sacred rule of teaching art. We did weaving and stitchery (everyone wanted to embroider something on their bell-bottom jeans and denim jackets), copper enameling, sculpture in various mediums, and, of course, drawing and painting. We worked a lot in clay, sculpting, hand building, and throwing pots on the wheel.

Our budget was limited and we were always trying to find ways to do things on the cheap. We combed the garbage dump searching for treasures to use for sculptures or to stamp into interesting shapes on clay, or for printmaking. We went to the lumberyard to get scraps of Masonite or wood to paint on or to use for sculpture. We went to the grocery store dumpster for scavenged cardboard, egg cartons, or vegetables and fruit past their prime to use as printing stamps. (Did you know that the cut end of a bunch of celery is a perfect rose?) With old newspapers and wallpaper paste we made giant papier-mâché sculptures, animals mostly.

When one of the girls and I took our huge baby elephant to an art show in Little Rock in the back of a Ford Ranchero, the rope broke and the elephant flew out of the truck bed like Dumbo. Two state troopers passing by thought it was a foreign car rolling down the highway, turned, and chased after it, sirens blaring. They were most helpful, catching it and tying it securely back down for us, but we had to find a store that was open on Sunday, buy paint and paste, and do some quick repairs before the show.

I announced on the first day of class that there would be no written tests, just a display of student work twice a semester, which elicited cheers, and I brought a cassette player to class so they could work to music, as we had done in college. The music made for a cheery, fun atmosphere, and a lot more work got done. The superintendent—we'll call him Mr. Birch—didn't like my methods at all and was constantly coming into class, telling me to turn off the music and make the kids sit quietly in their seats, which was impossible if they were working. We had a constant battle going on, but I was the hero to the kids, who were my coconspirators. One of them was always on the lookout, and when we saw Mr. Birch sneaking down the hall, we would quickly turn off the music and sit in our seats. It was a great game to the kids.

The only problem in my life, looming ever larger, was that more than ever I didn't want to be married. Larry and I had grown apart after he'd gotten home. For me, there was the stress of working and taking care of the baby—along with housekeeping, grocery shopping, cooking, laundry, paying bills, servicing the car, and never getting enough sleep. As for Larry, he was on the road several days a week, and his unhappiness at doing yet another job he didn't like took its toll. He was not a natural salesman. He didn't have the gregarious kind of personality it required; he had to force himself to get up and do it every day. He hated everything about it—the travel, being away from home, the phoniness of it all. Not to mention the memories he brought back with him from Vietnam, which he seldom spoke about. He had been quietly and deeply affected by the cruelty, brutality, and indifference to life over there, and the few details he shared with me were more than I needed to know. He told me of one incident that nearly cost a lot of people their lives, including his.

He was the paymaster and normally gave out the money in the afternoons, but on this day, for no particular reason, he decided to pay in the morning. So everyone was at one end of camp getting their money, while at the other end, a driverless, booby-trapped garbage truck was rolled into the compound and exploded. Most of the hooches where the men lived were destroyed, and the woman who cleaned the officers' quarters was in Larry's hooch and was killed. His quarters were destroyed. If he hadn't decided to pay early that day, a huge number of soldiers would likely have died. Running back and finding the maid in the rubble of his quarters was horrific for Larry.

He also told stories of being out in the field for weeks, living in a tank without a shower or clean clothes, so constantly wet in the rainy season that when they finally came in to base and took off their boots, their skin came off with the socks. They always had to be alert, even when asleep, and they never could trust anyone. The man who gave you a haircut in the morning could be the one setting out booby traps at night. The Vietcong even strapped bombs to children begging for food, who would then explode in the middle of a group of men handing out candy bars. Someone might leave a lighter on a bar top one night, and the soldier who picked it up and flicked it on would have his hand blown off. No one can live like that and be the same person he was before. Larry was not one to display his emotions, even to me, and Vietnam stayed buried deep inside him, where it gnawed a big ragged hole, one he tried to ignore.

Not long after he came home, his mother died. She'd had colon cancer and had worn an ostomy bag for quite some time, but it was still a shock for us. She was a funny woman, always cracking jokes and making fun of her bag, trying to make the best of things. She had raised nine children on a farm, and was a tough old bird. She'd had a soft spot for Larry, her baby boy, and he loved her a lot.

We and several other members of the family were in the hospital waiting room, taking turns going in to sit with her. Matt was a baby, and I was trying to amuse him while we waited. The doctors had told us Larry's mother didn't have long, but somehow we couldn't accept that—as one never does, I suppose. Her daughter was in the room with her, holding her hand when she died. It was frightening, and of course the daughter ran out into the hallway calling for the nurses and doctors, who came running with the crash cart, put the paddles on her chest, and shocked her back to life. It was so insane. They knew she was going to die, she had no hope, but they just wouldn't let her go. Doctors seem to look upon every death as a personal failure, when it is just simply nature. We don't play God when we take terminal patients off life support; we play God when we put them on it.

After she came around, we all crowded into the room, crying and nervous, but she was calm and peaceful. "I lifted up out of this bed and went to the most beautiful place," she told us, with a faraway look on her face, "where there were flowers in colors I never saw before, and there were trees and creeks that were like the ones here, except a hundred times better. I can't even describe them. I was on a path walking through this beautiful country, and I felt so good. I didn't have any pain at all, I had a lot of energy. I felt young. Across the path was a fence, and behind the fence were my mother and daddy and my relatives and all my friends who have already died. They were so happy to see me and I was happy to see them, and just before I got to the fence, I was jerked back here. Please don't let them do that to me again. I want to go back. I'm not afraid. I want to go."

We were all dumbfounded. I had only ever heard of one other near-death experience. They weren't widely written about yet, and the other person I knew who'd had one was my uncle B.F., my daddy's brother, who said almost the same thing when he was on the operating table having heart surgery. His heart stopped, and he saw his mother, and he was never afraid of dying again after that.

It was strangely comforting for all of us, what my mother-in-law said. A couple of days later she died again, and this time they let her go. Her death opened up a whole new world for me, if what she said was true, and I do believe it was. Death wasn't the scary hell and judgment scenario the preachers had always told us about. It was lovely and loving, just as I'd always hoped it would be.

Nevertheless, the death was hard on Larry, just coming from Vietnam a few months before. I tried to comfort him, but I didn't know how, and he was never much good at talking about feelings. He went to bed and stayed there, turning his back to me and sleeping until two or three in the afternoon, then eating, watching a little TV, and going to bed early at night. It was worse than the darkest times he'd had at Fort Campbell. Nothing interested him except hunting and fishing. Maybe it was a cure of sorts, spending long solitary days in the woods alone. It was an escape, and I guess he needed one.

Matt came down with a bad chest cold that the doctor said turned into pneumonia. While we were in the doctor's office, the baby threw up and aspirated his vomit, and the doctor hustled me out of the room. I sat outside for what seemed like an hour, as nurses rushed in and out. I tried to get someone to at least tell me if he was alive or dead, but no one would talk to me. Finally, they let me see him and he was more or less okay. After a while they let me take him home, but for that whole night we had to sit up with him and take his temperature every half hour. If it went above a certain number, we would have had to take him to the hospital. Larry had planned a hunting trip for that night, and to my horror, he went, leaving me alone with the baby. Maybe it was a way to handle the pressure. I can't judge him now, although at the time I certainly did. I called my mother and daddy, who came over and stayed up with me, and thank God the baby's temperature never went too high and he recovered.

Although I was only twenty-three, I felt like I was as old as my parents, and saw nothing stretching ahead for me except more years of the same—getting older, working for a low wage, and watching my husband constantly go out the door, to work or hunting or fishing, shutting me out of his life.

Larry and I were just two different species. He found peace in his solitude, living in his own head, spending hours alone fishing or hunting, while guns scared me and I was repelled by the dead things he brought home. I needed life. I wanted to have fun. I was young.

We both adored our baby son, but we'd met as children and had grown up into two totally different people. We were never going to be compatible, and an unhappy mother and father weren't good for Matthew. Or for us. As strange as this sounds, I always felt, in some part of me, that I was just marking time until my real life started. The breakup was my fault. I take total responsibility, but I got to the point that I felt like I was going to smother and die if I didn't get out of the marriage. I left him in October of 1973, and the divorce was final in February of 1974.

I was finally free.

Ten

Larry went back to school and became a senior nuclear operations manager for Arkansas Power and Light, a job he did until he retired, and he remarried a few months after our divorce to a woman with two children, although they never had any together.

I applied for and got a full-time high school art teaching job at Russellville High School in the fall of 1973. I loved Russellville. It was where I had gone to Tech and was much closer to my mother, so taking Matthew there every day was easier. There were two thousand students in the high school, there was more space, more money, and I even had the luxury of a working artist in residence, Polly Loibner, who was a local TV celebrity. She had her own studio where she gave demonstrations and worked with the kids in watercolor and puppetry.

My methods of teaching were the same as in Clarksville, music and no written tests, and the kids loved it. The only worm in the apple was the principal—let's call him Chip—who was a former football coach and didn't understand what art was good for when the money could be better spent on new uniforms for the football team. As an added bonus, he hated hippies with a passion, which of course was what most of my students aspired to be. He told me I couldn't wear jeans to class, I had to wear dresses, and I nicely explained it was hard to do that when I had to work with clay on the wheel, or crawl around on the floor, but he was adamant, so I openly defied him, which didn't help things.

I bought myself and Matthew, then two, a three-bedroom house in Russellville, and I used one of the bedrooms as a studio for my easel and paints. The house had a big backyard and I got Matt a red-and-green swing set. We had a fig tree that produced huge ripe figs. Matt loved to help me mow the yard, and we planted marigolds and zinnias.

Matthew liked to watch me paint, so I set up a little art table for him in my studio. He liked my oil paints in the tubes better, and once he took a tube of burnt sienna and rubbed it all over his body and clothes. I'm sure the neighbors thought I was abusing him, because he screamed bloody murder when I had to put him in the tub and scrub the paint off with turpentine. We smelled for days. But he didn't give up wanting to be an artist.

I had done a commissioned pencil portrait (for twenty-five dollars, real money) of a friend of mine on his motorcycle, which took several days, and as I had it lying out on the table ready to be wrapped and

Matt under the fig tree.

sent, Matthew got a crayon, climbed up on the chair, and "improved" it. After I redrew the portrait, to my horror the same scenario happened all over again, even though I'd just stepped away from the table for a minute to get some tape, but this time he only had a pencil and I stopped him before he did too much damage, and I could fix it. I knew then he was going to be some kind of artist. (When he was four, he drew several human figures, some of which were smaller than the others. He pointed it out to me and said, "These small ones are the same size. They just look small because they are far away." The concept of perspective was a difficult one, even to some of my high school kids, and I'd never seen such a young child understand it quite like that.)

The kids from my class quickly made our home their headquarters.

I would probably be thrown in jail today, but I let them keep bottles of Boone's Farm wine in my fridge, and they got so comfortable with me that one of the girls pulled out a bag of pot one night and proceeded to clean the seeds and twigs out of it. I didn't quite know what to do. I didn't want to seem prim or preachy, but I was uncomfortable. So I just asked her not to smoke in the house because of the baby. I had never tried pot myself, but I didn't want to push the limits of the teacher-

Me and Bruce, a visiting potter, in art class.

pupil relationship too far. We had great evenings sitting on the floor eating spaghetti, talking, and listening to Lynyrd Skynyrd, the Doobie Brothers, Jethro Tull, B. B. King, Eric Clapton, the Beatles, and the Stones. For me, music ended when punk rock took over, but that's what every generation thinks. I can hear "Black Water" by the Doobie Brothers today and I'm right back there in my hand-embroidered bell-bottoms and long straight hair, living the life.

I had, of course, started to date, this time having no intention of ever getting married or going steady again. One guy I was seeing was called John Cool, a bass player who was in a band at the Ramada Inn and had long black hair, a beard, and a day job running a used-car lot named Mountain Motors. He paid some of my students to make a hand-carved sign for his business, complete with flowers and peace signs, which I counted as an art project for them. He was divorced from Cathy, another hippie who owned a head shop called the CAT. John Cool and Cathy and I all got along, and she sold my paintings, as well as paid me to paint a mural on the walls of her shop. It turned out pretty well, and made me all fired up about murals, so I got my gang of students and we painted one on the walls of my bedroom, bright enamel trees and flowers, sun and moon, peace signs and stars, a blue sparkling river flowing through it all. The room had orange shag carpet, and one of my boyfriends—he was named Wild Bill; he grew pot and looked like an extremely relaxed version of James Coburn—gave me his old water bed, where little Matt and I slept snuggled together every night, lulled by the cool water.

Matt and me in our studio.

Jean Jewell, my old friend from Tech, lived a few blocks from me on the second floor of an antebellum house. The place had a veranda that stretched all around it, pots of flowers and vines growing everywhere, honeybees buzzing around them in the sweet sunlight, and a porch swing with soft faded cotton quilts to laze around on. She had an ancient pickup truck and would go into the woods to find roots and plants and other natural ingredients for her famous stews. One night several friends had to go to the hospital with food poisoning, but nobody blamed her. She was a true earth mother, the first in town to wear earth shoes, cook organic, and try to save the world from pollution. We and a few other friends convinced her boyfriend to pose naked for us, and we had a drawing class in her apartment every week, which was great fun.

Jean and I went to all the arts and crafts fairs, where I did pencil portraits for five dollars each, and Jean sold her clay pots. We took pictures of each other (sometimes nude) in the woods, standing in a brook

Matthew and me in an old house. Photo taken by Jean Jewell Moreno.

or in a tree, or through the open windows of a deserted house. We painted and thought we were great artists. I dragged Matthew along to most things, or my mother would keep an eye on him when I couldn't.

He was a good boy most of the time—except, like his mother when she was a little girl, he thought it was great fun to run off and hide from me. He did it once in McCain Mall in Little Rock, and I almost went crazy, chasing him through the mall, screaming his name, going into every store. I was about to call the police when I spotted a pair of small red tennis shoes peeking out from under a rack of dresses. I wanted to swat his little behind, but didn't, I was so relieved to find him. I paid for my raising, as my mother used to say, and wished sometimes I could just put him on a leash. But he grew out of that, thank goodness, and I have nothing to complain about with either of my boys. Neither of my sons has ever said one bad word to me. The worst thing I ever said to them was "Don't make me have to say 'Don't' to you" or "I'm going to count to three, and then you had better stop that." When he got older, Matthew once asked me what I would have done to them if they hadn't stopped, and I answered, "I don't know. I never got to three."

People assume I came to New York with Norman because I was dying to get out of Arkansas, but that is simply not true. I loved it there, and was having the time of my life. True to my vow never to go steady again, I had a string of boyfriends, none of them serious. I was seeing a guy named Gary with long blond hair and a thick golden beard, who worked as a potter at Silver Dollar City, a theme park in the Ozarks, and did beautiful work on the wheel. He had a VW van with flowers and peace signs painted on it and a mattress in the back, which was most convenient for going camping. I was also seeing Dick, a lawyer who at thirty-two was the oldest man I had ever dated. He was divorced with two children, and was a golf nut who took me to the country club for nice dinners and formal dances. There was another potter, Bruce, who had studied with the famous Bernard Leach in England; John Cool; Wild Bill; and a few other guys. Some I slept with, at least a time or two, and some I didn't. (It *was* the golden era of the late sixties and early seventies, after the pill was invented and before AIDS, when sleeping with someone was almost like shaking hands.)

I was a painter, so when my art class would start a new project, if I could, I would coerce my friends who were more adept in the other art mediums into giving a demonstration. I also made an arrangement with the Arkansas Arts Center in Little Rock, and they sent several artists a year to give workshops for free. (Bruce, mentioned and pictured earlier, was one.) It was always a treat when one of them came. One well-known potter named Scott came to do a demonstration, and apparently I had neglected to tell Chip the date Scott would be there. He drove up in his flower-painted van and parked in the faculty parking lot. He was the walking definition of a hippie—a little on the heavy side, blond hair down to his shoulders, a mustache, and little dirty round glasses. His clothing had a few layers of clay built up on it, and I imagined the shirt and pants stood quietly upright beside his bed at night, waiting for him to step into them in the morning. The kids were awed by him, and were fascinated to see the way the clay effortlessly came to life through his hands. Then good ol' Chip stormed into the room and yelled at me, "What's this hippie doing here? I'm not going to have any dirty hippies in this school, you hear me? Why wasn't I consulted about this?" He had seen the van in the parking lot and had rightly assumed I had something to do with it.

I tried to explain that Scott was sent by the Arts Center, which was paying him, and I had indeed told him at the beginning of the year that the Center would be sending a series of artists at no cost to us, but Chip wouldn't listen. He was so worked up that his face got beet-red and he yelled at Scott to get his dirty hippie self out of there. I had never been so humiliated in my life. Scott gathered his stuff and left, totally shaken. Chip—dried spittle frothing at his mouth—gave me a warning that if I ever tried to bring someone like that in again, I would be fired.

That began an all-out war between us. From then on, he waited at my door in the morning, and if I was five minutes late, he chewed me out. He would pop into my class unannounced and just stand there glowering, sending out poison gas with his presence. I continued to wear jeans, which was a huge bone of contention, and when we had our big end-of-the-year show of the students' work, he made me take out two or three fine drawings because they were nudes—even though all you could see was crossed arms and legs, a bit of a hip, a slight suggestion of a bosom. Fortunately for me, the assistant principal, Ellis, loved me and my work and stuck up for me. The superintendent, Harvey, also liked me, so they gave me another contract at the end of the year.

In my second year of teaching at RHS, the kids nominated me for Outstanding Teacher of the Year, and I won. It wasn't that I was the best teacher in the school—far from it—I just happened to teach the most fun subject. Chip tried his best to get the results thrown out, but he couldn't, which I imagine made him gnash his teeth at night. I think the happiest moment in his life was when I walked in at the end of the school year in 1975 and announced I was leaving to move to New York.

Eleven

There was another man I saw a bit of that year. Oddly enough, the same friend, Toni, who had introduced me to Edmond, called me up and said she was giving a fund-raiser for an attractive young man who was running for Congress. She said I should meet him. He was twenty-seven years old, single, and named Bill Clinton. I came in late, just as he began his talk, and he later said that when he saw me walk in, he forgot his speech—and then he forgot his name. I suspected he said that same thing to quite a few women, but it's a good line, so why not use it? He was the embodiment of charisma: when he talked to you, he had the ability to make you feel like you were the only person in the room. He looked you in the eye and never once glanced over your shoulder to see who else was there. The only other person I have met who had charisma to that extent was Jackie Kennedy.

Bill came up to me after his speech, and after the introductions, compliments on the speech, and pleasantries, he told me I had the old-fashioned kind of beauty that should wear cameos and he was going to get me one. That never happened, but then I never thought it would. It was just party talk. I was lucky to get that much attention. I could see that everyone wanted his ear, so I just stayed for a short while and then started for the door. When he noticed that I was about to leave, he said "Wait a minute, Barbara," walked me out to my car, and asked if he could see me again when he had more time. Why would I say no? To ensure he would remember, a day or two after we met, some of my students and I decorated one of our papier-mâché animals, a donkey, with a VOTE FOR CLINTON banner and took it to his headquarters, which greatly amused him.

He invited me a few times to campaign with him and his group in nearby towns, handing out cards and buttons and telling people why they should vote for him and clapping and cheering when he spoke. He was usually mobbed, mostly by women, but would always find a little time somewhere in the evening to talk to me alone. I stood next to him once in a receiving line, and was amazed at his memory for names and faces. One young man shook hands with him and said, "I'm honored to meet you, Mr. Clinton." Bill said, "I think we've met before." The other guy said, "No, I don't think so," and Bill studied him for a minute and said, "You were at Boys State with me in 1963." The guy was astounded; he really didn't remember meeting him. During his speeches, Bill could pull facts and figures easily out of some file cabinet in his head.

He also had a trick of holding and caressing my hand while carrying on a conversation with someone else in a crowd, which made me feel like I had some kind of inside track. Occasionally he would invite me to sit beside him in the car on the way to or from an event, which was a big treat, since there were so many people vying for his attention. But we were never alone. He was sorry, he said, but he had no time to take me out on a regular date. Everything was always a campaign event. "That's okay," I said, and really it was. I was busy enough anyhow, and just liked being in his glow once in a while. Then one night, late and unannounced, the doorbell rang. It was him.

Years later in New York, after all the scandals broke, a man I knew socially who was in politics said, "I guess he slept with every woman in Arkansas except you, Norris." "Sorry, Russ," I replied, "I'm afraid he got us all."

He was pretty hard to resist, I must say. So I didn't, although I stopped campaigning with him. I hated talking to strangers, handing out cards, and trying to articulate the reasons why they should vote for Bill. I had no idea what to say when people pinned me down on his policies. Still, when he happened to be near Russellville, he would call. What we had was by no stretch of the imagination a romance, with his heavy campaign schedule and his seldom being alone except in the wee hours of the morning. He didn't have the time, and I didn't like being part of his pack of admirers. I was still dating several other men—mainly the lawyer at this point, who later became a judge—and while I had no idea how many other women Bill was seeing, it was apparent by the number of starry-eyed followers that there were a lot of them. I liked him immensely anyhow, and had no illusion I would become anything more than a friendly warm place for him to go from time to time, and frankly I didn't want to be more. Even then, I knew he was going to be president one day. It didn't take a psychic to see his prowess as a speaker, his genuine concern for the people, and his huge ambition. Not to mention his love of women. And I wasn't the girl for that gig.

On election night, he invited me to headquarters in Fayetteville to wait for the returns, and I went with several friends. There were, of course, a lot of women there, but there was one I'd never seen before who seemed to be running things, rushing around answering phones, obviously in charge. Her name was Hillary, she wore enormous thick glasses, no makeup, and rather ugly colorless baggy clothing. Someone whispered that she was *the* girlfriend. I said, *"Really?"* surprised at first, but as the evening wore on, I could see there was something extraordinary about her. She had an intelligence that none of the prettier girls in the room had. If I ever had a pang of jealousy, it was for that, when I knew he and she must have had a relationship that was fired by intellect. I would have so liked to be able to talk to him about world affairs and politics, or art or literature, or anything, really. I had the conceit that I had a good mind, too. But we frankly never talked much. He was always exhausted and wanted to catch two or three hours of sleep, or he was dashing out the door on his way somewhere and had no time. I would have liked just once to have a leisurely dinner and sit and talk, but that never happened.

He lost the election, by a smaller margin than had been expected, since his Republican opponent, John Paul Hammerschmidt, was popular and had been in office since 1963. But it was clear he was going to make it big sometime, somehow. He had the hunger. I had illustrated a little memoir called *Idols and Axle Grease* by my friend Francis Irby Gwaltney, and I inscribed a copy to Bill with something like, "I'll see you in the White House."

By that time, I'd started to feel used. The last time he'd called at two in the morning to see if he could drop by, I'd said no. I was done, and that was probably the final time we saw each other in that way.

He moved to Fayetteville with Hillary to teach in the law school, and we didn't keep in touch too often, but when I decided to move to New York with Norman Mailer, I called him to say goodbye, and I don't know how it happened—maybe he'd had to come to Russellville for another reason entirely—but he drove up into my yard just as I was walking out the door with my yellow luggage, on my way to the airport.

"Are you sure you know what you're doing?" he asked.

"No," I said, and smiled, "but I'm doing it anyhow."

He carried my suitcases to my car, gave me a little kiss, and I drove away.

Several years later he became governor, and we reconnected when I had a show of my paintings in a gallery in Little Rock. He and Hillary had dinner with Norman and me in a Chinese restaurant and they invited us to one of his inaugurations. (Norman wrote a speech for him, but he never used any of it. I was sorry; it really was pretty good.) Through the years, we would occasionally bump into each other at functions in New York, or he would drop a note or call just to keep in touch. Norman liked them, especially Hillary, and would have supported her in the presidential primaries if he had lived. He said she had earned it. I still consider Bill and Hillary friends, if distant ones.

Twelve

I debated whether or not to include this next part, but I finally decided I needed to talk about one of the worst moments in this otherwise happy time, one that has colored my life over the years in small ways I may never be totally aware of. Maybe I just hope there is the off chance that the man in question will read this and understand, if he is capable of understanding, what kind of damage he willfully inflicted. It is something that happens to an astonishing number of women one way or another. You know what I'm talking about.

The older brother of one of my girlfriends, who lived out of town, was home visiting his family, and my friend invited me to their house for a barbecue. I hardly knew her brother, as he was several years older than us, but it sounded like fun. I don't know if my friend was thinking to fix us up, but I had no thought of romance with this guy. He wasn't my type at all, and I thought of it as just a low-key dinner with their family, all of whom I'd known since I was a child. She said her brother would pick me up, which was fine.

We had a nice time at the barbecue, although I spent hardly any time talking to the brother, and then it began to get late and I said I needed to go home. It was a Friday and Matthew was spending the night at my parents' so I could sleep late the next morning, and the brother drove me home. I got out of the car as soon as we hit my driveway. I didn't want to sit with him in the dark or make him think there was more to the evening than there was, but he said, "I'll walk you to the door." I said, in a friendly voice, "Don't bother. I know the way," but he got out anyhow and accompanied me, holding my elbow. It felt a little creepy all of a sudden, like I heard the music that swells in a horror movie to warn you something bad is about to happen, and I wanted to get inside quickly. I didn't want him to try to kiss me, so I said, "Well, thanks for the nice evening. Good night," and turned my key in the lock. Before I could turn on the light or shut the door, he shoved me hard from behind and knocked me to the floor. I was astonished; then I was confused. Then I was scared. I had always thought that if anyone tried to rape me, I could kick him in the nuts, or run, or scream, or do any number of things to protect myself. But I learned in short order that he was a lot stronger than I was and there was no way on this earth I could defend myself.

He proceeded to rape me.

At first I tried to reason with him. "Let's talk about this. Let's go sit down and talk," I said. Then, "Please don't do this, please," and then I begged him to stop. In the moonlight from the open door, I could see that he had a glassy look in his eyes, and he kept repeating over and over, "I'm going to make you scream. I'm going to make you scream." I somehow knew the worst thing I could do was scream, so I just gritted my teeth and endured. It was painful and lasted much too long, and then he left me, without a word, lying on the floor in the dark.

I was bruised and shaken, to say the least. Big purple marks bloomed on my arms where he had held me down. I was raw and burned. I pulled myself together, locked the door, and picked up the phone, but the receiver hung in midair from my limp hand. I didn't know who to call. I couldn't call my parents. They would have totally freaked out and probably tried to make me go to the hospital, and then the whole town would have known. I couldn't call the sheriff's office. They wouldn't have believed me. Some of them had played football with him, and nothing would have been done to him anyhow. He would just have said it was consensual, that I'd wanted it, and then they would have asked me who else I had been sleeping with and it would have turned into a trial of my morals, which at that point couldn't really withstand scrutiny. His family was prominent in the community, and I liked them a lot. They certainly wouldn't have believed me, and if they *had* happened to believe me, it would have torn the family apart and they would have wound up hating me, not him. So I told no one, not even my closest friends. I just filled the tub with the hottest water I could stand and tried to soak all traces of him away. It was a classic case of rape, like I had read about so often. Only this time it was me.

The kicker was that two days later, a note arrived in the mail. It said, "Thank you for one of the most exciting nights of my life." And he signed his name. I was so angry I shook as I burned it up in the kitchen sink.

He went back to his home soon after that, and thankfully I never saw him again. I never said a word to his sister. If she spoke about him, I would just change the subject, which I'm sure she thought was strange. To this day, I would leave the room if he walked into it. He got married and had children, and I sometimes wondered what kind of husband and father he was, if this was a pattern with him, or if I had done something to make him attack me like that. I know in my heart I didn't. I hardly even spoke to him all evening. I count myself one of the lucky ones who wasn't affected so badly, but it took something off my confidence forever. I never got into a car alone again with someone I hardly knew without thinking of that night, and now, even after all these years, instead of my hell dreams, I sometimes have nightmares of strangers in the dark.

Thirteen

An English teacher at Tech named Francis Irby Gwaltney (who wrote the memoir *Idols and Axle Grease* that I had illustrated) was a soldier in World War II with Norman Mailer. While I never had Francis (or Fig, as Norman called him) as a teacher, I was friends with him and his wife, Ecey (E.C., short for Emma Carol), another English teacher at Tech. Along with B. C. Hall and his wife, Daphna, we all subscribed to *The New Yorker* magazine and considered ourselves to be intellectuals—Russellville-style, anyhow. After I started teaching at the high school, we'd all get together once in a while to have a glass of wine (Russellville was in a dry county, so drinking wine was totally avant-garde—we had to drive thirty miles to buy it) and discuss literature and *The New Yorker* articles. We were big Walker Percy and Eudora Welty fans.

Often, Francis mentioned Norman. They had kept in touch after the war, and every couple of years they managed to get together. Francis became a writer after Norman published *The Naked and the Dead*. He said that if *Norman Mailer* could write, by God, he could, too. According to Norman, Fig had been a much better soldier than he had been, and Norman looked up to him. Fig was the inspiration for Wilson, one of the characters in the book.

Sweet, innocent Norman, straight out of Harvard, had somehow been assigned to an experienced, battle-hardened Texas outfit, and he tried to play dumb and be as invisible as possible so as not to be perceived by the good ol' boys as the Eastern Jewish intellectual he was. They were as tough as old leather, those Texans, skin burned a deep sienna from sitting around in the hot sun on the troop ship, endlessly sharpening their bowie knives on pieces of flint and painting their sores with iodine. One of them once said something about that "goddam New York Jew," and Fig jumped to Norman's defense.

"Who're you calling a goddam Jew? I'm a goddam Jew, too!"

"You ain't no goddam Jew, Gwaltney. You're from Arkansas."

"I am too a goddam Jew," the big, blond blue-eyed Southerner said, his chin thrust out, his fists clenched. He stood ready to jump in and fight, but the bully just said, "You a crazy sumbitch, Gwaltney," and backed off.

Of course Fig wasn't Jewish, but he endeared himself to Norman that day, and they became best buddies. Norman tried his hardest to keep a low profile, but once in map-reading class, when he was daydreaming, the harried officer who had been getting nothing but "I don't know" from the men asked him a question, and by accident, before he could think, he blurted out the correct coordinates of a position. He was busted. (Life was a little harder after that, but the officer was thrilled that he finally had someone who could read a map.)

IT HAS BEEN said that there are no coincidences in life, and I might just believe that. It was April 1975, and I had been divorced for more than a year. Frankly, dating a lot of different guys had begun to lose its charm, but I had no interest in getting serious about anyone. I liked having my own house and doing as I pleased. No man to clutter up my closets, no man to clean up after (except my big boy, Matt, of course). No man to tell me what to do, how to spend my money, what to cook. I was close to my parents, who adored Matthew and were thrilled to babysit for me while I worked. My life was pretty great.

Then I got a call from my friend Van Tyson, another teacher at Tech, who was having a film animation artist come speak to his class. He wondered if I wanted to bring my senior class over to the college to sit in. I was always up for something new to do with the kids, so we went, and it was interesting. But the most interesting bit of information I got that day was that Norman Mailer was next door in Francis's class, and Francis and Ecey were giving him a cocktail party after school. To which I had *not* been invited.

Although I've always loved literature, books were a luxury I treated myself to sparingly, but I had been a member of the Book-of-the-Month Club for several years, getting things such as Joseph Heller's *Catch-22*, or James Jones's *The Merry Month of May*. But for some reason, even though Fig knew him, I had never read one of Norman Mailer's books. Occasionally, I would forget to send in the Book-of-the-Month response card saying I didn't want the selection that month.

One such time was when Norman's *Marilyn* was offered. It was twenty dollars, more than I could afford, but there it was in my mail, and I couldn't resist opening it. After looking at the pictures and reading a few pages, I was hooked. "She was our angel, the sweet angel of sex, and the sugar of sex came up from her like a resonance of sound in the clearest grain of a violin . . ." Oh, my. This didn't sound like a rowdy war novelist at all. It sounded like a man who was sensitive and understood women, and who could write like the angels themselves. I read some of the sentences over several times, just to feel the words.

Now Norman Mailer was in Russellville! I called Francis and asked if I could stop by the party, just for a few minutes to get my book signed, and he said no, that he didn't want to bother Norman with that fan crap. Fig never minced words. One always knew exactly what he thought.

"Oh, come on, Francis," I said. "Don't be like that. I'll leave it in the car and won't bring it in if it doesn't seem right. I just want to meet him."

I had heard over and over from Francis what a genius Norman was and I figured I'd never have another opportunity to meet a famous writer. I had aspirations to write myself. Maybe he could give me some tips or something. So, reluctantly, Francis said I could come. Since they had all been in the war, I knew Norman was as old as my father (in fact, he was one year older), just as Francis was, not to mention that Norman had been married a bunch of times and had a lot of kids. The *last* thing on my mind was romance, I swear. I was just going to stay for a minute to see if he minded signing the book, and maybe have a teensy little conversation with him. I didn't even bother to change. I was wearing bell-bottom hip-hugger jeans and a soft cotton voile shirt tied at the waist, showing a bit of my belly button. I was also wearing huge platform shoes called Bare Traps that made me about six feet one. (I'm five feet ten in stocking feet.)

I was a little nervous when I walked in, realizing that everyone else was dressed up, and I wished I had gone home and changed. And then I saw Norman. He was sitting in front of the window, his curly, silver-shot hair lit by the sun as though he had a halo. (Saint Norman!) Amazingly, he was also wearing jeans, the most patched jeans I had ever seen in my life. There were patches on top of the patches. In fact, they were nothing *but* patches. His clear blue eyes lit up when he saw me. He had broad shoulders, a rather large head (presumably to hold all those brains) with ears that stuck out like Clark Gable's, and he was chesty, but not fat, like a sturdy small horse. (I once drew him as a centaur, which delighted him.) He didn't look old at all. Nor the least bit fatherly.

Me in the outfit I wore the day I met Norman.

He stood straightaway, came over to me, and to his surprise had to look up into my face. He always said he was five eight, but I personally think he was a hair under that, and I towered over him in my platform shoes. I introduced myself, we shook hands, and then he turned on his heel and walked out of the room. I was a little taken aback, but I figured he must have had a thing about tall women, so I just sighed and decided not to go out to the car and get my book.

I knew everyone there—all the English faculty, the men dressed in coats and ties, the women in little dresses or suits with tidy bows on their blouses and sensible low heels. Someone handed me a glass of white wine, and I started talking to Van. Then Francis came over and said, "Stay after the party and go out to Van and Ginnie's for dinner with us."

"Ginnie's making pizza," Van said. "Why don't you come?"

"Thanks, guys, but I think that's a bad idea," I said. "I don't think Mr. Mailer liked me much."

"Liked you?" Francis said in his gravelly voice, full of displeasure. "Hell, *he's* the one who wants you to go, not me!"

I didn't know why he was being so grumpy to me. If I hadn't known better, I would have thought he was jealous over Norman, that Francis was angry that Norman liked me and didn't want to share him or something. Anyhow, I didn't care. The fact that Norman wanted me to go out with them was a nice surprise.

The women teachers were all atwitter because Norman had brought along another pair of jeans just like the ones he was wearing, or even worse, which needed another patch, and they were all taking turns sewing on them, so pleased with themselves to be able to say "I sewed Norman Mailer's pants!"

But there was no sign of the great man. I guessed he was still in the kitchen, for whatever reason. I couldn't believe he was that shy. I went and sat on a low couch by myself, and finally Norman appeared. We looked at each other and I smiled. I patted the seat beside me, and he came and sat down while the other women gave me the evil eye, looking at me as though I was the hussy I was.

I don't remember the conversation we had on that couch—something trivial, I'm sure—but I do remember the intensity of his blue eyes, and his charisma—not unlike Bill Clinton's. He concentrated on me, that's for sure, and he radiated energy like a little steam heater. He couldn't sit still. Then, too soon, Francis came and got him so he could talk to the others, fearing I had trapped him long enough.

After a while, people started to go, but I stayed put. Another teacher had just polished off her fourth glass of wine and was determined to wait me out. We chitchatted until everyone else had gone, and then, in an awkward silence, knowing she had to go, she grabbed me by the arm and started pulling me toward the door.

"Come on!" she said. "They need us to leave so they can go to dinner!"

"I'm going with them," I said.

"Oh, no, you're not!" she countered, pulling harder.

Thank goodness I was bigger, because she was determined to haul me out of there.

Ecey, bless her, stepped in and explained that I had been invited, so all the poor thing could do was sadly turn and leave on her own, weaving a little as she walked down the driveway. Norman and I piled into the backseat of the car with Francis and Ecey and headed to Van and Ginnie's house in the woods.

As we drove, we were chatting, getting to know each other, and Norman asked me when my birthday was.

"January thirty-first," I said, "1949," which made me twenty-six. He got all excited and started pounding on Fig's arm.

"Fig! Fig! When's my birthday?"

"Well, Norman, don't you know?" Fig drawled in a voice that indicated he thought Norman might have had one drink too many.

"It's January thirty-first! We have the same birthday!" He was beside himself. It turned out that we'd also been born within one minute of each other, he at 7:04 and me at 7:05 A.M. I later checked it with his mother. A mother always remembers exactly when her child was born. He was also fifty-two, precisely twice my age, the only time that phenomenon would occur in our lifetimes. It seemed like some big portent had just been swooped in and dropped onto us by twittering birds.

Van and Ginnie's house was built over a brook, and as soon as we got there, Norman and I went out onto the porch to take a look. The woods, with the brook gurgling underneath our feet, were magical. It was so beautiful and peaceful. The air was sweet and fresh with the smell of pines, and dragonflies flitted under the little stone waterfalls in the brook like fairies.

We were at first shy with each other, and I still had those monster shoes on, but it didn't seem to matter to Norman. He rather liked it that I was tall, and years later he would make me put on high heels if I tried to go out in flats.

"Put on your big shoes. I'm not going to have people towering over you!" he would say.

The rest of the lucky dinner guests were milling around in the kitchen, which had a beautiful stone fireplace, watching us through the window, waiting for him to come in and talk to them. But Norman was in no hurry, and neither was I. I had wanted an intellectual man who would talk to me, and I finally got one. Norman could go on for hours on almost any subject, and this time it was one of my favorites—me. He rhapsodized about my eyes, my hair, my skin, my nose. Finally it got to be a touch too much, even for me. I had to cut him off.

"Well, you really know how to deliver a good line, Mr. Mailer," I said with an exaggerated Southern accent. "But that's all right. I've always bought a good line, well presented."

He roared with laughter, hugged me, and told me how marvelous I was. I had the passing thought that with that one remark, I had, perhaps, made a not necessarily small impression on him.

I did have to bring up the marriage thing, though. I wasn't going to get tangled up with a married man. (Little did I know just what a tangle I would find myself in.) He presented himself as separated from his wife, which was technically true, and it was only later in the evening that I learned he was separated from his fourth wife, Beverly, but not quite separated from his present companion, Carol, and they had a daughter, Maggie, who had just turned four, six months older than Matthew. Since I thought I would never see him again anyhow, separated from a legal wife was good enough for a flirt, especially such an enjoyable one.

Finally, someone tentatively came to the door and asked us if we wanted any pizza. There were only a couple of leathery cold pieces left by that time, so we went in and ate them, and he talked to the rest of the patient group. It got to be nine-thirty, and I told Van I had to leave to go pick up Matthew, who was at his father's house, by ten. My plan was for Van to drive me to Francis and Ecey's. I would get my car, pick up Matthew, and go home. I'm sure by this time everyone wished me gone. I'd monopolized the guest of honor much too long for their taste, especially Francis's. But Norman had other ideas. His plan was for him to drive me to Larry's, pick up Matthew, and come back to the party.

He drove, and I sat across the bench seat next to the door, not too close to him. We pulled into Larry's yard, and I went to the door to get Matthew, who was sound asleep. I carried him to the car, and Norman got out and took him, holding him while I drove, since he didn't know his way around those country roads in the dark. Watching him hold my sleeping boy touched me.

We went back to Van and Ginnie's, and I put Matthew to bed in the guest room. I don't remember how it came up, but someone there knew how to do tai chi, so we all did it. I was my usual clumsy self, which Norman thought was endearing. That night, it seemed I could do no wrong.

Finally we left, Matt still completely snozzed out, and Norman asked Fig and Ecey if he could drop them off, borrow their car, and follow me home. I think at this point they were both beginning to worry a bit, about whom I'm not quite sure, but they had to say yes.

I'd never before had a man over while Matthew was in the house. I put Matt to bed and then we went into the living room, where I offered Norman a glass of Boone's Farm's finest apple wine (I think it was a bottle, but it might have been a box), which I'm sure appalled him, but I didn't know that then. We talked for another hour or more, about my desire to write, my marriage, and my divorce, and then he began to tell me about his life, his five wives and seven children. (He referred to Carol, his present companion, as his wife. They had been living together for five years, and had a child, after all.)

He told me how he hadn't lied to me when he'd said he was separated, but he was in a place where he was being pulled in a lot of different directions. He then told me about another woman—I'll call her Annette—with whom he had been having a serious affair for several years and who was pressuring him to leave Carol for her. He didn't want to live with Annette, and in fact really wanted to break it off with her, but he didn't want to hurt her, so he had suggested that they not see each other for six months while he had time to think things through. He felt he was already half separated from Carol, living two weeks in New York in an apartment in Brooklyn, which he used as a writing studio, seeing Annette and various other "other" women, and then spending two weeks with Carol and Maggie in Stockbridge, Massachusetts. He'd been continuously married or living with five women in succession, each waiting in the wings to take over from her predecessor, since he was twenty years old—something else we had in common, our marriages at twenty.

It was all rather overwhelming, but I appreciated his honesty. I told him that the last thing on my mind was getting married again, after being with the same man since I was sixteen years old, and so we understood each other. At least I thought we did. That this was just a pleasant evening, an interlude in his lecture tour, was the unspoken meaning of it all. He said I was the nicest woman he had ever met, which I thought was just more of the line, but he might have meant it, at least a little; he said it a lot over the years, sometimes behind my back.

Then he leaned over and kissed me, at first just a casual, exploratory kiss; but the kiss ignited, and I knew I was going to make love with him. He was leaving the next day, I would never see him again, and I at least wanted to be able to say I'd done *that,* even if I hadn't been able to ask him to sign my book (which was still in the car). But I didn't want to go to the bedroom; too close to Matthew. I didn't want Matt to wake up and be scared by voices or strange sounds. So we did it on the living room floor. (Why did I always seem to wind up on the floor?)

It was a bit of a comedy, actually. I was jumpy and nervous trying not to make noise, listening for Matthew to wake up, and it was awkward and uncomfortable. I wouldn't fully undress or allow him to, as Matthew might walk in, and I was getting rug burns on my back. Finally, it wasn't that great. How could it have been? But then there are few great ones on the first try. Most guys never get *near* to great under any circumstance. Afterward, I was sorry we had done it, and I think he was, too. It was a slight downer to a magical evening for both of us, but he held me sweetly, and I felt close to him. As he was getting ready to leave, I thought once more about asking him if he would sign my *Marilyn* book, but after what had just happened, I couldn't. It would have been tacky. I'm glad I waited. It wasn't until the next February, when I was living with him in New York, that he finally signed it. The inscription read:

To Barbara

Because I knew when I wrote this book that someone I had not yet met would read it and be with me. Hey, Baby, do you know how I love Barbara Davis and Norris Church?

Norman, Feb '76

Fourteen

I couldn't wait to tell Jean Jewell, my earth mother friend who lived down the street, that I'd made love (what a strange expression for an intimate act with someone you hardly know!) with Norman Mailer. She was thrilled and wanted details, which I gladly supplied, and what particularly interested her was the fact that Norman and I had the same birthday, down to almost the same minute. She had a friend who did astrological charts, and immediately after she hung up with me she called the friend to get our charts done.

Among other things, the friend told her that Norman was going to die in 1978. This, as you remember, was 1975. That's why I have been leery of astrologers and seers and psychics ever since. I don't want to hear bad news. I was, of course, aghast at the prediction and didn't know whether I believed it or not. I read my horoscopes in the newspapers every day but had never taken them seriously. We tend to remember only the ones that come true. Still, even a stopped clock is right twice a day. I decided to forget it, but that was not to be so easy. Especially when 1978 rolled around. But that was three years away.

Norman had given me an address to write to, a post office box, which made me feel kind of sleazy. I was sure I wasn't the only woman writing to that box number. I worried over whether I should write to him at all, given his entanglements, but I didn't feel like I was breaking up a marriage. I didn't even know which marriage was there to be broken up, but whichever one (or two) it was, he made it clear it was broken before I came on the scene and wouldn't last whether I was in the picture or not. The bigger problem was that I didn't want to be just one of the harem, like with Bill Clinton, although it was way too soon to be thinking of being part of a harem or part of anything with Norman.

So between not wanting to tell him I had told Jean about our encounter (who then told some astrologist, who predicted he would be dead in three years) and trying not to assume a relationship where none existed, although still wanting to have some kind of one, I frankly didn't know what to say to him. "Thanks for a lovely evening"? "Glad to have met you"? "My rug burns have healed"? But he was easily the most interesting man I had ever met, and in spite of his age and his convoluted personal life, I did want to get to know him better, no matter where it led, if anywhere.

I finally decided to send him a little poem I had written, one that I thought said nicely that he was great but I understood ours was a romance that was not to be. I'd actually written the poem for John Cool, who used to write me poetry, but what the heck. It *was* the seventies, and I was much influenced by Rod McKuen. And why waste a perfectly good poem? It's so bad that I blush with embarrassment to recount it here, but it's a part of our history, so please be kind.

Ode to a First Encounter

You were there and
I was there
in a pocket
of sunshine
in a vacuum of space.

You poured your soul
into me
and I took it
knowing full well
I could not contain it.

And it was gone,
leaving me alone.

But I dared not follow,
lest I lose my own soul
and be lost forever
in a pocket of sorrow
in a vacuum of space.

What was I *thinking*? Obviously, I wasn't.

But he wrote back to me:

STOCKBRIDGE, MA
MAY 12, 1975

Dear Barbara,

Your poem was waiting when I got back, and I would have written to you then, but there wasn't a moment to think and some work to get out, and I thought I'd wait until things were quieter and there was time to write a decent letter.

But no, it's the other way and things are in a rush and if I keep waiting, another couple of weeks will go by. So this is just to tell you a few things.

(1) You were an oasis on a long trip

(2) Your poem was sad, and it was true—I knew what you were saying to me, and when we see each other again, maybe we can leave you with a somewhat different poem. I have to go to Denver for the Memorial Day weekend, May 24–26, and if you'd like I think I could stop off in Little Rock on the way back. Could you take off a day to meet me there or could you possibly stay overnight? I haven't said a word to Fig or Ecey that I might be in the area because we'd only have a day, and I don't want to share it. Depending on whether I do a lecture in the west or not, I'd be coming by somewhere between Tuesday May 27 and Thursday May 29.

Will you drop me a line right away—don't be like me!—and let me know how this strikes your beautiful auburn red head.

Cheers,
Norman

I wrote back immediately, YES, I'd love for him to stop off in Little Rock! I didn't worry about any of my concerns at all. (P.S. He'd sent back the poem, copyedited in red pencil. That should have been a clue, but I was too happy to care. Besides, it was a secondhand poem anyhow, so I figured we were even.)

A few days later, I ran into Francis at the Kroger store. After a few minutes of chitchat, I asked him if he had heard from Norman. He looked at me with a little pitying smirk—at least I imagined it was pitying—and said that yes, Norman had written him, but he hadn't mentioned me, so I shouldn't get my hopes up that I would ever hear from him again. Which, Francis said, to his mind was good, since I would have gotten in *way* over my head. He continued on in that vein for a while, how Norman was a busy, *famous* man, little girl, and just because he spent one evening with you doesn't mean he will ever call you again. He has *dozens* of beautiful, sophisticated women all over the place, all over the *world*. Why would he be interested in a girl from the sticks of Arkansas? The bottom line was that he (Francis) was just trying to protect me, he didn't want me to get hurt, on and on, yackety, yackety. I just nodded, never once letting on that I had plans to meet up with Norman in just a couple of days. So Norman really hadn't told him. I smiled and said, "Thank you, Francis. I totally understand. You're absolutely right. I know you're just looking out for my welfare, and I promise not to worry anymore. I'm just glad I got to meet him."

He smiled and patted my hand, as if to his mind that little incident was over and done with.

Norman came off the plane from Colorado—where he had been rafting on the Dolores River with his two boys, Michael and Stephen—carrying a big white stuffed dog that was dressed in denim overalls and a red shirt. He handed it to me with a grin, and it's fair to say I was speechless. I turned it over, and on its behind he had drawn a heart, in the middle of which he had printed our initials—NM + BN. It was so ridiculous and sweet I had to laugh. I discovered then and there that for the rest of my life I would never know what to expect from him.

We got his suitcase and went out to my yellow Volkswagen. He insisted on driving. It's a man thing some guys have, and I didn't argue, although it was the tiniest bit annoying, like having someone borrow your favorite pair of shoes. You know they are going to put their print on them somehow. It took him a few minutes to get the hang of the car, adjust the seat, which I was going to have to readjust, and we lurched out of the parking lot, our heads jerking, as he stepped on the clutch, gas, then the brake, trying to shift the grinding gears.

"You're not used to driving a stick shift, are you?" I blurted.

He got a little huffy and said, in his best Harvard accent, "I'm used to driving a *Porsche*."

A naughty part of me thought, "And I would bet money you drive it just like this." He had driven Francis's car kind of jerkily, too, the night we'd met, and Francis's car had an automatic transmission. He was one of those guys who have nervous feet on the pedals, he just

Norman at the Little Rock airport.

couldn't help it. (He indeed did drive the Porsche like that, although he would violently disagree. When I first saw it, the poor thing was riddled with dents and rusty scrapes and bumps covered with pieces of silver duct tape; we had an ongoing dispute during the next thirty years over who was the better driver. [I could write a whole chapter on his driving peccadilloes, like the time he wanted to get a closer look at a motorcycle and ran the guy off the road, but that would be dirty pool.] It was only near the end of his life one day, years after he had stopped driving and I had just finished the long trip to New York from Provincetown for the umpteenth time, with a few hairy moments like having to swerve to avoid a car wreck, that he told me he thought I was an excellent driver and he always had. It surprisingly made me cry to have him say that.)

I'd made a reservation at the Sheraton, and we dropped our bags off, then went out to lunch. He didn't know Little Rock, so I took him to a place I thought he would enjoy, the old Marriott Hotel, where the legislators and important people in town ate, near the capitol. The food wasn't that memorable. I think we each had a piece of bland fish with new potatoes and broccoli that was boiled gray, and I didn't recognize anybody well known—except for a man sitting across the room who saw us, got up, and marched right over to our table. I could see Norman going into celebrity mode, bracing to be assaulted by either a fan or a crazy person. Instead, totally ignoring Norman, the man turned on me and said, "Where were you last night? I waited for an hour at the studio for you!" Urps. He was one of the local TV weathermen, whom I had been out with a couple of times. (He was one of the never-slept-withs.) We'd had a dinner date for the previous night, which I had completely forgotten about in the excitement of Norman's arriving. There was nothing I could do except say that I was so sorry, I'd gotten my dates mixed up, and introduce the two of them.

They politely shook hands, then the weatherman walked away shaking his head, maybe a little impressed in spite of himself, but frankly more annoyed. Needless to say, he never called me again; ask me if I cared. The weatherman was shorter than I was, but unlike Norman, he didn't handle it well and made me take off my shoes and dance barefoot the one time we went dancing. He also liked me to pick him up at the studio after he did the six o'clock weather, and he wore his TV makeup when we went out, which I found to be a little pretentious. I guess he would have just had to put it back on for the ten o'clock weather, but still, how weird is that, to kiss someone and get makeup on my face that wasn't my shade? Norman found the whole thing amusing, as he seemed to find everything about me and my life.

After lunch, we drove around Little Rock and I showed him the sights, such as they were, the most important being General Douglas MacArthur's birthplace, a house preserved as it had been in 1880, now situated in the middle of MacArthur Park. There was a legend that during the Civil War, a group of runaway slaves took refuge in a room dug out underneath the park, and they all got diphtheria or something and died. People said if you walked across a certain area in the park, you could feel a chill, but I never found it. Nor did we that day, although we walked around, trying to feel the cold.

In the park was also the Arkansas Arts Center. The Arts Center was run by a man named Townsend Wolfe, who knew me well, or at least well enough, but he had never really given me the time of day, speaking down to me from his lofty artistic perch. This time, however, when I walked in with Norman Mailer, his eyes lit up and he was suddenly my oldest and dearest friend. He gave Norman a personal tour of the place and couldn't have been nicer to me.

There was a show of handmade silver jewelry going on, and a smooth silver ring with a moonstone that reminded me of a whale's eye caught mine. I pointed it out to Norman, and asked him if he didn't think it looked like a whale's eye. He studied it for a minute and then told Townsend, who had been hovering, that he wanted to buy it for me. I was aghast. I would *never* have admired it to him if I'd thought he would buy it! I didn't want him to think I was a gold digger who hinted for a man to buy her things. I protested. But Townsend took it out of the case and urged me to try it on. It fit the middle finger of my right hand like it had been made just for it. I was lost. But it cost eighty dollars. That was more than my monthly mortgage.

"No, really, Norman, you are sweet to offer, but no thank you." I took off the ring and firmly handed it back to Townsend. Norman could have gracefully backed out at that point, but he didn't want to. He really wanted to buy it for me. My father never bought my mother and me gifts at all when I was growing up, except for Christmas, and when we went shopping, we had to sneak our packages into the house so he wouldn't know we had bought things, or they would have a fight. I remember one horrible fight they had over a new shower curtain!

My father was a child of the Depression and had strict ideas about what one needed and didn't need, which was anything that wasn't replacing something totally falling-apart worn-out. Mom and Dad had those fights often, as she and I both loved clothes and things for the house. It got better when she opened the beauty shop and started earning her own money, and I began babysitting when I was eleven, but I never quite got over the feeling that buying things was bad. (I remember with the first money I earned, eleven dollars, I bought a watch, as my mother said I should get something I could keep forever to remember it. I have no idea where it is now.)

Even after Norman and I had been married for many years, I still sneaked my packages into the house, although he was always generous and couldn't have cared less. If I wore something different that he liked and he asked if it was new, I would say, "Oh, you've seen this before. It's been hanging in the closet for ages." I wonder what a psychologist would say about that? The poor man must have thought he was going crazy to forget so many of my outfits. Or perhaps he knew and just indulged me.

As far as the silver ring was concerned, never before had a man spent that kind of money on a casual gift for me. When I married Larry, I even paid for our wedding bands, as he was in school and I was the one working. I always had a strong sense of wanting to earn my own way; it was those early days of women's liberation. After I was divorced, I earned seven thousand dollars a year as a schoolteacher—a respectable salary for the time and place—and had an excellent credit history. Still, when I bought a house, I had to get a *man*, in my case my father, to cosign the mortgage before the bank would give it to me. The same with a credit card. I never had a credit card of my own until I had been married to Norman for many years. Until then, they were always in his name.

Protesting the ring got silly past a point, and I finally let Townsend write up the sale, but I was uncomfortable. Still, I loved the ring and didn't take it off for years.

As long as there has been literature and its naughty offspring, pornography, the sex act has been endlessly, exhaustingly described, but—like trying to describe pain or love—there are no words in any language to truly capture the phenomenon, and I am not going to try it here. Frankly, I had never been really attracted to many men in my life, even though I had slept with several. I was certainly attracted to Norman the first time I saw him, but it was as much mental and emotional as it was physical. I couldn't wait to hear what he would say next, and talking to him made me feel more intelligent, as I rose to the occasion of bouncing off his remarks.

Over the years, trying to one-up each other became our favorite game, much to the amusement and despair of our friends, but in the beginning that kind of verbal play was new to me. We were in the Hepburn-Tracy mold, he making slight fun of me and me turning the tables on him. Sometimes he would win, sometimes I would. For example, I had told him I was one of the champion table tennis players at church camp, so one night at a friend's house, he skunked me in a game because he had a nasty little serve that barely cleared the net. "You were the champ of church camp, huh? That's mighty Christian of you to let me win, then," he'd say, and I'd reply that Christians didn't go in for crooked cheap shots, and it would escalate from there. It all probably started with the remark I made about his driving, which just slipped out, and I got cheekier after that. To his credit, he was delighted when I got a good shot in at him, like his little protégé had done well.

I had never met anyone like him. He was fresh and enthusiastic about every subject, politics and religion being two favorites, but he had opinions on everything from how plastic was poison (it turned out that he was right, after decades of being laughed at) to how auto pollution was killing us (again, he was right). He had run for mayor of New York with some great ideas, like Sweet Sunday, which would be one Sunday a month when no cars except taxis and emergency vehicles were allowed in the city, and he proposed a better transit system, an electric monorail that ran around Manhattan that was nonpolluting. He had other ideas that were perceived to be totally off-the-wall, such as New York City seceding from New York, and becoming the fifty-first state, and people thought he was a clown who was running for fun, but over the years a lot of the ideas have turned out to be not so crazy.

Back to sex. As we went to the hotel, I was nervous and unsure of how compatible we would be in bed, given the last sad time on the floor in Russellville. But with all the inhibitions removed—Matthew safely at my mother and daddy's for the night—I was more than attracted to him, and he was determined to assert his reputation as the best lover in the world. (Where had I heard that? Maybe he'd told me?) Little Rock was only the beginning, of course. Through the years, no matter the circumstances of our passions and rages, our boredoms, angers, and betrayals large and small, sex was the cord that bound us together; it was the thick wire woven from thousands of shared experiences that never broke, indeed was hardly frayed and only got stronger, no matter how the bonds of marriage were tested. Even in the worst times we had many years later, when we almost separated—somehow, inexplicably, at night we would cling to each other, drawn like powerful magnets, the familiarity of our bodies putting salve on the wounds we had inflicted during the day, until over time the warring ended and the love remained. The only thing that finally brought it to an end was old age, illness, and death itself, but that was years away from where we were then, on this first night of our life together, and was quite unimaginable to my twenty-six-year-old mind.

He spent an extra night. For a girl who had previously never let a man who wasn't her husband spend the night in her bed—who couldn't, in fact, wait for them to get dressed and go home—it was something new. We woke up so entwined around each other that it was a task to disentangle ourselves in the morning. I had snuggled him against the wall, had him pinned there all night, and he was delighted. When we finally surfaced, rosy and happy, near to suppertime the next day, we went out to Cajun's Wharf, a great fish place where you could get peel-and-eat shrimp by the bucket, and fried catfish and hush puppies. We laughed all evening long, smug in our newfound attraction, as we peeled and ate an entire bucket of shrimp. By the time he left the following day, neither of us knew quite what had happened, or how it would play out, but we both knew it wasn't going to be a short-term thing.

JUNE 5

Dear Barbara,

Just got your letter. The timing was fine. I was in just the mood you were as you wrote it. We bounce into each other like sunlight. Off of red-rock walls. The time in Little Rock keeps reflecting back into the room for me so that no matter the hour or the place there we are swimming in that red gold light and there you are smelling like cinnamon. God, you're attractive. In

Brooklyn, we used to say fucky (as in the way I used it in *Marilyn*). Barbara Cinnamon fucky Brown Davis Norris—there's a moniker for you.

I miss you in a good way. I'm dying to see you again, tomorrow if I could, but I know it's there between us. It'll be the same whenever we're in a room with one another. I think something has started, I know we'll get together in July because there's a week when I have to do a tour for the book [*The Fight*] (It's published July 21) and we'll meet on the trip. But I want to see you before then. Maybe in New York or Chicago. Could you get away for a couple of days in the third or fourth week of June? It would probably be the middle of the week. When you answer this, put in a few pictures. The man is getting greedy about you.

I agree about the next to last one. I'd like to be right back there again. Right through the door. Lambent is the only word for such an afternoon.

I haven't written to Fig yet. Hate to take him into our yard. I may just invite him up to Maine by phone. I'll be able to tell by his voice.

Kisses and further
honey, Norman

Fifteen

It turned out to be Chicago. I had never been on an airplane before, and on top of that, I had to lie to my parents and tell them I was going with Jean to work at an arts and crafts festival. I hated to lie to them, but the plan was to wait until I got there and then call and tell them the truth—one, because I would already be there and they couldn't cry me into not going, and two . . . well, one is enough. But they had to know where I was in case something happened with Matthew. I was a conflicted, nervous, guilty, excited mess. I had again promised Norman not to tell Fig and Ecey that he and I were seeing each other. I think Norman really had Fig pegged as far as the jealousy thing went, but I just couldn't keep a trip as big as this to myself.

I was at the beginning of summer classes, taking an American literature course at Tech to complete my English degree, and we were reading *Moby-Dick*. My teacher, Ruth, wasn't much older than I was, and I had to tell her I would be missing a couple of classes and ask her if I could make up a test. I didn't want to tell her where I would be, but a part of me was just bursting to tell, so I hinted that I was going on a big trip to meet someone, and she weaseled out of me who it was. Of course, I made her swear that she wouldn't tell Francis or Ecey or anybody else, but the first thing Ruth did was call Ecey and ask her if they had spoken to Norman or me lately. When Ecey said no, Ruth said she thought she needed to talk to me. How Christian of her, to keep to the letter of the promise while doing the most damage. I don't think Francis ever got over what he saw as our betrayal. But for now, I couldn't worry too much about Francis and Ecey or *Moby-Dick* and Ruth. I was on my way to Chicago!

The closet in the back of my mind where I was cramming all the sinful things I was doing was pretty jammed, but there's always room for more. I couldn't even in good conscience pray for God to not let the plane crash, since I was on my way to commit adultery, but I did hope it wouldn't. It was hard to understand how something that heavy could float up in the air like that. I tried not to grip the seat arms too tightly, or gasp when there was some unexplained noise, so no one would know I had never flown before. This was in the days when people were allowed to smoke in the back rows, and I was in the row just in front of the smokers. The smoke made me sick, and the food was like an overcooked TV dinner, but I was too excited to really care. It was thrilling when the plane left the ground and headed, nose up, toward the sky, when the cars on the freeway became like chocolate sprinkles, and the Arkansas River a snake across a patchwork of farmland. I had a window seat and watched every mile of ground we flew over.

Norman was in Chicago doing publicity for *Playboy*, which was publishing an excerpt of his about-to-be-published book *The Fight*. He had to do a radio show just at the hour I arrived, but he had given me the address of the Blackstone hotel and told me to take a cab—which I had never done, either—and wait for him in the room. I was trying to pretend I wasn't a total rube as the cabdriver threw my bag into the car and I gave him the address, although there was no hiding my accent. He took off with a screech, and I fell back into the seat like I had been launched from a bean flip. I wasn't too interested in the scenery of Chicago—I was too intent on the erratic way the cabbie was driving—but I got an impression of tall dark buildings, which made the streets seem narrow and canyon-like. I didn't know about tipping, and didn't give him one, so he nearly ran over my foot when I got out. I went into the hotel and asked at the desk for a key to Norman's room, as he had told me to do. The clerk wouldn't give it to me.

"Who are you, Miss? I don't have any instructions to let you go up to Mr. Mailer's room."

I was so humiliated. I guessed there were dozens of crazy women who tried to get into famous men's hotel rooms all the time, and he just assumed I was one more, but I was well dressed, not like a floozy or anything. I was wearing a big straw cartwheel hat and a nice beige pants suit and tall wedge-heeled sandals. I tried nicely talking him into it, but he wouldn't budge and became rude. I wasn't used to being treated like that. It made me feel like I was nobody, like some hooker or something, and it was all I could do to keep from crying. There was nothing I could do except sit in the lobby with my suitcase and wait for Norman. The air around my chair was thick with the ice I was sending over to the desk clerk, who ignored me.

"What are you doing out here?" Norman asked, an hour later.

"*He* wouldn't let me go up to the room," I answered, glaring at the clerk, who promptly called for someone to help me with my suitcase. Norman was embarrassed he hadn't told the clerk I was coming. He hadn't thought there would be any problem. I was so happy to see him, though, it didn't matter, and he shortly made up for it.

I had brought along an African dashiki—a kind of batik short robe—that I'd bought in Mrs. Marshall's art shop, and when Norman saw it, for some reason he said, "Is this for me?" I, of course, had to say yes, and he put it on and wore it. I admit he did look cute in it. He had good legs, nicely muscled, if a little short and a tad bowed, and good posture. Cute little butt and a round belly I was particularly fond of—not too fat at all, nicely firm, like a soccer ball. I've always liked guys with little bellies, rather than those hard six-pack stomach things. Who wants to hug someone you bounce off like a brick wall? He was hairy, front and back, which I have always loved, too, and he walked with a kind of bearlike swagger, hands on his hips, which I thought was sexy. My own teddy bear. I was sorry to see the dashiki go, however, and I never saw it again. I have no idea what happened to it, but if he had come home to me from a trip with such a garment in his suitcase, I would have probably pitched a fit and then thrown it away.

Chicago was good practice, the hors d'oeuvres for New York, which came a few weeks later. It was a big city that wasn't too overwhelming but full of wonderful things I had never seen before. We went to fancy restaurants with flowers on linen tablecloths and maître d's in tuxedos, and I loved how the staff treated us like stars, seating us at the best tables, hovering around and offering us little treats as gifts from the chef. Norman knew a lot about wine, of which I was completely ignorant, and I discovered it was a totally different beverage than the sweet soda pop wine I had been drinking in Arkansas. "You don't have to get the most expensive French wine on the list. In fact, those are sometimes the most sour. Get a good medium-priced California wine. Merlot is good. Get a good merlot, or a chardonnay if you want a sweeter white wine. You never drink red wine with fish, you know, or white wine with meat."

"Why not? What difference does it make?" I really wanted to know. I could just about drink white, but red seemed beyond my capabilities.

"Red is heavier, and meat is heavier. You need the weight to wash down the meat. Besides, people will know you're a hick if they see you drinking the wrong wine, and won't respect you." Ah. The old "What will people think?" That I understood. Although I was surprised that Norman would care. He seemed like he didn't much care what people thought, but we all have our Achilles' heels, I suppose.

I didn't like red wine, but made myself sip it and pretend it was delicious, and after a while it got easier to tolerate. I have never liked any kind of liquor, except maybe a little rum in sweet juice punches like mai tais, or sweet amaretto over ice, and I usually put ice in my white wine. But Norman loved teaching me. He had a great time playing Henry Higgins to my Eliza Doolittle, introducing me to exotic things like escargot, which I ate enthusiastically, if with trepidation. I liked it, of course, for the garlicky butter sauce, as the snails themselves didn't have much taste, and I felt sophisticated pulling them out of their shells with the tiny, clever forks.

At one restaurant, we ran into a nice poet named Paul Carroll, who sat with us and talked for a while about the poetry center he had started, and about Allen Ginsberg, a poet I had hardly heard of who sounded absolutely crazy. (I met him later and discovered he was indeed crazy, but in a good way.) A lot of people smiled and stared at us, and I realized they were eavesdropping on our conversation as if they were at the theater. (That was one thing that always annoyed me, the way people would unabashedly listen in to our conversations in restaurants. Norman always loved to discuss things of a personal nature, too, in his big loud voice, and no amount of shushing him could ever get him to stop it.) I tried to listen with interest to Norman and Paul's conversation and not betray my ignorance of poetry. Norman used to say that I didn't open my mouth for the first three years we were together, which wasn't true at all of course, but I did subscribe to Abraham Lincoln's old adage "Better to keep your mouth shut and be thought a fool than to open it and remove all doubt." I resolved to read more poetry and try to wean myself from Rod McKuen.

After dinner, we went to hear jazz, another thing I had never done. In high school choir we had sung everything from show tunes to Russian dirges, and of course there was music at church and good old rock and roll, but I was totally ignorant of jazz and was a little nervous when we went into the smoky, dim club. Carol, Norman's companion at that time, had been an up-and-coming jazz singer in the fifties, and that was intimidating to me, too; I was an interloper in a world that was hers, with her man. I didn't mention my fears to him. I just pretended I was secure and confident, and he was happy to be there with me. I was wearing a tight pair of pale gray knit pants with an off the shoulder top and high-heeled lizard sandals, and my red hair fell in waves down over my shoulders. I instinctively knew that Norman needed a strong, confident woman, and that was what I was determined to be.

In a spotlight on a small stage, a man named Sonny Stitt was playing a saxophone, with a couple of other guys on the piano and bass. There was no beat, no dancing, just cool people sitting and drinking, nodding their heads to some rhythm I couldn't seem to pick up. Norman ordered a white rum and tonic, with a topper of water and *lemon*—very important that it's lemon, not lime. A rum and tonic Presbyterian, he called it. It was his drink for many years. (I later pieced together that during his turbulent earlier years, of which at this time I was more or less ignorant, his drink of choice had been bourbon. Only once did I ever see him seriously drink bourbon. It was on the campaign plane with Jimmy Carter when he was running for president, and Norman absolutely turned into someone else, as opposite from the man I knew as Mr. Hyde was from Dr. Jekyll—someone I didn't like at all, rude and snide and argumentative, not only with me but with others as well. He was so bad, I seriously considered getting another flight and going home, and I might have if it had been in any other situation. He was contrite afterward, and said he wouldn't drink bourbon again. He seemed to know what it did to him. They don't call it "spirits" for nothing.)

At the jazz club, I ordered a white wine, which I sipped the rest of the evening. When the band took a break, Sonny put down his sax and came straight over to us. He and Norman embraced like old friends (he embraced me, too, a good one), although I don't think they really knew each other well, if at all. (Celebrities are always happy to see one another; it is as if you are the only Little Person in the room and suddenly you see another one. Aha! A member of my tribe!) Sonny invited us to hang around until after the second set and then go out with him for a drink somewhere else, but Norman said that would be impossible.

Sonny tried to convince him, but to no avail, so he finally had to let it be and go back and perform again. We left well before the second set was completed. I later learned that before she met him, Norman's ex-wife (the one he was still married to) Beverly had once had a big affair with Miles Davis, so Norman wasn't keen on history repeating itself, I suppose. All that history with the wives! Well, I vowed to make a little history myself, and try not to worry about it.

The next day, we went to the art museum. I saw paintings and sculptures I had only seen in books. At the Arkansas Arts Center, I used to pack up my high school kids to go to look at a single Andrew Wyeth painting that they'd have on loan, and here were walls full of them! Norman bought me a necklace at the gift shop, a golden filigree pendant that was copied from a Spanish piece. He said he wanted to see me wearing it and nothing else, and later that afternoon I obliged. He kept saying I smelled of cinnamon—maybe it was some perfume I was wearing—and he jokingly said if I ever became a stripper, I should call myself Cinnamon Brown. (Remember the old game we used to play as kids, where you take the name of your first pet and the name of the street on which you grew up and put them together to get your stripper name? Mine would have been Blacky St. Mary, which actually is kind of better than Cinnamon Brown. His would have been Dukie Crown, which is also a pretty good one, come to think of it.)

When I got back home to Arkansas, I knew my life had already begun to change.

To Barbara Norris:

> . . . Cinnamon Brown, that's your other female, the tall jaunty slightly mysterious red-headed woman who can't walk into a bar without turning it on since there's a sexual voltage comes off you then of which you may even be unaware, and that lady, of course, is a distance away from Barbara who is looking to have one love till she dies and wants to make an art of that love so that she gives strength and gains strength and tenderness passes forward and back. And I, of course, love those ladies because there's one of them for each of me, Barbara for Norman since he is probably as tender as she is (that is saying a lot) and as much in love with the religion of love which is to make it with

one's mate and thereby come out to a place very few people visit and you can be true to that idea of love; then another side not so different from Cinnamon, a cold creation full of lust who might just as well have a name like Ace or Duke or some such hard-cock name far from Norman—and yet not a bad side, no worse than Cinnamon, for so much of the action is there, even an instinct for some of the better adventures.

I used to be that way when I was twenty-six; I still am. One past needs to be in love—the other can remain in love only so long as the love keeps changing, and so if it is the same woman, the ante keeps rising. There has to be more and more. Of course one cannot always name what *more* might be—it is rather that one has to believe it is possible. Then the two sides of my nature can come together. I know it is the same with you.

Sometimes I think of everything in the scheme of things which is not designed for us—the physical distance, Matt on your side and all my children on mine, my two years of chronology to each of yours, our cultures—for New York as you will see is a culture—and just as I might not be able to live for long in Arkansas, so might you not be able to endure the East; a cold and competitive place you will find if you live in it long enough, and then there's all you have to learn, and all I have to remember and to keep from losing, and yet I feel curiously optimistic, as if we will never lose the best part of each other for all those reasons, but only because there is finally not enough magic and/or balls in one of us or the other or both of us together to keep our opposites in that lovely tension which would not cease in Little Rock or Chicago. So I do not worry about our betraying each other . . . my happiness, and then my optimism is that at last I know a woman who understands love the way I do and has the same kind of confidence and the same respect—it soon becomes fear—that such a love can make in its resonance toward everything about it. This kind of love is dangerous in its essence possibly because its potential harmony is so great that every devil in you and me will be disturbed by it, and the devils in others will hate us. Still we have our chance. We have that lovely balance between us and that fucky imbalance which keeps us pawing each other and exploring each other and looking to surprise one another—there's such delight in the surprises, and that funny confidence we each feel where we're just happy to be with each other.

So I don't worry. I think we have a little time at least in this happy state and the confidence that if we have it in us truly, nothing will grind it down, and if we don't, well God we've been blessed a little already and I love Cinnamon Brown and Barbara Norris 'cause as you know they're both divine.

Hey, I miss you
right now,
Norman Kingsley

P.S. How did you know that Kingsley was my middle name? I wonder if I have a use for it at last.

P.P.S. Nope. It's no better than Ace or Duke. Call me Roger.

Sixteen

I did call my parents from Chicago, and it was as bad as I'd thought it would be—another round of "How can you do this to us? How can you do this to Matthew?" I was beginning to see that I couldn't talk to them about any of it. They forced me to sneak around, which made me feel horrible, but finally they began to understand that Norman wasn't going away in a hurry. He was one year—almost to the day—older than my father, and while they didn't know many of the particulars of his reputation, they knew enough to be worried for me. I was learning more about him every time we talked. He was certainly candid about his past, but it seemed like the stories he was telling me were about somebody else, maybe an older black sheep brother who'd gotten into pointless fights, had gotten married a lot of times, and had—God forbid—in a drunken, drugged-out bout of psychosis, stabbed one of his wives. I just couldn't reconcile that wild man with the funny, smart, loving man he was when he was with me. It wasn't possible he could be capable of that kind of behavior, or at least not anymore. I knew in my gut he was a good man, and my gut had seldom been wrong; whenever I had gone against it I'd always been sorry.

In return for telling me about his foibles, he wanted to hear stories of my past, especially the boyfriends—it seemed to turn him on—but I frankly didn't have all that much to tell him, and when he kept insisting on more, I made up a couple of affairs that never happened and embellished the ones that had. Later I was sorry I had done that, and finally confessed I had made some of it up, but at the time he was so disappointed that I had nothing else to tell him, and I wanted to please him. Maybe he didn't want to believe how young and naïve I was.

My first act of rebellion had been to marry Larry, but when we divorced, that was bad, too. My parents' generation was of the era that believed "You made your bed. Now you have to lie in it." Forever. You married the first person you went to bed with, as a matter of course. The principal fear that kept you in line was "What will people say?" Well, people in that small town said plenty. When word got out that I was seeing Norman Mailer, I was the center of gossip, and when I actually quit my job and moved to New York to live with him, that is all anyone talked about. (The reactions were pretty mixed between the people who felt sorry for me and the people who felt sorry for him.)

One older woman whom I knew only slightly gave out the word that I was putting Matthew up for adoption, which really hurt me. I don't know what was worse, the stupid gossips or the friends who raced to tell me everything that was said. For some people, there is a perverse pleasure in the pain of friends. As our old friend Gore Vidal famously said, "It isn't enough to succeed; your friends must fail." Even my dearest friends thought I had lost my mind and that I would stay in New York awhile and then come to my senses and move back to Arkansas.

After Chicago, Norman called almost every day and wrote wonderful letters several times a week. We exchanged a lot of pictures, and a huge box of his books arrived. I dutifully set out to read them all in order, starting with *The Naked and the Dead,* and for the most part succeeded, which was a big mistake in a lot of ways, as I was in no way ready to have that plethora of ideas and bombast of language thrust into my brain all at once. I absorbed as much as I could, though, enough to know whom I was dealing with a little bit better. I liked *The Naked and the Dead.* It was a good war story that had funny, true moments. I laughed out loud in some places. ("What is this stuff?" one of the soldiers in the chow line says. "Owl shit," answers the tough mess cook, giving him the evil eye. "Okay," the soldier says. "I just thought it was something I couldn't eat.")

The Prisoner of Sex struck me as humorous, but he didn't write it that way. "Those feminist bitches have destroyed my credibility with women," he said. I could see how people could take a lot of what he said in a bad way, as he never thought of the consequences. He just said what he thought was the truth at the time. To me, the humor and irony was inherent, but you can't transfer the twinkle in the eye to the page, so a lot of people treated everything he said as perfectly serious, like his famous comment that women should be kept in cages. Who would think he was serious about that? But feminists saw it as him making fun of them. He didn't help his own cause a lot of the time. I always told him I was a feminist. I had run across gender abuse myself, and was certainly for a woman's right to have the same salary as a man and all the rest of it—rights he supported, as well—but he never accepted that he had to be serious with the subject. He didn't couch his language at all; he threw it out there with force. I could understand his frustration.

Once I overheard two women talking about him in the bathroom of a theater where we were watching a play, and they were calling him a sexist pig and a misogynist and other bad things. I usually just ignored things like this, but they were right in my face, putting on lipstick, so I interrupted them and said, "Do you know Norman Mailer?" They said no. "Have you ever read anything he's written?" I asked. Again they said no. I said, "Well, I'm married to him, and if you are going to call someone names like that, you should at least know what you're talking about." They just stared at me, and I walked away, I was so angry.

After we were married, Gloria Steinem said in print that anybody who would marry Norman Mailer couldn't be healthy, well adjusted, conscious, or aware, because for such a woman Norman was unmarriable, which I totally resented, since she knew nothing about me and had, in fact, been friends with him. Close friends. Germaine Greer, who almost had an affair with him (I'm a little fuzzy on the details), and who was his nemesis in the famous debate at town hall, was quite nice to me the one time we met in London, and even gave me a copy of her book about women painters, as I was a painter. I sympathized with the fact that these painters had never gotten any credit, but it didn't make them more interesting to read about. "She was a decent painter, even a good painter; she was ignored; she died." End of story.

Some of Norman's political writings I frankly skimmed, and while I thought they were brilliant, it was just too much to take in all at once. *An American Dream* was disturbing, in light of the incident with his second wife, Adele, and his violent history with Lady Jeanne, his third wife. I found *The Deer Park* unbelievable. I didn't like any of the characters; they didn't seem real to me; every woman was, or wanted to be, a prostitute. I found *Why Are We in Vietnam?* to be just about unreadable, although it had some beautiful writing about Alaska and a lovely passage about a long train ride in it. I never thought dialogue was his strong suit. I once pointed out that people didn't talk like he wrote, and he said they did, so we were at an impasse. I do believe that no one else can write like him, sentence for sentence, with brilliant passages such as the descriptions of Provincetown and Maine in *Tough Guys Don't Dance* and *Harlot's Ghost*. And no one can say he doesn't use wonderful, unusual metaphors, but we had long arguments about the need for plot. "There's no need for a plot," he would argue. "Life doesn't have a plot. Life is existential. You never know from one minute to the next what is going to happen, and there are no clear endings."

"That's exactly why a book needs a plot," I would answer. "Nobody wants to read a book to get real life. You want to *escape* from real life when you read. You want to have a beginning, a middle, and an end. You want there to be a conclusion, where the guy gets the girl, or the house is sold, or the murderer is caught." But he was unmoved by my arguments.

Slowly over the years I've reread the volumes, and they seem like entirely different books from that first green reading. I've come to have more respect for his work. One of the reasons Norman was attracted to me—or so he once believed—was that I had never read his work when I met him, and I liked him for himself. As I used to tell him, I would have fallen for him if he had been a truck driver. He would ask, "But would you have married me?" And I'd say, "Of course not. The hours are too long, and you would be away too much. There would be too much temptation on the road to cheat." He liked the dishonesty of that.

The first time I met Ethel Kennedy, the first thing she asked was, "Would you be with him if he weren't Norman Mailer?"

I thought for a minute. "Well, I know a whole lot of people who aren't Norman Mailer, and I'm not with any of them, so I guess not."

It's a silly question. If I had weighed three hundred pounds, or had looked like Groucho Marx, would Norman have been with me? If he hadn't been the writer-celebrity and personality he was, he would have been someone else entirely, and I might have been attracted to him, but probably not. Interesting puzzle. In my memory, that's where Ethel's and my conversation stopped. There was nothing else to say. So funny, how women reacted to me when I first came to New York. Lizzie Hardwick, a writer who had been married to Robert Lowell, took me aside when we were first introduced and, with that croaky little giggle she had, said, "Now, don't let that man make you pregnant!" Bella Abzug gave me her home phone number and told me to call her, at any hour of the night, if I needed to get away from him, and she would come and get me. I just stared at them. I had no idea what they were talking about.

Before I met Norman, I had been toying with the idea of going back to school to get my MFA in art and teach in college, preferably at Arkansas Tech. My ambition at the time was such that I didn't want to move away. I just wanted to be able to work more seriously with older students and have more pay. I loved living in Russellville with my son, I loved my little house with the murals on the walls, my water bed, my orange shag carpet, my parents and my friends, but for some inexplicable reason, I checked out schools in the East. I had written to the Rhode Island School of Design and MassArt in Boston for applications to their MFA programs. I had filled some parts out but hadn't yet sent the applications off. I was also thinking of going to the University of Arkansas, which made a lot more sense, but that would have been my last choice. I was drawn to go east. If I did go to one of the Eastern schools, I would have to get loans and scholarships or a working fellowship, and find a place to live for myself and Matthew, day care for him. It was a huge undertaking. I, of course, discussed it with Norman.

> Well, gorgeous, I read your letter, studied it, thought about it, have dipped into new ink, and present my first thoughts.
>
> The idea of you being in Massachusetts is exciting as hell. It's also easy for me to welcome you and disruptive for you. Nonetheless, I think you ought to start working at it—applications, so forth. If you want, wait till you see New York, or maybe even fly back to Boston with me for a day and you can see how you like it, and how you like the school. How you like the East.
>
> I think that's important. The feeling I have about you and me is that we will beat the odds against us only if we fulfill the innermost idea of love—which is that we continue to be good for each other, and feed each other our strength and our talent and our warmth and our wit. Nothing can break us if we do the thing so few people can do for each other—which is: each give fire to the other's courage. (So often one finds love, and then looks for a cave where one can feast on it—soon such love grows stale.) I've always believed that people don't find happy

love if they're looking for it to solve their problems—they just find an intensification of their problems. We find our good love about the time we deserve it. I like to think we may each have arrived at that place (took me twice as long as you) where we deserve each other. That would be great if it is true. It is going to put, however, every demand on us—because, for once, I want to be in love without guilt, and want a woman to love me without guilt. I want us only if we succeed with each other (not every instant, of course, but over the whole). I don't want us ever to be loyal out of duty. I want us, rather, to be loyal to the best idea we can have of each other.

You see, I ask you for feats, bit by bit. But I don't think you would have been drawn to me if that was not what you wanted. So I think you should come East with the full hope that it brings us together and the full awareness that you are prepared to live it alone if you and me become less grand than we are at this instant.

What a joke. There I'll be probably slaving away in Stockbridge working my dull axe (my pencil) while you're the new beauty of Boston.

God bless you, love. Days are getting nearer. Ain't you nifty, ain't you sweet.

The thought of talking to you soon is half as exciting as the thought of fucking you, and that means it's very exciting.

Yeah,
Norman

P.S. I can't remember who took the pictures. It was on the lecture tour, I think, and then mailed to me. Anyway, they're recent and date from last winter or spring.

P.P.S. It's cloudy out, but I find it a fine morning.

I loved those letters. It was like having him there with me, as I read them over and over with a cup of coffee in the morning, the ink fresh and immediate from a pen in his strong, square hand. His handwriting was sometimes hard to read, but he made an effort to make it as legible as possible. At any rate, soon he sent me a ticket to New York. Norman liked to tell the story of the first time he got off the plane in Berlin, how he took a deep breath and got a hard-on. That's metaphorically what happened to me in New York. I got off the plane, and immediately I knew this was my town. I had never fallen in love with a place so quickly before. Even the dense air at the airport and the energy of the crowd in the dingy buildings were exciting. Norman was waiting at the gate, and when we got into the taxi, he grabbed me and gave me a kiss that lasted all the way to the front door of his apartment in Brooklyn. We talked about the Taxicab Kiss for years. It was the most astonishing kiss I ever had or ever will have. I think he would have agreed.

Norman had been regaling me with descriptions of the magnificent apartment he had there (it sounded like the Taj Mahal), with its soaring glass skylight, the view of the skyline of lower Manhattan, the harbor, and the Statue of Liberty. How from the roof deck you could see New Jersey and Staten Island and the Brooklyn Bridge, as well as the Manhattan and Verrazano bridges, and how he had decorated it like a ship, so it felt like an enormous yacht. I was so excited. I couldn't wait to see the wonder of this place. I missed most of the scenery coming in from the airport because of the kiss, but the few glimpses I had weren't so spectacular. It looked like a bunch of dirty row houses in some slum, graffiti on the walls of the buildings closest to the highway. But I knew we were going to a great neighborhood with tree-lined streets and this palatial apartment.

The neighborhood was sweet, with trees and rows of nineteenth-century brownstone houses. We carried my bags up a set of brownstone steps into the house, and then up three long flights of stairs. The hallway was painted dark green and the carpet was a dusty midnight-blue wool. The last flight of stairs leading to the top floor, Norman's palace, was carpeted in red. "Of course," I thought. Red. It was fitting for the king. The door was painted a rather ugly flat blue, and as I stood there panting, trying to catch my breath from the climb, Norman opened it and stepped back with a flourish—ta-da!

The first thing to hit me in the face was the heat. The ceiling over half the apartment was an enormous A-frame skylight through which the sun was beating as if the window was a magnifying glass. The windows had all been shut for weeks, and all the oxygen had been burned out of the room. I could hardly draw breath. He rushed around opening the door to the little terrace and climbing a ladder (a ladder!) to reach the second level to open the skylight windows. I stood there and tried to take it all in. The view was as spectacular as promised, but the Taj Mahal, the apartment wasn't. It was much smaller than I had anticipated. Much. I was used to living in a sprawling three-bedroom two-bathroom house with a dining room, living room, den, laundry room, and big yard, and this was the top floor of a New York brownstone. Not a bad size for an apartment in the city, but for someone used to space, it was tiny.

Aside from the soaring skylight, the apartment was basically one big open room with two small separate bedrooms in the back, a teeny galley kitchen with white metal cabinets and orange walls on one side, and on the other, a bathroom with dark blue tiles that was smaller than most coat closets, just large enough to squeeze in a small black sink, a five-foot tub, and a toilet. There were nets everywhere. Old fisherman's nets (that still carried a whiff of the sea) hung from the ceiling around a bed in a corner of the living room, and one entire wall was bookcases crammed with books. Books were in piles on the floor, on chairs, on tables. The furniture was, to put it kindly, dusty and worn, and the place was filled with odd things, like strange dried fish heads hanging on the walls, or a grimy, slowly disintegrating sculpture made from black stockings that was hung from a hook in the ceiling. A quarter of the living room was filled with an enormous red, white, yellow, and blue LEGO sculpture (also terribly dusty, as was everything in the place) cordoned off by a low fence.

There was an open area between the bathroom and kitchen that was like a jungle gym; a trapeze was suspended from a beam in the middle of the space under the peak of the skylight, with a hammock slung across the abyss above it, two stories up. A tightrope was stretched at knee height on metal legs that were screwed into brass plates set into the hardwood floor. There was a climbing rope and a ship's ladder that folded down so one could climb up to a little room over the living room, and above the kitchen there was an open loft with two beds that folded into the wall, like ship's bunks. Another ladder went up to yet a third level, a crow's nest that was in the high peak of the roof, and you had to walk an exposed plank that stretched across two open stories to reach it.

One of the two bedrooms in the back was papered in red and held a bed, a chest, and a lovely antique dresser. The other one was papered with cartoon ships and sailors, as if for little boys, and crammed with old filing cabinets, a chair with the stuffing coming out, and assorted broken lamps and boxes of junk. The place looked like it hadn't been cleaned in many months. Many. I wandered into the filthy kitchen. I wasn't sure what color the floor was, but it was brownish and sticky. I opened the fridge and shut it immediately. Someone had spilled a bottle of soy sauce in there in the not so remote past and then unplugged the refrigerator. The whole thing reeked. I was speechless. Norman stood expectantly, beaming.

"Well? Isn't it everything I said it was?"

"Oh. It is. It's wonderful. It's amazing. Can I go out on the terrace?" I had just about gotten my breath back, but between the smell of the fridge and the heat, I was a little sick, and sweat was pouring down my neck. I went out, and the view was indeed spectacular. I started imagining myself cleaning the place and reorganizing it, and I began to relax a bit. I am a lot like my mother, who is a total neat freak. I could see now that Norman was the furthest thing from that. It wasn't that he was just messy. I don't think he even *saw* the mess. He truly had no idea it wasn't perfect just as it was. There would be a lot of work to do, and I would have to do it carefully, so as not to offend him.

I stood looking out at the city across the river, at the tall rectangular shapes of the new World Trade Center towers, the tallest buildings on the horizon. The river was so close, it seemed like we could run down to the water and swim across.

"Aren't those two towers the ugliest things you've ever seen?" Norman said, coming out to join me. "They've totally ruined the skyline. Look at the rest of the buildings, how lovely they are, reaching up to heaven, like the points of artists' paintbrushes, and then there's those two Kleenex boxes stuck in the middle of it like two big buck teeth. World Trade towers. What a monument to the corporation."

"You're right. The older buildings are better. These new ones are so cold. All that glass and steel. I like wood and stone more."

"Oh, definitely. Right. I made up a law about the phenomenon. I call it Mailer's Law of Architectural Precedence. It goes, 'If the building you are in is less agreeable than the building across the street, then the building you are in was put up later.' "

It must be said that the brownstone in Brooklyn where he lived was much more agreeable than the Kleenex box high-rises in Manhattan, and it had been built much earlier, in 1836, the same year Arkansas became a state. His apartment was the servants' quarters then, the house a one-family dwelling, and now there were four families living in it. His furniture—an overstuffed moss-green velvet couch, a claret-colored velvet wing chair, low wood tables, and nice Oriental carpets—was worn and a little shabby, but it was all good stuff and comfortable. Now that I'd gotten over the shock, all the place needed was a good cleaning and maybe a few pictures on the walls—definitely the dried goose fish and broken lamps thrown away. Maybe a few of the chairs re-covered. There were lots of possibilities. I didn't dare plan for too much right away, as it was only my first day in the place, but I couldn't help it. Decorating was one of my passions.

Norman took me to Montague Street, the main drag of Brooklyn Heights, for a Chinese lunch, the first time I'd ever had real Chinese food. He was so happy and excited to introduce me to new things. Brooklyn Heights was a small, sweet neighborhood with mom-and-pop shops, interesting bookstores, and friendly people. Norman had been preparing me for weeks, talking about the coldness of New York, how every woman on the street would be more beautiful and chic than I was, how intimidating I would find it, but that wasn't the case at all. If you grow up as a self-assured, beloved person, you will be that same person no matter where you are. As far as all the beautiful women went, of course there were beautiful ones, but most were just like the women on the streets of Russellville or any other place. I never felt inferior to any of them, then or ever, and part of it was that Norman always made me feel special.

Norman's sister, Barbara, invited us for dinner at her place in Greenwich Village, and I met his mother, Fanny, for the first time. I was astounded at how much the three of them looked alike; Barbara was a petite, pretty version of Norman, with curly salt-and-pepper hair and lively blue eyes, and his mother was an older version of them, still energetic and bustling in the kitchen. Norman had concocted a story of how I was Francis Gwaltney's niece who had come to New York to see if I might want to move there, but I don't think they bought it. It was impossible not to see the sparks flying between us, and with his track record, they were no dummies. Barbara's husband, Al Wasserman, a producer for *60 Minutes,* had snow-white sideburns,

Norman's sister, Barbara, and Al.

with darker hair in a comb-over on top, and told funny jokes in a Jewish accent. He had done some great documentaries, one of which had won an Academy Award.

The only member of the family I met who wasn't so great was Bouncer the corgi, who did his best to bite me all night. They had to put him in the bathroom, where he had obviously been put many times before, as the door had a good-size chunk of it chewed out. They told me it wasn't personal, he had tried to bite every one of Norman's children, and even snapped at Norman's sister occasionally. At one point, I forgot he was in there, went into the bathroom, and nearly got my leg taken off. They had to hold him while I used the facility, which was pretty embarrassing.

The surprising, wonderful thing was how warm and close and normal a family they all were. I immediately liked them, and I think they liked me. Barbara was a good cook. She had made pot roast, and Norman's mother promised to teach me how to do it. I'm sure they had a lot of questions, but refrained from asking them, and I played my part as Francis's dutiful niece who also was a schoolteacher. I could tell Norman was happy, though, that we got along so well. They didn't seem to think it was strange that he was there with me, and no one mentioned his wife. None of Norman's kids were there that night, but there would be time enough to meet them. I kept telling myself this was just a visit. I would be going home in a couple of days, and might never be back. But we both knew better. We had gotten even closer during the week; it had been nonstop fun, going out to restaurants and getting to know New York, and long hot nights in bed. As the time came for me to go back, neither one of us wanted it to end. By the last couple of days, we stopped pretending.

"Why don't you move here and try it for a while?" Norman said. "You can always go back to school later. Stay here in the apartment until you figure out what you want to do. You might decide to try modeling, or if you want to teach or write or paint, you can do that."

I hadn't thought about modeling since I had sent my pictures to Eileen Ford when I was eighteen. After the divorce, I thought I was too old, and obviously with a child it would have been impossible to come to New York and try it, but everywhere I went people kept mistaking me for a model. On the street in Manhattan, a photographer came up to me and asked me who I was with, and I didn't know what he was talking about. He handed me his card and told me I should think about modeling. He wasn't the first one, and actually being in New York, the idea began to take root once again.

Norman and I were walking down Fifth Avenue when I told him I had to stop and buy a pair of flip-flops or something because I had a wicked blister on my foot from my shoe, so we went into Saks Fifth Avenue, where I got a pair of sandals. A pushy saleswoman took one look at him, smelled a live one, and descended on us. He wound up buying me two dresses, a beautiful Diane von Furstenberg black knit dress in a lotus pattern, and a Saks label long evening dress in a dark blue velvet print. The saleswoman was beside herself, bringing things out for me to try on, and he loved the fashion show I did for him. We drew a little crowd. (It was embarrassing when I went into the dressing room, though, because I hadn't worn any underwear, and the woman insisted on coming in with me. That was the last time I made that mistake—either not wearing underwear to shop in or letting the saleswoman into the dressing room.)

"You should be a model," the saleswoman said as I was sashaying around in my new outfits. Norman agreed with her, and he decided then and there to take me down the street to see an old friend of his, Amy Greene, who ran a business out of Henri Bendel's called Beauty Checkers, which taught a woman how to put on makeup. Amy was in her forties, at the peak of her beauty, and had been a model when she was young. She was married to Milton Greene, one of the most famous photographers in the business. They had befriended Marilyn Monroe when she'd come to New York to study at the Actors Studio, and Marilyn had lived with Milton and Amy for a time in their house in Greenwich, Connecticut. Norman wrote about them in *Marilyn*. I knew Milton's photographs from the book, and the idea of my meeting Amy and maybe actually becoming a model was exciting for both Norman and me. We had lunch with Amy, who is nothing if not honest. "Kiddo," she said, "you're beautiful. Your skin is to die for, but you're three years too old, so you'll have to lie, and you need to lose fifteen pounds. I wouldn't let you go see Wilhelmina like you are. She would just turn you down."

Oh. That was honest. I weighed about 130, but I was five feet ten, so it wasn't like I was obese. Still, I took her at her word. Models were skinny. Wilhelmina was one of the two biggest model agents in New York, the other one being Eileen Ford, who had turned me down when I'd sent those pictures years ago, so I knew it would have been pointless to try her again. I told Amy I'd go back home and lose the weight. I thought as long as I was there at Beauty Checkers, I might as well get some pointers, so Amy did my makeup while Norman waited. I thought I was pretty good with makeup, but Amy wanted to do something different from the browns I used. She chose odd colors of yellow and purple eye shadow, which were not my colors at all. I didn't want to say anything, since she was Norman's friend and all, but it was kind of appalling. My eyes looked like two pansies. Norman wasn't as nice about it. He took one look at it and growled, "Could you please wash your face and put your regular makeup back on? My reputation is bad enough in this town without people thinking I beat you up and gave you two black eyes!"

Amy took it with good grace, we redid the makeup, and when the time came, she called Wilhelmina for me and made an appointment, but I'm getting ahead of myself. First, I had to face my parents, my son, and the town of Russellville and tell them I was moving to New York City.

Seventeen

It was about what you would expect. "How can you do this to us, after all we have done for you?" my parents said. "How are you going to live? Who is this man? Isn't he married? How can you take Matthew off so far away from us?" And many variations of those questions. I didn't know the answers myself, but the thing I did know was that I was either going to move to New York to be with Norman or die. I didn't care how much of a sinner I was. I had seen my future with him and I wanted to be there, in the middle of all that excitement, no matter what. I planned to sell my car and house and to cash in my teacher's retirement, which would give me about five thousand dollars—enough, I figured, to last until I got a job. I had no idea what ultimately would happen with Norman. He had made me no promises and I had asked him for none, but he was as anxious as I was for me to come and live there. Of course, I knew he was unhappy in his present marital situation, but he never said straight and plain he was going to leave Carol, who was in Stockbridge, waiting for him to come back and take the family to Maine for the rest of the summer.

The plan was that I would leave Matt with Mother and Daddy until I got settled and got a job, whatever it turned out to be, and then I'd come back down in a few weeks or months and bring him up to live with me. I was going to get my own apartment. I would stay with Norman for a while, but I wanted to have my own place in case for some reason it didn't work out. That, and at least it would give Mother and Daddy the illusion that I wasn't living in sin, although I certainly would be.

I went back to Arkansas, and the next month was a flurry of quitting my job (which gave both Chip, the principal of Russellville High School, and me enormous satisfaction), selling my house and car—my beloved yellow Volkswagen Super Beetle, which I still wish I had kept—and saying goodbye to all my friends and boyfriends. None of them could believe I was moving to New York to be with a man older than my father. Norman had talked to Francis about it by that time, and he was quite upset, as we had feared. He and Ecey were worried for me, of course, but I think they were just as worried about him. Here he was breaking up his fifth marriage, leaving another child behind.

That was something I didn't like to dwell too closely on. I hadn't met any of the children yet, but of course I knew about them—all seven of them. He had broken up with every one of their mothers before any of them was older than six, and now the oldest one, Susan, was my same age, twenty-six, and the youngest was Maggie, four. I knew in my heart that if it hadn't been me, he would have broken up that last marriage in any case. As he had told me, he was being pressured by Annette to make a choice between Carol and her, but Annette seemed to have been forgotten. (Part of their pact was to not speak for six months, either.)

In fact, for some incredible reason, I didn't worry about anything, or any other woman. Norman made me feel that secure, that loved. As soon as I got home, all I could think about was getting back to New York and Norman. The one fun thing I did do during that month of July was go to Memphis to a Rolling Stones concert with a boy I had been dating named Bob, who had long wavy blond hair and blue eyes, because we'd had tickets for a long time, but I wouldn't sleep with him, which was quite upsetting to him. He, too, was in shock that I had plans to move to New York. He gave me a turquoise ring and told me that he would be waiting for me when I came to my senses. But there was nothing anyone could say to stop me. I had never been so single-minded about anything in my life, or so sure of what I was doing.

So, once again, for the seventh or eighth time in four years, I moved. Without a backward glance, I gave away or sold all my furniture and clothes, keeping only a few suitcases for the trip and a few clay pots and paintings and mementos from my students and friends. The one thing Norman said about my packing was, "Don't bring any of your Arkansas polyester clothes up here." As if they had never heard of polyester in New York! But I had no choice because most of what I had was polyester, and frankly I liked it. It fit nicely, was easy to wash, and didn't wrinkle. I also made a lot of my own clothes, and it was easy to sew. Even the big designers such as Oscar de la Renta used Quiana nylon and polyester in their designs. Still, I left most of the homemade things behind, aside from the pants. I never could get pants long enough. I had no idea if I could really become a model or not, but I went to work starving myself and riding my bike, and by the time I left for New York, I weighed 115. I visited a couple of photographers, including Bill Ward and Lee Rogers, and collected a few pictures to show Wilhelmina when the time came.

I tried to explain to Matthew that I was going to go away for a while but would come back and get him and we would go to live in a big city. I don't think he understood at all what I was saying, but he didn't worry too much about it. He loved my parents and felt safe with them. No matter what, I didn't intend to be without him for long. I think my mother and father thought I would get it out of my system and move back in a few weeks. At any rate, they didn't have a choice. I was one determined girl.

The only one who wasn't that concerned about me was me. And Norman. He was off on another adventure. He had a new willing Eliza Doolittle he was going to make into the next star, and whatever happened would be all good. He was feeding my moving frenzy with long letters and phone calls from a phone booth in Maine, where he was living for the summer with the family. They were mountain climbing, hiking, and swimming, living in an unusual house situated over a fjord with a deck that cantilevered out over the water. He told me a rite of passage for the kids was to jump off the deck into the water eighteen feet below, and how he was trying to get up the courage to dive off it. I was so jealous, wanting to be there with him. It was torture, knowing Carol was with him, sleeping in the same bed, and worrying that he would change his mind and decide he wanted to stay with her after all. But still, the letters and calls kept coming, reassuring me. I proceeded to make my plans.

Darling,

. . . God, I adore you. Time keeps coming back from our week. Lovely thoughts and lovely little swoonings of all that big and lovely joining meat and then the vaults and the whispers and the bells that do not stop and the hours of talking through sugar-time—you can't be as naturally smart as I think you are because I'm not smart enough to realize it.

I've been tempted to break all I said and call you anyway, but

I'm going to hold out. I think phones are a nasty addiction like nicotine. They use up real love for a quick electric charge and they're noxious to the heart. So even though I'm dying to hear about Matt's reaction when you came home and your parents and the world—that world of Russellville—slowly coming to focus on you whether you realize it or not—I'm going to wait for you to write.

Tell me in detail if you feel like it. And for God's sakes tell me of any and all fear because there'll be moments—there will have to be. I have no fear about us over this year and years to come—I think we will not have boils and bends and the harsh kinds of trouble so much as we will be like the weather with one another. And you, stand-up lady, are golden as the sun. All the same, for now, right now, there has to be something of the dream-like about the next two weeks and fear may even come in moments when and if you don't feel real or selling the house becomes all too real. Like tasting pennies. Just remember it will work out. Things may be in one state or another two weeks from now, but by George, come Friday, Saturday, then Sunday two weeks and two days from now—we'll be together again for another week, and since we're natural athletes at love (although rookies in the major leagues) we ought to feel pretty good at the chance to break all those honey records we put up last time. Yes, some of those records were twice honey.

Darling, I just had a picture of how you look in the morning with that incredible beauty in your face as if you'd been fucking a stag in your dreams and he said something lovely as he left you in my arms. Did I ever tell you that your hair is as red as the last rays of a sunset on a hot summer night and your eyes are the golden umber of the last rare cloud before it gets dark? Well, it's something like that if just as lovely and never so full of corn. God I look forward to the next days we can spend in loving each other.

Cheers. Rum and
nectar
Yes, I adore you,
you guessed.
XO Norman

He was waiting for me at the airport when I arrived in mid-August. He was going to spend a week with me until I got settled, then go back to Maine to the family for another few weeks, when I would be all alone in New York.

Eighteen

Fanny Mailer was under five feet tall, had maybe been five feet one at her peak, but had shrunk with age and had the dreaded arthritic widow's hump. Still, she was capable and full of energy, and for some reason took a liking to me. She had grown up Jewish in New Jersey. Her father owned a kosher butcher shop where she and her three sisters worked hard from the time she was a small, indefatigable girl. She'd also had an older brother but didn't mention him much; she and her sisters were the close-knit heart of the family and they did most of the work. Fanny was the youngest, but we never knew exactly how old she

Fanny.

was, as all the sisters shaved a few years off their ages. She might have been five or more years older than we thought. Besides running the butcher shop, her father had also been a sort of unofficial rabbi, with a long flowing beard, who would take over services when the regular rabbi was away, and they'd kept a kosher home.

The Christian kids they'd gone to school with had been mean to her and her sisters, calling them kikes and making fun of them, so she had bad feelings about all Christians, but she was curious about the way our lives were lived, the beliefs we held, and the way our services were conducted. She loved to hear my stories of having to swim in dresses, or the "sin list," the deeds that would send you to hell. I, in turn, was fascinated about her religion, the dietary regulations, having to use two sets of pots and pans and dishes, not eating meat and dairy together, and what *"mikvah,"* "shiksa," and other funny Yiddish words meant. (*"Schlong"* is another good one, and *"meshugana,"* like Meshugana Ike, the grade B version of Crazy Eddie.) She told me the stories from her childhood, like the time her mother and a friend fell into the path of an oncoming railroad train; the friend was killed and her mother's arm was cut off. How could that happen to someone? I never understood why they had been so close to the train, and in fact Fanny never understood that, either.

In those first weeks and months I spent in New York, she and Barbara were my only friends. Fanny and I used to spend every morning together. I would go over to her apartment on Willow Street, which was two blocks away, for tea. I'd zip up her dress or find her contact lenses, which she was always losing, and then we'd sometimes go to lunch at an old-timey restaurant near the promenade (called the Promenade Restaurant) and have meals of pot roast or stuffed cabbage. Not as good as what Fanny made, but not bad. Other times we would eat and shop at A&S, a department store that was about a mile away on Fulton Street. She wore stockings with elastic garters, and her little calves were so skinny the hose were constantly rolling down her legs, so she would have to stop and pull them up every half block or so. We laughed about it, but she wouldn't think of wearing pantyhose. She wasn't used to them, and they were all too long for her anyhow. We were like girlfriends, and had a great time together.

By the time I'd been there awhile, I'm sure she knew what Norman's and my relationship was, but we didn't discuss it. I had the feeling she didn't really care. He had been around the mulberry bush so many times with other wives and women that I imagined she thought I was just one more and would soon be gone, so she might as well have fun with me while she could. I went with her to synagogue, and the whole congregation was buzzing about it. "Who is that tall redheaded shiksa with Fan?" they whispered. We giggled over how mystified they were. She cryptically introduced me as her friend. And I was. I really don't know what I would have done without her during that time.

Fanny and me in Ptown.

I spent the first days after Norman went back to Maine cleaning the apartment. I got down on my hands and knees with an S.O.S. pad and scrubbed the kitchen floor until I could recognize the terra-cotta color of the tiles, and worked on the soy sauce fridge for a whole day. I was afraid to throw anything out, even the fish heads, but it all got a good scrubbing. I was dying to paint the place. I have never liked primary colors, and he had done the whole place up in red, white, and blue, to match the Lego Vertical City of the Future, which was on the cover of *Cannibals and Christians* and took up much of the living space, but I didn't dare even broach the subject. (The LEGO city itself was dirty but uncleanable. I tried it, and it was so fragile the pieces fell apart.)

But finally all the cleaning I could do was done, and I realized that it was late summer, Norman was still in Maine with the family and would be for another few weeks, and I was alone; I didn't know exactly when he was going to come back, or what was going to happen when he did. I didn't want to push him for any commitments. I knew that would drive him away, like with Annette, whom he hardly mentioned. So I pretended to be stronger and tougher than I was. He liked strong and tough, and in a way I was deceiving him, but in the acting, I did become stronger. Still, it was hard on me, and hard on him, knowing I was so close but yet so far away. I missed my son and worried he was going to forget me. He wasn't much on the phone. He was always in a hurry to get back to his toys or TV or whatever he was doing. I told Matthew stories of New York, and all the things we would do when he got here, and I hoped he understood how much I loved and missed him. I wondered at times, when I hung up the phone after an unsatisfactory talk with him and my parents, if I was doing the right thing, but then I would look out at that view and I knew that there was no place in the world I wanted to be more than right there. Just walking the streets gave me energy, a solitary kind of purpose, as if I were finally entering my real life.

AFTER WE'D BEEN apart a couple of weeks, Norman arranged for me to come and spend the night in Maine in a little motel near where they were staying. I flew to Boston and then Bar Harbor (the first time I had ever been on a small plane, which was frightening) and checked into this seedy little motel. He came over in the morning and spent the day with me, but had to go back home by dinnertime. I had dinner alone, read for a while, went to bed early, and then got up the next morning and took the little plane back to New York. It wasn't a good visit; we both felt too guilty. He had to lie and make up some excuse for being away all day, and I had to lie to his mother about visiting friends in Boston for the night. I felt bad about Carol, too. Although I was in love with her man and would have done anything to get him away from her, that didn't mean I liked myself for it, and for the first time I left Norman with a sense of myself, ourselves, as bad people. I wrote Norman a letter as soon as I got home.

WEDNESDAY

Hello, Darling—

Whether or not you will read this is something I haven't decided yet, but I need to write it down to get it out of my system, if nothing else. For the first time since I've gotten here I am in total misery. The plane ride back was awful—I sat next to a little old lady who talked constantly about her children, grandchildren and dear departed husband, who were all geniuses, fantastic artists (at 4½ years) etc. etc. Then I called your mother who was out, Matthew, who didn't have time to talk to me because he was playing, and my mother was busy working. Even you seem far away from me now. Neither of us was at our best these last two days—there were too many things on both our minds. You have this terrible confrontation with Carol to constantly dread, and I know there must be times when you are not sure if I am worth it. We haven't been together long enough to establish a middle ground. We don't have fifteen years of shared experiences and children to bind us together when one of us is a bit off and we start to get dull. You were feeling blue this morning when I left because that marvelous high we give each other hadn't come—and you knew how much we both needed it to tide us over until the next time we are together again. Norman Mailer, I am deeply in love with you. I am saying this to a man with whom, if you count on your fingers, I have spent slightly more than three weeks—but in that length of time, or even the first time we were together if you prefer, I found in you, and in myself when I am with you, a life-giving force that I take from you and return in a current so strong it frightens and exhilarates me at times into a pitch nearing frenzy. Never before have I met a man with whom I could so completely let go—all of the animal instincts that have been lying dormant these years have been touched by you. You have the power to look into my head and sort through the dusty stacks of whatever miscellany has collected in the 26 years of my narrow existence, and find—occasionally—something worth taking a second look at. If there were no other reasons I would love you for that alone—

but there are other reasons. Both of us are enormously physical people. With us sex is as much a need to be satisfied as hunger. Your body has become an obsession with me. More so each time I see you—you charming little chunk of muscle, hair and musk—you have me wrapped around that splendid cock of yours. You can't possibly have an inkling of the feelings you have unleashed in me. There are times when I start coming and can't stop that I want to scream and ask God to please let me remain intact because every nerve in my body is on fire. And you were surprised when I said I was jealous. There are times when I turn a fetid pea soup green because it should be me jumping off the deck with the boys and climbing mountains with you—being there out of the way when you're writing, in case you need me—sleeping with you every night, lying close to you, feeling my soul leave my body to glide over and briefly enter your body—making us one while I waver on the edge of dreams. Yes, I want you. I am a greedy, selfish bitch at times, and if I could get you by tearing hair and scratching faces, I would—believe me—but you wouldn't want me on those terms, because the only way I will truly have you is for you to have me in the same way—to give you as much (or more, for you are even greedier than I, my dear) as I get from you. That's why we get so upset when one of us is a bit off—we want all of it all of the time. But the middle ground will come in time.

So here it is a few hours later. I feel much better. Your mother called and invited me over for dinner. She was quite upset when I didn't come home last night—I guess I didn't make it clear I would be away all night. We had a good (low calorie, bless her) dinner and I told her all about my adventures in Boston with Martin and JoAn. It eats at me to have to lie to her, but by the time I've finished the story I believe it myself! I did have a good time with you in Bangor, and in spite of the horrible sense of loss that kicked off this letter, it was worth it. Seeing you under the worst of circumstances is infinitely better than not seeing you at all.

It's beautiful here tonight. The sunset was fabulous. I went for a walk around the neighborhood at dusk, and the feeling of tranquility I got has carried over and given me a tired sweetness. All the poisons have worked themselves out now.

I've thought carefully, and have decided to go back on the pill. I hesitated because you were right—I've noticed subtle changes for the better taking place in me since I've been off the pill, but the alternatives are repugnant to me—I believe they will kill something between us. And I know this is not the time for the baby—he will come in his own time—God! What a boy he will be! I know I'm not pregnant, but I don't know what I would do if that were the case. I cannot conceive of killing our child, or of bringing him into the world when even a small part of us doesn't want him. I hope it's a decision we don't have to make.

I'm tired now, and going to bed. I feel drained, but not as lost and desolate as I was. I miss you terribly, but that is something I've lived with since I met you.

Goodnight,
Darling. I love
you.
Barbara

MOUNT DESERT

Darling,

Looking back on it, my Love, we were stacking a few odds against us last Tuesday. I was sick with a cold I'd been holding off by way of much Vitamin C—it doesn't stop the cold so much as put a manhole cover over the symptoms until you stop taking the C pill & let the nose begin to weep. And that infection on my chin was backing up. Once in the Army I almost got blood poisoning. Had an infection on my knee—a mean-looking scab—much like my chin presents now and then the lymph gland in my groin began to swell. I was a day away from blood poisoning when they stuck me in the hospital.

Then add getting up very early in the morning and leaving a note that I'd be gone for the day for writing—a lie I'd never quite told before. Ah, baby, there was heaviness in me. And when we made love right away, I felt this godawful dead space in me after I came. So empty. In all the time I've known you, I never felt anything like that before. I literally wondered in the half-hour preceding breakfast how we could uncover enough to talk about for the rest of the day. And all that dull heavy stupid guilt.

So we spent that afternoon and evening chasing after magic and secretly furious with each other and ourselves when it would not come, not the way we were used to it. And all the while there was never enough energy. I felt as if I were chasing after my own energy all day.

I know now how I could relive that day. I'd recognize that it always takes us the first day to get started. Then after the first day, it starts, and we're in that place where all we want to do is find a way to separate out six or eight hours to spend in one room in bed or else there won't be time to do it all, every last ambitious greedy thing we want to fuck, tease, implore, shake and slyly elucidate out of each other and then go again. No wonder it takes a day to begin. Next time I have a day alone with you, and only a day, I swear we'll take hours before we even touch each other—I want every part of us to wake up to the fact that we're together before we even kiss once. Can you imagine what a sweet torture that will be? I don't know if we're near to that, but it's our next step so long as we are forced to see each other for only a day or overnight. There's too much between us for it to be ready all of it at once from all the crossroads of our body and the knots in our nerves right from the start after days or weeks of not seeing each other.

It's like I want to wine you and dine you and just get the tip in, and then, please Gawd! just let an elephant step on my ass.

I've been lying around with my cold finally come, and happy with your letter—sometimes it's as if you speak with my private critical sense of things—and enjoying the recollections of yesterday on the mountain. I don't know when I've been more tired than going to bed last night, but my body feels so honest today. I think I would like to spend a week in that park with you—we could have some long and crazy walks, and some of the cliffs are as close to rock climbing as we're likely to get. I wonder if you would be too tired in the evening to revolve me in the sleeping bag?

I love you angel.
Norman

Nineteen

Norman had strong ideas about birth control. He thought the pill was absolute poison for women. Maybe that was why he had so many kids. (You think?) I don't know that he was wrong. It certainly has been under the microscope, and anything powerful enough to alter a woman's ability to conceive has got to do strange things to her system. Not that he totally influenced me. If I had wanted to be on the pill, I would have been, but I'd been on and off it for years—on it when I met him—and it wasn't good for me. It made me bloat and gain weight. So when I went on the diet to get ready to meet Wilhelmina, I got off the pill and we tried using other methods, none of which we liked. After I lost the weight, I went back on the pill, thinking I would just work harder and keep on eating less. That didn't work so well, so I got off it again, at his suggestion, to dire consequences.

> . . . And the pill. God, I admire you for living seriously with everything I say. I think you must stop it. It's insanity for us to have a child right now—and that means we'll have to live on our sexual wits to keep from impregnating you before we can begin to do anything about it, but there are ways and we'll talk about them. The first thing, apart from love and fidelity and commitment and children is that there's something evil about the pill as if one's most beautiful fucks go directly to the devil. Besides, I think the pill is terrible for a woman's health, and if she's in love, it's next to cancer. No, we'll have to splice the rope and do without it . . .

It was madness, but the week he arrived for the second time in New York, I got pregnant. I was terrified. Here I was, fresh off the boat, so to speak, all alone and nobody to confide in except his mother or sister, whom I obviously couldn't tell. He couldn't just up and leave the family in Maine and come and be with me. It would have been too disruptive for everyone. So it was a tough time for both of us, me not knowing if he was really going to be with me or what, and him worried about and wanting to be with me while having to be the consummate dad—hiking and sailing and pretending everything was normal. He swore to me he was going to leave Carol, but it wasn't something he could do overnight in the middle of summer vacation. We discussed it and decided that whatever happened with the baby, he would split his time between New York and Maine—then Stockbridge—until after Christmas, and then on the first of the year he would come and live with me full-time, and we would go back to Arkansas and bring Matthew to live with us. What would make it bearable was that we had two big trips to tide us over until he moved. In September, there was the Muhammad Ali boxing match in the Philippines—the Thrilla in Manila—and then we were going to Rome for a month in October and November because he was writing a movie script for Sergio Leone, based on a book called *The Hoods,* that Leone was calling *Once Upon a Time in America.* Our life together was just beginning; we were like two excited kids. And then I got pregnant.

He called a few friends, among them Amy Greene, who had also become a friend to me (and is to this day), and José Torres, a boxer who had been the light heavyweight champion of the world, to tell them I was there alone and needed a friend, but not that I was pregnant. No one knew that. Of course, Norman and I talked on the phone every day and continued to write letters. Again, I pretended to be stronger than I was. I had learned that tears had little effect on Norman, and in fact were repugnant to him. So I did my crying when I was alone, and brazened out a kind of humorous cheerfulness on the phone and in letters to him.

Then one day something odd happened. It sounds like a twisted fairy tale, but I swear it was real. It was the middle of a hot early September afternoon, and I had just lain down to take a nap on the bed in the living room. It's possible I might have dreamed it, but it didn't seem like a dream. A small blue fairy-like thing flitted in and out of the edge of my vision, twinkling like a little bell. "It must be a bluebird," I thought, and I sat up in bed, thinking it had flown in through the open door to the balcony. I peered around the room, but couldn't see it anywhere. Then I lay back down and it popped up again, flitting just around the periphery of my vision, over my head, never close enough for me to see clearly what it was. When I tried to look at it directly, it disappeared.

The sun set and the light faded into twilight, the magic hour, and the bluebird glowed brighter. All of a sudden, I simply knew. It wasn't a bird; it was the baby. It was trying to decide whether to come into me or not. I lay there, and tears flowed from my eyes. I prayed to God. I couldn't ask Him for forgiveness—I didn't want to be forgiven. That would mean I would have to forsake my sin and leave Norman, and I wanted desperately to stay with him—and yes, one day have his baby, but I knew that now wasn't the time. I selfishly wanted to take the trips, I wanted to be a model, I wanted to have some time to get to know Norman, for us to be out in the open about our relationship, to get married and make a life together.

I began to talk to the baby and tell him (I knew it was a boy) that I loved him and wanted him so much, just not right now. I went back and forth between talking to the baby and talking to God. All I could ask for was the wisdom to make the right decision, whatever it had to be. I asked God to help me, to have mercy on me, and to let it all work out. I knew it was greedy of me to want a man who already had seven children and such a tangled past, but I also knew without question that it was right for us. We both knew it, as if it had always been inevitable. I slipped into a deep sleep then, and woke to the doorbell ringing.

It was José Torres and four or five of his friends, stopping by to keep me company with a big bag of food. I didn't know what Norman had told them, but I pretended I had a little stomach flu, and they stayed for quite a while, laughing and telling funny stories, playing music and cheering me up. No one could laugh like José. He slapped his knee and fell off his chair laughing, which made everyone else laugh, too. I will always have a soft spot for José, who has now passed over like so many of our old friends, bless him. He was the kind of friend who would pick up dinner and visit a person he hardly knew, just because his friend asked him to.

A few days later, I met Chuck Neighbors, who was the literary agent for B. C. Hall, my old creative writing teacher at Tech. B.C. had published several novels and some nonfiction, and he'd called Chuck to see if he might represent me as a writer, too. B.C. knew I had been working on a novel I'd started in his class when I was a senior and my first husband, Larry, was in Vietnam. I still didn't know if I was going to be able to model or not. Amy was trying to help me get more pictures to show Wilhelmina before she sent me up there, as she thought the ones I had brought from Arkansas weren't good enough. Racking my brains for a way to make some money, I thought I might be able to write magazine pieces, or perhaps even get a publisher for my book, which I was calling *Little Miss Little Rock*.

Chuck and I agreed to meet at the Riviera restaurant in Greenwich Village. He was wiry with a wispy goatee, protruding ears, and dark, longish curly hair. He seemed to know a lot about everything, had gone to school in Texas and could do a credible Texas accent. We got along. I agreed to show him the novel, and we talked about what kind of pieces I might do for a magazine.

In the middle of dinner, I began to feel a bit sick and strange, and I couldn't quite get any of the food down. I went to the bathroom and discovered I had started to bleed. I sat on the toilet for quite a while—oblivious to people knocking on the door—feeling a little faint, listening to trickles. When I got up, the bowl was filled with blood. There was a dark clot in the middle of it. I knew it was the baby. He had heard me and decided to go back and wait for a better time. I said, "Thank you, God. Thank you, baby." I cried, washed my face, and came back out and told Chuck I wasn't feeling so well. He got me a cab to go home. He did become my agent, and later, after I had been modeling for a year and more, I wrote a piece for *Cosmopolitan* magazine called "Getting My Book Together" about what is involved in becoming a model. Chuck and I have been friends ever since, and that piece was the inspiration for my second novel, *Cheap Diamonds,* which came out more than thirty years later.

Two years after this, in 1977, I did indeed become pregnant with our son John Buffalo, and Norman and I were thrilled about it. I used to tell John when he was little that he had been up in heaven, manipulating the situation so his father and I would meet each other so we could have him.

"Can you imagine the trouble you had to go through, John," I used to say. "You had to make sure I forgot to send in that Book-of-the-Month card saying I didn't want *Marilyn*. Then you had to arrange Dad's schedule so he would be in Arkansas right at that time. You had to get the film animation artist to come to Tech on the day Dad was there, get Van to invite me to bring my class, and then make me crash the party for Dad and pick out those tight jeans to wear!"

What I left out was that he had also kindly waited for two years before he came back, and this time, his timing was perfect.

Twenty

SEPTEMBER 12, 1975

Darling,

It's storming here now and my sailboat is bucking up and down on its mooring like a horse in a steeplechase. I took the kayak out a little while ago to ride the waves, and tried it for awhile close to shore (chicken to have to swim back in this water from too far out) and finally miscalculated and tipped. It felt good.

Listen, I've wanted to tell you my side of the week, for it's stayed with me in force, as if I'd been steeped in tea. Indeed my feeling for you is almost that hue. Sometimes when we're fucking, or even when just holding you, I can close my eyes and feel you as a rich red presence in my arms, and of course I don't mean just your hair but your aura. It's as if orange and red and fine rose-red waves come off your heart, and at such times I see into your emotions and feel a little awe at what we are getting into for it's a true woman I'm holding then, as big as her heat and her love for me could grow to be as strong as fire and as wrathful if I ever betray it. But what a marvelous love is that woman in you, big girl, the woman who is just beginning to emerge, and I feel cool in the center of this fire, nice and strong and cool as if my emotions are made of some kind of steel and it's fire I need to give them a better shape.

I can be walking through the woods up here and think suddenly of you and me kissing in that cab as if we had invented the embrace and discovered the taste of flesh and fruit. Your lips have changed so much since I have known you. Sometimes I feel all of the woman in you coming to me through your mouth even as your soul is shaking like a leaf in the sweet eye of your sex where the come begins to free itself like wet wings stirring up to fly, and then I'm nicely at sea and floating up to your fuck storm.

It's like fucking in sunlight, and all the tender red of your heart comes through my closed eyes and it's a fall into all the sweet choices—do we fuck, or lay in that funny heaven of being half asleep for hours and glued each to the other's spine?

Ah, darling, I've never felt more confident that we won't use each other for too little. We may fuck up, we may get into storms with each other, we may yet disagree profoundly on what we want the other to be, but that's ahead and we will live in it and find our arts living in it. I feel optimism thinking of you and a little scared at the possibilities that I'm in true good fortune and have a woman equal to me, as bad, as good, as brave, as dumb, as full of sugar and don't we love to turn the lights down low and let the fire come up. Bitch, you don't need this letter, but I'll come to collect for it before too long.

I love you,
Norman

Hey, read the Rainbow by D. H. Lawrence. Skim it till you find the passage about the passionate bridegroom who gives a different night entire to each separate part of his beloved's torso, limbs and feet.

Summer was finally over and Norman brought the family back from Maine for the kids to go to school, and told Carol about me. He didn't have a choice. She called the house one day and I picked up the phone. I know she was in shock over it, since she knew about the other woman Norman had been seeing, Annette, and I'm sure she knew of several others. But "Barbara" was somebody brand-new. I was relieved on the one hand that she finally knew, but the woman side of me felt bad (only a little, but it was real) for her.

Carol and I have had a tumultuous relationship over the years. There were times when we would have cheerfully thrown each other under the moving wheels of a Mack truck, but there was also something inexplicable in each of us that kind of liked the other. When I had John, she called me in the hospital and we talked for an hour, for the first time, like old dear friends. It was a short-lived hiatus then, but today, we *are* old dear friends, two survivors, members of a small club, if you will. Not the only members. There were four others, after all, but the only ones who like and understand each other. I'm not going to spend time talking about Norman's ex-wives. They are women who gave birth to the children I love. They have their good points and their bad ones, as do I, and whatever their relationships were with Norman, they were different from mine. I'm not going to talk about the numerous girlfriends, either, but you know who you are, and there are many more of you than you think.

One night, not long after Norman had moved in with me for good, the phone rang at three in the morning. I jumped up out of a dead sleep and ran to the living room to answer it, instantly awake. A strange female voice demanded, "Let me speak to Norman."

"He's sleeping," I said sweetly, like the nice Southern girl I was brought up to be.

"Well, wake him up. He will be very glad to hear from me."

"Honey, if he was that glad to hear from you, *you* would be here instead of me." And I put down the phone and went back to bed.

So here was Carol, having yet another woman in Norman's life shoved in her face. But at least it was finally out in the open. The one thing Norman kept saying he wanted to do was clean up his life and stop sneaking around, stop lying, stop living in guilt. He was tired of juggling a lot of women, sick of all the time-consuming deceit. He was in his fifties and felt he had wasted a lot of his prime years when he could have written more books. He wanted to get serious about his work, and he wanted to try monogamy, something he had never done. He wanted to see how deep a relationship could go when there were no others, no cheating, no deceit. He wanted to try it with me. Until they had moved back from Maine, he hadn't told the family about me, and was still spending half the time in Stockbridge with Carol. But after she found out, there was no reason not to tell the kids, no reason not to spend more time in New York, so he began to gradually introduce them.

Betsy was the first one I met. She was sixteen. Norman sent me alone to the apartment she shared with her mother, Adele, his second wife, who thoughtfully (or whatever) was out. Betsy was exotic, with a head of fabulous curly dark hair like her father's, and a sweet smile. She was sophisticated for her years and didn't seem to mind that here was another of her father's girlfriends, this one not that much older than she was. She showed me some of her poetry, we talked about her boyfriend, and we've been great friends ever since.

Kate was the second child I met, thirteen at the time. I went to her apartment on Seventy-second street in Manhattan, again by myself, on a day when she'd had a small growth removed from her neck. Her hair had gotten caught up and tangled in the bandage, and I took it off and put a new one on for her. She looked like a perfect mix of her mother and father. She was well mannered and sweet, with a creamy British complexion, at that wonderful age in a girl's life when everything is poised to bloom.

Her mother was Lady Jeanne Campbell, Norman's third wife, the granddaughter of the newspaper magnate Lord Beaverbrook. Jeanne's brother Ian was the Scottish duke of Argyll and lived in a castle in Inverness. Kate showed me a picture of it on a postcard, with a small arrow pointing to a window, in the vast rows of windows, where she stayed when she went to visit. She had drawn a balloon above it that said, "My room." Jeannie was striking, with erect posture and a smile that could be welcoming but at the same time brought to mind a cat with feathers caught between its teeth. She had the most incredible voice, a beautiful, aristocratic English accent. I am weak before good upper-class British accents, and hers was the best, not a hint of Scottish in it. I've been to Scotland only once, but I could hardly understand anything they said. (I'm sure they thought the same about my thick Southern American accent.)

Jeannie got married again after she and Norman divorced, and she had another daughter, a beautiful dark-haired girl named Cusi, who was eight when I met her. Cusi was wise beyond her years, and was balancing her mother's checkbook when I arrived, which they said she did all the time. Jeannie rather enjoyed the fact that Norman had a young girlfriend, I think, and invited me to Thanksgiving dinner that year while he would be in Stockbridge. I said yes, and I so appreciated it. I still had few friends in town and was alone most of the time while Norman was away. But Jeannie also had a wicked streak, and told Norman that she had invited several attractive single men to Thanksgiving as well, so he should be careful, he might lose me. He said he wasn't the least bit worried, pompous man that he was. I liked her enormously, but we never got to be real friends. It just wasn't in the game plan. But Kate is one of my best friends today, as is Cusi, as are all of the kids.

Betsy, me, Danielle, and Kate.

I went to Provincetown to meet Michael and Stephen on a cold November evening in 1975. I'd taken the bus from New York and Norman had driven from Stockbridge, where he had spent Thanksgiving. As the bus topped the hill on Route 6, I had a view of the curve of the town around the bay in the setting sun; I gasped and fell in love with Provincetown at first sight. I had never seen another town remotely like it. The salt air was clean and invigorating with a hint of fish, and the muted voice of the foghorn was comforting at night. It sounded like music when it mixed with the sound of waves washing the beach. No one ever sleeps better than they do their first night in Provincetown. In summer the population of the town swells to seventy thousand or more, but in winter only about three thousand diehards dig in for the long, dull evenings that start in the middle of the afternoon. The most poetic and eerie description of it I know is in *Tough Guys Don't Dance,* which Norman wrote in 1983.

> . . . the land I inhabited—that long curving spit of shrub and dune that curves in upon itself in a spiral at the tip of the Cape—had only been formed by wind and sea over the last ten thousand years. . . . Conceived at night (for one would swear it was created in the course of one dark storm) its sand flats still glistened in the dawn with the moist primeval innocence of land exposing itself to the sun for the first time . . . artists came to paint the light of Provincetown . . . but then the summer ended and most of the painters left, and the long, dingy undergarment of the gray New England winter, gray as my mood, came down to visit. One remembered then that the land was only ten thousand years old, and one's ghosts had no roots. . . . no, there was nothing to domicile our specters who careened with the wind down the two long streets of our town which curved together around the bay like two spinsters on their promenade to church.

Provincetown was indeed spooky and bone-chilling in the winter wind. We would spend part of every summer there for the next thirty-three years (Norman had come originally with his first wife, Bea, in 1943), and we would live there year-round the last ten years of his life, but the first time I came was magic. Of course it was magic. We were newly in love and everything was magic. We rented a small attic apartment with yellow painted floors, blue walls, and a view of the bay. Across the road was Ciro's, an Italian restaurant situated in the basement of an old house, which had warm lighting and low ceilings that just escaped being claustrophobic.

In the middle of the first night, a nor'easter blew in with fierce howls. The electricity went off, as it tends to do often there, and the only light in town was from the glow of snowflakes as they whipped about in the air. Norman and I bundled up and took a walk from our apartment, which was almost in the middle of town, to the far end, about a mile and a half away, to the spot where the Pilgrims first landed and signed the Mayflower compact. In the dark, walking with our heads bent against the wind, we could almost believe that it was three hundred years earlier, no electric lights, no illumination except the occasional flicker of a candle in a window and the luminescence of the snow in the cold, salty air. Then we reached the big motel at the tip of land's end, hunkered down in the dark like a great sleeping beast. That brought us back to reality. Norman used to say, in his guided tour spiel that he loved to give our guests who had never been there before, that the motel had been erected to commemorate the spot where the Pilgrims had landed, before they'd had to hotfoot it over to Plymouth because they'd killed a couple of Indians and stolen their winter cache of corn.

We took Michael and Stephen to Ciro's for dinner, and I remember what I was wearing, a black suit with a straight skirt, a necktie, and white shirt, and a big black hat with a wide sweeping brim. It was an outfit out of a Raymond Chandler novel, my hair swept down in a Lauren Bacall wave. I always loved hats and wore them whenever I could. Hats add drama to any situation, not that this one needed any added drama. The good-looking blond boys were nine and eleven. Michael, the older one, had startling blue eyes like his father, and Stephen's were green with a glint of the imp. I ordered fried zucchini, which was at least close to my beloved fried squash (I so missed Arkansas cooking), and veal parmigiana, heavy on the garlic. While I tried not to slurp the spaghetti and get it on my shirt, Michael and Stephen, chesty little studlets that they were, entertained me with stories of playing baseball and football.

After the dinner, they went home and told their mother, Beverly, Norman's fourth wife, that Dad had this neat new friend, a tall redhead, and I'm sure she groaned. Although they hadn't lived together for six years, he was still legally married to her, and would be for another five years until he could get the marital situation straightened out, which is too complicated to put into a sentence here. I'll do a whole chapter about it later. Beverly and I were actually pretty friendly in the beginning, until I got pregnant. (In her bed, no less. How rude is that? At her request, we were staying with the kids in Norman's and her house in Provincetown in the summer of 1977 while she did a play in Connecticut. One night we even piled all the kids into the car and drove up to see her, and she was really good in the role.) But then when I got pregnant and Norman pressed her for a divorce, it got ugly. However, that's down the road. It's hard not to get ahead of myself.

To continue with my meeting of the kids, Susan was Norman's old-

Michael and Stephen with Dad.

est child, a girl only six months my junior. Her mother, Beatrice, Norman's first wife, married a Mexican man when Susie was two, and moved to Mexico City. Sue grew up there and Spanish was her first language. I've never met Beatrice but have immense respect for her because after she moved to Mexico, she learned Spanish, went to medical school, and became a doctor, a psychiatrist. Susan is a psychoanalyst and now lives in Chile. She is another one of my close friends, and the great thing about our relationship is that we feel free to totally be honest and say anything to each other without worrying about hurting the other one's feelings. That goes back to our first meeting, which was in New York at her aunt Barbara's, also that same November. We went out alone for lunch to get to know each other, and over soup and hot homemade bread, she said, "I feel like you've taken my place with my father."

I was a little stunned by the directness of this, and said, "Well, Sue, what exactly *is* your place with your father?" I tried to make a joke of it, but I thought I knew what she was talking about. As the oldest, she'd

Susan.

had four stepmothers, not to mention several serious girlfriends to contend with, but no one had been as young as I was. Now he had someone her exact age, someone who was there with him all the time while she lived thousands of miles away and saw him once or twice a year. That was the hardest thing for her, not being around him all those years. The other kids at least saw him on a regular basis, but she was too far away. He was not good on the phone, either, so there weren't many phone calls. I still don't see her often enough. She married a man from Chile, Marco Colodro, who is much like her father—older, powerful, handsome, divorced with three children, and they have three of their own. (Sue is the analyst to the family. We always go to her for advice. Everyone else is in the arts somehow, so of course we all need an analyst.) That first day, we talked it out over our bowls of soup, and then went to Bloomingdale's. There has never been any problem that couldn't be fixed by two women bonding over shopping.

Maggie was the baby—four years old, just six months older than Matthew. I'll never forget the first time I saw her, when she came to visit with her nana, Myrtle Bennett, who later came and worked for us when I got pregnant with John. Maggie was an adorable little elf; her blue eyes seemed to take up half her face. She was scared and shy, and I could see it wasn't going to be easy, so I decided to take it slow, to gain

Maggie.

her trust when it came. Maggie had wild curly hair, long enough so she could sit on it, like a Liddle Kiddles doll, and her face was a perfect sweet miniature of Norman's!

Danielle, eighteen, was away in college at Bowdoin when I came to New York, and was the last one of the kids I met that November at a dinner at Barbara's. She had similar coloring to Betsy. (They had the same mother, Adele, Norman's second wife, who is half-Spanish and half–Peruvian Indian.) But while Betsy had black curly, wiry hair, Danielle's was long and almost straight, which I so envied. She was a beauty with eggplant-colored eyes; she was lively and funny, and she quickly became another great friend. She's the kind of girl who can sit next to you on the couch and in ten minutes learn more about you than some of your nearest and dearest friends know. She was a strong, healthy girl, and a good athlete, like I wasn't, but she was also an artist, like I was.

All of the kids look like Norman in different ways. All of them have a talent for writing, too, although some of them prefer to do other things. Danielle and Maggie are painters, but both are good writers.

Sue is an analyst who writes professional papers; Betsy is a talented writer and poet who is working on a memoir; Kate is an actress but has her masters in writing and writes a lot of her own material; Stephen is an actor and is working on a screenplay. Everyone else is a writer in some larger way. My son Matt is a writer-director with a degree from NYU film school, and his senior thesis film called *The Money Shot* won the Wasserman award, which is NYU's version of the Oscars. Michael is a movie producer who has written screenplays, and John Buffalo is a playwright-screenwriter, as well as an actor. Norman's sister, Barbara, worked at Simon and Schuster for many years and edited a book called *The Bold New Women*, for which she wrote the preface. She is currently writing her memoir. Her only son, Peter Alson, is a journalist who has written about gambling and published two memoirs.

Peter's true vocation is poker playing, and he has been in the World Series of Poker several times. Peter was only six years younger than me and was at Harvard when I came onto the scene. Being the only child of Norman's only sister, he always felt like one of the kids, and was closest to Danielle until the boys got old enough to hang out with him. It was odd to have all these grown-up children, some of them my age or nearly my age, in the role of stepchildren. If any of the kids—except Maggie, of course—were unhappy that Norman and Carol's re-

Peter Alson.

lationship was ending, they didn't tell me. I'm sure they were all confused, unsure of what was going to happen. But they were too well mannered to even be impolite to me, although what they said to one another I can only imagine.

The one thing Norman always did throughout all the changes of wives was to keep the family together, especially in the summers, so they truly thought of themselves as brothers and sisters, not a collection of half siblings. Maybe by the time I arrived they were all shell-shocked from a surfeit of stepmothers and it was a relief to have someone young they could play with. I don't know why we all got along so well, and I don't want to analyze it too much. It just happened, and I was so grateful for having a large, wonderful family. Norman used to say that if the two of us were in the water drowning, the kids would save me first. I'm glad we didn't have to find that one out.

I always respected the kids, and tried never to say anything bad about their mothers in front of them, although Norman didn't share that characteristic. In fact, when one of the kids did something to displease him, he always started chastising them by saying, "You're just like your mother . . ." and then he would rant on about whatever bad thing the kid had done that was just like the mother of the moment. He did the same thing to me about *my* mother even, and once, fed up, I said, "Why don't you ever say we are like our mothers when we do something good?" He didn't have an answer to that, but he never gave up the pleasure he got from the comparisons, although it drove all of us crazy.

I began to meet his friends, too. He didn't have a lot of literary friends like I thought he would. He was friendly with people such as John Cheever, John Updike, and Saul Bellow when he saw them, and while we sometimes went out to dinner with Kurt Vonnegut and Jill Krementz—Kurt's girlfriend, later his wife—Norman's closest friends were from other walks of life. Like Harold and Mara Conrad. Harold was tall and suave with a black pencil mustache. He was a tough reporter in his youth who worked the sports desk for the *Brooklyn Eagle*, among other papers, and he then was a fight promoter who spoke with a gruff Damon Runyon accent. His wife, Mara, was a dancer and actress in the musical comedy genre, a long-legged blonde who took a lot of Gwen Verdon shows on the road. She had beautiful legs, the straight posture and carriage of a ballerina, two rows of big white teeth, and bottle-blond hair, with a strong dash of Lucille Ball in her personality. She played, among other things, Marilyn Monroe's girlfriend in *Let's Make Love,* and a wild jungle girl (with incongruous red lipstick) in the 1950s *Prehistoric Women.* Hanging in their apartment was a cool picture of her in a leopard skin from that movie.

Anyhow, when I first came to New York, Norman wanted to play a joke on Mara, who was a practical joker herself. We cooked up one with the help of Harold. Norman told them he had met a new girl he was crazy about but there were some problems, so he wanted them to take a look at her and give him some advice. He took me over there dressed in a sexy red dress (that I had borrowed from Sarah Johnson, one of my students in Russellville), a cheap blond wig, and a lot of makeup. He told them my name was Cinnamon Brown from Texas (Waco, no less) and that I had come to New York to get into pornographic movies.

We rehearsed at home, with great glee, and I was prepared, even though I had never seen a pornographic movie. (Norman asked me in Little Rock if there were any theaters that showed them, and I just said, "Huh?") At the Conrads', I swept in, brash and loud and trampy, and

Me as Cinnamon Brown.

the two of them had their mouths hanging open, even Harold, who had met me and was in on the joke. (I was having so much fun, saying bad words like a naughty child and pretending to be someone so totally different from myself. I was using words I had never said out loud until I met Norman! At that moment, Norman decided I was going to be a movie star.) We went on and on with the charade, pretending to get into a big fight about my choice of career, him trying to stop me, and me adamant it was what I wanted to do more than anything else in the world. At one point he said to Harold and Mara, "Cinnamon *can't* be in pornies. She has no tits!"

"Tits, what are tits?" I answered. "I have a *great* pussy!" At that, Mara took Norman into the next room to talk to him while I went and changed into the elegant Diane von Furstenberg dress Norman had bought me at Saks. I took off the wig, brushed out my long red hair, and toned down the makeup.

The Diane von Furstenberg dress.

In the other room, Mara was saying, "Look, Norman, you're in way over your head. You can't be with a woman like that. She's too much for you. She'll kill you. Just let her go and be in the pornies if she wants to. She'll be great at it. She'll be a big star and make a ton of money. And *you* have to stay away from her, got it?"

"But I think I love her," he whined.

"Snap out of it! She'll never love you. She's trouble, and you don't need more of that." He nodded sadly, and they came back into the living room, where she took one look at me sitting there talking with Harold, and said, "Who are you? Where is Cinnamon?" She was genuinely confused.

We laughed until tears rolled and our stomachs hurt. She kept saying, "I can't believe it! You had me. You totally had me!" At that moment, in walked Don King, the fight promoter, who had that hair that looked like he had just plunged down an elevator shaft, as Norman described him in *The Fight*. And of course we had to tell him all about it. (The problem is that I think the only sentence he heard was "I have a great pussy," because he chased me around for years after that evening.)

The next week, we were invited to Harold and Mara's house for dinner again, and we couldn't wait to go, mainly—for me—because Mara always made great fried chicken and mashed potatoes. As we rang the doorbell, we started laughing again at how we had so totally gotten one over on her. She opened up the door and was standing there—stark naked. We screamed. She ran through the house doing pirouettes and saying, "You'll *never* get one up on me!"

Twenty-one

Fanny by this time knew that I wasn't Francis Gwaltney's niece, and I don't think she cared. It was never mentioned again. She did make one small gesture toward saving Norman's relationship with Carol, which I think she felt was her duty because of Maggie. When we told her we were going to the fight in Manila, she took me aside and said, "Darling, I want you not to go." She held my hand as she said it, and I knew she was torn. Here was her beloved son, who could do no wrong in her eyes, breaking up another family, the *fifth* one, leaving another child, which went against everything in her upbringing. But she had gone through so many of his breakups and remarriages (and one of Barbara's) that it wasn't something earth-shattering like the first one must have been. Plus, she liked me, and she wanted him to be happy.

I didn't want to hurt her, but I said, "I'm sorry, sweetheart, I really am, but I'm going with him. We love each other, and we are going to be together." She stood up, gave me a hug, and said, "Well, I had to try," and that was that. From then on, she was totally in my corner.

The flight to Manila was twenty-two hours long. We got to the airport two hours before we had to. I was discovering Norman's penchant for being on time, which translated to being early for everything. Before we took any kind of a trip, whether it was halfway around the world or to Provincetown, he would go into his travel mood, which was nervous and angry and crotchety. I tried not to talk to him and risk getting my head taken off. Packing was a huge chore for him, and he was so nervous about being late that we were always early for everything. I learned to take a book along everywhere and just relax. I thought of it as free time, no phones, no kids, just my time to sit and read. Even traveling to Manhattan for dinner got him into a tizzy. I can't count the times we arrived so early that we had to go looking for a bar in which to have a drink and kill a half hour so we wouldn't be too early to someone's house. Once, we arrived and the hostess was in the bathtub.

I told him it must be in his genes, that on the first big trip the Jews ever took, they got lost and wandered in the desert for forty years, so of course he was afraid of traveling. He didn't think that observation was quite as funny as I did. Other than that, I never used the Jews as reference for anything, I was pretty sensitive, and he didn't have a sense of humor about it at all. He wasn't a practicing Jew religion-wise, and there are those who thought he wasn't Jewish enough in his writing, but he certainly thought of himself as Jewish. On the other hand, he never missed an opportunity to bring up the Christians—Baptists in particular (as he brought up my mother)—to explain why I did "bad" things. Like one Christmas when I was cooking a turkey and I put tinfoil over it to keep it moist. He thought I should leave it uncovered and baste it every twenty minutes like his mother did, which I wasn't prepared to do, so I didn't.

"You're cooking this turkey like a Christian!" he yelled when he saw I wasn't going to take off my little tinfoil tent and baste.

"Well, what the fuck holiday do you think this is!" I yelled back. Christmas was always problematic, but more about that later. Now we were on our way to the Philippines, still besotted with love on the long twenty-two-hour flight.

My fear of flying wore off after a while and I stopped listening for pings and getting a pounding heart at each little bump. There was an unending parade of food in our first-class cabin, which Don King had paid for—shrimp and caviar, wine, champagne, ice cream sundaes, dinners of steak or chicken or anything else we wanted. One meal rolled into the next one, chocolates and cookies and nuts passed around by beautiful Filipino stewardesses every few minutes, purple orchids decorating everything. Glutted and exhausted, we finally tried to sleep, and I was delighted that the seats reclined all the way down, so we could lie flat.

There was no chance of snuggling, as there was a console between us, and in his sleep, Norman knocked over a glass of water that dumped right onto my head. I leaped up out of a deep sleep, with my clothes and hair all wet, not knowing what was going on, and I had to dry off as best I could with a towel and then sleep wet. I couldn't even be mad at him since he didn't mean to do it, and he felt so bad. Actually, looking back (after I'd dried), it was funny. Kind of. In those days everyone dressed up for flying, and I was wearing the black suit and big black hat (although I wasn't sleeping in the hat, of course) that I later wore to meet Michael and Stephen. I was pretty disheveled at the end of the flight, rumpled and bleary-eyed, with my contact lenses gummy from my having slept in them. (They were hard lenses, and meant to be taken out at night. Soft ones hadn't yet been invented.)

As we stepped off the plane, there were hordes of photographers waiting to snap our pictures. Great. That's all I needed, with makeup smudged in dark raccoon circles under my eyes, clothes rumpled as if I had slept in them. (Oh. I had.) In the newspapers I looked like the last zombie in a horror movie. At least Norman was wearing something appropriate, a khaki safari jacket and pants that were always wrinkled anyhow, so he looked normal, while my suit and hat were more suitable for a New York winter.

The first person I saw as we entered the airport was Larry Schiller, a photographer who had worked on *Marilyn* with Norman and who would figure in our lives over and over throughout the years. He was hurrying up to us, saying, "Do you need money? I've just exchanged a lot of money," and he handed us a stack of bills for which we traded him dollars.

The hotel was meant to be a tropical paradise; the lobby was full of trees and flowering plants set around a pool. Boxing figures of all kinds were lolling around, drinking pastel drinks with little umbrellas in them. Ken Norton, who later became heavyweight champ, was there, and Larry Holmes, who was Ali's sparring partner and who also later became champ. I couldn't get over how big they were in real life, close up. Lazy power came off them, like pumas, even when they were sitting doing nothing. Ken Norton struck up a little conversation with me, and Norman got all chesty and right in the middle of it. Angelo Dundee, Ali's cornerman, came up, and he and Norman hugged and pounded each other on the back, and I met Bundini Brown, an assistant trainer and cornerman for Ali. Norman knew everyone, it seemed, and they were all interested in his new girlfriend. Don King ambled over smoking a cigar and asked us how the trip had gone. I inched a little closer to Norman. Don had a habit of being particularly huggy with me, and I was wary.

Harold and Mara Conrad were there, too, so it was like old home week. After the Cinnamon Brown night when I'd first met Mara, we had seen them often, always with a lot of laughs. Mara loved antique-clothing shops and thrift stores, as I did, and we spent a lot of fun times sifting through bins of old sweaters looking for cashmere and rifling racks of chiffon evening dresses from the fifties.

Norman, me, and Don King in the Philippines.

Mara came up to me in the lobby and said, "See that woman over there?" She pointed to a knockout blonde who was nestled in a good-looking man's arms. "That guy wrapped around her is her husband, who's in Frazier's camp, and he's been here all week screwing everything that's warm and moving. His wife just arrived today, and as she came in, she announced, 'The main event is here! You can forget all about the preliminaries!'" Apparently they had a great marriage, and she knew about the other women but didn't care. I told Norman the story and he loved it. "That's the kind of woman who really loves her man," he said. I was appalled.

"What are you saying? That's the kind of man who doesn't love his woman!" It really bothered me that he admired that kind of behavior. "You'd never do that to me, would you?"

"No, of course not!" He changed his tune fast. "If I'm going to be with you, I'm going to be true to you. I mean it." He was so sincere, those blue eyes piercing right into me. I believed him. Even though he had a track record six miles long, I really thought we had too much going between us for him to risk ruining it. He wanted to change. He sincerely wanted me, just me, he kept telling me over and over. I was twenty-six and I would be young and sexy forever. Well, at least I would forever be twenty-six years younger than him.

The days were backward to the time in New York—midnight was at noon—and we slept all day and stayed up all night. Ali and Frazier trained all night, as it was better they worked on the schedule their bodies were used to. We didn't even try to change our schedules. We just found new ways to amuse ourselves all night. Norman got hold of some body paint and painted my body like a weird Helmut Newton African tattooed woman or something, and took pictures. Then I painted him, and finally we had the fun of washing it off in the shower. We were like two naughty kids, up all night playing, but we still managed to get up during the day and do a few tourist things as well.

Norman had been in the Philippines during the war, and the government gave us a car and driver to take us out into the bush to see if we could find the spot where he had bivouacked. He thought he remembered exactly where it was, as he had been in the reconnaissance unit. We headed out of Manila, with our driver, in a huge stretch limo on a beautifully paved four-lane highway, but a few miles outside the city the pavement simply ended and we hit the dirt with a hard whump! And then we were on a narrow little pig trail through the jungle. Broad leaves slapped the windows and sides of the car as we drove through, and children appeared and disappeared in the dense foliage. People hung out of houses made of bamboo and reed that were up on stilts, grass mats rolled up and hanging over the windows. They had probably never had a big black limousine come crashing through their neighborhood before, and I'm sure it was terrifying. I had never felt so much like a rich American in my life. I wanted to duck down and hide from the faces peering in the window. I wanted to say to them, "This is not who I am! I'm really not rich at all! This is a borrowed car!" I was ashamed to be there, riding in such a car, while the people hardly had enough clothes to cover their bodies.

Finally, we rolled into an open field that had a large tree in the center of it, and we got out. Norman thought it might be the same place they had bivouacked thirty years before, but even if it wasn't, it was a tree much like one he remembered, and in the spirit of the occasion, we pulled out a picnic basket, spread a cloth on the grass, and had a picnic under the tree that once had (maybe) sheltered a young Norman Mailer when he was hatching the plot for *The Naked and the Dead*.

Belinda Ali was a big, beautiful woman who looked like the female version of Muhammad Ali. She and Muhammad had gotten married eight years before, when she was a virginal seventeen, and they had four children, but she was not the woman he had with him at the fight. That was another beautiful, tall, thin woman named Veronica Porsche. He had been going around introducing Veronica as his wife to everyone, including the press, and it got into the papers in the States. He was a womanizer, and I'm sure Belinda knew the score about him. (Although I wouldn't swear to it. It's amazing how wives can not know what's going on under their very noses. I know this the hard way.) But this was too much for her to ignore. He was introducing Veronica as his *wife*.

Word got out that Belinda was on her way to Manila. Norman and I were supposed to go over to meet the champ that night, so we were waiting to see what was going to happen with Belinda. Belinda flew the twenty-two hours to get there, and I would imagine she slept little. She was driven to the hotel from the airport. She closeted herself with Muhammad for about thirty minutes. It could have been longer. I can't remember exactly, and we heard from someone who was outside the room that she was screaming at the top of her lungs every minute she was there. Then she went back to the airport and flew the twenty-two hours back to America. This all happened the day before the fight.

Nobody told us not to go for our meeting with Ali, so we showed up and were ushered into his suite. The air felt thick and heavy. It was an effort to breathe. He was sitting in a chair in the middle of the room, like the king on a throne. Veronica was there, wearing a long, beautiful white caftan, walking back and forth, wandering, seeming not to know what to do with herself. In the background, a screen had been set up and an old Ronald Reagan movie was playing, *The Killers,* with Angie Dickinson, where Ronnie plays a bad guy and Angie plays a femme fatale. We sat on the couch with several other people, his trainers and handlers and assistants, nobody speaking, as if we were waiting for some play to begin.

A group of children came in. I'm not sure where they were from, but in my memory they had on school uniforms. Ali took the time to say hello to each of them, perched each one on his knee, and gave them a personal message, like "You have beautiful eyes," or "You're going to be a fighter one day, with muscles like that." On it went. We didn't say a word. We watched Ronnie and Angie scramble over rocks, have a shoot-out with someone. Ronnie got hit and died. Then the kids left, and there were still a lot of us in the room waiting, looking to Ali expectantly to say something, to give us words of wisdom.

He took a tired, deep breath and began a sermon, one about the different kinds of hearts. Veronica paced behind him, back and forth, back and forth. "There is the heart of paper," he began in a quiet voice. "It is beautiful, but soft, and the rains of despair beat on it and weaken it until it is nothing but a shapeless mass of sodden waste. There is the heart of glass, beautiful but cold, and although the sun shines through it, making it light up the corners of a dismal room, it is fragile, and the winds of evil blow it over and it crashes into a thousand shards. . . ." He went on . . . and on . . . about the different kinds of hearts, and we all worked to keep our eyes open. I pinched myself, bit my lip, did every trick I knew to keep awake, but I didn't succeed too well, and Norman just about managed to keep looking interested. It was hot in the room, and dark. Perfect for taking a little snooze. The soft voice went on for another hour, more maybe, but finally he was done and someone gave the signal that we were all to leave.

Ali stood by the door to say good night to everyone. As we walked by, Norman put his hand on Ali's shoulder and told him that he was the true champ, he was the greatest, and he was going to win the next day. Ali nodded. Somberly. Norman continued on that he knew what Ali was going through with the women, but it would be all right in the end, that he would wind up with the woman who was meant to be with him, and he tried to offer more heartfelt good things from the well of his experience. Ali looked him in the face and said, "You know, with the troubles I got, if I was a white man or a businessman—I'd be dead." Norman nodded. I shook hands with Ali. He pulled me into a little hug, whispered into my ear, "You're so beautiful," and off we went into the night, leaving Ali in the doorway.

It was a moving experience, being there in his presence, which was overwhelming in the charismatic way that truly great people have. I've met more than my share of celebrities, but most of them are smaller than life, if you get that. Like movie stars, on the screen, are bigger than life, but when you meet them, they might be tiny. The glamour of the lighting and the distance between the screen and the audience is gone, and they are just like anybody else. Some are nice, some not so nice. There have been a few, like Clinton or Jackie or Norman, Fidel Castro, certainly Ali, that were larger in person than in pictures. There is a special electricity—for want of a better word—that permeates them.

Frankly, I hadn't been all that in love with Ali's behavior toward Frazier in the days leading up to the fight. He'd called Frazier a gorilla and had talked about how dumb he was, what an Uncle Tom he was, which I know hurt and angered Frazier. Norman said it was just to get interest in the fight going, but it was so ugly that I wondered why Ali had to take it to those extremes. I certainly couldn't criticize him for having someone there who wasn't his wife, since I was in the same boat myself, but the way he was introducing her as his *wife* really rankled and made me sympathetic to Belinda. At least Norman wasn't pretending we were married. We were good, honest adulterers.

I also felt for Veronica, who was under such scrutiny and didn't deserve the contempt people were placing on her, hypocrites that they were. I can't imagine what percentage of the population has had affairs, but I'm sure it's high. I think the unusual couples are the ones who marry as young virgins and happily never sleep with anyone else ever again. Somehow that didn't seem natural to me, and at the same time, I desperately wanted just that. Fidelity was the goal, but it was hard to attain.

The fight was held at ten-thirty in the morning, because of the time difference in the States. Norman sat close to the ring, but I was relegated to a seat farther back, and sat with Mara, which was comforting, as I had never been to a fight and the whole thing was pretty scary. The crowd was raucous. I was afraid I was going to get lost and separated from Norman, and I tried to keep my eye on him all the time. Mara was dressed in a big feathered blue hat and a dress to match, and I wore a straw hat and a rose-colored batik sundress I had bought in one of the shops. It was a good thing, because it was so hot in there that I could hardly breathe. Someone said the temperature was 104. Someone else said 125, and I believed them.

Testosterone glowed in the air like phosphorus, and the smell of sweaty bodies was at a level I could just about tolerate without fainting. The crowd parted, and four men came in carrying a . . . well, a throne is what it was, a big gold chair that sat up higher than everyone else's. Behind the chair, in a procession, was President Marcos surrounded by a phalanx of bodyguards, walking in formation. The chair was put into place, the president was installed on it, and the fight began.

Mara and I had pretty good seats, right behind the press, and I could see the faces of Ali and Frazier. Ali came out with a flurry of punches that I could tell really hurt Frazier. I was shocked at the power and the viciousness. It was brutal beyond my expectations. How anyone could be hit with punches that hard and remain standing was a mystery. My head was still full of all the hearts in Ali's sermon and Belinda taking that plane trip back and how she must have been feeling right then, knowing her marriage was over. Was she watching the fight? Was she rooting for Frazier? Was she scanning the crowd to catch a glimpse of Veronica? I'm sure she would have liked to be hitting Ali herself. I know I would have if I'd been her. Could he just forget about it while he concentrated on the fight, or was it bothering him?

The sweat started to trickle down my front. The crowd was going crazy. First it looked like Ali was winning, then it looked like Frazier was. Ali had said that Frazier was like a wolf, and I could see that. He got in close, attached himself to Ali's chest, and wouldn't let go. I couldn't believe the amount of punishment the human body could take. From time to time, they held on to each other like lovers, resting, then one or the other would push away and they would go at it again. It went on and on. I thought it was never going to end. I thought one of them was going to fall down dead. They both had puffy faces, and blood was everywhere.

I recently watched the film again on HBO, and I didn't see this happen, but in my memory a man in the corner took out a blade and cut one of Frazier's eyes, and blood spurted out so the swelling would go down so he could see. Maybe I'm remembering another fight (or maybe I'm remembering *Rocky*), but I do know Frazier's eye was swollen to the point that he could barely see anything. I thought at times I was going to faint from the heat and the brutality, but I just sat down and closed my eyes for a minute, and then they popped open again. I had to see what was going on. Mara was jumping up and down, as though she were right in the ring with them, yelling and punching the air and giving Ali directions. Her hat kept falling off; she kept putting it back on.

Finally, it was over. Frazier's corner stopped the fight after the fourteenth round, which was fine with me. I didn't see how either one of them could go one more round. I didn't know for sure who had won, but Ali was called the winner. Then he fainted, and there was a commotion over that. I tried to see Norman, but in all the tumult I lost him. Mara somehow got separated from me, too. I was sure I'd be trampled into meat loaf on the floor and nobody would ever see me again.

Then, miraculously, Norman appeared, and we somehow made our way out of the crowd and located one of the cars that took us back to the hotel. I was exhausted, and with not much sleep the night before, all I wanted to do was take a cool shower and go to bed. Norman was so excited that he couldn't sit still, so he went off to talk to the men about the fight. It was one of the most exciting fights of his life, I could tell. While I was relieved to get back to the hotel, I understood the significance of it all. The first fight I had ever seen was one of the greatest fights of all time, and I thought they were all like that. Come to think of it, most of the fights I've seen in my life were Ali's fights, and while they weren't all great, like that one, they all had the Ali magic somehow, even the ones he lost, the ones that he never should have fought, like the stupid one with a kickboxer that almost ruined his legs. After he retired, I don't think we ever went to another fight. Not one I remember.

That night there was a party at the palace for the fighters and the guests, but first, we were invited to a cocktail party at the home of the owner of Philippine Airlines, Benny Toda. I had never seen such a grand home (until I saw the Malacañang Palace a little later). There was an Olympic-size swimming pool in a glass room, and all around it were platters and bowls of fresh fruits, fowl, meats, fish, vegetables, and sweets of all kinds—a cornucopia of the world's best offerings. More food than the people living in the jungles had in a year was being picked over by a crowd of the richest and most powerful people in

Manila. There was no way it could all be eaten, and I wondered what would happen to it, if it would be thrown away or what. I hoped it might be given to the poor people roaming the streets, who all looked like they could use a good meal, but somehow I doubted it.

Gorgeous girls in teeny bikinis were swimming , and we were in the middle of it all, talking to everyone, playing the part of American celebrities, which Norman was and I wasn't, but nobody knew that. I was treated like a celebrity anyhow. I stuck close to his side, unsure of how to handle myself in this crowd. I was wearing an outfit I had gotten in Russellville, white palazzo pants and a long brown-and-white tunic top, and looked okay, but all the other women wore expensive haute couture gowns they had picked up in Paris or London or New York, and jewels. A lot of jewels.

Imelda Marcos was wearing a lovely native design dress of pale green silk, with above-elbow-length sleeves and high shoulders that fluttered like butterfly wings. Her silk shoes were dyed to match. Someone introduced Norman and me to her, and he was totally charming, flirting madly, showing his dimple with the little smile I called his twenty-five-cent smile. (No matter how mad I got at him, he could give me that smile and I would reach into my pocket and pull out an imaginary quarter to give him, which would mean I had forgiven him. He got away with a lot because of it.) If he was throwing twenty-five-cent smiles away at her, I could tell he was smitten, but then she was the president's wife, so I figured he was entitled.

Up close, she was still beautiful, with smooth satiny skin, perfect hair and makeup, and while she obviously was not a kid, she was well preserved, as though rich cream were massaged into her pores every day. She spoke perfect English, and included me in the conversation, too. She was interested in where I was from and how I'd gotten there, how I had met Norman. I told her that my best friend in college was from the Philippines, and she wanted to hear all about Aurora, who had a sister named Imelda. Norman gave me a look like I shouldn't be monopolizing so much of the first lady's time, but on I went, oblivious. Then it was time to go to the palace, and Imelda invited Norman and me to ride with her in her limousine.

She got into the backseat and motioned for me to slide in beside her. Norman perched on the jump seat facing us. She sat rather close and companionably linked arms with me as we kept chatting. She was gracious and included Norman in the conversation, too. He later told me that he thought she had a crush on him and had invited me to sit next to her in order not to make me jealous, but I'd heard that she had a girlfriend and liked women, so I think maybe that was the real reason. At any rate, it was not the worst, to drive up to the palace in the car with the president's wife. Everyone was straining to see who we were, and flashbulbs went off everywhere, practically blinding us. We went inside a step ahead of Ali and Frazier, who arrived within minutes of each other. They both were wearing sunglasses. Their faces were swollen like blood sausages and they looked awful. (They should have been in the hospital, but they were the stars of the evening and had to work for their salaries, which I'd heard was six million for Ali and at least two and a half million for Frazier.)

The president, Ferdinand Marcos, met us and took us on a little tour of his library, where he signed for Norman a couple of books he had written, telling him that while he didn't pretend to be the writer Norman was, he was a good writer, and he wanted his books to be in Norman's library. He asked Norman to send him some of his own books, which Norman did after we got back home. He was good about fulfilling promises made like that, whether it was to a president or a fan.

I was naïve about the world and had no idea what kind of people the Marcoses were then. The Philippines were an exotic and foreign place to me and I would have never even thought about the country except for my friendship with Aurora, who came to America from Manila when she was three. The poverty was evident everywhere you looked, and the contrast between Benny Toda's opulent house, with its pool and glut of food, and the rest of the country was glaring, but as their guests, we didn't dare say a word of criticism. It would have done no good and would have been ungracious. They joked about martial law, as if it were some minor inconvenience, and Imelda spoke about "her people" as if they were children. We just listened and didn't comment.

As part of the guest entertainment that week, it was arranged for us to float down a river in a canoe, where we saw the actor Hugh O'Brian and his wife or girlfriend floating in the opposite direction. We waved madly at them, and they at us, even though we didn't know one another at all. We jumped out of the boat and swam in our clothes, ducking in and out under a waterfall. It was paradise, just like in the movies. Later, we went shopping, which is my favorite activity, and although I would discover in time how much Norman detested it, we enjoyed picking out trinkets for the kids together. He loved masks. There was one on the bookcase in the apartment he had gotten from Africa during the Rumble in the Jungle, the Ali-Foreman fight the year before, and over the years he sometimes gave me masks for Christmas. We got a big carved wooden mask with scary sharp teeth in a grimace for the apartment, and several small animal carvings as gifts for the kids. They were mostly elephants, made of some kind of shells, not too kitschy—well-crafted, nice souvenirs.

The airplane trip back was the same as the trip over, lots of food and orchids. By that time we knew more of the other passengers, so people stopped by our seats and chatted. Then we landed in Hawaii and the pilot announced that everyone had to get off with all their luggage and go through customs. Customs? We had totally forgotten Hawaii was the United States.

When it was our turn, for whatever reason, they took one look at us and went through our luggage like they were the bomb squad and we were card carrying Weathermen. Norman said the two of us must have looked suspicious, him older and dressed in rumpled khakis, me in tight jeans, a shirt I'd gotten in Manila tied at the waist, which was my style, and my straw hat; I'm sure we did. They lifted out all my clothes and shook them, dirty underwear and all, and practically took Norman's briefcase apart. Then the man doing the search let out a groan, like he had stuck himself with a sharp object. I looked to see if somehow he had cut himself, but he brought his hand out of a pocket of Norman's briefcase holding a tiny bit of paper. I had no idea what it was, but it proved to be a marijuana roach. A teeny-weeny one. Too small to smoke.

The man snapped his fingers, and before I knew what was happening, we were hauled off to separate rooms and two big hairy women told me to take off all my clothes. I didn't really know what was going on, but I was scared and did as I was told, and then one of them told me to spread my legs. I didn't want to do that for sure, but they didn't give me an option, and before I had time to cringe, they flashed a light in the place where only my gynecologist had previously shone one, although they didn't actually touch me, for which I was pathetically grateful, and then they told me to get dressed.

As I was sitting beside the open door waiting to see what would happen next, two little old sportswriters were hustled by, several stern officers behind them, herding them like befuddled sheep. I forget their names now, maybe it was Murray and Al, but they were the cigar-chomping kind of reporters that had names like Murray and Al and spoke in broad Brooklyn accents. One of them yelled out to me, "Barbara! Ya gotta get Norman to tell 'em we're okay! They think we're some kind of terrorists or something!"

"Oh, Murray," I called after him, "you don't want our help. They think we're drug runners!"

When the inspector found the roach, everything turned upside down and they began to go through our luggage again with a fury. Linings were ripped out of the suitcases, our cute elephants and all our souvenirs were smashed open to see if we were smuggling drugs inside them. Norman kept saying, "We don't have drugs! I didn't even know that roach was in there! It's been in there for months, years probably! Why would I have left it in there if I had known? I would have thrown it away!" He had been strip-searched, too, which he was most annoyed about, although they hadn't laid a hand on him, either. I think they just wanted to look at us and assert their power and scare us, which they certainly did. We were humiliated and angry.

While all this was going on, the rest of the passengers didn't know what was happening, just that there was some delay, so our two friends Murray and Al were worried that they were going to miss the flight. One of them said to the other, "If they don't hurry this up, we're going to blow the plane," which was Brooklynese for "We're going to *miss* the plane." Some official walking by had heard them, and that's when they were immediately nabbed for strip-searching as well, poor things. It was pandemonium. Finally, after our luggage was in shreds and all our souvenirs had been smashed and they hadn't found so much as a leaf of pot or anything else, the boss of the airport was called in, and thank God he knew who Norman was.

"I'm sorry, Mr. Mailer, for the inconvenience," he said, as if we had merely been asked to change our seats or something. "How was the fight?" the man asked. Norman, as jolly as he could be in that situation, gave a blow-by-blow description for the man, and then the boss told the underlings, who were noticeably frustrated that they had failed to find large quantities of drugs, "These people are okay. Let them go." I think if there had been any more marijuana in his bag, or if we had lipped off to them, or if the boss hadn't known who Norman was, we would have been thrown in jail. But it was the weekend and everyone wanted to go home. They didn't want to have to deal with something this trivial. We eventually got back on the plane, shaken but wiser.

Coda: for the next few years, every time we took an overseas trip, our luggage was searched. I think we'd been put on some list, but finally it stopped—until the shoe bomber and that ilk arrived on the scene, and then travel was never the same again for anybody.

Twenty-two

When we got home, Norman went to spend a few days in Stockbridge, which I understood he had to do, but it was getting harder for me than it had been before. I felt connected to him now, and I was so afraid he was going to change his mind and say that he liked the situation as it was and he wasn't going to leave Carol after all. But I couldn't let him know that, so I put on a good show of not minding a bit, which I knew he admired, and went with Amy and Milton Greene to their home in Connecticut for the weekend. Milton had agreed to photograph me. I would finally have some good pictures to take to Wilhelmina done by Marilyn Monroe's own photographer. He also called a photographer friend of his, who agreed to take some more pictures as well, so I was feeling pretty good about modeling.

Their house in Greenwich was light and beautiful, perfect in every detail, just like Amy. Amy was a honey blonde and tiny, probably five feet at her tallest. Once when we were sitting on the couch, I reached out and spanned her foot with my fingers, from thumb to little finger. I could comfortably reach an octave on the piano, and there was her little foot the same length. "Amy, your foot is an octave long!" She loved that. She had such a hard time finding shoes that fit, at least she could have the conceit that she was walking on octaves.

Marilyn Monroe had once stayed with them in that house when she'd come to New York to study with Lee Strasberg at the Actors Studio. I didn't know then how involved I would later become with the Actors Studio myself, but I didn't know much of anything then, just that I wanted desperately to be a model and start to make some money so I could bring my son to New York. I'd been away from Matt for nearly a month and missed him terribly; every day we talked on the phone and he kept asking when I was coming home, which broke my heart. But I felt I was getting a step closer to getting a job by Milton taking my pictures. Sleeping in the room where Marilyn had stayed, putting on my makeup at the dressing table she'd once used, I felt like I was on my way to somewhere. It was a mirrored table from the thirties, which Amy later gave to me, and she said Marilyn used to mix her face cream and makeup on its surface. It's a good trick; it makes the makeup more transparent and dewy. I still do it—only I mix it on my face, first the moisturizer, then the makeup. I hate making messes, especially on my dresser top.

It was a chilly, rainy afternoon and the leaves were putting on a grand show in glorious red and yellow and rust. The light was diffused by raindrops, perfect for pictures. Milton handed me an umbrella and we walked out into the yard, where I sat on a small bench and he took several shots. Then he said, "We got it." We took a few more shots inside, with me in a great antique hat I'd gotten in a vintage shop in New York for five dollars, a black straw hat with ostrich feathers circa 1914. (The tag on the hat must have been the original price tag, because even in 1975 a vintage hat like that would have been more than five dollars. I asked the salesgirl, just to be sure, if that was the right price, and she said yes, so I gave her my five and left. I'm sure she got reprimanded by the owner, but I could hardly argue with her that it was too cheap.)

Posing for Milton Greene.

My life was spinning so fast that I'd hardly had time to unpack from the Philippines and take a breath, but I was so happy when Norman came back from Stockbridge after the weekend and showed me in no uncertain terms how glad he was to be back with me, and how excited he was to take me to Rome.

Norman had been asked to write a movie script for Sergio Leone, the director who had done the Clint Eastwood spaghetti westerns *A Fistful of Dollars, For a Few Dollars More,* and *The Good, the Bad and the Ugly.* We'd met him in New York at Nicola's, our favorite Italian restaurant, with his translator and several business associates. Leone didn't speak a word of English, but as he had come up with the perfect formula for the American western, he wanted to apply himself to the perfect American gangster epic, and had acquired the rights to a book called *The Hoods* by Harry Grey. He was going to call it *Once Upon a Time in America*. I don't think he had read any of Norman's work, not in the original English for sure, but he wanted the best American writer to write the script, and someone had told him Norman was the best. Leone was a large, rotund man with an egg-shaped head. He smoked cigars and had rather lazy, bulbous blue eyes he fixed on me until I was uncomfortable. During the dinner, they agreed on a plan, whereupon Norman and I would travel to Rome and spend a month while Norman wrote the script and had conferences along the way with Sergio.

It was now early October, and I still didn't know for sure what was going to happen. My daily calls to my parents and Matt were getting to be a little charged.

"When are you coming back?" they asked every day.

"I don't know. I'm not sure what's happening."

"When are you getting a job?"

"I don't know. I can't really get a job until we get back from Italy."

"We wish you would come on home and stop living like you are. Everyone is talking about it here."

"It's nobody's business what I do. Just ignore them." But I knew they couldn't do that. They had lived all their lives in the glass house of "What will people say?" and they couldn't change now. Why I kept calling them every day, I'm not sure, except that I was lonesome for them and I felt so guilty about leaving Matt, even though I knew I was going to bring him up to New York as soon as I could get settled and get some kind of job. The ugly rumor that I was putting Matt up for adoption really wounded me more deeply than I'd thought possible, and I wondered if people did believe it. I guess I wasn't immune from "What will people say?" after all. So it was a relief in some ways to be going to Italy, where I could be with Norman every day and not have to be browbeaten over my behavior.

Partly to appease my parents and partly to show Norman my independence, I found my own apartment before we left for Rome. I would be in the same building as Norman's mother, Fanny, who got the apartment for me. It was a one-bedroom with a tiny kitchen and a view of the courtyard, for $250 a month, a fortune to me at the time. My mortgage on a three-bedroom house had been only seventy-five dollars a month. I had come to New York with five thousand dollars from selling my house and car and furniture, plus my meager teacher's retirement, and it was amazing how fast that went. I didn't want to take money from Norman, although he offered. If I could hold out, I just knew I was going to get work sometime soon.

There was no furniture in the new place, but Fanny knew a man who owned a storage warehouse, and he let me come and pick out some things that his customers had abandoned. I got a gray velvet couch, a nice wooden table and chairs, a bed, a daybed for Matt that I put in the living room, some rugs, and several lamps, plus kitchen stuff, bedding, and so on, all for only a few hundred dollars. The man even threw in a couple of leather shirts I saw and loved. The best were the lamps. One was a standing lamp made of chalk that was in the shape of a king, or maybe it was Jesus. At any rate, it was a guy with a beard who was wearing a gold crown, and it weighed about fifty pounds. The apartment was a sweet, funky little place, and Norman and I stayed there a few nights to christen it, so to speak.

My mother and father sent up some of my artwork, my TV, my sewing machine, and several other things, bless them. They were happy to do it, because at least they could finally tell everyone I had my own place. It was great for Fanny, too, because while Norman was away, we hung out together a lot. Norman had confided that she had said to him I wasn't much of a cook, so she was teaching me the dishes Norman liked. Other times, we went shopping or just sat and talked on the Brooklyn Heights Promenade.

If Fanny was upset that Norman and I were off on another trip together so soon, she didn't say anything. We got to the airport two hours early as usual, and again hit the skies for another long flight. Leone's driver picked us up and took us to the outskirts of Rome to a place called Eur, where Leone had his production offices, and installed us in a modern hotel in suburbia, where there were few shops or restaurants. Norman went to Leone's office every day and worked, and I soon realized there was nothing for me to do in Eur. Finally, tired of sitting around reading, I got up my courage and took a taxi into Rome by myself and explored the streets, looked in shops and galleries, and went to a famous coffee shop that someone told me de Chirico went to every day for coffee at four in the afternoon.

I had done my senior thesis on the surrealists, and de Chirico was one I loved. I knew he was old, but I just wanted to meet him. (I had no painting for him to sign, unfortunately. Probably just as well.) But he wasn't there. They said he usually came in about that time, though, so I lingered over a cup of cappuccino and one of those pastries that look so much better than they taste. Then, when it was obvious he wasn't coming that day, I went out and sauntered down a side street, no destination in mind.

The street had no shops, was just a deserted street of apartments, and I was about to turn around and go back when, a block away from where I was standing, a man ran out a door. Then three shots echoed in the narrow, empty street. Pop! Pop! Pop! The man fell, and blood gushed out of him, making a puddle on the sidewalk. No one followed him out of the building, and I saw no one else on the street. The man just lay there, unmoving in the quiet, the blood slowly creeping toward the gutter. I was paralyzed for a minute, adrenaline pumping at a great rate; then I turned and ran to a larger street, where a cab materialized. I jumped in and told the driver to take me to Eur. He couldn't understand me. I was nervous and just wanted to get out of the neighborhood before someone came after me. I wrote down the name and address of the hotel for the driver, and he still didn't know where to go. Finally, I was so frantic to get out of there, I practically grabbed him and shook him. He pulled out a map and I was able, somehow, to show him where it was. When I got back some time later, of course I told Norman all about it, and to my dismay, he was skeptical.

"That couldn't have happened. Maybe you just thought you saw a man being shot. Maybe it was a movie. Maybe he tripped and fell."

"But I heard shots! I saw blood coming out of him! He didn't move!"

"It could have been a car backfiring. It could have been sound from a television. Maybe something in his pocket broke. I'm sure if it was a murder we'll hear about it on TV. You're letting this Pasolini murder get to you." Pier Paolo Pasolini, a famous film director, had been killed a few days earlier, on November 2, in a bizarre way. He was run over several times by his own car. Nobody was sure who did it, but there were rumors of a gay lover and maybe that Pasolini had staged it himself, although you'd think a person committing suicide would find an easier way to do it. It was all pretty sordid. It was everywhere in the news, and while I was certainly not unaffected by it, I wasn't so overcome that I was seeing murders everywhere.

I watched the news for the next few nights, but there was no mention of any murders, no men getting shot in shadowy small side streets in Rome. Norman probably just didn't want me to be frightened and worried, but I began to think maybe I *was* crazy and actually hadn't seen it at all. The whole thing was a scene out of *Gaslight*. But I had no choice. I had to just let it go. I don't know to this day what happened. It was just another one of life's little mysteries.

Norman wasn't happy in our modern hotel in Eur, either. It was too far from the center of Rome, where Norman's oldest friend, Mickey Knox, lived. When Norman and Mickey met, *The Naked and the Dead* had just come out and Norman and his first wife, Bea, were in Hollywood while Norman tried to write movie scripts. Susan was born while they were out there in 1949. Mickey had been an up-and-coming young actor who'd been blacklisted during the McCarthy era a few years after he and Norman had met, and consequently had moved to Rome. He'd made a good living there ever since, doing dubbing, translating, and acting. He and Norman had even been brothers-in-law at one time, as Mickey had married Joan, the younger sister of Norman's second wife, Adele. Joanie was a famous fashion model for Oleg Cassini. They'd had two daughters, wild little Italian beauties named Valentina and Melissa. He and Joanie were divorced, but we saw Mickey and his girlfriend Carol, an English teacher, almost every night for dinner.

It was great fun, although Norman became disgruntled with the lack of variety in the food, and once, after we'd been there a couple or three weeks, when Mickey said he was taking us to a great fish place, Norman grumpily said, "Mickey, the Italians don't know *what* they're doing with fish! There's no such thing as a great fish place." (I do admit that after a month of wonderful Italian restaurants, I, too, was happy to get back home and have a hamburger.)

Traveling back and forth to the city every night from Eur was a chore, especially if I also wanted to go to the city in the daytime, so Norman asked to be moved and they put us up in the Hotel Splendide at the top of the Spanish Steps on the Via Sistina. Our room had a small balcony that overlooked the city. Outside the door were the Spanish Steps, where artists and young people hung out all day. I had my portrait done on the steps by a sketch artist like I used to be myself in summers at the Ozark Folk Center. I liked the Conté crayon the artist was using and asked him where I could get one. He didn't understand English, so people kept coming over and trying to help out until quite a crowd had gathered. Finally, someone spoke enough English to tell me where the art shop was, and everyone clapped and cheered. I went there and bought the crayon and a pad and did some drawing myself, back in the room. (I later used that crayon to draw Henry Miller's portrait which was used on the cover of *Genius and Lust*.)

Norman had to ride in to the office in Eur every day, but at least I didn't have to deal with cabs and trying to find my way in and out of the city. I spent my days walking the streets (avoiding small empty backstreets), loving the big piazzas with fountains everywhere and pigeons cheekily hopping around, blanketing the ground. There were other kinds of cheeky animals, too, called easy boys, handsome young men who would come up to you and begin speaking in English. If you didn't answer, they started in French, then Spanish, and finally German. They knew a smattering of everything, and their aim was to pick up young (or not so young, but rich) women tourists and get what they could from them. I was pretty adept at sloughing them off, but once a rather young one I had just rejected reached out and grabbed my breast. I had a flashback to the time I was raped and was so outraged that as he turned to leave, I gave him a hard kick in the pants. It was a stupid thing to do. He could have turned and attacked me, but instead he ran away, and that made me feel good, like I wasn't just a helpless woman.

Another time, a handsome older (probably thirty-five) man struck up a conversation with me, and was highly insulted when I said I wasn't interested in easy boys, that I was there with my boyfriend. He said "I am no easy boy. I own a boutique. Come, I'll show you." And he grabbed my hand and started walking fast down the street. I was a little frightened, not sure what he was up to, but the streets were full of people, and a couple of blocks down, he turned into a delightful little boutique where he was greeted as the owner. I spent a nice hour trying on clothes and bought a couple of dresses. Come to think of it, even though I didn't go out to dinner with him, he accomplished the same thing as if he had been an easy boy, didn't he? He made some money off me.

Right beside the hotel at the top of the Spanish Steps was a beauty shop called the Femme Sistina. I passed the window every day, and one day I saw a lipstick in the display that I liked and went in to buy it. The shop was owned by a charming woman named Lisette Linzi Terracina, who asked me if I had ever done any modeling. I said no, but that I really wanted to, and was in fact going to try to do that when I got back to New York.

"Would you like to do some pictures for us?" she asked. "It would be in an Italian magazine for salons. You have wonderful hair." I was so flattered that of course I said yes, and the next day I went to a studio with Lisette and posed for a whole afternoon while the stylist did several different hairdos on me. The pictures were good, and Norman, proud of me, took them to show to Sergio. Leone laid them out on his desk in a row and studied them for a while. Then he grunted, shuffled them into a stack, and put them into his desk drawer. Norman was horrified.

"Wait a minute, Sergio. I can't let you have those," he said. "Barbara needs those to show to Wilhelmina when she gets back to New York. They are for her work." Leone either pretended he didn't understand or he really didn't, but either way, he wasn't giving back the pictures. Norman went and got the translator, who finally got across to Leone that the pictures were not meant as a gift to him. He gave them back with ill grace. Norman said that at that moment, he felt something shift in the relationship.

Norman had been working steadily on the screenplay, which had turned into two movies, the original one and the sequel. Then, ugly items started appearing in the press. Someone reported that Norman Mailer had brought an eighteen-year-old girl (!) to Rome and was holed up with her in his room, ordering in room service and writing the script on toilet paper. It was laughable, but people took it seriously. His friend Mickey Knox was incensed. He and Norman's secretary were prepared to testify that Norman worked at the studio every day, everyone knew that. What could this all be about?

Modeling for the Femme Sistina.

Soon Norman got word that Leone was unhappy with the script, and he was canceling the deal. The script hadn't been translated, so there was no way Leone could have even read it, but it must have been the producer who didn't like it, and they were not going to pay. Mickey said that Leone did movies for children, and he didn't know how to handle a sophisticated script in well-written, full-bodied English like this one. There was hardly any dialogue at all in Leone's westerns, so I could see the problem. Our month in Rome, so wonderful in so many ways, turned into a nightmare.

Norman's contract clearly stated that he would get paid for the script whether or not it was made into a movie, but Leone was determined not to pay him at all. He said the script was useless. We came back to New York and sent it to Peter Bogdanovich and Billy Friedkin, two top directors at the time, both of whom liked it. In fact, Friedkin wanted to make the movie, and tried to buy the script, but Leone wouldn't sell. Nor would he make the movie, and he wouldn't pay. Norman sued for his money, about seventy-five thousand dollars. Leone called Mickey and tried to get him to testify against Norman, and Mickey went crazy. He told Leone in no uncertain terms that he would never lie about his best friend, and that Sergio should pay Norman what he owed him.

The lawsuit dragged on for a few years, and finally Leone was ordered to pay, but by then the money had been mostly eaten up in lawyers' fees, so the only thing we got was the professional satisfaction that Norman had, indeed, written a good script. Leone went on to get another screenwriter—several other writers, actually—and made the movie using the same title, *Once Upon a Time in America*, with Robert De Niro. We never did know exactly why Leone had such a drastic change of heart. I can't believe it was because he couldn't have my hairdo pictures, but Norman was always convinced that was the turning point. He said there was something in his eyes as he handed back the pictures that said, "You'll be sorry."

Twenty-three

We got back to New York just before Thanksgiving, and true to his word to Carol, Norman spent it in Stockbridge and I went to Lady Jeanne Campbell's for dinner. She cooked a lovely, if not exactly traditional, dinner of turkey and little rubber dumplings called spaetzle. Jeannie was famous for not being much of a cook, but she did everything with such panache that you didn't care how it tasted. She had indeed invited several single men, but none of them offered Norman any competition, and the people at the dinner who were the most interesting to me were her daughters, Kate and Cusi.

They had a nanny who used to be a homeless person. She'd taken up residence on the steps outside Jeannie's door on Seventy-second Street, and every time Jeanne went in or out, the woman said, "Good morning, Lady Jeanne," or "Good evening, Lady Jeanne." One day Jeanne noticed the woman had numbers tattooed on her arm, obviously from a concentration camp. Jeannie couldn't help herself, she invited her in and somehow she stayed. The poor woman resided in fantasyland part of the time, but she loved the girls and for the most part was harmless, if rather ineffectual. Jeannie was like that, always trying to help someone.

After Thanksgiving, Norman came back from Stockbridge, and Christmas suddenly exploded everywhere. The windows of New York's fanciest department stores were a fairyland of inventive displays, one more clever than the last. Ropes were set up outside Lord & Taylor, Bloomingdale's, and Saks to keep the lookers in line. I went into FAO Schwarz and vowed that the first thing I would do when Matthew got up here was take him there and let him get any toy he wanted. He was going to love New York so much! I couldn't wait to bring him up here, which we were planning to do before Christmas.

I called Amy and showed her the pictures. She said that with those Milton had taken, I had enough good ones, and she called Wilhelmina. Amy said Willie could tell from these that I was model material, and she was pretty sure she would take me on. I wasn't so sure. The letter I had gotten from Eileen Ford all those years before, in 1968, the one that said I should pursue another career, still haunted me. I hadn't told anyone back home at the time that I had even written to Eileen Ford, and it was a good thing. It would have been pretty embarrassing if they knew I had been turned down flat. Larry would have been upset because it had been a last-ditch attempt to have a life other than marriage and living in Atkins, and I thought I had blown it forever, but here I was, at twenty-six, trying again.

Wilhelmina was a beauty from the Netherlands and had an exotic accent that had been cured in years of cigarette smoke until her voice was textured like suede. She had deep brown eyes and chestnut hair, was wearing a black turtleneck and black slacks, and had a pair of little half-moon glasses on her forehead when I walked in. I handed her my envelope of pictures and stood waiting while she positioned her glasses onto her nose and looked at them.

"How tall are you?" she said, looking up from the pictures.

"Five feet ten."

"No. You can't be. Step closer to the desk." I did. "Well, if you're not, you're close." What an eye! I wasn't really five ten. I was five nine and three-quarters, but I'd always rounded it up for good measure.

"How old are you?" This was the part I dreaded. They didn't take girls older than twenty-three, and I would have to lie.

"I'm twenty-three." I had the look of guilt on my face, and was ready to walk out if she asked to see my driver's license, but she only nodded, studying the photos.

"Your hair's too red. We'll have to dye it brown. Redheads don't sell." That was a shock. I thought my red hair was my biggest asset. I didn't know what to say. I most certainly didn't want to dye my hair brown and be like every other girl on the street, but I didn't want to walk out the door, either.

"Could we wait a little bit on that?" I said. "I really like my red hair, and maybe it will sell. Surely there are other redheads that make money, aren't there?" She looked at me for another long moment.

"Well, you at least need to get a good haircut. There's too much of it. It's too long and shapeless. I'll call Pierre at Pierre Michel. You go over there right now and tell him . . . tell him . . . oh, hell, tell him you're with us."

I wanted to grab her and hug her but she was not the kind of woman who invited strangers to hug. I'd never been scared by a woman before in my life, but I was close to it with Willie. She stuck my pictures back into the envelope and handed them to me. "Go back and talk to Kay, get all the paperwork done, then go see Pierre. He's on Fifty-seventh Street. He'll be waiting for you." She handed me a piece of paper with the address on it.

I went back and talked to Kay, a heavyset young woman with a beautiful face, and got all the paperwork done. Then I went down the elevator and ran as fast as I could up Fifth Avenue toward Fifty-seventh Street. The Christmas lights had never looked so bright, the air was clean and cold, and everyone on the street smiled at me when I told them "I've just been taken by Wilhelmina!" I couldn't help it. I wanted everyone to know.

Pierre was French, young, and handsome, and made me feel like I was part of a special club. I didn't know what kind of haircut Willie wanted for me, and frankly I didn't want a haircut at all. I had spent two years growing my hair out from a bad short haircut, and I liked it long. I thought long would be more versatile, but apparently not.

"Willie suggested that I should give you a wedge, like Shaun Casey has," Pierre said, holding up a picture of a girl I had seen in Wilhelmina's. She was on the cover of *Glamour.* I hated her hair. It was pouffy on top and layered short in the neckline, like a mushroom. It would look stupid on me. My head was too small and this would make it look like a peanut in a Beatle wig. My face must have shown how disappointed I was.

"Uh, Pierre, could we keep it just a little bit longer? I don't think I look so good in short hair."

"Okay. I'll just do layers around your face, some bangs, and not too short in the back." He went to work, and when he was done, it was a lot shorter than I thought it would be, just a tad longer than a mushroom. It was about chin length, and the ends stuck out all over the place. The top was layered. I really didn't like it at all. But what did I know? It was chic—at least he said it was—and I would have to learn what was chic and what was not. I went back to the agency. Wilhelmina liked the haircut, and thank God didn't say anything else about dyeing it brown.

There was only one other little thing we needed to discuss. "So, what name do you think you'd like to use?" she asked. I was a little surprised.

"I guess Barbara Norris. That's my name."

"Yes, but that seems so . . . ordinary somehow. We need a name that people will remember, something that is catchy and exotic. Not so girl-next-door and old-fashioned."

"Well, when I paint, I sign my paintings with just the name Norris. Maybe I could use that." I actually liked the way it looked in paint, which was why I did it. Barbara was harder to paint with a brush.

"Norris. Norris. That's good. Yes, like Twiggy or Apollonia or Pope. Models with only one name are big right now. Okay. Norris. We'll try that."

She then introduced me to my booker, who would be the person making all my appointments for me, a girl named Gara. I was to call her several times a day, since new things came in all the time. Gara would be my den mother, the one who would help me get started, the one who answered all my questions. At this point I didn't even know enough to know what the questions were. I wanted her to like me, and I think for the most part she did. She gave me a chart that showed the numbers and cross streets of Manhattan, and she made a few appointments for the next day. Then she helped me put my pictures into a temporary book, a brown plastic binder that said Wilhelmina on the cover, and she gave me a brown faux leather appointment book, which also had the Wilhelmina logo inside. I would later get a nice leather portfolio with a shoulder strap that I carried to appointments, the book that told everyone on the street that I was a model. I was excited and scared all at the same time.

Norman was thrilled when I got home and told him all about it. His Henry Higgins strategy was paying off. He liked the idea of the name change. He was always big on funny nicknames. If I did something stupid or clumsy like, say, slip on a banana peel, he would say, "I'm going to call you Slipsy from now on. Slipsy McNorris, how ya doin'?" Or whatever it would be for the moment. He never remembered the nicknames more than a few minutes, and there was always a new one for every occasion. He had funny pet names for the girls, too. Maggie was Magatroid Magoonspoons, Sue was Susu McGoosoo, Danielle was

Goosey Patako, and Betsy was Fats Svengado. Kate was Katie Katoosh. He loved playing with names and words, and spouted silly doggerel and bad wordplay jokes that made us all laugh. He loved limericks. (There was a young lady named Alice . . . Uh, you've probably heard that one.) He even wrote a nonsense poem called "Cousins" that was included in a book called *Wonders,* and I did a little illustration for it.

My favorite things he did, which went on for many years, were the twat poems. Every morning when we woke up, he would sing a version of the same silly little song, sort of to the tune of "Bill" from *Show Boat*. It started out "She's just my twat . . ." and then he went on with some kind of funny verse that always ended with "She's just my twat. I love her an awful lot." So we started our days with giggles.

I didn't mind that Wilhelmina wanted me to change my name, but I told Norman, "If I use just the one name, Norris, for my modeling name, that's great. But I think I need a second name. A person can't go through life with just one name. What about driver's licenses and stuff? I can't use the name Davis. There's too many *s*'s: Norrissss Davissss. Not good." He thought about it.

"How about Church? You're a good Christian; you spent half your life in church. It's a solid English name, and that's where your family is from. How about Norris Church?"

And that was it, with about that much thought put into it. So I began to use my ex-husband's last name for my first name, which was weird, to say the least. I called Larry and asked if he minded, and he didn't mind at all. I think he rather liked the fact I was going to use his name. It would prove to be even more weird down the road, when I took Norman's name after we were married. I realized that my identity was composed of my two husbands' names with me nowhere in it, but by then it was too late. (Plus, Norris is usually a man's name, and that has caused endless confusion. Once someone looked me straight in the face and called me Mr. Mailer. I said, "Do I look like a man to you?" He was befuddled and nervously apologized, but somehow it was easier for him to call me Mr. than to wrap his head around the fact that Norris was a woman. What an idiot.) If I had it to do over, I would be Barbara Davis, then Barbara Mailer, no matter how boring the fashion world thought it was, but now it's too late.

Twenty-four

Just before Christmas, we went to Arkansas to get Matt. Norman called Fig and asked if we could stay with them because my parents wouldn't let us sleep in the same bed, and Norman wasn't about to sleep on the couch. Fig and Ecey were still a little sore that we had deceived them and sneaked off together, as they saw it, but they said yes. What else could they do? I dreaded confronting my parents, but it turned out they were so happy to see me that nothing else mattered. They met us at the airport, and Matthew came running up to me and hugged my legs. "I knew you would come to get me!" he said. Poor little guy. I'm sure there were moments when he wasn't sure I was going to come back, but we were together again, and he stuck to me like a cocklebur all the way home in the car.

Norman was cordial to my parents, as they were to him. He told them we were in love and were going to be married when he could get his personal life straightened out, but it was complicated. I'm not sure if they knew exactly what the complicated personal life entailed, and he didn't go into details, but they knew he was married and had seven children.

My father had a man-to-man talk with him alone, along the lines of, "She's a lot younger than you are. She might get up there and meet someone younger and leave you." And then he had a talk with me and said, "Norman is even older than I am. One of these days he will be an old man and you will have to be his nurse. Are you prepared for that?" I don't think either Norman or I were thinking much past bedtime then, but many years later, as I was nursing my elderly husband, my father's words kept creeping back into my head. At the time, I said, "Daddy, we love each other, and yes, there's a big age difference, but do we pass up twenty or thirty years of happiness just because he is going to get old? I might die first. You never know." When I was diagnosed with cancer twenty-five years later, those words came back to haunt me as well.

You never know what life is going to hand you, but if I had it all to do over, I would do it all again. Norman would have, too. I know that because just weeks before he passed away, I asked him if he would do it all again, and he said yes. He reached out and got my hand; with a little difficulty, he took my ring off and then put it on my finger again, saying, "With this ring, I thee wed." A lot had happened in the almost thirty-three years we had spent together, but for better or for worse, the love was real, and it was always there.

When we got back to New York after the Christmas visit, Matthew took one look at Norman's apartment with big eyes, then ran and climbed up the ladder as fast as he could, like a little monkey. The ropes and ladders and the small upstairs rooms were a perfect little boy's playhouse, once I got over the fear he was going to fall.

Almost as soon as we got back home, Norman left for Stockbridge, to spend Christmas with Carol and face the difficult task of telling her he was leaving her. He took my Italian photographs to show her, which I thought was not necessarily the best thing to do, but he did it. Norman was a young fifty-two, vigorous, full of ideas and energy. He was setting fires and jumping across roofs to escape the flames, and he needed someone young and a little wild to hold his hand and jump across with him. I wasn't as wild as I let him think I was, but I was young and ready to jump.

Beverly was so far back in his history that I hardly thought of her as his wife at all, even though they were still legally married. I think part of her was secretly glad when he left Carol for me, as they understandably weren't friends, and I'm sure Beverly thought I was just one more girlfriend who would soon be gone. The other wives were buried even deeper in the layers of paleontology, and it was hard to even think of them as having been married to Norman, it had been such a long time ago. That was a different man from the one I knew.

As far as Annette went, I never met her, but Norman had told me stories about her, how tough she was, how she fancied herself as his bodyguard, and she had once gotten into a fight with Elaine Kaufman in Elaine's restaurant. When the six months of their separation were up, he told her he had met someone totally new that he was living with and he wouldn't be seeing her again. In answer, she sent him a message through his then secretary, Molly, that she had a gun and was going to kill us both. He took her seriously enough to change the locks on the apartment door, as she had keys. I can't imagine why it was such a shock to her. If a man tells you he wants six months of no contact with you, that is a clue he doesn't want to be with you. Or at least it would have been to me.

I did take Matt to FAO Schwarz for Christmas and loaded up on toys. Norman got him a complicated Erector set that was way too advanced for a four-year-old, but Matt kept it under his bed, and years later he put it together. Fanny took a liking to Matt as she had to me, and didn't mind babysitting him. He was a good little boy, inventive and quiet, with a full life going on inside his head.

From the time he was small, he imagined complete scenarios, lined up his little soldiers in rows, and played all the parts of both sides in a war. It was entertaining to watch him obliviously talking and moving his soldiers around, crashing planes and rushing ambulances to the crash sites. It was almost as if he had been in a real war in a past life and was reenacting it. He could draw really well, too, precocious for his age, and he drew German soldiers with insignia on their uniforms that looked remarkably like the real ones I looked up in books. I always believed he had been either a German soldier or a Jew in the last war; sometimes he had nightmares about things he would or should never have known about. He would wake up screaming, saying he was being put into an oven. I'm a total believer in reincarnation, and often young children still retain remnants of memories of their last lives. I was in awe of him, and so glad he was here with me, safe. I enrolled him in nursery school at Open House, not far from our apartment, and every day when we walked home, we would stop and get an ice cream cone at Baskin-Robbins or a small toy at the drugstore. He particularly liked Boney Benny, a rubber skeleton, and had several of those. If anything, I worried at his enthusiasm for horror movies—he loved Frankenstein, Dracula, and the Wolfman, as well as all the superheroes. From the time he was able to think in those terms, he wanted to make movies.

Norman came home to Brooklyn on New Year's eve. It was snowing, and we went to Gage and Tollner on Fulton Street in Brooklyn—a restaurant that had opened at the turn of the century and still retained its Victorian flavor—to celebrate, just the two of us. Although I had never been happier, and he seemed to be just as happy and relieved to have finally made the decision, it must have been a little bittersweet for him. Now Maggie would begin the ritual of coming to visit, just as the other children did. He had left them all, the wives and the seven children. I should have been worried that I, too, would be next in line for heartbreak, but I wasn't. He so totally convinced me that I was the love of his life, that I was the one he wanted to be with, that it never entered my mind he would do the same thing to me.

As naïve as it was, as farfetched as it seems looking back now, I was right. He never left me, in spite of some heartbreak along the way. Whatever qualities I had, they were something he needed, and for whatever reasons, I was the one he stayed with. A lot of people have tried to figure that one out, it was such an unlikely pairing. Some have said that I have a calm centered quality that appealed to and balanced his fiery personality, or that I was his Marilyn Monroe (although Marilyn and I were nothing alike in any way I could see). I do know that I ran his life like a tidy ship—I took care of the kids, the bookkeeping, and bill paying, and got the insurance we needed. I looked after his mother and his children, keeping in touch with them by phone when they weren't with us, making sure we all got together from time to time for dinners or outings, and organized the summers. I shopped and cooked and saw that he always had clean clothes in his closet and a car full of gas. I hung pictures, painted rooms, and did minor repairs on the house. I rewired lamps and did other small jobs. I put in bookshelves. I dealt with the workmen who did things that were beyond me. He was always grateful and said that I allowed him to write and not have to deal with life, and that's certainly true.

Once, early in the relationship, when he was at work (he didn't have a phone in his studio), I needed him for something. I forget what now, but at the time I thought it was important, so I went and knocked on his door. He was not pleased. He said, "When I'm writing, pretend I have gone to South America. What would you do if I was in South America? You have a brain. You can deal with whatever comes up." I apologized and said, "Okay," and I never knocked on his door again.

I realized then that he would never be a partner for me, like a lot of marriages were, but in truth, I enjoyed taking care of everything. I would not have liked to be married to someone who made me depend on him. We agreed on most things such as politics and religion; he liked my taste in decorating, he was generous, and he seldom questioned any purchase I made. His mother said I was down-to-earth and level-headed, like she was. (He told friends I had more common sense than anyone he'd ever known besides his mother, and I equaled her.) Fanny said I knew when to overlook things (or as Norman used to say when he had done something particularly egregious, "Rise above it!") and not fight, although Norman loved fighting better than anything, which I never truly enjoyed. He would say that I did like fighting, and we certainly fought a lot. I'm sure our friends were exhausted by all the fighting, the repartee, the one-upmanship we engaged in all the time.

When we were alone, we got along fine for the most part, but if we were out with friends, or at a dinner party, it was a game we invariably played, one of us making a comment, the other one topping it. People's heads would swivel back and forth, as if they were watching a tennis match. Sometimes I did enjoy the back-and-forth, especially if I won, but I did get terribly weary of his bad-boy behavior, like the time he invited an old girlfriend to dinner when I had a fever and he expected me to entertain her. I cooked a nice meal and tried to be gracious to her and the girlfriend she had brought along for protection, but she was flirty with him, snarky to me, and when Norman mentioned I hadn't been feeling well, she said "Oh, I hope it's not cancer" in a tone of voice that indicated that was *exactly* what she was hoping for.

After she left, I complained bitterly, and he told me for the umpteenth time to "rise above it." I said that he should marry an angel—if he could find one that would have him—that I had no wings with which to "rise above it." At times like those, the fights were real. He did things like that purely for the novelistic curiosity of seeing what would happen, I think. Although I would prefer to believe that he was a curious novelist than to think he was just an insensitive clod.

Clod or angel, there are many reasons we lasted for thirty-three years, aside from the physical passion, which was as intense decades into the marriage as it was at the beginning, if not as frequent. As trite as it sounds, I think we stayed together because we really loved each other, we loved our kids, we loved our life, and we were comfortable together. We had each found someone whose quirks and habits we could live with, like a key in a lock. Besides, if I had left him, as I seriously considered only once, I would have always wondered what he was up to, and would have been miserable in my curiosity.

Twenty-five

Even though I was in a big agency, getting work as a model wasn't automatic. I had to go to appointments called go-sees with photographers, sometimes four or five in a day, to try to get them to give me work or tests, which are photographic sessions in which the photographers try out lighting and new ideas, perhaps discover the next big talent, and models get pictures for their books. I had the pictures from Italy and the ones from Milton Greene, which I showed to everyone, but I had no tear sheets, which are magazine pages from real work, and I didn't have a variety of looks, no fashion shots at all, only beauty, or head shots.

Most of the models were younger than I, all of course beautiful, single for the most part, and the photographers, with few exceptions, were all youngish men. I was at a disadvantage before I even knew it because I couldn't date the photographers and get them to take my picture, and I didn't go to the parties that were being given every night, or go out to the clubs and network. The name of the game was hooking up, and I had Norman and Matt and the family. Wilhelmina and her husband, Bruce Cooper, had parties at their house almost every weekend, and I didn't go to those, either, for the same reasons.

Wilhelmina called me into the office early on and told me I needed to move to Paris for a year of seasoning. It was traditional. A new girl would go to Paris, a rich playboy would meet her at the airport in a limousine with a bottle of champagne, and the girl would spend a year working for French magazines, which were much easier to break into than American ones. The girls would have a ball with all the men, and then come back to New York with sophistication, experience, and a book full of beautiful tear sheets. I told Willie it was impossible for me to move to Paris. I wasn't going to leave Matt again, and I knew if I left Norman for a year, he would find someone else.

So I just trudged around New York with my few pictures, doing a lot of testing and getting small ads for things like bras for A&S or sunglasses for Gloria Vanderbilt, a little work for Clairol, but no big jobs. I was making sixty dollars an hour, the beginning rate, and when I started working more, I would be raised to seventy-five dollars an hour. It seemed like a lot when they first told me how much I would be making, but when you get only one or two hours a week of real work—if that—minus your taxes, commission, and expenses, it isn't so much. I had to start taking money from Norman, as much as I hated to.

In the beginning I pretended it was a loan I would pay back, but he just laughed and said don't worry about it. That was one thing about Norman, he was generous to a fault. Not only with me but with all the kids and exes. Any old friend who was down on their luck and needed a hundred bucks could come and get it from him. His attitude about money was, "Money is cabbage; it will always come when you need it," and for him, somehow it always did. Not that he didn't work hard for it. In the years when the writing wasn't enough to support the enormous family, when we had as many as six children in college and private school, he also went on the road and lectured, sometimes doing as many as twenty lectures a year at colleges and other venues. He wrote magazine pieces and did anything he could to make an extra buck.

I occasionally went with him on the road (he did meet *me* when he was on a lecture tour, after all, no fool this girl!), and he was a phenomenon onstage. He came alive in the spotlight. No matter what his mood, when he got up in front of the audience, a switch turned on and his eyes were luminescent, his brain crackled with energy. He became even more articulate than normal, speaking in full paragraphs and pulling facts and figures and quotes out of his head that always astounded his audience. He spoke mostly about politics and the state of the world. Sometimes he would read from his work. He always had a great deal to say about what was wrong with this world, one thing being plastic. Plastic was poisoning the human race, and everyone just laughed when he said it, but now, by golly, they are discovering that plastic is, indeed, poison. Not to mention how it never disintegrates and is clogging the landfills.

Another thing he spoke often about was television, and how it was making all the kids become ADD and have no attention spans because every seven minutes the program they were watching was interrupted by a commercial, so their heads were spun in a totally different direction. No wonder kids couldn't sit for an hour in class, or read a book without having music or TV or something else to distract them. I was in total agreement with his ideas, most of them.

A big truck of books and his stuff from Stockbridge came to the apartment soon after he moved back, most of which we put in the basement. He tried to write at his desk in the living room, but it was too distracting with the phone and Matt and me bumping around in the house, so he moved downstairs to a small room that we owned on the floor below to use as an office. It was a little claustrophobic but had a big window with a view of the city, and a teeny kitchen with a fridge, a small sink, and a four-burner stove. A person could live there, although not too comfortably. I arranged my modeling appointments so I could take Matt to nursery school and pick him up, and on the evenings we went out, he stayed with Fanny. I cooked a lot, though, and we enjoyed quiet evenings at home. We were beginning to find a rhythm to our life together.

We still split the time between my apartment and his, more at my place since Matt had come to live with us. One day, we were set to take the afternoon train to Harvard, where Norman was lecturing, and Matt was going to spend the night with Fanny. Maggie had been in for a visit with her nana, Myrtle, and we had spent a nice few days with the kids, who were both imaginative and creative and got along well, but Myrtle and Maggie were going back to Stockbridge that morning on the bus. I'd said my goodbyes because I had to run into the city for a little modeling job in the morning, and was walking Matt to nursery school first. When we got outside, Matt said, "Oh, I forgot my lunch!" It was on the kitchen counter. I told him to wait right by the door and I'd run up and get it.

As I approached the apartment, the most god-awful noise came from inside, sort of a mix of groan and yell, one that I'd never heard before, which literally made the hair rise on the back of my neck. I fumbled with the key, got the door open, and rushed into the bathroom. It looked like the set of *Psycho*. Norman was standing in the tub with blood rhythmically spurting out of his hand with every pump of his heart, splattering against the wall. I grabbed a towel and wrapped it around his hand, and it was soaked in two minutes. Norman got out and sat on the floor, pressing hard on the wound, trying to no avail to staunch the bleeding. The white porcelain knob of the shower was broken; evil, bloody shards lay on the bottom of the tub. The shower knob had been rusted shut, and since I always took baths, I'd never even noticed. Norman had never taken a shower at my place, either. He had always waited until he got home. When he tried to turn it, he thought, with typical macho zeal, "If that girl can turn this thing on, I can, too," and he strained until the porcelain knob broke and sliced a major artery in his thumb.

"Go up to my mother's and get some tape," he managed to get out. "But don't tell her I cut myself." He was beginning to turn the color of flounder belly. I ran out the door and up the stairs. I couldn't wait for the elevator. I knocked on his mother's door, and trying to be cool, I said, "Um, could I borrow some tape, please, Fan? Norman cut his finger a little bit."

She smiled and said, "Of course, darling, but you'll have to wait. Myrtle is in the bathroom."

I got hysterical. "I can't wait! Norman's cut his thumb half off!" I yelled, and ran through the apartment and flung open the bathroom door. Myrtle was sitting on the toilet, her eyes as big as moon pies. I started throwing everything out of the medicine cabinet onto the floor, not caring if it broke or not. Finally, I found the tape and raced out the door, Fanny hot on my heels.

When we got downstairs, Norman was still on the bathroom floor, and he now was the color of the gray bathroom tiles, which were covered in even more blood. Fanny let out a moan, and he said, "For God's sake, Mom, get out of here!" I wrapped a robe around him and then tried to get him up off the floor. I couldn't. He was too heavy and he couldn't help himself. We both tried to stop the bleeding by wrapping it with tape, but the tape just slid off the wound in the gush of blood. If we didn't get him to the hospital soon, he was going to pass out, and then we'd be in big trouble. This was before 911, so I went to the phone and picked it up, but drew a blank on who to call. My mind was half gone. Fanny said, "Call the car service," so I dialed the familiar number and told the driver to get over here fast and come up and help us.

We managed somehow to get Norman into some sweatpants and a shirt, and put sneakers on his feet.

I had totally forgotten about Matthew in all of the ruckus. He finally got tired of waiting and came inside with someone who lived there, and then he climbed the stairs to the apartment, since he couldn't reach the elevator buttons. He was standing in the living room in his coat, holding his lunch, thinking we had all lost our minds, I guess. At that point, the doorbell rang and it was the driver.

"Go upstairs to Grandma's house," I said to Matt. "You can stay home today. I have to take Norman to the hospital." I started to put my arm into my coat sleeve, and bumped Fanny, who was putting her arm into the other sleeve. Norman said, "Oh, for Pete's sake, Mom. Go upstairs and stay with Matt. We'll be back soon. I'll be fine. Barbara will call you." Fan didn't want to let us go alone, but Norman insisted, and the driver helped us down to the car.

When we got to the emergency room, the receptionist asked me if we were married, and I honestly said "No," not realizing they wouldn't allow me to go back with him to the doctor's office. I decided right then that there are times it might be necessary to lie. I sat outside in the waiting room and tried to read an old *Reader's Digest* for a couple of hours, not knowing what was happening to him behind the doors, until finally he came out with his hand in a cast. He had cut the tendon almost in two, and it was just luck that he hadn't cut the whole thumb off. Thank God it wasn't his writing hand.

"The first thing I thought when I first cut the hand was, 'I've blown the train trip,'" he said. "The second thing was, 'I've blown the lecture,' and the third thing was, 'I've blown the thumb!'" He was wan and exhausted. They had put his hand under a running stream of cold water for about an hour, which had been excruciating, then they had sewn it up and put it into a cast.

"You're going home and going to bed," I said, totally wrung out myself. I'd called and canceled my little booking, which upset everyone, but it couldn't be helped.

"No. I promised I'd go to Harvard and do this lecture for the Advocate, and we're going. We'll take a plane." And we went. He was weak from the blood loss, a little peaked and shaky, but once he was onstage, he was the old performer. He waved the cast around and made a joke of it. It healed and he had complete use of the thumb, but he had a scar, and half his thumb was numb for the rest of his life; still, he didn't take any time off. He went back to writing the next day, pushing himself, by force of will, to take the discomfort and pour it into the writing.

Twenty-six

The tall ships came to the harbor of New York in July 1976, the bicentennial of the Declaration of Independence. We had an afternoon party at Norman's apartment, and watched the ships from the roof terrace while eating ham and baked beans and coleslaw, Norman's favorite party foods. Dotson Rader was there. He was a friend of Norman's who was a writer, a young radical in the sixties, and someone who had lived with Tennessee Williams for fifteen years or more. He was cute and funny, and from the moment I met him, he became my surrogate brother. His father was a traveling evangelist, and Dotson, his twin sister, Michelle, and his family had lived the life of nomads, moving all over the country, setting up a tent and having revival meetings, something I knew a lot about. We used to sing gospel songs whenever we got together, and he is still one of my dearest friends. At the tall ship party, he was regaling everyone with stories of the healing services his father used to hold, and he grabbed Betsy, who was the closest to him, to demonstrate his father's technique.

"Here's what he would do, Betsy," he said. "You look at me right in the eyes, then we pray to God for healing, and then I tap you on the forehead with the heel of my hand and . . . In the name of the Father and the Son and the Holy Ghost, BE HEALED!" He smacked her maybe a little too hard on the forehead, and she lost her balance and fell down onto the floor. "Oh, my gosh, I'm so sorry! Betsy, are you all right?" It was a most dramatic display of the power of prayer, and I'm quite sure Betsy was healed if there was anything in her that needed healing. That party was a memorable one.

Norman loved parties, and we soon became famous for them. Our apartment could comfortably hold about fifty people, but I know there were times when we had two hundred or more. The first time I helped give one, I had only been in New York for a few months and we were just becoming known as a couple. Norman told me that he had a recipe for coleslaw that was like nectar and ambrosia. Everyone just ate it until they were sick. I had a hard time believing that. *Coleslaw?* But I guessed he knew what he was talking about. I told him I could make a good ham and baked beans and corn muffins to go with it, so that was the menu. We did the shopping, and he piled the cart with twelve heads of cabbage. I would have bought two, maybe three at the most, but he said, "No, no, no. We need *twelve*," that people would bring people and you never wanted to run out of coleslaw.

"Norman, how many people are coming? Are you sure everyone will eat this much food at ten o'clock at night? Won't they have had dinner already?"

"Of course they'll eat it. It's famous. And by the time they get here and have a couple of drinks, they'll be hungry again."

I was unsure, but then New York social life was not exactly like Russellville social life, so we began chopping. It took us the better part of the day, as we did it all manually with a big sharp knife, and it included carrots and onions and red peppers as well as cabbage. "You have to slice it *thin*," he said, and demonstrated. "Thin like paper. And throw out the chunks that are too thick near the stem. It has to be almost transparent in order for the dressing to soak in." He always had a special way of doing everything. His mantra in the kitchen was, "Here, let me show you a little trick." He had me cut away all the white parts in the center of the red peppers, too. That part was bitter. The carrots had to be peeled and sliced in thin, long strings until the carrot was a skinny stick, and then that had to be peeled into nothing. Onions were chopped into tiny bits, not too much. The dressing was a secret, chiefly because he never wrote it down and it was different every time, but it included mayonnaise, teriyaki sauce, Worcestershire sauce, lemon juice, and some other ingredients that are too secret to put down here (and too secret for me to remember). Obviously, we didn't have a bowl big enough for it all, so we mixed it up in our biggest cooking pots, and then distributed it into several of our largest bowls. It took up most of the fridge. I put the bulk of it in a huge decorative antique footed urn from the living room that looked like it had been unearthed in Rome or Greece, and centered it on the dining table.

The party was for our friends Doris Kearns and Richard Goodwin, who had just gotten married. Doris had been an assistant to President Lyndon Johnson and was writing a book about him that would be called *Lyndon Johnson and the American Dream*. Doris has always been one of my favorite people in the world, and her husband, Dick, was a speechwriter and adviser to John F. Kennedy and Lyndon Johnson, among other things. He has a swarthy complexion and long curly black hair, and the kids called him "the pirate" behind his back.

As Charlotte Curtis later wrote in *The New York Times,* I was wearing "little wisps of white silk," and it seemed like half of Manhattan was there. (I couldn't believe a *Times* reporter had actually written about the party. It was the first time I'd come in contact with the press, and I didn't like it. I remembered from reading *Marilyn* that she once said about reporters that she supposed they thought they were talking to her clothing, and that seems to be the case. They sure weren't thinking about anybody's feelings. It was something I never got used to.) Anyhow, I was wearing a white silk top and pants, and I kept introducing myself to people as the hostess. The room was so packed that nobody could move. Drinks were passed overhead through the crowd, and the guests had to link arms to get their drinks to their mouths. I met so many people that night, some who became friends and some who became social friends—some I never saw again. Arthur and Alexandra Schlesinger were there, as was Gianni Agnelli, Ali MacGraw, Pat Lawford, and Allen Ginsberg. Bob Dylan came with Joni Mitchell and an entourage. Jackie Onassis came and we never even knew, it was so crowded. Woody Allen, Kurt Vonnegut, and Jill Krementz were there. I can't remember everyone. People told me for years afterward they were at that party, and I had no idea.

As far as I could tell, the coleslaw remained untouched. A bit of the ham was picked over, but the beans and corn muffins weren't eaten, either. The bar was going great guns, though, and at about one o'clock I sneaked into my room to sit at my dressing table, regroup, and refurbish my lipstick. I looked longingly at my bed, heaped with coats, wishing I could get into it and forget the hordes on the other side of the door. But I went back out, with fresh red lips, and carried on.

At about four, the last person left and Norman, who was nicely oiled, fell into bed, but I, tidy compulsive that I am, decided to put away the food so I wouldn't have to look at it when I got up a few hours later. I picked up the bowl of coleslaw and . . . I still cringe as I write this . . . dropped it on the floor. The bowl smashed and the contents quickly soaked into the rug. The whole thing, maybe eight or ten of the twelve cabbage heads, lay on our Oriental rug, among the broken pieces of the (possibly) priceless Greek or whatever bowl. I scraped up coleslaw and pottery and cried. I tried to wash the greasy dressing out of the rug, but it wouldn't come up. I was so tired that I was practically hallucinating. My bits of silk were stained with teriyaki mayonnaise.

It was about six by the time I finally got to bed, sliding in next to Norman, who was blissfully snoozing away, unaware that nobody ate any of his coleslaw. I was just drifting into unconsciousness when the doorbell rang. It was Hunter Thompson. He had left late, and in fact had been one of the last to go, so I was going to politely tell him the party was over, but he was feeling pretty rough and hungover and asked if I could make him some bacon and eggs. The way he looked, I thought his very life hinged on those eggs and bacon. I can't believe I was compos mentis enough to do it, but I staggered into the kitchen and made him bacon and eggs plus toast and coffee. Then he climbed up the ladder and flopped into the hammock that was slung over the crevasse under the skylight, and fell asleep. I worried for a minute that he would fall out and get a concussion, but figured his head had had worse things done to it, so I went back to bed.

When I emerged a few hours later, he was still up there. Finally, about three in the afternoon, he woke up, flipped out of the hammock, hung by his hands from the ropes, and dropped to the floor. He said "Thanks for a great party, Norris" and walked out the door, just like it was the most normal thing in the world.

My parents came to visit and took Matt back to Arkansas for the first part of the summer of 1976. They stayed at my apartment, and I tried my best to show them the wonders of New York so they could see why I loved it so much. I made them climb the Statue of Liberty, up into the torch, and we went to the top of the World Trade towers and the Empire State Building, which made my mother and me dizzy with vertigo. We walked across the Brooklyn Bridge. I dragged them around the Metropolitan Museum of Art and the American Museum of Natural History until they begged me to just let them stay home and rest one day. We took them to our favorite restaurant, Nicola's, on Eighty-fourth Street, and Sammy, the waiter, reeled off a long list of delicious specials. My father turned to me and whispered, "What language is he speaking?" I'm sure Sammy didn't understand my father's thick Southern accent any better.

They stayed four days and then with thin excuses said they had to leave. New York was just too much for them. I hated to see Matt go, but they were thrilled to have him back home again, and his father wanted to see him, too. Matt knew he was coming back in August to go with us to the Cape, so he wasn't so worried.

I kept on doing a bit of modeling, and then in July, I got a call from my mother saying that Matt had somehow contracted salmonella poisoning and was in the hospital. My heart started pounding and I got on a plane as fast as I could, praying with every mile that he would be okay. As far as the doctors could tell, he might have eaten an egg that was bad, or chicken that wasn't quite cooked. Nobody knew for sure how he got it, but he was pretty sick. I was in the throes of guilt, thinking if he had been with me this wouldn't have happened. I slept on the floor beside his bed at the hospital for a week.

By the time we brought him home, he was over it, but washed out from the experience. He needed a rest, not a long flight back East, but we had rented a house in Wellfleet on Lieutenant Island for August and part of September, and Norman and the kids had been up there for more than a week without me. Matt wanted to go as much as I did. It was our first big summer together, and it meant a lot to everyone. Norman and I spoke on the phone every day, of course, and he was anxious for us to come home. The girls—Betsy, Danielle, and Kate—declared they were old enough to hold down the fort, but cooking and taking care of the family was a huge job, and I know they needed us to get there.

Finally, Matt was much better, and on August 9, he and I flew back and went to the Wellfleet house in the marshes of Lieutenant Island. Although we were all still getting to know one another, it also seemed like Matt's and my addition to the family was welcome and seamless. Norman was like our drill sergeant, organizing the day's activities. When we were on vacation, he hardly worked. It was his time to be with the kids, and he threw himself into it. We started off the day jogging in the mornings. (He'd wake everyone up with a cheery ditty he'd learned in the army, "Drop your cocks and grab your socks! Out of your fart-sacks, you bastards!") Oy. Matt and Maggie were too young to jog, and Betsy, Kate, and I always brought up the rear, while Norman, Danielle, and the boys led the pack. I was secretly jealous of Danielle's athletic prowess, and tried to pretend I was much more of an athlete than I was. In reality I hated everything about jogging. I think it is bad for a woman to have her insides and her breasts jostled up and down like that. It can only lead to trouble down the road, when age and gravity helps pull everything earthward. While I can't wholeheartedly blame the jogging I did, everything of mine has certainly gone south, and I like to think that has to be a part of it.

We also canoed among the marsh grass and found horseshoe crabs, went swimming, took long hikes in the dunes, and had picnics. We biked on the bike trail and walked the two miles to the pizza parlor on the highway. Our family car was the old silver Porsche, believe it or not, the one with the duct tape Band-Aids and dents all over it, and one night eight of us piled into the car and went to Provincetown to pick up Bob Lucid, a professor at the University of Pennsylvania and a dear friend of Norman's, who was coming for the weekend. Lieutenant Island was only an island at high tide. The road became dry at low tide, and we had to time our trips in and out accordingly.

That night, there was a simultaneous chess tournament in town with Nat Halpern, one of the grand master chess players who lived in Ptown, and Norman and Bob were playing in the tournament. We picked up Bob, wedged him into the car—Lord knows how (thank God he was skinny)—and then dropped him and Norman off at the chess tournament while I took the kids—Michael and Stephen, Betsy, Danielle, Kate and Matt—to eat pizza and see a movie, one of those stupid beach movies where some monster eats the kids, like a *Jaws* knockoff. Maggie stayed home with Myrtle.

As it turned out, Norman was one of the few who won at the chess tournament, which put him in a good mood, and then all nine of us crammed ourselves back into the Porsche for the thirty-minute ride home. I had Michael and Stephen sitting on my lap in the front seat, which quickly made my legs go numb, and the others were stacked on laps in the tiny two seats and the console in the back. What were we thinking? No one used seat belts or child seats in those days, but I'm sure there were rules about this kind of thing, and if we had been spotted by a cop, we would have been in big trouble.

Of course we got to the road too late, and the water had already covered it. We had two options: one was to leave the car, wade through the water, and hope it wasn't too high, and the other was . . . well, we had one option. It was a warm night and the water was covered with glowing green phosphorescence. We parked the car off the road and piled out like clowns from a circus car. My legs were so dead from the weight of the boys cutting off my circulation that I fell to the ground, and everyone had to rub them to get the feeling back. That pins and needles feeling you get when they come back to life was excruciating. Then Norman put Matt on his shoulders and we all held hands as we started wading across. It was probably a hundred yards to the other side. We had to feel the roadbed with our feet to keep from falling off and getting into deeper water, and it was touch and go.

When we were about halfway across, the boys started singing the theme song of *Jaws*. Dada. Dada. Dadadada dadadada . . . Something slithery brushed against my leg and I started screaming, so all the kids started screaming, and we tried to run though the water, half of us falling in and getting totally soaked. Poor Matt was hanging on to Norman's head for dear life, bouncing around, and he nearly fell off into the water. We finally made it and then had to walk about a mile to our house, our shoes sodden with seawater and packed with sand. I rinsed myself and Matt off, the other kids took showers and got themselves to bed, and I left Norman and Bob talking over a huge bottle of red wine. In the morning, when I got up to make breakfast, Bob was still there, sound asleep in a chair beside the fireplace, tenderly hugging the empty wine bottle.

The summer brought us all closer together, in spite of the lateness of my and Matt's arrival and the fact that the house was in a salt marsh and the drains smelled vaguely like baby urp. The girls accepted me as something between a girlfriend and an older sister. We all shopped and cooked, did mountains of laundry, and took care of the smaller kids. Michael and Stephen were normal rowdy boys who half loved me and half were wary of me, now that I was a figure of authority. The kids really knew after that summer that the guard had changed.

I met Carol for the first time the week I arrived in Wellfleet. She had rented a house down the road to be near Maggie. I was watching out the window as she drove up into the yard and got out of the car. I was nervous. Norman talked about her constantly, and she had achieved epic status in my imagination. I knew she was a great beauty from seeing her pictures. I wanted to look good, but not as if I were trying too hard, so after changing outfits several times, I finally put on a pair of jeans and a T-shirt and some big earrings.

She was as beautiful as I had imagined, wearing a low-cut silk top and pants (I remember a lot of cleavage, something I didn't have much of), and sandals, with shimmery toenail polish. Her skin was tanned to a dark bronze, which made me envious, as I never got a tan. My milky skin only burned and got freckles. She was wearing copper eye shadow, the same color as her toenails, and looked alarmingly like Elizabeth Taylor. I'm not sure what she thought of me, but we hugged and said, "Oh, you're so beautiful!" over and over, and we both meant it. Of course, there was tension (how could there not be?), and for years we were jealous of each other, but with the passing years, we have somehow become friends. I wish we could have been friends from the beginning. It would have made things so much easier on Maggie, but that was not in the cards.

Carol.

It's funny now to compare notes and realize how our relationships with Norman paralleled, how he had done the same things to each of us, told the same jokes, made the same comments. One of his little tricks was to come up to Carol at a party where she was talking to a handsome man and whisper in her ear, "You've lost your looks," hoping to throw her off in case she was enjoying herself too much. I'm not sure how she reacted, but he did the exact same thing to me. I just said, "Yeah, thanks, pal. I'll work on it," and I'd go on talking. I used to tease him that the reason he got married so many times was that he kept running out of stories and jokes, and had to keep getting a fresh audience. Maybe there's more truth than poetry in that.

When we got back to New York from the summer, I managed, with the help of Chuck Neighbors, to get *Cosmopolitan* magazine to print a story I had written about my experiences of becoming a model. It was called "Getting My Book Together." I wanted Francesco Scavullo, who did all the covers for *Cosmo,* to do my picture for the article, and they agreed. They even let me do a cover try. I went up to Scavullo's studio wearing a pair of khaki blouson pants and a white shirt, with a pair of L.L.Bean rubber and leather boots—don't ask me why, I thought it was terribly chic—and he did pictures of me in that outfit first. Then Way Bandy, who was the top makeup man in New York at the time, did my makeup, and Harry King, a famous hairdresser, did my hair. I felt like one of the big girls. I wore a pink silk low-cut top with skinny pants. I apologized for my flat chest, but they said, "Don't worry about it, Norris. They'll airbrush some boobs on. Never fear." I didn't make the cover because Helen Gurley Brown said my hair was too short. I gnashed my teeth over my lost long hair, but there was nothing to do about it.

Wilhelmina loved the piece and for many years had it photocopied and handed to every new girl who came in, along with her street guide.

THE WINTER OF '76–'77 was a particularly snowy one, and I didn't have a warm coat. I'd left all my coats, which weren't heavy, behind in Arkansas, and the winter before, I'd made do with a black velvet coat with a fur collar I'd gotten in a vintage clothing store in the Village on Bleecker Street for twenty-five dollars. While it was striking for evening, it wasn't warm. I'd also gotten a purple wool cape in Italy, which was dramatic but not warm enough for the deep cold. Then I ran across some old pictures of Carol and Norman, and she was wearing a fur coat, a gray fox or whatever, and I got green-eyed fur lust. But how to broach the subject with Norman? I couldn't let him know how jealous of her I was, and I hated to ask him for money. He had started having his secretary send me a check for a hundred dollars every week, which paid the rent and a few extras, but I wasn't making enough at modeling to really fill in the gaps. It was tricky. I couldn't ask him for a fur coat head-on, but one night when we were out in a snowstorm, he put his arm around me and felt me shiver. "Is that the warmest coat you have?" he said. I said yes, but maybe I could find a warmer one at a vintage store or something. He took a look at the purple cape, like he'd never seen it, which was entirely possible, given his obliviousness to his environment. "We have to get you something warmer than that!"

"How much would a fur coat cost?" I asked. "Not that I'd need to have a *fur* coat, but they're really warm. Maybe I could get a secondhand one or something. I'll look around." Oh, I was so crafty!

I saw the wheels begin turning in his head. It would never occur to him on his own to get me a fur coat, but once an idea got into his head, he did it up in a big way. He asked one of his friends, who knew someone whose uncle or cousin or whatever was a furrier in the Garment District, and found we could get one wholesale. Norman said he would take me down there and just look and see what they had, no promises. I modeled in the Ben Kahn fur ads for *The New York Times,* and I knew a coat like those would be way beyond my wildest dreams, but I was sure we could find something reasonable for wholesale.

The place was called D'Cor and was run by a guy named Buddy. His assistant was a woman named Rita, who wore too much eye makeup, but then so did I, and we liked each other immediately. She started off showing us the cheaper furs like rabbit and raccoon, none of which Norman liked at all. I tried on a mink, which he didn't like, either. Too plain. Then he saw a coat across the room. "What's that one?" he said. We'd told Rita we didn't want one that was too expensive, but the one he was looking at was a full-length red fox. Rita winked at me and went and pulled it off the hanger. I put it on, and it was like a slot machine in Las Vegas had gone off. With my red hair, it was perfect. Norman was so transparent. I could see him thinking of me wearing that coat and nothing else. I could see it, too. I didn't dare hope he would go for it, so I didn't carry on too much, but after I tried on a few others, he said, "No, that's the one we want. I'm not going to have you walk into a place in a drab ugly coat. It has to be the fox." And he got it. I could hardly breathe, I was so excited. They were going to take a couple of days to embroider my initials "NC" into the coat's champagne-colored lining, and then it would be all mine.

When I finally brought it home, the first thing I did was put it on with nothing else underneath. Needless to say, it was a huge hit. He loved sweeping into places with me in that coat and tall high heels. There was a picture of us in *Playboy* at a party at Studio 54 with me wearing that coat when I was nearly nine months pregnant. There were pictures in all the social columns of me in the coat. I wore it everywhere. I hated to take it off. I had that coat for thirty years, and it was worth every penny he paid. I'm sure he would agree.

Several years later, during the period when furs were getting splashed with red paint by crazy nuts, I was a little nervous. It was such a spectacular target, and sure enough, one night as I was standing in the street, my mind somewhere else, waiting for the light to change, someone came up behind me in a car and slowly and carefully ran into me. The heel of my shoe got crunched under the tire, and it was a wonder I didn't fall and really get hurt. I was in such a rage that I yelled and screamed at the people in the car, who just laughed as they got out. I'm not sure if they were fur nuts or just nuts. If there had been a cop around, I would have called him, but I was also a little afraid of them. There's a fine line for a woman alone between standing up for herself and being foolhardy. It did take some of the bloom off the coat, though, and even if I hadn't been a fur nut target, I felt like a target of some kind. Besides, it was beginning to show its age. The elbows were nearly bare and it was becoming shabby, so I finally had to put it away, but I still have the shreds hanging in the closet. I can't part with them.

(P.S. One Christmas when I was about thirty-two, I had Robert Belott shoot nude photographs of me in the coat, and I gave an album of them to Norman for a Christmas gift. He said it was the best present he had ever received. They were classic Victorian sepia nudes, not pornographic by any means. I totally trusted Robert. He was my favorite

In the red fox, with the naughty bits blocked out.

photographer and a dear friend, and I told him that no one—*no one*—else was to see these pictures, not even his assistant. He swore.

Then one day several months later, my downstairs neighbor, who was in advertising, called and asked if I knew there were nude photographs of me being circulated in some photographer's book. I called Robert, got quite loud, and reluctantly he promised to take them out. "They're just too good to not let people see them," was his argument. "You can't ask Picasso to put his work in the closet!" He was frustrated. Still, I think he took the pictures out of his portfolio.

Years and years went by, and we kept in touch. Robert left photography and opened a bed-and-breakfast in Florida called the Cypress. Recently, a remark dropped in a conversation with a mutual friend let me know that my nude pictures had graced the bar of the Cypress for many years. Actually, at this point, I don't mind. It's kind of flattering, being the nude girl above the bar. I told my daughter-in-law Sasha, Michael's wife, who is a gorgeous singer, that she should get some done while she is still young enough. When you are old and wrinkled, you will always have those pictures to remind you that once upon a time, you were a hot naked babe in a red fox coat.)

Twenty-seven

I think of that winter of '76–'77 as our first real year together. We had become closer than ever, the family had accepted Matt and me, and our life was coalescing. After our big party for Dick and Doris Goodwin, where we more or less came out to society as a couple, we started being invited to a lot of dinner parties and social functions. I was beginning to learn about fashion—being in it all day, of course—but I still didn't have much of a wardrobe. I had no evening dresses at all, and a lot of the functions we were invited to were black tie. I made do with a few things I'd gotten in my favorite vintage store called Fonda's, on Lexington Avenue in the thirties, a long black Scott Barrie skirt with different tops, mostly, and I managed to kind of pull it off, chiefly because I was young and skinny, but it was catching up to me. We were in a social set that wore couture and designer, and while I couldn't afford that, I didn't want to look like some down-at-the-heels hick, and Norman didn't want me to, either. One of his pleasures was to walk into a party with me looking glamorous in the coat, but I couldn't wear the coat all the time.

Then one night we were invited to Oscar de la Renta's house for a small dinner. He had also invited Sam Walton, of Walmart, which hadn't yet become the behemoth it is today but was already getting well known, and I supposed they wanted us in part because I was from Arkansas. Oscar was my favorite designer in the world, and I was a wreck over what to wear. I went to Bloomingdale's and searched through the evening dresses, but everything was way too expensive. Anything designed by Oscar himself was totally out of the question. Then, wandering through the lingerie section, I came across an ivory satin gown with a filmy silk jacket, like Jean Harlow might have worn, and it wasn't too expensive, so I got it. I figured with a long strand of fake pearls and glitzy earrings and the red fox coat I could pull it off. My hair had grown back a bit by this time and was pretty glamorous. So off we went to Oscar de la Renta's house for dinner. Oscar's chic

French wife, Françoise, took my coat and said how beautiful it was, and then there I was, left in my nightgown. I hadn't even worn a bra or pantyhose because of the lines.

They indeed had seated me next to Sam Walton, who was nice and so down-home. We liked each other immediately, and talked about how nobody in the North could understand us, and how stupid some of the people were. I told him of talking to the headmaster of a private school for fifteen minutes about my work as an art teacher, the problems of education and whatever, until finally the headmaster had asked me where I'd taught, and I'd said "Arkansas." "They have *art* in Arkansas?" He'd been incredulous. Sam laughed. He could relate. People always underestimated him, which was sometimes to the good. In fact, he cultivated it. He drove the same old pickup truck he had driven for years, and could talk bird dog with the best of them. We had the best time talking about Arkansas, just like Oscar and Françoise knew we would. Norman, of course, was always the center of attention at any dinner party. He came alive at the table much like he did onstage, and for years we were invited everywhere just for the entertainment value.

The de la Renta house had lush velvet and gold and embroidered cushions and furniture everywhere, Oriental carpets, luminous paintings of Arab sheiks and desert tents full of pillows and carpets and couches, not unlike the ones in the room below the paintings. I felt like I was in Morocco or Zanzibar or somewhere hot and sandy and exotic, only without the heat and the sand. Oscar had a soft accent and brown eyes that melted every woman into a puddle. He and Françoise couldn't have been more gracious to Norman and me.

At the end of the evening, Françoise took me aside and whispered into my ear, "My dahling, we have to get you some clothes. Call me tomorrow and we'll go to Oscar's showroom and pick out some things. You can fit the runway samples. It will not be expensive." She did it in a way that didn't humiliate me, and I always loved her for that. I did call and go with her the next day to the showroom, and it was a wonderland of the most beautiful clothing I could imagine. Norman had told me to get anything I wanted within reason. He knew I needed things for the life we were beginning to lead, and so I came back with a huge bag of runway samples. I still have a lot of them, and regret the ones I gave away over time. Twice a year I would call Françoise, and then Boaz Mazor, Oscar's assistant, and get a few new things for the coming season. I was still struggling to find my "look," as Wilhelmina said, but I was getting closer. At least I knew better than to go out in a nightgown again.

Twenty-eight

I did a go-see for a Mexican TV commercial for Raleigh cigarettes, and was astounded when I got it. I think Wilhelmina was, too, but it was good news for me, as I wasn't making that much and it was a small windfall. I'd never been to Mexico, although Norman's oldest daughter, Susan, lived there. I thought I'd get to see her, but unfortunately she was in New York while I was down there and we missed each other. Norman used to spend quite a bit of time in Mexico when Sue was small. He sometimes stayed for weeks, and told me lots of stories of his time down there.

One story I love is of when Sue was driving back with him and his second wife, Adele, to New York when she was about three or four, and for some reason she started talking about angels, *los ángeles*. Norman, who was then trying to be a staunch atheist, said there were no such things as angels. "Can you see angels, Sue? Do you hear them?" "No," she had to admit. "Well, then, if you can't see them or hear them, there aren't any angels. They don't exist. It's like a fairy tale." Sue was crestfallen. After a few minutes of deep thought, she said, "Papa, Grandma exists, doesn't she? We can't see her or hear her, but she lives in New York. So maybe *los ángeles* are real, but just live in heaven." It gave him pause, and that may have been one of the first cracks in his atheistic beliefs. Another crack came from author James Jones, who believed in reincarnation. Jim said it was the only thing that made sense to him, and Norman finally had to agree. He certainly had done a complete turnaround and firmly believed in God when I met him.

MY PLANE CIRCLED Mexico City, which was obliterated in soft gray fog. It lies in the bottom of a bowl, with mountains all around, and the pollution was bad. In fact, when Sue got pregnant with her first daughter, Valentina, she and her husband, Marco, moved to Chile to escape the smog. It was indeed a little hard to breathe sometimes, and if I stood looking down the street, everything got hazy after a block or two and then became gray. But the excitement of being in a commercial outweighed anything else. Cigarette commercials were not done in the United States, but Mexico didn't care. There was already so much pollution that smoking a cigarette was like taking a breath of ordinary air.

The first afternoon was devoted to getting fake fingernails. In those days, the way they did it was to mix up a powder and goop it over forms on each fingertip. The forms had to dry, then the nails were filed and shaped to the correct length. It took hours. In this case, the correct length was about two inches long. I had never had real nails in my life. I kept them clipped short, being a painter and working in clay and other art materials, so I wasn't used to them at all. It was sort of glamorous at first, having these long red talons, but after I left the salon, I realized how helpless I was. I couldn't push elevator buttons. I couldn't dial the phone. I couldn't button my blouse. I tried to pick my nose and nearly slit my nostril. Washing my hair was problematic, too, and by the time morning arrived I was going a little nuts with them. I had small nicks where I'd tried to scratch in my sleep, and it is a miracle I didn't put my eye out.

Nevertheless, I arrived at the set dressed, with a clean face, like they'd asked me to do, and then the makeup man began to cover my entire body with dark body makeup. I looked like a redheaded Mexican, which was a little strange. If I put my arm down on a chair, or leaned against the wall, it left a dark print, so I had to be careful. I couldn't touch my dress. I only half kiddingly told the producer, who was a dark, handsome young man, "You come all the way to New York to get a pale-skinned redheaded model, and then you turn her into a Mexican! Why did you go to the bother?" He laughed, but never did explain why they chose me for the role if they wanted someone Hispanic. I wasn't going to argue, though.

The premise was that I wandered into this beautiful hacienda all alone, wearing an evening dress and lots of jewels. I looked around the room with great appreciation, touching a handsome leather-bound book, or running my finger around the rim of a crystal goblet here and there. (Now I could see why they wanted those long elegant nails.) Then I picked up a pack of Raleigh cigarettes, and took one. Holding it in my fingers, I turned, and in the doorway was an impossibly handsome male Mexican model in a dinner jacket. Our eyes met and there was some voice-over in Spanish I couldn't understand about the cigarettes or whatever.

It wasn't difficult, but we did a lot of takes, different angles, and shot for the whole day. I was tired and most anxious to go out for real Mexican food that night, as I loved it, or at least I loved the Tex-Mex kind we had in Arkansas, but the producers said no. They took me to an English pub–type place that served boiled beef and Yorkshire pudding. It was dreadful. After the next day's shoot, I asked again to go to a real Mexican restaurant, and again they said no. I might get the turista, they said, and we couldn't afford to lose the time. So we went for Chinese, which was again awful. I was in Mexico, starving for Mexican food. I passed women making tortillas on the streets and my mouth watered. I panted after the drinks they made from melons and fruit in stands on the sidewalk, but my producer watched me like a hawk. Not one bite of Mexican food could I have. Then, the last night, we had finished. The commercial was in the can and everyone was happy with it. Nobody cared if I got diarrhea or not, so my producer said, "Okay, we'll take you out to a good, real Mexican place."

It was called something in Spanish that translated to the Peeing Dog, and on the sign outside was indeed a picture of a dog with its leg raised. I was a little dubious, but I ate and ate and ate, tacos and enchiladas and chicken with mole sauce. Then we all went dancing at a club. I think the name of the place was the Camino Real, and we were having so much fun that I didn't notice the time. Oops. I was supposed to call Norman. It was now about three in the morning in New York, and I didn't want to wake him and face his wrath, so I just slipped into bed and didn't even check my messages, I was so worn out.

Bright and early, the phone rang. It was him. "Where were you last night?" he barked. "I tried to call you at two in the morning and they said you were out. Who were you with? That good-looking producer?" I was half-asleep, and tried to answer him, "No, I mean yes, but there were other people there. We went dancing and I forgot what time it was." Oh, boy. The more I kept talking, the more in trouble I got. Well, in a way it was good for him to be jealous for a change. I was the one who was always fending off women who were trying to get to him, so a dose of his own medicine went down pretty well. He was so glad to see me when I came back, and I think it made him appreciate me more, at least for a while. When the commercial started airing in Mexico, Sue's fiancé, Marco, would say to her, "Susan! There's your mother!" I think she was only half-amused.

I was beginning to make my own friends and enjoy our social life. My picture started appearing in *Women's Wear Daily*, once I had the Oscar de la Renta wardrobe, and we went out several nights a week. One woman I met who became one of my best friends was Pat Lawford, President Kennedy's sister, who was also a great friend of Dotson Rader's. We were both tall and redheaded, and we made each other laugh. She and Norman were terribly fond of each other, too, and we saw her frequently.

During one memorable dinner at her house, I was seated between her brother Teddy and Oleg Cassini, a suave, handsome designer who used to design for Jackie when she was first lady. I was working double time at the charm. I would talk to one for a while, then turn and address the other. It was lively and funny, but both of them were acting a little peculiar. I would almost say they were giddily overflirtatious. One would lean in and whisper a joke, look at me meaningfully, and I'd laugh, then the other one would do the same thing. I was having a good time, but at a certain point, I needed to go to the ladies' room. I scooted my chair back and said, "Excuse me, gentlemen. I'll be right back." As I stood up, I saw them look at each other in shock. Then I saw them, red-faced, fiddling with their shoes. It became apparent that they had been playing footsie with each other, both thinking the stockinged foot they'd been rubbing was mine. I had to giggle and tease them about it. They laughed, too, making a huge joke of it, not the least bit ashamed. Pat thought it was hilarious. "He's my brother, kiddo, and I dearly love him, but you have to watch him." I promised to do just that.

Twenty-nine

The summer of 1977 came quickly, and Norman and the kids decided they wanted to go back to Maine, to the house where they'd spent summers before I'd come into the picture. It would be a little weird, me going into the house where Carol had been with them before, but Norman was never sentimental about anything. He certainly didn't mind, and if he didn't, then neither did I, by golly, so we rented it for August. Then Beverly asked if we would stay in the Ptown house with the boys while she was in Hartford doing a play in July, so we packed up a rented van and all went to Provincetown.

Their house was right on the water in the east end of town. It had once been part of a group of houses on the very tip of the Cape they'd called Helltown back in the old whaling days. It was mostly a bunch of shacks where sailors had gotten drunk and slept with prostitutes, and thieves had often built fires on the beach to confuse ships, which would then go into shallow waters and founder, so the thieves could rob them. Then, in the nineteenth century, as whaling began to die out and Provincetown proper became the center of things, Helltown was abandoned and the shacks were floated across the bay and situated on the beach as the basis for houses. Norman and Beverly's house was one of these. The living room was part of the shack, and the ceilings were so low that it made me feel like ducking my head when I walked in. But it was a beautiful house, with four bedrooms upstairs and a huge deck that fronted the bay. The only real problem was that the house was smack on the street. When you walked out the kitchen door, you had to look both ways or you would be run over. I worried about the kids a lot that summer. In fact, one day a little girl was riding by on her bicycle outside our kitchen door, and someone opened the door of their parked car just as she got even with it, and it hit her. She was wearing braces, and her poor little mouth was all cut up. All I could do was put some ice on it and try to comfort her until her parents and the ambulance arrived.

Carol also had rented a little place in Ptown for the summer, and

Adele had an apartment down the beach. We didn't really socialize, but we'd stop and talk on the beach or see one another at parties. If not exactly one big happy family, it was civil, for the kids. Ptown is heaven for kids in the summer. The sand flats at low tide stretch out for a quarter of a mile or more, and you can let the kids out to run and play without a problem. The beach is full of shells and beach glass, and small creatures like hermit crabs. Every Mailer child at one time or another has offered painted shells for sale on Commercial Street. I was Maggie and Matt's biggest customer, and still have some of the shells in my treasure box.

Norman and I had never spoken in terms of trying to have a child since I'd had the miscarriage when I'd first come to New York, but we knew that we wanted one. Our lives were so much about the kids, how could we not want one together? I'd been on and off the pill, as it caused me to gain weight, and we were pretty lax about using birth control. We kept taking chances until we finally stopped using anything at all after a while. We just figured if it happened, it happened, and in July that summer it happened—while we were staying in Beverly's house. Beverly came back home from doing her play in Hartford, we piled all the kids and our stuff into a rented van and the Porsche, and hit the road for Mount Desert Island, Maine. I knew by the time we had been in Maine for a week or two that I was pregnant, but I didn't want anyone to know. I was worried about what the kids would say, and having lost one before, I wanted to be sure before I told anyone. Norman was thrilled about it, which made me so happy. I hadn't been sure if he would be, but given his philosophy about sex and love and children, I shouldn't have been surprised.

The house we rented was called Fortune Rock and was built by Clara Fargo Thomas of the Wells Fargo Fargos. She was an eccentric woman whose lover, George Howe, was the famous architect who designed it. She had passed away three years before, and Norman had been the first renter. The main feature of the house was a forty-foot-long living room that was cantilevered out over the water and had walls of glass panels on three sides. At high tide, the water was eight feet below the deck; at low, it was eighteen, but was still deep enough to jump into. I'd of course heard all the stories of the family ritual of jumping off the deck, and was dreading having to do it, but I was still pretending to be bolder and more athletic than I was, so when we unpacked, the first thing—the absolute first thing—I did was put on my bathing suit and run and jump off the deck. It was terrifying, and the water in Maine is so cold that it shocks the breath out of you and numbs you in just a few minutes, but I got so many brownie points from Norman that it was worth it.

View from the deck at Fortune Rock.

The house was spooky. Clara had been a painter, and all the walls were made of plywood oak covered in her murals, which were rather primitive, in blue and green, black and white, and browns mostly. Large Picasso-esque eyes were painted above the spigot in our bathtub, which made a nose, and the drain switch made the mouth. These paintings were everywhere. You couldn't escape them. Danielle and I made fun of them, but Betsy, who was tuned to the spirits more than most people, said, "You two better stop talking about Clara. She will haunt you!"

To get to Norman's and my room, you had to go down a long hallway that at the end had a life-size photograph of a young beautiful Clara, her hair falling down her back in long waves. The eyes in the picture followed me down the hall, as if she were standing there accusing me, and I half regretted our little jest about the artwork. The boys, Michael and Stephen, of course totally pooh-poohed the ghost thing. They weren't scared of anything.

The family in Maine, 1980.

But soon after my conversation with Danielle, I was lying in the bathtub, looking at the eyes staring at me above the faucet, when the hangers in the closet started tinkling against one another. The window was shut and there was no air at all moving in there. The closet was freestanding, and we had stored our suitcases on top of it. As I stared at the hangers, which were slightly moving and making a quiet noise, one of the suitcases came crashing down. It hadn't been teetering on the edge of the closet. It had been lying flat, and there was no reason for it to fall. I jumped dripping out of the tub and ran into the bedroom and got Norman, but when he came in, the hangers were quiet. He put the suitcase back on top of the closet, and I think he believed me when I said a ghost had moved it.

He said that one time something had tripped Carol, who took a fall for no discernible reason, and she always thought Clara's ghost had pushed her. It seemed Clara was jealous of Norman's women. Then a few days later, I caught Michael with a butter knife, trying to open a locked closet in the living room. No one had ever been in that closet, and I was about to tell him to stop it when the door swung open and . . . It was almost like music from *The Phantom of the Opera* swelled. . . . It was full of Clara's paints and brushes. I felt a woe come over me, and I said to Michael, "Oh, Mikey, you've done it now. Clara will get you. She didn't want us to find her paints!" I was only half kidding.

That night, after we had all gone to bed, Michael went into the kitchen to get a drink of water, then yelled and ran down the hall to our room and jumped onto the bed. There was a mirror above the kitchen sink, and he swore when he'd looked in the mirror, there was Clara standing behind him, her long white hair hanging down her back. It took awhile to get him to go back to his room. But the ghost of Clara was with us the whole summer. She might have liked Norman, but she definitely didn't care for me.

ONE OF THE things we did almost every day was hike some mountain around Mount Desert. My favorite was a route called the beehive that had a few ladders (iron bars driven into the rock that necessitated a vertical climb), but not too many. Another favorite was an easy trail, practically a stroll, that ended at Jordan Pond, where there was a tea-room. We got tea and hot popovers with butter and jam and sat in Adirondack chairs out on a long sloping lawn in the golden sunshine where the smaller kids ran, played, and rolled down the slope to the edge of the pond. Some trails were more challenging than others, obviously, and, as when we were jogging, Betsy and Kate and I were often in the rear.

As strange as it seems, the one thing I did that I didn't have to pretend too hard to like was rock climbing. We hired a guide to teach us, and Norman, Danielle, Michael, Stephen, and I climbed Otter Cliffs, a vertical climb of about eighty feet, rappelling down first. We had to trust our guide with our lives, because the first step off the edge of the cliff, supported only by a single rope, was a big leap of faith. But once in flight, bouncing down the cliff, the feeling was pretty phenomenal. I could understand for the first time why people engaged in dangerous sports; the adrenaline rush and the feelings of being a superwoman were intense. For some reason—I suppose it was my long spidery arms and legs—I was pretty good at it, and felt like a real jock when I made it to the top. I wasn't particularly afraid of the height, being so close to the rock, and I even at one point unhooked my rope for a minute to untangle it. I used to tell my son John that I took him rock climbing when he was in my belly, and that's why he's such a good athlete.

Near the end of the summer, the whole family trained every day on the trails around Bar Harbor for our biggest hike, Mount Katahdin, a drive of several hours that required an overnight stay in a motel, which was a treat for the kids. Michael, Stephen, and Matt had a room of their own, which Norman had to visit a few times to calm them down from jumping on the beds and making general mayhem, and the three girls shared a room. Myrtle Bennett, Maggie's nana, had come with us to Maine at Carol's request, to take care of Maggie, and she was a godsend that summer, helping with the cleaning, laundry, cooking, and everything else. She was from Honduras and had come to work for Norman and Carol when Maggie was just born. She and Maggie shared a room.

Before the sun rose, we arrived at the bottom of the trail, ready to climb. Even though we had been working all month building our stamina, it was an all-day ordeal, and we were taking Maggie and Matthew, who were six and not quite six. It started off fine. We each carried a backpack with a sandwich, oranges, chocolate, water, a sweater, and whatever else we thought might come in handy on the mountain. Norman didn't want to be bothered carrying his sweater, so I tied it around my waist. I had been having not exactly morning sickness but a general malaise in the mornings, and I wasn't feeling as well as I was pretending to. The girls kept glancing at me as I trudged up the mountain, stopping to rest more often than the others, and they were solicitous. They later told me they had been saying all month that they bet I was pregnant, while I'd thought I had them fooled. Once, I stopped and gacked a bit, and Danielle, Betsy, and Kate looked at one another and nodded their heads wisely, which I picked up on. "Well, I might as well tell you now. I'm pregnant," I said.

"We knew it! We knew it!" they squealed. I'm sure their feelings about having yet another sibling were mixed, but they never let on if they had any misgivings, and they would all love John like little mothers. At this point we were pretty far behind the others, who had stopped to wait for us, and it was beginning to get colder, so I put Norman's sweater on over my own. At the next rest stop, Norman asked me for his sweater back, and I selfishly didn't want to give it to him. "I've carried it this whole way because you couldn't be bothered, and now it's freezing, and I'm keeping it!" I was so bad about it, I don't really know why. I can only blame the hormones. He yelled at me for being so greedy, and then stomped off, and I felt like a big jerk. He was freezing in only a shirt, and I had his sweater and mine, too. My better angel won out. I caught up to him, apologized, and tried to give it to him. He said, in a gruff voice, "No, keep it. Not for you. For the little one." I broke into tears, and he hugged me. I guess I just needed a little attention paid. But I kept the sweater.

We climbed down into and up the notch, which was the next thing to rock climbing without ropes, and started across the knife edge, a sharp edge of rock that in places was as narrow as three feet. It fell sharply off on either side in a forty-five-degree angle, gave us vertigo, and made us feel like we were going to plunge down into eternity any minute, but one way or another we all made it. Then we got to the top, rejoiced, ate our lunch, and had to immediately start the long descent on a trail called the Bubbles, which was a dry creek bed paved with smooth stones, before it started to get dark on us. We still had six hours to go. That Bubbles trail looked easy at first—there were no verticals at all. But in the long run it was the most difficult, because with every step, our feet slid off the smooth round rocks, twisting our ankles, and after a few pounding hours of it, we all were exhausted. A bonus was when we saw a moose sticking its head out of some brush, curious at this noisy band of humans. Matt and Mike and Steve ran ahead like little mountain goats, but Maggie was totally worn out, and the rest of us had to take turns carrying her. I vowed if I ever got off that mountain I would never go back on it again.

After twelve hours of climbing, we finally staggered to our car and drove back to the hotel in the dark. The next morning, every muscle in my body was so sore that simply getting out of bed was a monumental task. I had to stop this pretending to be a jock. I was pregnant, and I hated physical activity. I would tell Norman the truth. But it could wait. He thought I was heroic, a real mother courage, and I didn't want to dispel that image. And next summer was a long time away.

Thirty

Somewhere in the back of my mind was the prediction Jean Jewell's friend had made that Norman was going to die in 1978. Here it was, close to the end of 1977, and the baby was due to be born in April of '78. It began to weigh on me. We had a friend named Al Morrison, an astrologer and a psychic who published a little pamphlet every month called an ephemeris, which was the "void of course" moon schedule. I'm not sure exactly how it works, but there are days when the moon wobbles slightly off its course, which can be predicted, and those are the days that nothing goes right. You drop your egg on the floor in the morning and mash your finger in the car door, you are late and get scolded, or have a fight with your husband; if everything in your day goes wrong, look at this pamphlet, and nine times out of ten you say, "Of course. The moon is out of phase." I made an appointment with Al. I think he charged twenty-five dollars at the time. I wanted to ask him only one question. He lived in a cluttered walk-up in the Village, as I remember it—or maybe it was the West Side—full of books and years of papers and magazines. There was one chair available, and as I walked through the door toward it, he said, "You're pregnant." It was not a question.

"How did you know that?" I was a little shaken. Only a few weeks along, I wasn't showing yet at all, and nobody outside the family knew.

"Because you have two auras." Oh. If he'd wanted to impress me, I was impressed. I told him about the prediction the other astrologer had made two years previously, and he looked in some books, took his time, and said, "It's possible." My heart sank. I'm sure the misery wafted off my two auras, and I started to cry. He continued: "But just because it is possible doesn't mean it is fated to happen. The signs that point to death also indicate financial reversal, and our fates aren't written in stone anyhow. We can always change them. There is such a thing as our will, too. We aren't simply the pawns of some uncaring force in the universe."

"But it's possible."

"Anything is possible." I gave him the twenty-five dollars and left, not comforted at all, but not desolate, either. I had a will, and I would will Norman to live, no matter what happened. I would watch him like a hawk and be ready to throw him out of the way of a car on Broadway if it was bearing down on him. I would watch his health, cook good meals, and make him go to the doctor if anything at all was wrong. I would never tell him about the prediction.

Soon after, I had a talk with Wilhelmina and told her I was pregnant. She knew I wasn't that serious about the career. I booked out for two months every summer and numerous times during the year to go do things with Norman, so I don't think she was surprised at all, and probably was relieved that she didn't have to let me go. We parted on a friendly note, and a couple of years later, she called me to have lunch and I agreed to do an occasional job here and there on a special basis, but for now I had only a few more bookings and then I would be done.

One was for Ben Kahn furs, and although I was only a couple of months pregnant, I had gained enough weight to make inaccurate the measurements they had previously taken, and they were not pleased with me at all. I thought they were going to refuse to work with me, but they didn't, and the pictures turned out fine. I loved the coats, but none of them was as great as my red fox.

Then I had a booking with Robert Belott for an album cover. I already had the beginnings of a little belly but was wearing a loose-fitting dress, and it didn't show in the pictures. Norman stopped by the studio to pick me up. I can't remember what the circumstance was, but Robert asked him if he would take a few shots with me, and the winds must have been blowing right, because he said yes. Those pictures are the best ones we have, great moody shots in sepia and black-and-white. In one, Norman is blowing a bubble, with a bored look on his face. I can't remember why he was chewing bubble gum; he never chewed gum. Maybe Robert gave it to him. In others I'm sitting on Norman's lap, oozing sex, my burgeoning boobs right in his face. I was nearly three months pregnant at the time, and my belly was just beginning to bloom. We hung several of them on the wall, where they have been for the past thirty years. As a favor to me, Robert took pictures of Fanny as well, beautiful head shots that are treasures and are also on our wall of family photos.

Me, three months pregnant, and Norman.

Robert was also a painter, his style more hard-edge design than my realistic one, and he'd started a painting of three women who were joined together by a black-and-white stripe motif, but he couldn't seem to do the faces. He asked me if I would do them, and it was great fun to paint again. There was one teensy little problem with it. He had done his part in acrylic and I did mine in oils. I repositioned the arm he had done, and I realized that after a while the oil was going to turn transparent and the acrylic arm would—pentimento, ghostlike—show through. I tried to fix it so it wouldn't, but I have no idea what it looks like today. (We sold that painting to Billy Friedkin, the movie director, in my first show. I'm sorry, Billy, if the girl in your painting now has three arms.)

I couldn't model anymore and knew I would have to find something else to occupy my time and to make some money, so this was a good way to transition back into painting, with my easel set up on a chair in the kitchen. I still loved to write, too, and returned to the novel I'd started in B. C. Hall's creative writing class. I had written about three hundred pages longhand in a spiral-bound notebook, but was afraid to show it to Norman. He kept asking to read it, though, and finally I typed up about a hundred pages and gave it to him. He took it downstairs to the small office while I paced the floor, waiting. When he came back up, he was slightly disturbed. "Well," I said, "what did you think?"

He handed it to me and said, "It's not as bad as I thought it would be. But you're nowhere near ready to show this to anyone." Oh. I knew it wasn't great literature on his level, but the way he said it took away any illusions I'd had that I could seriously write. I put it back in the drawer and concentrated on painting for the next twenty years. The kitchen was no space to work, but luckily, Edie Vonnegut, Kurt's daughter, had a studio in the East Village that she wanted to sublet for a year, so I took it and had a great time getting back into painting. It was wonderful to have my own little getaway place again, too. I guess it is an only-child thing, but I need several hours a day to be alone and work, and I like to know when I put something down that it will be there when I go back to pick it up. When Edie came back, we shared the space for another two years, and I had a show at Edie's gallery, Central Falls, in SoHo. Actually, I had three or four shows there. Edie and I had a great camaraderie, and it was the most productive time I ever had painting. I sold a lot of work and started doing commissioned portraits.

Carol and Maggie had moved to New York, and Myrtle started splitting her time between us. It was great for me, and great for Maggie, too, to be closer to Norman. At first, I didn't really trust Myrtle. I thought she would be on Carol's side and not like me, maybe she'd report back to Carol what went on at our house, but that proved not to be the case at all and we came to love each other. With Norman's help, she got her own apartment in Brooklyn and brought her five children up from Honduras to live with her. I think the youngest, Ruth, was maybe twelve at the time.

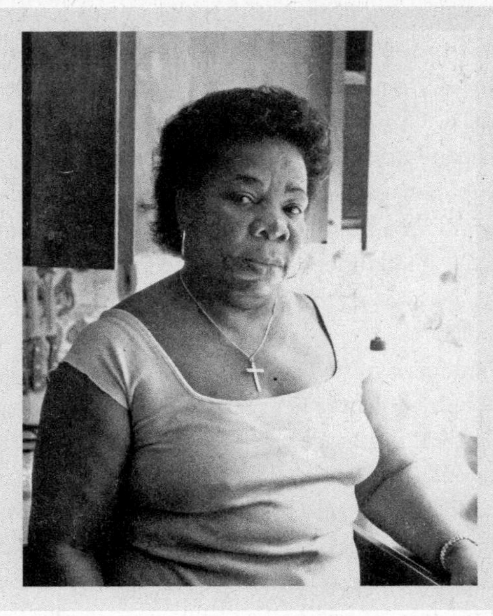

Myrtle Bennett.

Beverly was living year-round in Provincetown with Michael and Stephen, but after Norman moved to Brooklyn, she sent Michael to live with us, as he and Beverly were not getting along at all. Michael was twelve, an age when a boy needs a man as a role model, and Beverly and Norman both felt Michael needed more time with his father. Then the following year, Stephen joined us, and the boys went to Saint Ann's.

Up until this point, I hadn't really done much to Norman's apartment except clean it, but with the baby coming and the boys living with us, we needed more room. Michael was in the little bedroom above the living room, Stephen was in the crow's nest, but Matt couldn't continue to sleep in the living room, and we had no place for a crib, so one day Myrtle and I decided to clean out the second bedroom, which was crammed with old file cabinets and junk, and rearrange the apartment. Norman loved to tell a story about what happened that day.

Myrtle and I had spent all day scrubbing, rearranging furniture, throwing out the fish heads, broken lamps, old newspapers, magazines, and other detritus. (I was obviously more secure at this point and realized that Norman wasn't really attached to the stuff; he rarely noticed his environment at all, in fact.) We carried the file cabinets down to the basement, moved the bed from the living room into the bedroom, took down the whiffy fishnets, and generally changed the whole apartment. The place sparkled. A pot roast bubbled on the stove, and fresh flowers were on the table. At the end of the day, Myrtle left, both of us exhausted, but I was so anxious to see the expression on Norman's face and ready to be praised for my hard work.

Just before he was due to come home, the doorbell rang and it was the cleaners, delivering one of his suits. I was about to take off the plastic covering and hang it up when I heard his key in the door, so instead, I laid it down on the bed and ran into the living room to see his first reaction. He walked in, and I stood there expectantly, waiting for my doggie bone of appreciation and love, but all he saw was the suit lying on the bed. He said, "Look at what you've done. That suit should have been hung up. It's going to get all wrinkled! What do you do all day? Can't you even hang up my suits?"

A red curtain of rage descended over my eyes, and before I could think, I hauled off and punched him in the jaw. Hard. He staggered back a couple of steps, then turned and leaned his head against the wall. I was afraid to say anything. I waited for him to hit me back or yell or something, but he did nothing except stand there pressing his head into the wall. Finally, he turned back to me and saw, as he liked to tell it, my eyes round with horror, my mouth in an O. Then he started to laugh.

"What do you think I was doing?" he said, with a not-so-nice grin. I shook my head, afraid to say anything. "I was praying," he said, " 'God, give me the strength not to smash that beautiful girl's face.' " I finally found my voice, now that I was pretty sure he wasn't going to hit me back.

"I didn't mean to do that. My hand just flew out by itself. I'm sorry. But you have no idea how hard I've worked all day. Just look around."

He then noticed the candles and flowers on the table, which had been moved to a different spot, dinner cooking on the stove, the new, cozy bedroom for Matt, and realized why I had been so mad. So he apologized and we made up and had a nice dinner with the kids. As unbelievable as it was, I had to recognize that when he came home from work, he was still somewhere else, off in his head, and I stopped expecting him to see anything that wasn't put directly under his nose. He needed awhile to transition from work, unwind, and come back. And I also realized then that he would never hit me, no matter the provocation. I resolved never to provoke him again. If I could help it. (Of course I did provoke him again, countless times over the years, and I hit him plenty of times, too, but he never, ever hit me.)

PHOTOGRAPH BY JILL KREMENTZ

NORMAN WAS THE one who called my parents and told them I was pregnant. I just couldn't do it. Of course, they were upset. Having a child out of wedlock was still a big deal in Arkansas in those days. Girls were "in trouble" and looked down on if the man wouldn't marry them. Everyone still counted on their fingers if the baby came too soon after the wedding, and abortion was illegal. But in New York, it was getting to be not such a big deal at all. Movie stars had babies out of wedlock all the time. Even the term "out of wedlock" was beginning to sound quaint. Even so, Norman Mailer having his eighth child with the sixth woman, to whom he wasn't married, still caused a flurry in the papers. There was a picture of Norman and me in *People* magazine at some party where the photographer had gotten down on the floor to get the best angle of my burgeoning belly, and of course everyone back home saw it. My parents were so ashamed. But Norman told

Mother and Daddy he loved me and he was going to marry me, and then he set about trying to do it.

The first thing he did was call Beverly, who at that time was living in Provincetown all year, and tell her he wanted to talk. She came to town, and Norman went downstairs to sit in the car with her and tell her about the baby and say that he finally wanted to get a divorce. I don't know why it was such a surprise. They hadn't lived together in eight years. Norman hadn't pushed her for a divorce before, he said, in spite of Carol having Maggie, because he'd known how ugly it would get, so he had just let things drift along as they were. Now he wanted to sort it all out and start afresh.

Beverly totally flipped out, and as he told me when he came back upstairs a little shaken, she had nearly run over him when he'd gotten out of the car. In Norman's telling, he'd leaned back in through the window to say something and she'd gunned the motor and driven off. He said he'd pulled his head out of the car just in time to keep from being decapitated. That started a legal battle that lasted for nearly three years. Of course, the newspapers and magazines were full of it, and since it was all being done on the Cape, we were constantly going back and forth to Barnstable.

Al Morrison's prediction about financial reversals proved to be accurate, too. We had seven children in private school or college, not to mention three alimonies, and had gotten so behind on our taxes that the IRS had taken a lien on the Provincetown house. Beverly considered it to be *her* house, and no matter what the IRS said, she was adamant that it would go to her in the settlement—along with the Brooklyn apartment and everything else Norman owned. She was basically asking for us to be out on the street with nothing. And 1978 was just around the corner, hanging over our heads. Well, over my head, since no one else knew about the prediction.

Norman had started working on a project with Larry Schiller about Gary Gilmore, the Utah convict who had murdered two people and been sentenced to death. He was the first person executed after ten years of a moratorium on executions in the United States, the first since 1958 in Utah. Gilmore had refused to appeal the decision, which caused a furor in the courts and the press, as no one had ever done that before. His attitude was, "You sentenced me to death. I've been accepting sentences all my life, I didn't realize I had a choice. Now you have to carry it out." The press was full of it. He was on the cover of *Time* and *Newsweek* and in every paper in every state. Gary Gilmore was shot to death on January 17, 1977, and Schiller had the rights to the story.

We were in Provincetown for a winter weekend not long after Gary had been executed, when Larry called and said he wanted Norman to write it. Larry had already done an incredible amount of work, securing rights to stories, doing interviews, and now Norman started going back and forth to Utah, meeting and interviewing Gary's uncle Vern and aunt Ida, his cousin Brenda and her husband Johnny, and all the lawyers and the families of the victims. I accompanied him to Utah a few times; we went skiing in the spring, and I finally managed to get down a mountain, not prettily, but without half killing myself, though after I got pregnant in July, I stayed in New York most of the time when he went.

With money so tight, I gave up my Willow Street apartment. I didn't mind, really, but my apartment had been a little place of refuge Matt and I had had that I now missed. With both Michael and Stephen living with us, the place was just too small. The boys were lively young teenagers, being pulled between their mother and father in the divorce, and they often took out their frustrations on Matt, who was so much younger. It was not a good time in our lives. I loved the boys, but had to protect my small son from their bullying. I don't think they ever really hurt him, but he was creative and sensitive, and they would sometimes do things like snatch away a drawing he was working on and tear it up, make fun of his Southern accent, or break his toys, which broke my heart.

The noise level was high most of the time, with music or the guitar or loud voices. Their friends were over a lot, and I couldn't keep them from climbing around the apartment. Once, Stephen and some of his friends were jumping into the hammock, ignoring my yelling at them to stop it, and one of the girls fell and hit her head. I rushed over to her, lying on the floor, and she looked up at me, smiled, and said, "I remember you. You were in my dream." Alarmed, I called her parents, who came and took her to the hospital, and she was ultimately fine, but my nerves were pretty shot, I have to say. I worried about what would happen when the baby arrived.

We had another addition to the circus at this time as well, Judith McNally, who became Norman's secretary and worked for him until her death in 2005. His previous secretary, Molly, and he had parted company, and it had not been amicable. She and her partner, Mary, who did Norman's typing, had decided they didn't like the Gary Gilmore project and had refused to work on it, so Norman had had to hire outside researchers and typists (while still paying Molly's and Mary's weekly salaries). That couldn't go on for long. Molly resented me as well, and went out of her way to let me know it. For example, if we were going on a trip, she would make Norman's airline reservation but not mine, so I had to call on my own and try to get on the same flight in a seat next to him. The final straw came when he had to go to California, and Molly, annoyed at him about something, routed him through Dallas, which had a three-hour layover, instead of booking a direct flight. He didn't check his ticket until he got to Dallas, and he inquired if there had been direct flights available. Of course there were. There were direct flights to L.A. from New York practically every hour. He called her from the airport and fired her, and she immediately wrote herself a check for the balance of his bank account, which was about three thousand dollars—not a vast amount, but real money for us in those days. And then she took a hammer and destroyed all the office equipment.

After that debacle, I tried to help him as much as I could. I took over paying the bills and other minutiae of running his life, a lot of which I was already doing—which might have been part of the problem with Molly. But the new Gilmore project, which he was calling *The Executioner's Song*, was too vast and he needed a full-time secretary and research assistant badly. He put a blind item in *The Village Voice*, "Well-known author seeks amanuensis."

"That'll weed out half of the people who have no idea what an amanuensis is, and the others will either look it up, which is good, or will already know, which is better." He received a big stack of résumés from *The Village Voice* post office box, we weeded them down to about ten or twelve, and called the finalists, who came in for interviews. A couple of them were possibilities, most were marginal, and one was simply unbelievable. She was a hefty blonde (a color found nowhere in nature) and she came for the interview wearing a low-cut short skintight black dress with black fishnet stockings and red spike-heeled shoes. This was just before Christmas, and I was already pretty big in the belly. I answered the doorbell, took one look at her, she looked at me, and she knew she had done the wrong thing. The interview didn't last long, that's for sure. Then, when we were about to despair, Judith McNally rang the bell. She was wearing a tidy gray wool suit with a little robin's-egg-blue blouse. Her long brown hair was pulled back into a bun. She was smart and thin and as crisp as a new package of crackers. And she lived only two blocks from us. She was perfect.

So the household was formed. In the daytime, Judith worked down in the little office on the floor below our apartment, Norman rented a studio down the street, and Myrtle was with us most days. Michael, Stephen, and Matt were in school, so it was quiet during the day, but at night it was chaos. The situation with Michael and Stephen wasn't improving, and I couldn't seem to get through to them. Norman didn't back me up at all. In fact, he was annoyed that I couldn't handle them, and blamed me for their misbehavior. It got to the point where something had to give.

I've always been able to express myself better in writing, and it seemed like nothing I said to Michael and Stephen had any effect, so I wrote them a heartfelt letter, asking them to be kinder to Matt and telling them how much I loved them and what good big brothers they could be to him if they only tried. I said they should try to look at it from his point of view. He had been taken from his home when he was three, where he'd been an only child, and brought to a place where he was one of eight children and his two older brothers teased him mercilessly. He was teased at school because he was dyslexic, and then teased at home. He was miserable, and I couldn't do anything to protect him.

I really think the letter helped. They hadn't seen themselves as being that bad, and to their credit they felt awful. Norman certainly thought the letter helped. Although nothing could dampen their energy and exuberance, I think they were kinder to Matt after that and stopped teasing him quite so much.

The trapeze hanging from the skylight rafter was one huge problem, though. It was right in front of the kitchen, and one boy or the other was always swinging through the house on it. I had to time my entrances and exits to the kitchen so I wouldn't be crashed into by a flying boy. Then one day, as Stephen was standing up on the trapeze bar in his socks, pumping, flying higher and wilder, he slipped off and flew into the air for real, crashed, and went skidding all the way across the living room floor. I dropped a cup of tea I was holding and ran to him, but he was fine, just shaken and bruised a bit.

Shortly after that, one of the ropes on the trapeze broke, fortunately not while someone was standing up on it. We never put it back up again. The tightrope had long been put away. And the rule about no friends jumping into the hammock was strictly enforced. It was just too dangerous. Finally, Beverly moved from Provincetown to Brooklyn Heights, a block away from us, and Stephen lived with her most of the time. Then Michael eventually went to Andover to boarding school. Now Michael and Stephen are my dearest loves and I don't know what I would do without them. Michael even produced Matt's first film, *The Money Shot*, and they have great affection for each other.

Matt on the trapeze.

PHOTOGRAPH BY JILL KREMENTZ

"Matt is so talented," Michael said while they were filming. "He's a great filmmaker."

"Mike's always there for me. He's a great producer," Matt said.

"Who are these people?" I said. Everyone is a teenager once, and everyone grows up.

Judith had been on the job just a few weeks when she came in one morning looking considerably different. We had slowly been getting to know each other, and I like to think there's nobody I can't talk to, from hillbillies to presidents, but she was hard to decipher. She was intensely private about her life, and while she did say she was single and lived alone, she had a boyfriend. Her usual office attire was something a little drab and colorless. Her hair had been a wren's-nest-brown, and she wore no makeup on her pale Irish skin. She was efficient and did her work with the minimum of talk, and while they weren't buddies, Norman had respect for her, and they were beginning to find their relationship.

I don't know what possessed her to make the change on this particular morning, but I sat up in my chair and almost spit out my coffee, because in walked Judith, with her long hair dyed a brilliant shade of red, best described as "*carnevale,*" and she was wearing Day-Glo pink spandex pants and a tight sequined T-shirt. She had painted her long fake nails a neon green, and her makeup matched the ensemble.

"Judith? Is that you?" Norman came out of the kitchen to stare, too.

"Well, I thought it was time to let you see the real me. I've started managing my boyfriend's group, and I've had to start looking the part." It was hilarious to hear Judith's precise, tidy voice coming out of the woman standing in front of us. Her boyfriend was in a duo that performed in punk rock clubs, and she had become part of that world. I can't remember if it was Judith who introduced us to Legs McNeil, a writer who started a magazine called *PUNK,* and coined the term for the music of the eighties. It might have been Martha Thomasas, another applicant for the secretarial job, whom Norman hired on a part-time basis for research, but we were soon introduced to a different kind of crowd.

Martha took us to CBGB's to hear Shrapnel, a band that Legs was friendly with, and the Ramones, whom nobody at that time except the hip underground crowd had heard of. On the night we went to CBGB's we wound up going back to the Ramones' apartment after the show and hanging out with them for a while. They were knocked out that Norman Mailer was there, and we were knocked out that we were there, too. The music was so loud that even with earplugs in our ears it was painful, and hanging out with them involved watching them drink and get stoned while we tried to have a conversation with them. Still, it was kind of fun to be able to say, "Oh, yes, I used to hang out with the Ramones."

When Sue and Marco got married a year or two later, we had Shrapnel come and perform at the party we gave. They were set up on the balcony above the kitchen and had a girl singer named Joey with them who was lovely but pallid; her hair was orange and her skin was the color of buttermilk. Her teeth were in need of attention. Her hands shook. I had a bad feeling about her, and with sorrow I heard that she overdosed some time after that.

Ultimately, Judith and the boyfriend broke up, she found one who was an executive for an envelope company, and her wardrobe went back to something a little more normal, although she kept the red hair and the fake nails. She was the most enigmatic woman I have ever met. She worked for Norman for twenty-seven years, and I don't think I ever really knew her.

WHEN I FIRST met Norman, he was having a feud with Gore Vidal. I'd never read Gore's books, and didn't know exactly why they were fighting, but his name kept coming up in stories and conversations with Norman's friends, and in the press. Then I found an old magazine, *Intellectual Digest*, October 1971, with an article by Gore, and I understood Norman's animosity. The article was originally written for *The New York Review of Books*, July 22, 1971. Gore was reviewing *Another Country*, by a feminist writer named Eva Figes, and out of nowhere he came and smacked Norman squarely in the face. To quote from the essay: "There has been from Henry Miller to Norman Mailer to Charles Manson a logical progression. The Miller-Mailer-Manson man (or M3 for short) has been conditioned to think of women as, at best, breeders of sons; at worst, objects to be poked, humiliated, killed."

The piece is littered with references to M3, as in, "M3 knows that women are dangerously different from men, and not as intelligent (though they have their competencies: needlework, childcare, detective stories)." Or, "Until recently, M3 was damned if a woman was going to be paid as much as he for the same job." He quoted from Norman's essay "The White Negro," taking it out of context to make it seem as though Norman was advocating the murder of women.

It was an ugly piece all around. Norman was not only enraged by the article—who, after all, wants to be compared to a crazy murderer, the most famous crazy murderer of the time?—but it also accused Norman of being anti-gay, which was astounding. "He [Norman] links homosexuality to evil. The man who gives in to his homosexual drives is consorting with the enemy." To be unfairly accused of being anti-homosexual—by a close homosexual friend, no less—was too much. Norman had lived in Provincetown for many years. Why would he have chosen to live in a place that was the gay mecca of the East if he thought homosexuals were evil? For the final five years of his life, Norman's assistant was gay, and a former assistant was a lesbian. Gay men have always been among our closest friends, as Gore himself once was one of Norman's.

After the article was published, Norman didn't speak to Gore until they were on the Dick Cavett show together a few months later. The show turned into a fiasco because Norman confronted Gore in the greenroom before they went on camera and butted his head (Norman was a famous head-butter in those days; his skull was like concrete), and there were some ugly comments back and forth on the air. Norman tried to talk about the article Gore had written comparing him to Charles Manson, but he got sidetracked by Gore and Dick, so he never got to fully explain why he was so angry. Gore acted as if he couldn't understand why Norman would take offense. Cavett seemed at sea as to what was happening, but he was clearly on Gore's side, as Norman was the aggressor, looking positively wild, and the audience was on Gore's side as well. Janet Flanner, an elderly author who was the third guest on the show, was in the middle, poor thing, seemingly afraid Norman was going to hit her when he leaned toward her to make a comment. The whole thing was jaw-droppingly bizarre, but instead of

Norman being able to get across why he was so mad at Gore, he just appeared to be *mad,* as in "as a hatter."

After the debacle of the Cavett show, he vowed if he ever saw Gore again, he was going to punch him. They managed not to run into each other for six years. Then one evening while I was pregnant, we were at the home of Lally Weymouth, Katharine Graham's daughter. I was wearing a long white maternity dress that had a draped Greek feel to it. I spotted Gore across the room and knew if Norman ran into him, there would be trouble, so I warned Norman that Gore was there. I thought he would leave the party, but instead he marched right over to Gore. They exchanged a few hot words, then Norman threw his drink in Gore's face. That wasn't quite enough, so he threw the glass as well. It bounced off Gore's head, and Gore sat down and was made much over by everyone, who grouped around him on the couch as if to shield him.

I'm not saying beaning Gore on the head with a heavy glass was something Norman should have done, I'm just saying he didn't do it for nothing. I stood a few feet away and watched (like a tall marble statue, someone at the party later said), horrified and helpless. Was there something I could have done to stop this? I don't think so. It had gone past any cajoling I could do. While Gore's essay might not have caused Norman's bad reputation with feminists, it had added gallons of fuel to the fire. We never understood why Gore had written it. The next day the incident at the party was in all the columns, and magazines such as *People* picked it up. Of course, we were never invited to Lally Weymouth's again, although she later said that it probably had made her reputation as a hostess.

Thirty-one

The baby was due on April 17, and I had gained sixty-five pounds. I was hungry all the time, and craved things like chocolate cheesecake from a bakery on Montague Street, ice cream, and hamburgers and french fries. I had starved myself so long while modeling that I went a little crazy, eating everything I wanted. Norman said that when I swept into a room wearing one of the big evening dresses Myrtle had made for me, I looked like a frigate in full sail. During the pregnancy, we hardly slowed down at all in our social life. It seemed there was a party almost every night, and Norman wanted to go to them all.

One night, when I was nearing my ninth month, we were at François de Menil's, whose family had one of the biggest and best art collections in the world. The house had more art than a lot of museums, with famous works hanging in every room. The crowd included actors and writers and artists such as George Segal, who zeroed in on me, came over, and straightaway started rubbing my belly. I took a step back. I really hated it when strangers took the liberty of petting my stomach like it was a cute little dog or something, and I knew Norman would go berserk if he saw it. But to the contrary, Norman came right up and said, "There is no other man in the world I'd let feel your belly besides George." George, of course, was the famous sculptor who did the plaster people, and I had admired him my whole teaching career. I always did a segment with my students using his techniques to make plaster masks and sometimes complete figures. (One memorable one was a man sitting on a child's tricycle.)

He was doing a series of pregnant women and asked me to pose for him. Naked. I wasn't inclined to do that, as I was due to give birth soon and I didn't like the idea of going into labor while encased in a plaster cast, not to mention the fact I was fat, but I promised I would do it later, and in fact I wound up posing for him several times. (Yes, sometimes naked. It was all totally professional, but nevertheless his wife, Helen, had timed his movements down to the second and would appear at the door just as he finished the last bit to see if we wanted tea or something. No fool, that woman.) If you're curious, you can see me in several of his books, one showing the steps to making a finished sculpture.

I left George talking to Norman and went poking around in the different rooms. There were several floors full of art to peruse, and I wandered into what looked like a small library. On one wall was a gigantic buffalo head. I stopped, my heart racing. I had never been close to a real buffalo before. I'd had no idea how big they were. This thing took up most of the room. Its shaggy coat was rough and soft at the same time. Its small glass eyes watched me, as if the rest of the buffalo were reclining, through a hole, on the other side of the wall in the next room. Norman and I had been trying to come up with a name for the baby, and we were seriously considering naming him Buffalo—why, I won't tell, as it has been a secret all these years, one that only John and I now know—so seeing the buffalo head was a portent of sorts.

As I communed with the buffalo head on the wall, a voice behind me said, "You are going to have a boy, and you are going to name him Buffalo." I jumped and whirled around. There hadn't been anyone in the room when I'd gone in. On the couch sat a small man, elderly, perhaps in his late seventies or more. He had longish white hair, was wearing a black three-piece suit, and his hands rested on a black gold-tipped cane. In my memory, he was wearing spats and had a bowler hat, but I think that is probably my imagination embroidering an already unbelievable scenario. I looked at him, speechless. He might have been the devil, or an angel, or a mystic, or just an old man with a wicked sense of humor and a cane. I didn't know and didn't want to know. I had always been afraid of everything that smacked of the supernatural, my Baptist roots still dug firmly into the ground. So without speaking or looking at the buffalo head again, I walked out the door. I didn't see the man at the party again, not on any of the floors of the house. But his voice stayed in my head. I can hear it still.

A few nights later, we went to a party hosted by Alice Mason, one of the biggest real estate mavens in New York. It was only two days before I was due to deliver. By that time, I was so huge I was uncomfortable, but I still put on a pair of stiletto sandals and a black-and-gold maternity dress the size of a pup tent and swept out the door. Alice was famous for her dinners. Wearing a red Galanos or some other beautiful designer dress, she and her daughter, Dominique Richard, gave a dinner every month as a thank-you to her clients, and invited interesting people. I always knew I would have a good seat at Alice's table, and we were regulars.

This night, it was too much to stand on those high heels during the cocktail hour, so I took my glass of ice water and sank into the couch, sighing with the effort. I put my feet up on the coffee table, hoping to ease the pain from the straps on the shoes biting into my swollen flesh. Dotson Rader came over and looked at me in horror. "Oh, lovey! Your poor feet!" he exclaimed. "Here, let me rub them." While it was a little embarrassing to be in the middle of a swanky party and have someone rubbing my feet, it felt really good. Just at that moment, Norman came charging over and said, "Take your hands off my woman's feet!" I thought at first he was kidding, but he was really upset. It was so sweet. He was jealous of Dotson! I do love Dotson, and always will, but it wasn't like we had a romance going. He was like my brother and my best friend. Dotson and I just gave each other a look, and he got up.

"You're going to have that baby tonight," he said.

"Oh, no, it's not due for two more days." I couldn't imagine the baby coming early. Matthew had been two weeks late. (I hadn't taken into consideration Norman's propensity for always being early, or Larry's for always being late. I think there must be something to that.) We got through the party, went home, got into bed around one, and at two in the morning I woke up needing to go to the bathroom. Before I could get out of bed, my water broke. I nudged Norman. "Wake up, sweetie. My water just broke."

"I know it did," he murmured. There was no way he could not have noticed. He was awash. "Just lay back down and take a little nap. It won't be coming for hours yet." And he turned over and tried to find a dry spot.

"Take a nap? Take a *nap*? You get up right this minute!" I yelled. "We have to get to the hospital, *now*!" I jumped out of bed and went into action. I called my doctor, I called Fanny to come over and stay with Matt and the boys, and then I began to clean up and get my stuff together. With my encouragement, Norman finally dragged himself out of bed and staggered to the bathroom, where he started to shave.

"Shaving? You're *shaving*? Get your clothes on and take me to the hospital *right now*!" I called the ever-ready Heights Car Service, and in five minutes a car with a driver named Snake was outside. Snake was happy; he had just won the lottery. The boys at the car service, who were such gamblers they would bet on which pigeon would take off first from the ledge, had had a little bet going on when I would deliver, and Snake had called it—April 16, the early morning shift. The rumor was that Snake had done time in prison, for what I never found out. He was taciturn, always had a cigarette hanging out of the corner of his mouth, and had homemade tattoos of snakes running up both arms. I always sighed with resignation when his car drove up, as it was not the most comfortable one, the springs popping through the seats, and I'd torn an evening dress or two on them, but this time I didn't care. He was going to have to clean up a little puddle of water.

We made it to New York Hospital in record time. Norman and I got out and walked to the admissions desk, water still dribbling down my legs, pooling on the floor. The woman in charge couldn't have cared less. When we told her we didn't have insurance, she said flatly she couldn't admit me. I was looking around for something to throw at her, but Norman happened to have a check on him, so on the spot he wrote a check for two thousand dollars. If we hadn't had the check or, God forbid, if we hadn't had two thousand dollars, I guess I would have had the baby right there in the waiting room. So up we went. By now it was around three or four o'clock and the pains had started in earnest. A nurse came in with a pan of water and a razor to shave me, but I wouldn't let her.

"There have been millions of women down through history who gave birth without having their twats shaved and their babies were fine. It's too awful when the hair grows back in. No. You can't do it." I'd had the worst time when I'd been shaved last time. I broke out in razor rash and itched like crazy for weeks, and there was just no reason for it. Was the baby going to choke on a hair or something? It was ridiculous. She was not amused.

"I'm going to have to call your doctor if you can't cooperate, Miss Church." She emphasized the Miss, I thought. That did it.

"So call him." She did, and the doctor said I didn't have to be shaved. She flung the water into the sink and left in a huff. It was now getting to be daylight, and the pains had intensified. Norman sat beside me, not knowing quite what to do, so he tried to distract me by telling me stories of all his other children's births, how all the other women had reacted. After about an hour of this, I asked him if he could just not talk for a while. That is one of the hardest things he has ever tried to do, just not talk. For want of something to do, he got up and fussed around my bed, trying to make me comfortable. I was up on my elbows, huffing and puffing, and he took my pillow and fluffed it up. Then he put his hand on my forehead and pushed, in an effort to try to get me to lie back on the pillow and relax. Of course, as I was up on my elbows, all he accomplished was cracking my neck. I'm afraid I yelled an ugly word at him and threw the pillow. Poor man. He didn't know where to put himself.

"I think I'll go down to the cafeteria and get some ham and eggs," he finally said, dying to get out of that room. Just at that moment, I had a tremendous pain, and the nurses came rushing in. I hadn't taken any anesthetic. I had been so drugged for the birth of Matt, and I wanted to be awake for this one. By that time the pains were pretty good ones.

"Oh, no you don't!" I yelled at Norman. "You're not going anywhere. This baby is coming right now!" And it was true. They rushed me next door to the delivery room, where the doctor was waiting. They got Norman into a gown and mask, and then the doctor took one look and said *"Push!"* and I pushed. It felt as if my body were being ripsawed in half. "It's almost here. Push one more time!" A steam whistle scream that I never dreamed could be inside me erupted, nearly shredding my throat, and the baby popped out like a watermelon seed. Instantly, the pain stopped. "It's a boy!" I knew it would be, of course. I'd known for years.

The doctor laid the baby on my belly as Norman stepped up to get a look at him. I'll never forget the look on his dear little face. It was as if a grown person, not an infant, were looking out at us. His eyes were clear, his mouth was in a little moue, with the top lip stuck out, and he frowned as he looked at the two of us, who were grinning at him like maniacs. He blinked at the lights and the room as if he were saying, "*What* the heck is going on? Who *are* these people? Where *am* I?" Then a light dawned on his face—"Oh. My. God! I'm a BAAAAABY!"—an astonished look that made everyone laugh.

They took him away to clean him and put silver nitrate drops in his eyes, which must have hurt like the dickens because he cried and squeezed his little eyes shut, and when he opened them again, he was truly a baby. The aware person had retreated somewhere inside and an infant was in his place. The afterbirth was one more pain, and then they cleaned me up and wheeled me to the recovery room. I told Norman he could go and get his ham and eggs, he had done his job brilliantly.

Baby John Buffalo with Norman and me.

PHOTOGRAPH BY JILL KREMENTZ

Thirty-two

We did name him Buffalo, as the old man had predicted. John Buffalo. The sturdy old name John balancing the peculiarity of the Buffalo. The origin of his name is his secret to keep or tell. He was a happy baby, and all his brothers and sisters loved him, as well as his nana Myrtle Bennett and his grandma Fanny. I once caught Fanny whispering in his ear, "You're going to be a great man one day." She turned to me a little sheepishly and said, "Well, I used to do that with his father, and it worked. So why not?"

I worried that the kids—Matt, particularly, who was six and a half—would feel displaced by John Buffalo, and I tried to compensate by doing special things with him. Matt and I went out to lunch every weekend, just the two of us, and to the Metropolitan Museum to visit the knights, or the American Museum of Natural History for the dinosaurs, or to a movie, and to antique-toy stores, where we bought old G.I. Joes for him and antique Barbies for me. Matt never appeared to be in the least jealous. He was a terrific big brother from the beginning. The first night we brought John Buffalo home from the hospital was a chilly April evening, and Matt kept going to look at the baby, worried he would be cold. Finally, he came in and said, "I wrapped the baby up. He was cold." He proudly led me in to see how nicely he had done it, and the baby was wrapped head to toe in a blanket, which I immediately threw off so he could get some air. I explained to Matt that you had to leave a little space for his nose so he could breathe.

Matt carried him around, helped me feed him, and played with him constantly. As they got older, he made up games for them to play. He took paper bags and made hats and they played Civil War or Revolutionary War (although John always had to be the rebels and the British), and they played G.I. Joe endlessly. Matt had a collection of the bigger Joes, and John desperately wanted one, so I made Matt give him one of his treasured Joes. John promptly tore its arms off, and I felt terrible, remembering once when my father made me give away my beloved Barbie to a little girl who was dying. He thought I was too old for dolls, and it would be a good, Christian thing for me to do, but I loved that Barbie and I didn't even get the moral credit, because I didn't really want to give it to her. You can't force your kids to be generous if they don't want to be. But for the most part, John and Matt were best friends from day one and are still.

John and Matt.
PHOTOGRAPH BY
JILL KREMENTZ

My parents softened after the baby arrived, and finally came to see him when he was four months old. I was changing his diaper when they walked in the door, so I scooped him up and brought him out, diaperless, to show them. I proudly held him up, and John let go a long arc of golden pee right onto my father's spotless shirtfront. Daddy laughed with delight and took the baby. And I never heard them say another word about how I had disgraced them.

Norman's divorce from Beverly rocked on, frustratingly slow. It was a worry hanging over us, disrupting our lives. We had to plan everything around the long trips to the Cape, the delays, the canceled court dates. The year 1978 was half over, and then it was three-quarters over. I had only a few more months of worrying about Norman's dying. Then one day, the courtroom drama turned particularly bad. Norman had been under a lot of pressure going back and forth to Utah, the IRS was about to take the house and sell it at auction, and the

My daddy, Matt, and John Buffalo.

newspapers were still reporting every little thing that was said in court. On this day, Beverly was recounting something that Norman thought was a total misrepresentation, and he started having an anxiety attack. He was having difficulty breathing, so he got up and walked out of court, me right after him. We sat on the stone steps of the courthouse and he unbuttoned his shirt collar, loosened his tie, and said he felt like he was having a heart attack. Oh, God. This was it. This was going to be the moment he died, and I would be left with a tiny baby and all the responsibilities and he would still be married to Beverly. "I'm going to call a doctor," I said.

"No. Don't leave me. Just sit here and let me get my breath." He was as pale as new milk curd, and his face was slick with sweat. I desperately wanted to get some help, but he was adamant. He took my hand and looked into my eyes. "Listen to me. If I go today, or anytime soon, I want you to finish *The Executioner's Song*." What? Me? "I know you can do it. In spite of what you think, I know you can write. I've got the research all laid out, and Judith can help you. It's almost finished. It's a simple style that you can do. You know you can. Promise me you'll finish the book." I'd given up on my novel, but he had read plenty of my letters, from the one to Michael and Stephen to ones I wrote to him all the time. If I ever had anything serious to talk about, I always wrote him a letter. I knew that way he would hear me. If I just talked to him, his mind would be racing to his next reply, or he wouldn't really hear what I was saying and we would have a fight. But if it was on the page, I knew he would get every nuance. "I promise I'll do my best, sweetie, but you are going to finish that book yourself. Let me get you some water." I went and got him a cup of water, and after a while he began to feel better. We went back in, and somehow he got through the rest of the day.

HE DID FINISH the book, and in April 1980 it won the Pulitzer Prize, his second, which gave him an emotional boost, to put it mildly. Then, in late October, after nearly three years, the divorce war was over. Beverly got a little too much for Norman's taste, not quite enough for hers, but it was done. We kept our apartment and he bought her another one in Brooklyn Heights. Rather than seizing the Provincetown house, the IRS had given Norman a chance to sell it and pay them off. After the taxes were paid, he was going to give Beverly half of what was left, and put his half into a college fund for Michael and Stephen, but she wouldn't agree. She still wanted the house, free and clear. Finally, it seemed the lawyers had convinced Beverly of the urgent need to sell, and on the appointed day, Norman, taking Michael with him, went to the lawyers' office to sign the papers. Beverly didn't show up. The sheriff had to come to the house and forcibly remove her, which of course was in all the papers, and the IRS took the house and put it up for auction. (Coincidentally enough, a relative of the IRS agent had the winning bid for the house, which was about half of its appraised worth. What a small world! I mean, what are the chances?) What was left barely covered the tax debt. There was no college fund. But Norman was at last free to marry. Again.

Thirty-three

"MARRIAGE-GO-ROUND! Norman Mailer is not a cheap bigamist," the papers screamed, "he's a TRIGAMIST!" It seemed that every week I was calling my mother and father in Arkansas to say, "I hate to have to tell you this, but before you read it in the papers . . ." and I'd relate the latest in the ongoing saga of my life with Norman. Although Norman's divorce from Beverly was final, she didn't like the settlement and was suing for more money. It seemed to me that in her mind that meant she was still married to Norman until he gave her what she wanted. Fortunately, the law said differently, so we started making plans for the wedding. Or *weddings,* as it were, as Norman was going to marry *two* women, hence the trigamist headlines.

On Friday, November 7, Norman was going to marry Carol, to legitimize their daughter, Maggie, who was at that time nine. He would fly alone to Haiti the same night to get a divorce on Saturday (we'd researched it, Haitian courts grant quick divorces and are open on the weekends), then fly back on Sunday and marry me on Tuesday, November 11. Which was also Veterans Day, an appropriate coincidence, as he was certainly a veteran of the marital wars.

I'm not going to pretend Carol and I were all sweetness and light about this arrangement. I was in favor of him adopting Maggie to make her his legal daughter, while Carol had made it clear she would prefer to be married to him longer, for a year or so, and then "quietly" divorce, as if that would be possible with the ravenous press, but that was not his plan. He felt bad that he hadn't divorced Beverly years ago when Carol had gotten pregnant, and he wanted to marry Carol to "honor their years together." He didn't want Maggie to be his only child whose mother he had never married, even if it was for only twenty-four hours. I truly sympathized with Carol—she hated publicity and was intensely private about her life, and now she was right in the middle of this media frenzy—but when you fall in love with somebody like Norman Mailer, you have to understand publicity is a given.

Since divorce papers can't be signed before a marriage, Norman had to trust that Carol would go along with the plan and sign the divorce agreement immediately after the wedding ceremony. The press was having a fine old time, constantly calling the house (every wire service in the Turkmen Republic and such places had our home phone number, it seemed), so Norman thought the best thing to do would be to call Liz Smith, who was a dear friend and the fairest columnist there ever was, give her quotes, and that would defuse the others. I think I told Liz something like, "Of course it is all a bit disconcerting, but I understand why Norman wants to do this, and I am in support of him." And I was, finally. Really. It would have been horrible for Maggie to be the only child whose mother was never married to her father, and his years with Carol had lasted longer than some of the other marriages. Besides, Carol had never caused Norman a lot of headaches or publicly gone after him for more money or said ugly things about him in the press, as some of the others had, and she deserved better.

Still, as I watched him walk out the door that Friday night, I had a brave face, but I knew he was on his way to marry a woman he still had feelings for. (He would always have feelings for her. It was something I learned to live with, like arthritis.)

After I had a loud, cleansing cry, I layered on the makeup, put on one of my best dresses, and went out to meet Louie Cabot and his then wife, Maryellen, who had kindly invited me to the ballet that night. Rudolf Nureyev was dancing, the first time I had ever seen him, and we sat in the front row, where I had an unimpeded view of his powerful musculature and graceful moves. That pleasure aside, I vowed never again to sit in the front row. It took all the magic out of the show. We were privy to the grunts of the dancers as they jumped and executed difficult moves; we saw the sweat fly from their faces; and the shoes that from afar seemed a part of the foot, so soft and pliable, clattered alarmingly loud across the stage. I prefer to be farther back and imagine that the dancers are magically flying. At any rate, it was a diversion from the business that was transpiring at just that moment with Norman and Carol, who were being married by a friend of ours, Judge Shirley Fingerhood, in her offices. They had written their own vows, which were on the order of, "I want to honor the years we have spent together and the love that created this beautiful child, Maggie." I'm sure if I had been there I would have been weeping.

After the ballet, I came home and checked on my sleeping children. Then I went to bed. Alone in our room, I lay awake, wondering if Carol would indeed allow him to marry me, or if she had changed her mind and decided to be Mrs. Mailer for a while and let me stew, as she had stewed for the past ten plus years while he was married to Beverly or living with me. But my worrying was for nothing. She signed the papers. Carol was a decent woman, and she knew that I, too, had a small child who was waiting to be legitimized.

Norman came back from Haiti two days later, Sunday, with the promise that the decree would be delivered on Monday. We couldn't plan a wedding without the divorce papers in hand, and we had tickets to fly to London on Tuesday night, where Norman was acting in the movie *Ragtime* for Milos Forman, playing the architect Stanford White. I didn't dare even tell anyone the wedding might happen. I let it be known that we would probably get married when we got back from London. Norman had secretly gone by himself on Monday morning to Tiffany's and bought me a ring, one that made my heart sink when he presented it to me with a flourish. It was a thin band of tiny alternating diamond and ruby stones, which seemed to me like the cheapest ring he could find. It wasn't my style at all. I am a big girl with big artist's hands, and a ring that delicate was just not something I would have picked for a wedding ring. Although I didn't want to be ungracious, I let my feelings be known. I couldn't help it.

"Why couldn't you have just bought a plain gold band? That would have been much better than this. I don't care about diamonds [which was a big fat lie, I'd been hoping for one], but I am not going to wear these teeny diamond chips. And I hate rubies. Have you ever once seen me in a red piece of jewelry? Don't you know me at all? How do I take my coffee?"

"Your coffee? What does that have to do with anything?"

"Do you know how I take my coffee in the morning?"

"I don't know. Black?"

"*You* take yours black! I drink it with milk and sugar. See, you've never even noticed. You don't know the smallest thing about me." I was in tears, for a lot of reasons that had nothing to do with the ring or the coffee, I'm sure. He was furious that I was being ungracious about his choice of ring, so in a foul humor, we went back to Tiffany's to change it. We were so angry with each other that he walked down one side of the street and I the other. As a compromise, we got a plain gold band and added another little diamond and ruby band as a guard on either side, which made it look more substantial. Then we went back home and waited. There was nothing all day, then late Monday afternoon, the doorbell rang. It was the papers from Haiti.

Tuesday morning dawned, a cold, bright November day, and I woke up early to find Norman sitting on his side of the bed holding his head in his hands. I studied him with sleepy eyes. He looked so depressed. A feeling of woe came off him, as if he would rather do anything today than go through another marriage; as if he were thinking he couldn't keep on having children with women and marrying them, there had to be a stopping place. The woe crept into me. I thought, "Maybe I should tell him to forget the whole thing." Maybe he was sorry he had left Carol and wanted still to be with her. Maybe he just didn't want to be married at all, to have no responsibilities and do as he pleased. I had been looking forward to this day for years, but if even a little part of him didn't want to marry me, then I didn't want to marry him.

"Sweetie? What's the matter? Are you okay?"

"All my life, all I have ever wanted was to be free and alone in Paris." He said it so sadly. I was right. He didn't want to marry me. Should I offer to step aside and let him go to Paris? Was that what he really wanted? I leaned up on my elbow and gently put my hand on his arm.

"Look, sweetie. What would happen if you were free and alone in Paris? You would be walking down one of the boulevards and you'd sit at a sidewalk café to have a cup of espresso. A pretty girl would walk by and you would give her one of your twenty-five-cent smiles. She would smile back and stop to talk. You would invite her to sit and buy her a cup of coffee. You'd go to a museum, and then take her out to dinner. Soon she would be living with you, and then she would get pregnant, and you wouldn't be free and alone in Paris anymore, would you?"

John Buffalo, two and a half, came in, sleepy-eyed, climbed into bed with us as he did every morning, and snuzzled down under the covers. Norman laughed and said, "You know me too well. It's scary. Okay. Let's go get married and legitimize this little bugger."

Norman, me, and the "little bugger" Buffalo.

So we kicked it into high gear. I called my mother and daddy and my closest friends. Pat Lawford sent over a case of champagne. Jan Cushing, who was my eight-months-pregnant matron of honor, had a wedding cake delivered. I ran out and bought a champagne-colored satin suit, and Judith got on the phone with our other friends and family. "What are you doing today at five? Want to come to a wedding?"

Norman and I rushed to get the marriage license. David Dinkins (later the mayor) was the city clerk who gave it to us. We invited him to the wedding, as well as Mayor Ed Koch, both of whom came. Everyone came. It was all a big crazy blur of our friends and family. Michael, unfortunately, was away at school in Andover and Sue was in Mexico, but most of the kids were there. Matt and John Buffalo, of course, Betsy, Kate, and Danielle. Stephen, fourteen at the time, was the best man. John wore a little burgundy velvet sailor suit with a white satin collar. During the ceremony he kept asking, "When are we going to cut the cake?"

We hadn't thought about pictures at all, but Dotson wanted to take pictures, and the only film we had in the house was an old Polaroid camera, which jammed after the first one, so our only wedding picture was of me, Norman, and Father Pete Jacobs in the kitchen after the ceremony. Norman looks like he is in shell shock, I am smiling so wide my face is about to crack, and Father Pete looks worried because he

Norman, me, and Father Pete Jacobs at the wedding.

was always in trouble with his church. He couldn't marry us, of course, because Norman was Jewish and I was Baptist—forget our checkered marital pasts—but he was a friend and we wanted him to do something, so he read a poem—for which he was reprimanded when his church found out. A rabbi named David Glazer performed the actual ceremony, and for years I heard he told everyone we were members of his congregation. I was so grateful to him, I didn't even care. If he had asked us to join his temple, I would have.

It would have been nice if my parents had been able to come, but they were so thrilled that we were finally getting married, it didn't matter. I was no longer the tootsie; I was the wife. What a difference it made, not just in my feelings, but in the way the world treated me. Now we got invitations to Mr. and Mrs. Norman Mailer, not Norman Mailer and guest. I could say "my husband"; I was Mrs. Mailer when I called a restaurant for reservations; I had the same last name as my son. A hundred little things changed with the signing of one piece of paper. We had been living together for more than five years, talking about it every single day, and finally we were married. I had never been so happy.

We left the guests eating cake and drinking champagne, and off we went for a week in London. I spent my wedding night, high over the Atlantic Ocean, staring at my wedding rings, which sparkled in the overhead reading light. I had changed my mind about the tiny rubies and diamonds. Never underestimate small stones. They have their fire, too.

The morning after our arrival, I was as emotionally worn out by everything that had preceded the trip as I was by the jet lag. Norman had to get up early and be at Shepperton Studios by seven o'clock to shoot his big scene, but I was going to sleep all day if I could. He had been gone only a short while when the phone rang. It was Milos Forman.

"Norris, are you asleep? I'm sorry, but can you come out here at once? Norman is in a scene where he is enjoying a show of dancing girls, and he just pointed out that Stanford White would not be at a table alone at such an event. He would have a beautiful woman there with him. I want you to be that woman. I want you to be in the picture."

I jumped out of bed, threw on clothes, and ran out to the waiting car. The movie was based on the book *Ragtime* by E. L. Doctorow, which was set in 1906 and centered on the killing of the famous architect Stanford White by socialite Harry K. Thaw, who was married to Evelyn Nesbit, a former showgirl and ex-lover of White's. Thaw discovered Evelyn was not a virgin on their wedding night, and she then implied that White had raped her at age sixteen. Thaw became obsessed with the architect and finally shot him at close range in Madison

Square Garden, which White had designed, in the middle of a show, *Mamzelle Champagne*.

I was to play the girl at the table with Stanford White, his date of the moment, and as soon as I got to the set, they hurried me into period costume and did up my long hair into a Gibson Girl do, and there I was,

Norman and me in the scene from Ragtime.

guzzling ginger ale champagne with Norman at the table while Donald O'Connor led the chorus girls in a song called "I Could Love a Thousand Girls." It was a tricky scene, as Norman/Stanford gets shot and killed. He had been outfitted with a small blast pack taped to a metal plate that protected his head—underneath a wig that looked like his hair—and was attached to a tube that snaked down his neck, under his clothes, and ended under the table, where a special effects man was waiting to pump fake blood out the head wound and onto the floor. They could do only two takes, as they had only two wigs and suits of clothes, so it had to go perfectly. Norman was to stand, turn, and fall with his right side next to the floor so the tubing wouldn't show. My job was to kneel beside him and scream bloody murder. The rehearsals went fine, and they packed Norman's ears with wax and cotton so the sound from the blast wouldn't damage his hearing.

"Action," Milos called out, and the band started the song; the dancers began to dance. I took a sip of my ginger ale and laughed with Norman/Stanford, who was wearing a big bushy mustache, the only thing on him that looked at all like the real White. Thaw, played by Robert Joy, rushed up with a maniacal look on his face, shot the gun, the blasting cap went off, and Norman stood, turned, and fell perfectly. The only thing that went wrong is that when he fell, he whacked his head on the heavy silver champagne bucket next to the table and there was a real cut with real blood coming out of his forehead. I was screaming my heart out, looking at the real wound, and then Milos said, "Cut! That was perfect." Norman didn't move. I nudged him. "Norman? The scene is over. You can get up." He remained perfectly still. I thought he had knocked himself out on the champagne bucket for real, and started shaking him. He resisted me, trying to remain motionless. Finally, Milos came over and yelled, "Norman! It's okay! The scene is over." Norman couldn't hear him and thought I'd just been overacting. He'd been trying to remain dead. I was never so relieved to see someone open their eyes. We got him cleaned up and did a second take just in case, but the first take was the one they kept. Our honeymoon had started with a bang.

Thirty-four

Soon after publication of *The Executioner's Song,* Norman wrote a script for a four-hour NBC miniseries that was based on the book. I had left the modeling agency after Wilhelmina had tragically died of lung cancer in 1980. I'd then signed up with William Morris, thinking I needed a real acting agency, especially after my spectacular screaming performance in *Ragtime.* Who knew where that might lead? I was studying acting at Herbert Berghof Studio in the Village, and while my agent had sent me on several auditions, I hadn't gotten many parts, just a couple of day player bits on soap operas—parts called "under fours" because they were under four lines of dialogue. *The Executioner's Song* was a perfect opportunity for me to continue my acting career. The only problem was that there was only one small part that might even be feasible for me in the movie, the role of a girl named Lu-Ann who worked in a factory and had gone out on a date with Gary Gilmore when he'd first gotten out of prison. She was not a particularly attractive girl. She was a bit sour with a no-nonsense approach to life, but they have a date, Gary gets drunk on beer and tries to put the make on her, she lectures him, like a schoolmarm, on having to work for what he gets, and he scares her.

Larry Schiller, who was directing the film, said I was too glamorous for the part; he wouldn't even let me read for it. But I *had* to be in the movie, I just had to! Like Lucy Ricardo, I was going to weasel myself into the movie or bust. If Larry thought I was too beautiful, then I would show him. I have never, at least not while compos mentis, gone out in public without my makeup on, but on this day I not only didn't put on makeup, I greased my face with cream to make my complexion shiny and ugly, and I combed my hair in the style that used to be beloved by poor Arkansas girls in the fifties. The top half of it was piled in a kind of biscuit thing held up by bobby pins, and the bottom hung down long, with a white part separating the two halves. The girls who wore it usually had bangs, too, and little spit curls in front of their ears, but I didn't go that far. I cut off a pair of jeans and put on a baggy blouse with elastic around the neck, and flip-flops. I didn't even recognize myself.

Then I went up to the Helmsley Palace on Madison Avenue, where Larry was staying. The men at the desk immediately came out to greet me, and I asked for Larry Schiller. They asked my name, and I said Lucille McGillicuddy. I said I was an actress, there for an audition. They stepped over to the side and had a little confab, while I looked them and the place over, like it was the first time I'd ever seen a big hotel, or anybody wearing a necktie, for that matter. Finally, they must have decided to let Larry deal with it rather than risk a scene, so they let me into the elevator and I rode up to the fifth floor and knocked on his door. He opened it and looked me full in the face for an entire minute or more, uncomprehendingly, until I started laughing. Then it dawned on him who I was, and he grinned that possum grin of his and said, "You have the part."

We started filming in Utah in the fall of 1981, with Tommy Lee Jones playing Gary Gilmore and Rosanna Arquette playing his girlfriend, Nicole. Tommy Lee would go on to win an Emmy for this performance, but he played Gary as an exuberant boy who just got let out of detention rather than as the depressed, psychotic man I think Gary actually was. Convicts speak of flattening time in jail, and if you flatten enough time, you, yourself, become flat, but it was Tommy Lee's choice to make him manic, and it worked for the film in the end.

In our scene, we start in the bar and then go for a drive in my car. We were filming in November, although it was supposed to be summer, and it was freezing that night. I was dressed in a short-sleeved thin top, and Tommy Lee was wearing a T-shirt with the sleeves cut out. They had done my hair up in a beehive and used blue eye shadow and red lipstick. I looked better than I had at the Helmsley Palace, but not by much. In the bar scene, Tommy Lee was drinking real beer, and by the time we had moved to the car, he was feeling pretty relaxed. He had just gotten married, and his wife, Kim, was there that night. I remember her standing on the sidewalk and waving as we drove by, and him saying, "Look at her in those little bootsies. Isn't she a cutie?" She was indeed a cutie, and I was happy he was so in love. It was so cold that both of us were shivering in our summer outfits, and between takes we grabbed our coats from the backseat and huddled under them for warmth. We had to suck on ice cubes so our breath wouldn't fog in the air, which only made us colder. At some point, someone brought us cold Chinese food, which we ate for dinner, and by the end of the night, Tommy Lee had gone through I don't know how many cans of beer. The last take, where he gets angry and throws the beer can out the window, was verging on being really scary. But we had it.

Thirty-five

When word first got out that Norman was writing a book about Gary Gilmore, he started getting letters from prisoners. A lot of them. Most were on the order of "Why are you wasting your time on that bum Gilmore when my story is so much better?" (P.S. They all were innocent.) One letter he got was different. The guy said that he knew Gilmore, and if Norman wanted to know what being in prison was really like, he was the one to tell him. It was signed Jack Henry Abbott, and Norman showed it to me and said it was surprisingly well written. I never intruded into Norman's writing or research unless he asked me to read something, but I hated the whole idea of him getting so involved in the lives of prisoners. I felt like all of them were con men. Still, Norman and Jack started a correspondence, and Norman found Jack's letters to be most helpful for *The Executioner's Song*.

Over time, more and more letters came from Jack, one or more nearly every day. Jack described how life in prison worked, the brutality, the relationships with the guards, how you had to demand respect, how you were either a stand-up guy or a punk. The lowest level of person in prison was the snitch. Most snitches didn't live long. In due course, Norman told Jack he thought the correspondence could make an interesting book. Norman would write a preface for it. The book was called *In the Belly of the Beast*, and others thought it was worthy of publication as well.

Jason Epstein, Norman's editor, brought it to Random House, where Erroll McDonald, another editor there, took it on as a project. The novelist Jerzy Kosinski was also interested in Jack and had corresponded with him for years. Bob Silvers, the editor and one of the founders of *The New York Review of Books*, Lionel Abel, the essayist, and other major players in the publishing world also championed Jack's writing. They compared him to Jean Genet, a French convict who turned his life around and became a successful novelist and playwright. Genet had been helped by Jean Cocteau, Jean-Paul Sartre, Pablo Picasso, and other prominent artists in France. In much the same spirit, Jack's admirers wrote to the Utah parole board saying they thought Jack was a real talent who could have a career as a writer. They all would help him.

Jack was due for a regular parole hearing, but nobody seriously thought he was going to be let out. He was a career criminal whose Chinese mother had been a prostitute and his father a G.I. who had abandoned them. He was a troublesome boy and went to reform school when he was about twelve; his mother committed suicide somewhere along the line, and he became what they called a state-raised child. After reform school, he went to prison in 1963, when he was nineteen, for breaking into a shoe store and stealing checks, which he then wrote out to himself. Three years into that sentence, he killed an inmate in a knife fight and was given an additional sentence of three to twenty years.

In 1971 he escaped from a Utah prison and held up a bank in Denver, but he was caught the next month and got another sentence of nineteen years. He had a record of psychiatric testing that pronounced him paranoid with the potential for sudden violence. At one trial, he leaped out of the witness box and grabbed a juror's throat. In another instance, he stabbed a doctor in the nose with a sharpened ballpoint pen. The doctor had been sewing up the arm of a prisoner whom Jack had just knifed. At the time he was writing to Norman, he was thirty-six and had spent all but nine months of the past twenty-two years behind bars, fifteen of those in solitary confinement.

I learned these facts much later from an article in *The New York Times* by M. A. Farber, but at the time Norman didn't confide anything at all about Jack or his past to me, and I'm not sure exactly how much he knew. I was opposed to any help Norman was proposing to give Jack, and any discussion always ended in a fight. I hadn't read Jack's letters, and I certainly didn't know Norman had offered Jack a job as his research assistant, or just how committed he was to supporting him, but when we found out Jack was getting out of prison, neither of us was really expecting it. In fact, I didn't know about it until one night when I was cooking dinner. Norman put on his trench coat and told me from the open doorway that he was going to the airport to pick up Jack.

"I've invited him for dinner, honey. It's his first night out of jail, and I think he should have a good home-cooked meal, but don't worry, you won't have to see him again." I was practically speechless. But not quite.

"What are you going to do with him? Are you supposed to take care of him and babysit him? He's not going to know anybody, and who knows what he'll do? I'm not having him over here around the kids, that's for sure. Didn't you learn anything from writing about Gary Gilmore? Somebody who has been in prison his whole life can't just change and be a normal person overnight. I wish you had talked to me about this."

"Then we would have argued for weeks instead of a few minutes. I think he can make it. He's talented. His book is going to do well, I know. He'll have plenty of people to help him. Frankly, I was as surprised as you were when they told me he was getting out this early. I thought the chances of him getting parole were slim. I don't know what happened. But now I've got to go get him. So, please. Just let him come tonight, and then you will never have to see him again. I promise. Please?"

I was on the landing watching as Jack climbed the three flights of stairs to our apartment. I saw the top of his head first, the hair neatly parted down the middle. He was wearing a dark blue pin-striped suit with a vest, a white shirt, and red tie, and little round glasses. It was a color Xerox of what Norman wore all the time. He came up to the door, smiled, and stuck out his hand. "I'm Jack," he said. He was about as tall as I am, slim, neat, and nervous. I couldn't tell what his ethnicity was. He had a slightly exotic look, with tan skin, and was much more attractive than I had anticipated. I wasn't afraid of him at all. In fact, there was something rather moving about him, dressed up in his Norman suit with those little glasses.

John Buffalo, who was about two and a half at the time, came running out of his room, straight up to him. Jack introduced himself and held out his hand, which John shook. "Hi, Jack. I'm John Buffalo, but they call me Buffy. Want to see my toys?" He took Jack's hand and led him to his bedroom, where he started to show him all his G.I. Joes. Jack sat on the edge of the bed and talked to him for quite a while, looking at his figures. I kept an eye on them. Then I said dinner was ready, and we all sat down to eat, Norman, me, John, Matt, and Jack. He ate every scrap on his plate and had seconds. I think it was roast chicken and mashed potatoes, and Jack said it was the best meal he had ever had in his life. The thought passed through my head that it might well have been, and that made me sad.

Norman and he did most of the talking, and I could see Norman intimidated him a bit. Still, he had his own intellect, and if he disagreed with Norman, he wouldn't hesitate to say so. He had brought an advance copy of his book, and after he ate, he asked if he could give it to me. He wrote, "To Norris, who gave me my first home-cooked meal; introduced me to the great Buffy! love, Jack." He was staying at a halfway house on the Bowery, and I called a taxi to take him there. He could learn the subway another night.

Norman went to see him the next day, to make sure he was settled and everything was okay. Jack had meetings with his editor, Erroll McDonald, and others at Random House, and the book was due to be published July 18, in about six weeks. He started calling us every day, and usually it was me who picked up the phone because Norman was at his studio, working. Sometimes Jack just wanted to chat, or ask for advice, such as, where did he go to buy toothpaste? Where did he get stamps? He asked if I would go shopping with him, as he had almost no clothes, so we went to Macy's, and it was so overwhelming that he almost couldn't function. Just buying a pair of jeans was monumental. "Is there somebody who issues them to you?" he said, eyes wide, looking at the stacks and racks of clothes.

"No. You just find your size in something you like and go try them on. Over there, in the dressing rooms."

"You mean they let you take and try these on? With nobody watching?"

It was a concept he could hardly grasp. We picked out a couple of pairs of jeans and a few shirts and T-shirts. Then we went to a coffee shop for lunch. Again, he seemed at sea, looking at the menu.

"So what do you want, Jack? You can have anything you want. I'm treating today. There's burgers, eggs, soup, pasta. You can get meat loaf or chicken. Order anything you want."

"What are you having?"

"I think I'll have a hamburger deluxe, with tomato and onion and french fries."

"I'll have what you're having." He always had what I was having whenever we went out. Any choice was overload for his system. I was determined not to get involved with him, but Norman had little time or inclination to go shopping with Jack, or answer his questions—there were so many. If Jack was supposed to be a research assistant, the job never materialized. It was all Jack could do to navigate through his days. I don't think he would have been capable of taking on job responsibilities as well, and I couldn't imagine having him around the apartment all day.

One day the phone rang and it was Jack, in a total rage. Someone at the halfway house had stolen his shoes, his new black lace-up shoes like Norman's. He was going to find the thief and kill him. I got scared. There was something in his voice that said he wouldn't hesitate to do just that. I had already seen flashes of Jack's temper. Once, we went to the Metropolitan Museum, and he was smoking a cigarette when we walked up to the door. The guard said, "Put that cigarette out." It wasn't an angry voice, but not particularly friendly, and I saw Jack tense, as if he were about to punch the guard. I said, "Hey, Jack, you know nobody gets to smoke in the museum. It's not personal." He put out the cigarette, but kept glaring back at the guard.

Another time, we stopped at a newspaper kiosk to buy cigarettes. The man was rushed and slapped the change down a little too hard on the counter. Again, Jack tensed, as if the man had personally threatened him. Again, I had to explain that in New York, people were just in a hurry, they weren't out to offend anyone, it was nothing. But the hair trigger of his temper was always cocked; he was on the lookout for anyone who might disrespect him.

After a couple of weeks of this, it frankly got to be too much for me. I couldn't go on babysitting Jack every day. I had the kids, I was painting and showing at the time, still taking my acting classes, and I had the house to run, not to mention Norman's and my social life. I had a dear friend, I'll call her Gretchen, who I enlisted to go with us on some of the outings. I wasn't trying to set her up with Jack as a romance, Lord knows. I just needed someone else to be a friend to him, to help me as a buffer so I wasn't always alone with him, and Gretchen was unmarried and had the time. The three of us went out to a few places. She did like him, and he liked her.

I had no idea what was going to happen to Jack in the long run. I just wanted him to get from one day to the next without any major troubles. Soon after the shoe-stealing business, his suit went missing as well. Again Jack called, in hysterics, but soon after, he called back and told me the director of the halfway house had only taken it for safekeeping. Still, he was angry the director would do that without asking him, and I worried he was going to try to hurt the man. There was the feeling of lava boiling down inside Jack, and I was certain that one of these days something was going to cause it to erupt.

When he had been in New York a couple of weeks, we had our first dinner party with Jack. We invited Pat Lawford, Dotson Rader, and Norman's old friend and mentor, Jean Malaquais, and his daughter, Dominique, who was about fifteen at the time. Jack had read some of Dotson's books, and agreed with his radical left position about the Vietnam War and the government. Dotson later said he thought Jack might be gay because of the direct way he stared, unblinking, into his eyes, which is sometimes construed to be sexual interest—or it might have been the prison code for intimidation, or a way of keeping himself from being intimidated, as Jack was certainly intimidated at that dinner. Dotson said Jack seemed like the repairman who came to fix the fridge and then was asked to stay to dinner. He clearly didn't belong. Norman, uncharacteristically, seemed to be holding back, letting Jean Malaquais take control of the conversation. Pat hung out in the kitchen with me while I cooked, but at the table, she joined in the discussion, at first a little hesitantly.

Jack considered himself a Marxist, like Jean, and the two of them got along well. But then Jean started criticizing America, our foreign policy, the "imperialist culture," on and on. He had nothing but bad things to say. Jack ratcheted it up a notch, calling America a fascist hellhole run by pigs, and so on. Pat, who of course was President Kennedy's sister, was now furious. I had told her who was coming for dinner, but I don't think she fully realized who Jack was, or that a convicted felon can't vote. She turned on Jack and said, "When did you last vote?"

"I don't vote," Jack replied.

"Don't vote? But you criticize! If you don't like the way this country is run, the minimum duty you have is to vote."

"It's pointless to vote because voting is a fucking fraud, and the whole thing is a dirty scam run by the rich capitalist pigs."

Then Jean chimed in with his views. "It doesn't matter which bourgeois president America has," Jean added, shrugging his shoulders in a French manner. "They are all the same. All for the almighty dollar, no care at all for the people." Pat's fuse was good and lit. Norman picked up the bowl of potatoes and tried to pass them to change the subject.

"Want more potatoes, Pat?" I'd never seen him this nervous.

"If you hate America so much, why don't you *leave*?" Pat asked Jack.

"I want to," he answered.

"Good. Where do you want to go?"

"Cuba." Given JFK's history with Cuba, that was almost enough to give Pat a stroke.

"*Cuba!* Splendid. I'll buy you a ticket. *One way!*" She got up and announced she was leaving. Dotson stood up with her. Norman was alarmed and tried to calm her down. For some reason Dominique, Jean's daughter, chimed in at that point, trying, I think, to put balm on the situation by explaining her father's views, but it only put more gas on the fire.

Pat turned to her and said, "You're only a kid and you already have your mind nailed shut." She and Dotson left.

Dotson later told me privately that he had looked into the eyes of two killers in his life, and they'd both had eyes like Jack's. Pat had said in the car going back, "Why would Norman have that person in his house? Poor Norris! Did you see his eyes? He has a killer's eyes. Don't ever let me be in the same room as that man again." Later, when Jack killed Richard Adan, she said, "That could have been Norris or one of the little boys. Norman needs to have his head examined."

As I had feared, the socialization of Jack was deteriorating. He wasn't ready for the dining rooms of New York society, that much was for sure. Whether he was ready for socializing at all was in doubt. That night was the first real inkling we had of what we were up against. We had a big problem on our hands.

Summer came, and we moved to Provincetown, which brought some relief from the daily calls and frequent visits from Jack. Gretchen continued to see Jack from time to time, and I think she was falling for him a bit. He could be charming in a little-boy way. He had read a vast amount and was knowledgeable about many subjects. Jack was self-educated, you could tell, because he sometimes pronounced a word strangely, as if he had read it but had never heard it spoken aloud. I usually corrected him, and he was grateful.

Norman felt that we couldn't totally abandon Jack, so he invited him to spend a few days with us on the Cape. We were renting a big house that summer, and Jack had his own room on the water. He loved being in the middle of our family, and would sit on the deck for hours, just looking out to sea, soaking up the solitude and light. One night, the girls—Betsy, Kate, and Danielle—went to the movies, and Jack asked if he could tag along with them. It never occurred to any of us that we should be afraid of him. While he sometimes bragged about his misdeeds, like the time he killed someone in prison who had disrespected him, stuck a knife in his chest while he was watching a movie in a theater, it always seemed like a little boy bragging. I never quite believed it, but that was probably just me in denial that he could really be as bad as he was telling me. (Once, while we were sitting at an outdoor café called Café Blasé, Jack gave me a lesson on how to kill someone with a single knife blow. He said it should be a sharp knife, and you put the tip between the person's second and third shirt buttons and push hard, one quick thrust. That sends the knife right into the heart, and it's over immediately. I think he really thought it might be useful information for me one day.)

He stayed with us a few more days, and then went back to New York on the bus, but life in the city was worse for him after the cool tranquility of the sea. New York was hot and gritty, and everyone in the city was testy, a bad combination for someone as paranoid as Jack.

I got a call from him not long after he left, and he was really agitated. He told me several things people had said to him or done to him, much like the museum guard incident, and he kept saying, "I'm going to blow. I'm going to blow." I thought that meant he was going to leave town. He'd talked often enough about skipping out and going to Cuba, which would have been a terrible thing to do, as he would have been arrested and sent back to jail.

"Try to stay cool, Jack," I said. "It's just the weather. People in New York get hot and cranky. They don't mean anything. You can't take off now. Your book is coming out soon, and when that happens, you are going to be a big star. It will be a bestseller and make a lot of money. Everyone knows it will. Just hang in there. Please don't do anything stupid. The last place you want to go is Cuba anyhow. I don't think they would welcome you there with open arms." We talked of the time when he'd get out of the halfway house, get an apartment, maybe a place in the country with a dog (he wanted a Doberman), and start a regular life. I think Norman, too, was counting on the positive reception of the book to change things. Boy, were we naïve.

A FEW DAYS after that conversation, at about ten o'clock on a Saturday night, I got a call from Gretchen, who was crying and sounded awful. She and Jack had made plans to go out that night, and he'd stood her up. Never called or anything. She was really upset. I said, "It sounds like you've gotten a crush on him, sweetie. You haven't slept with him, have you?" She had not, although she'd made up her mind that she was going to do it that night if he made the move. But he never came. Never called. The following day was a Sunday, the day that *The New York Times* was reviewing Jack's book. The review turned out to be a rave, but that elation was forgotten when our phone started ringing with the news that Jack had killed Richard Adan, a waiter at a restaurant on the Lower East Side called the Bini Bon, and had disappeared.

The phone rang constantly all day. The FBI put a stakeout around our residences in Brooklyn and in Ptown, in case Jack tried to come there. The kids were all upset, rightfully so, especially the girls. I had never felt like he would hurt any of our family, but then maybe that was just my naïveté. The authorities tapped our phones, in Ptown and in New York, in case Jack called us, but he never did. They tapped Gretchen's phone, too, and there they lucked out. Jack began to call Gretchen.

A detective named Bill Majeskie was in charge of the case. He was a sweet-faced boy in his early thirties, not at all the type of tough detective you would cast on a TV show. He came to the house in Provincetown and talked to us, and just when I was thinking he was too young and innocent to be involved in something like this, he crossed his legs and I saw a gun strapped to his ankle. I was in the real world. Majeskie talked to Gretchen, taped Jack's calls, and made a big map on his wall of Jack's whereabouts. The pushpins and marker line went all the way to Central America, and then back to Louisiana, where they finally captured him about six months later.

I remembered Jack talking incessantly of his plan to get to Mexico and then somehow to Cuba, but that never happened. It had been too hard to make his way in the backcountry of Mexico. He'd been starving and dirty and had had no money or means to get to Cuba. So he'd returned to the United States and gotten a job working for four dollars an hour in the oil fields of Louisiana, where he was identified, picked up, and shipped back to New York.

Norman, of course, went to see him after he arrived, and he acquired a well-known attorney named Ivan Fisher to represent Jack. Ivan wanted to see me alone in his office, which was a fancy place on the Upper East Side. His office contained the longest leather couch I had ever seen, comfy, worn brown leather that pulled you in. As soon as I sat on the couch, he leaned back in his chair and grinned. He is an enormous man, six feet seven or thereabouts, with the girth to go with it. He has large prominent eyes, and the habit of kicking one crossed leg back and forth while he talks. After the pleasantries, he said, "We're going to have Jack back out on the streets before you know it. Don't worry about a thing."

"What makes you think I want Jack back out on the streets?" I was flabbergasted. "Jack doesn't belong out on the streets. He is going to do this again and again if he gets out. I want Jack to go back to jail. Forever." Ivan's smile dropped off his face.

"But you don't want Jack to go down for murder, do you?"

"Jack murdered somebody! I don't care. It wasn't premeditated, I'm sure, but I don't want him out on the streets. He is too nervous, too volatile. He can't deal with the pressure. He thinks everyone on the street is waiting to kill him. He would do it again, I know it."

He sent me back home in the long white limousine he had at the time. That rocky introduction started a friendship for Norman and me with Ivan and his girlfriend, later his wife, Diane, who became my best friend in New York.

I never went to see Jack in prison. I just couldn't. I had nothing to say to him. I couldn't give him any words of comfort. I couldn't say it would be all right, because it wouldn't. It was going to end badly, as it was always destined to, before Jack had even one brief moment of seeing clear blue sky in his sad life of looking through dingy glass.

The trial started, and of course we went every day. I couldn't let Norman go by himself, even though I dreaded waking up, knowing I had to go. Getting through the press was like running a gauntlet. I was shoved and whacked in the head by cameras as reporters lunged for Norman. Norman was never cool under pressure, and tended to get angry and say stupid things when goaded, and the press are experts in goading. I knew what Norman was trying to say when he said "Culture is worth a little risk," but I wouldn't have put it that way. It is true that if no one in prison ever had the chance of redemption, it would be a sorry fact, but to throw out a statement like that was like throwing meat to hungry dogs. "I Would Help Killer Again," was another ugly headline.

Norman probably would have helped Jack again, but in a different way, I'm sure. That's the way Norman was. He tried to help people; he got pleasure from it. He always felt guilty that he hadn't made more time to spend with Jack, that he'd let me go out with Jack day after day while he'd worked, but, frankly, I don't think it would have made much difference if he'd spent every waking moment with Jack. The truth was that Norman and Jack didn't really like each other on a personal level, and it was tough spending time with him. While some of Jack's letters were indeed brilliant, there were also his forty-five-page letters in which he ranted on about whatever he was in a rage about at the moment—capitalism, religion, whatever.

It's no secret Norman always had a huge ego; he believed he could change the course of a river by the strength of his personality, but he was sometimes naïve in the extreme. He didn't consider that while a violent person can be a philosopher of violence, he is nevertheless still a violent person, and just because he is a talented writer doesn't mean he doesn't also have a screw or two that are too loose to keep his head together. While I don't believe Norman was inherently a violent person, in spite of certain episodes in his history before he met me, Norman was intrigued with it. He had analyzed violence, studied it his whole life, played with it in his imagination.

I hadn't read "The White Negro" when I met him, but that was the document that a lot of people used to point out how crazy and violent he was. That plus the fact that he had stabbed his second wife, Adele—no small event. Of course, I knew about that when we got together, or pretty soon after, but I never for a minute worried about my own safety. At the time of that tragedy, Norman had been going through a period in his life when he and Adele had been drinking heavily and doing drugs, and it seemed to me that it was another person who had done those things.

He would tell me stories and I'd listen, like it was bedtime fiction. I wanted to believe—in fact, I did believe; I couldn't have been with him otherwise—that he had changed, that he had gone through the fire and come out cleaner and forged of stronger steel. I knew how much he loved me. I knew he was inherently a good man, that all he wanted to do was help someone better himself, but the one thing Norman never had was the ability to understand that not everyone was like him. Not everyone could pull himself out of the grasp of mental illness by an act of willpower and come back to win Pulitzer Prizes and lead a good life. There was evil in the world, not theoretical evil but real, pulsating, visceral evil, that couldn't be explained away, no matter how much talent the person had. Norman flirted with the idea of evil, and he certainly considered the devil to be as real as God, but I don't think he ever understood that it was a force that was equal to a raging forest fire against the match flame of his will.

I was friends at this time with Susan Sarandon, and she and Chris Walken wanted to go to court to watch the trial one day. I don't know if they were thinking of doing a movie with Chris playing Abbott and Susan playing me, but there was an element of research to it. Actors always want to watch real life. They soak it up like sponges and use it later in a character, whether it is the exact character or not. At any rate, Norman said they could come with us, not realizing the chaos that would ensue when we showed up with the two of them. Our pictures were on the front pages of all the papers, and I really feared for our safety going through the mass of press outside the courthouse. No bodyguards in those days.

A friend of mine who was a photographer wore a miniskirt to court one day and was walking around the courtroom before the trial began, talking to some of the press and sketch artists who were friends of hers, and someone mistakenly printed that it was me, flitting around the court in a short skirt talking to reporters, trying to get myself into the papers. It was humiliating, but there was nothing to do about stories like that. Every day brought some new indignity, some new lie to contend with.

Time magazine said that Norman and Jack should be shackled together in prison; several other articles said Norman should be sent to prison as well. We got death threats; our children were threatened. All of the other people who had helped Jack, who had written letters supporting him, just faded away, and Norman was left to take the brunt of the ugly publicity all alone. What nobody seemed to understand was that a private citizen, even a famous person, can't just go and get someone out of jail. There has to be a reason why a prisoner is released.

Later we found out, through a letter from another prisoner, that the reason Jack had been let out early on parole was that he had turned snitch and ratted out several of his fellow inmates. From the article by M. A. Farber in *The New York Times,* we learned that Jack had given a secret, sworn statement at Marion Prison on December 12, 1980, that had provided information about other inmates and had made a series of accusations against the Marion Prisoners' Rights Project, a lawyers' group. The group had instigated one of the longest inmate work stoppages in the history of the federal prison system, and Marion Prison was trying to ban them as "agitators." Jack Abbott was desperate to get out of prison. He felt he was going to be murdered at any moment, even by the lawyers.

The people who wrote letters in support of Jack were never told any of this by the parole board, and were never told about Jack's long history of violence. Jack's supporters didn't know that his medical records were full of references to paranoia and his potential for violence. From the *Times* article, we learned that Dr. Steven Shelton of the Menninger Clinic in Topeka, Kansas, stated as early as 1973 that the prisoner was a "potentially dangerous man" with a "hair trigger temper." And in the same article we learned that Thomas R. Harrison, the chairman of the Utah board of pardons, said at Jack's parole hearing, "Here's a man who has a great deal going for him, and against him is one outstanding factor. And that's an extremely violent temper, explosive at times." Addressing Jack, Harrison said, "The street is a real world, too. There are going to be disappointments; there are going to be people who rub you the wrong way, who make you angry. And it's of great concern to the board how you're going to react to this situation."

Jack replied that no one had given a damn for him since he was a child and that he "grew up in a cage where you've got to fight your way through all that. . . . The only way you can do that is by getting angry. It's a rational anger, but it isn't anything else. I'm not violent to where I'm going to go out and be a maniac, if that's what you mean." Harrison replied, "What we're interested in is your potential for hurting somebody. You say there is no such potential, right?"

"No, no," said Jack. "No. There won't be nothing like that."

Perhaps it's true that Harrison was swayed by the letters Norman and the others sent speaking of Jack's talent, or the fact that he was publishing a book; possibly Harrison just wanted to believe that it was feasible for a man to change, and here was a chance to prove it. I'm sure he knew as well as anyone how many men who walked out those doors on parole walked right back in again. Conceivably Jack's release was just part of the deal, an exchange for names he had given to the parole board. For whatever reasons, Jack was let out early, but it wasn't simply because Norman Mailer wrote a letter.

In the thick of the threats and news stories, I seriously thought about taking Matt and John and going to Arkansas for a while, until the trial was over and the press stories died down, but I couldn't let Norman stay and take it all by himself. Norman said, "If someone wants to kill us, they will kill us no matter what we do. I'm not running away from my responsibilities." I couldn't run away from his responsibilities, either.

Of course, eventually it was over. Jack was convicted of manslaughter and sentenced to fifteen years to life, but we got new friends out of it—Jack's lawyer, Ivan Fisher, and his wife, Diane; and Bill Majeskie, the detective who caught Jack, and Bill's wife, Evelyn. I think it was a lesson for Norman in the true nature of violence and a shock for him to see just how little he could influence the life of someone else with the force of his personality. I hoped with all my heart that he wouldn't drag the family into anything as dangerous ever again, because I realized more than ever that I could never influence Norman by an act of will, no matter how angry I got or how I tried to reason with him.

A small coda to the story: many years later, Jack committed suicide in prison. (There was doubt as to whether it was really suicide or someone helped him along.) I had a friend named Rosamond who had recently passed away and who had been quite a powerful psychic. Over the years she'd predicted a lot of things for me that had come true, such as health issues and the births of both my grandchildren. Not long after she died, her cousin Kiana had a dream. In the dream, Rosamond came to Kiana and said for her to tell me that a man named Jack H. was on the other side, and he wanted to send me a message. He wanted me to know he was sorry he messed it all up and caused me so much pain. Kiana asked if it might be an old boyfriend, but the only Jack H. I ever knew was Jack Henry Abbott.

Thirty-six

After Abbott was sent back to jail, the newspapers found new headlines. Norman threw himself into his work. *Pieces and Pontifications* came out in 1982, and in April 1983, *Ancient Evenings* was published to mixed—mostly bad—reviews, but it reached number six on the *Times* bestseller list and got a huge amount of publicity. Norman was on the cover of *New York* magazine as the pharaoh (which I privately think he had to have been in a past life; there is no other explanation for him). It was another fat tome that almost nobody finished, but it is my favorite of all his books. I have read it seven or more times in one draft or another, and every few years I pick it up again, always finding new things I didn't remember, surprising bits of magic I'd forgotten. I think it is a tour de force, a densely woven tapestry of a great tale, but the only two reviewers who understood it at all were Anthony Burgess and Joan Didion. I don't think a lot of them even read the whole book.

Instead of going to Maine, we spent July in New York. I put John in a YMCA day camp, and Matt went to visit his father and grandparents in Arkansas for a few weeks. Norman was working on a book he was calling *Tough Guys Don't Dance,* a kind of noir thriller set in Provincetown, and he had to finish it in two months because with everything else that had been going on, he had let the deadline get too near.

It was boiling hot in the apartment, and because of the configuration of the windows, we couldn't get air-conditioning; fans just smeared the hot air around. I hardly saw Norman at all. He worked from late morning until around nine at night, when he'd come home for dinner, and then we'd fall into bed to sleep, fitfully, in the heat. But it was a happy time, too, for us.

One day there was a particularly brilliant sunset, and as I always did on good sunset days, I called Matt and John to the window to look at it. "Boys! Come and look at the sunset!" They would drop their toys or whatever they were doing and troop over to the window, and we would all three put our arms around one another and watch until the red ball of the sun dropped behind the horizon. Then they would go back to playing. On one such day, I had the conscious thought that this was the happiest moment of my life, that everything I'd always wanted I had, right here in Brooklyn with my family and Norman, and I was content. There have been a lot of those moments in my life, and I am grateful for all of them.

I had been showing my paintings at a restaurant/gallery called Central Falls in SoHo, the same place where Edie Vonnegut, my studio mate, showed. It was run by a sweet guy named Bruce Goldstein, and I always did well, usually selling at least half of the paintings.

Me and my painting Hot Springs.

I'd just taken down a show, and Aurora Huston (née Young), who you'll remember had been my best friend in college, wrote and asked if I wanted to come to Arkansas and have a show at a gallery she was representing called the Sketch Box in Little Rock. It would be a chance to see my old friends and have some fun, maybe sell some more paintings. Jean Jewell would be there, too. It had been way too long since Aurora, Jean, and I had seen one another.

Aurora.

I packed up all the paintings I had left from the Central Falls show, and Norman, Matt, John, and I went down. Dotson Rader and Pat Lawford also came. They wanted to see Arkansas and were always up for a little adventure. We all stayed at a motel called the Lagniappe, which is Cajun for "a little extra." At that time, Bill Clinton was in office as governor, and I invited him and Hillary to the opening. We also gave a small dinner for the gallery owners at a Chinese restaurant that the Clintons attended, and Norman got along well with them both, Hillary especially. He later said, "That might be the brightest woman I've ever met." I wasn't even offended. I had known a long time ago how bright she was. I was delighted that they liked each other, and I was happy that Bill and I could still be friends. I guess there was a little part of me (maybe not so little) that wanted to show Norman off and let Bill know I was capable of having a relationship with someone who was an intellectual, too, and while I don't think he was eating his heart out, he was maybe impressed a little. If he was anything, Norman was impressive. But then so are Bill and Hillary. I was so proud of them years later when they gained national prominence, and my New York friends thought I was some kind of psychic genius because I had been telling them for years that a man from Arkansas named Bill Clinton was going to be president one day.

Dotson Rader and me in Arkansas at the Razorback football game.

It was great fun to see them again, to get to know Hillary a little bit, and the show was a big success. A lot of my family came to the opening party, and my mother and my aunt Ella Belle, a teetotaling Assemblies of God Christian who had probably never tasted alcohol in her life, took a glass of champagne off a tray, and she and my mother giggled like two little girls as they tasted it and made sour faces, my father looking on at them with disapproval. Dotson and Pat, who was dressed to the nines in jewelry and designer clothes, mingled and had a great time. Dotson and I sang gospel hymns, as we were prone to do at the drop of a hat, but down there everyone else knew them, too, so it wasn't as exotic as it was when we sang at parties in New York. People just thought we were acting a little strange.

Norman loved to tell the story of how one little old blue-haired lady came over to him at the reception and said, "Oh, Mr. Church, you must be so proud of your wife!" He then grumbled that he finally understood why all of his wives complained about being in his shadow.

The Clintons had us over to the governor's mansion for a drink, and Pat was clearly taken with young Bill. She was nothing if not politically astute, and to her, he was the perfect man to run for president. Pat danced around the subject, easing into it, but finally leaned in and asked him if he thought he might ever run for national office, and he admitted he had thought about it (he'd been thinking about it since he was eight), but it was too early for him. He wanted to work at being governor awhile longer, make contacts, really get things prepared before he made the big jump. (He'd won the governorship in 1978, lost it in 1980, and regained it the previous year, 1982. He went on to serve for ten more years.)

Pat's green eyes glowed. I could see the wheels already turning,

Me, Norman, and Bill Clinton.

planning what she was going to do to help him. Pat liked winners, and Bill was clearly a big one. Norman was warming to the subject, too, and the discussion was lively. Then, a uniformed policeman came in and said he was sorry to interrupt us but he had just received an emergency call that Mrs. Lawford's son had been rushed to the hospital. He didn't spell out that it was a drug overdose, but there were few other things it could have been. Pat had to leave immediately. She was as angry as I had seen her since the night with Jack Abbott. She turned to all of us, fire shooting out of her green eyes, and said, "If he's not dead when I get there, I'm going to kill him." (Fortunately, she called later to say he was all right.)

TOUGH GUYS DON'T DANCE came out in 1984, again to mixed reviews. I always dreaded when a book came out. It seemed to me that most reviewers wanted to kill Norman. With one breath they would say he was our greatest writer, and with the next they would say the book he had just written was crap. He pretended to have rhinoceros hide, but he was hurt by it—of course he was. To devote several years of your life to a book, as he often did, and then have someone who has scarcely read it and who has few credentials rip it apart? It makes one want to do serious damage to the reviewer. (Er, any reviewers reading this are excepted, of course. All of you are lovely.) He still could quote hurtful reviews from decades past, like the one in *Time*, for his second book, *Barbary Shore*: "Paceless, tasteless, and graceless. He is marooned on an intellectual point of no return." For some reason that one really got to him. When he got the chance to make *Tough Guys Don't Dance* into a movie, he jumped at it. He needed a break from writing and the judgment of book reviewers. Not that the judgment of Hollywood reviewers was any kinder, but it would be different, at least.

Menahem Golan, of Golan and Globus, an Israeli company, had a lot of money at the time and they were making deals all over the place. One of their deals was with Jean-Luc Godard, for a movie based on Shakespeare's *King Lear*, and they wanted Norman to write the script. Norman agreed, on the condition that they give him the money to direct *Tough Guys Don't Dance* as a movie. He had done three underground films (which is a rock-and-roll term for "Norman's improvised home movies starring all his friends and family") back in the sixties, and the time spent making those movies was some of the happiest of his life. Maybe I was just jealous because it was before I came into the picture, but I have never been a fan of those movies, even though he looks cute in them and there are some surprisingly good moments. There are also some embarrassing moments, such as the outfit he wore in *Maidstone* that consisted of cutoff jeans, a leather vest with no shirt, and a top hat. And moments that were pretty horrific, like when Rip Torn whacked him on the head with a hammer. With blood streaming down his head, Norman bit Rip's ear in retaliation and sent him to the hospital with an infection. It's a wonder neither one of them was killed.

At any rate, Golan said yes, he could direct *Tough Guys Don't Dance,* and Norman set to work writing *King Lear* for Godard. It was a disaster from the beginning. At the time he began the project, we were doing a workshop of Norman's play about Marilyn Monroe, *Strawhead,* at the Actors Studio, with his daughter Kate playing Marilyn and me playing Amy Greene. (It was set during the time when Marilyn lived with Milton and Amy in Connecticut.) Jeannie was in it, and Adele had a small part. It was a real family production. Stephen was one of the stagehands, and Ben Stiller (Jerry Stiller and Annie Meara's son, before he became the famous Ben Stiller) was running the lights. Godard came to see one of the rehearsals and brought a woman with him who was dressed in leather, furs, and jewels, dripping with European disdain for Americans. Norman had forgotten his glasses that morning, so I was to bring them when I got to rehearsal, but I also forgot them, to Norman's great annoyance, and I profusely apologized. Godard overheard our conversation and said to his companion, in an arch, suggestive way, "She forgets his glasses because she does not want her husband to see his daughter playing Marilyn Monroe." It was creepy in the extreme, but we ignored it, as Norman still had to work with him.

Godard and the woman returned to Europe, and Norman worked on the *King Lear* script while we did *Strawhead* at the studio, which was a big success. Kate had been a star in theater at Brown and was incredible as Marilyn. She had studied her walk, her hand gestures, her facial expressions. . . . She got onstage and *became* Marilyn! *Vanity Fair* had her on the cover as Marilyn, and there were articles about it everywhere. After that incident, Godard then got the bright idea that he wanted Norman to act in the movie as King Lear, with Kate in the role of Cordelia, Lear's daughter, except they would be called Norman and Kate Mailer. Already it was getting a bit strange.

Godard flew Norman, Kate, and her present husband, Guy Lancaster, to Switzerland to film, and on the first day it became apparent he wasn't going to use Norman's script. He was quite open about the fact that he had never read *King Lear,* either the original by Shakespeare or Norman's version, and he had no intention of using what Norman had done. Godard's concept was a King Lear who was a modern-day film director named Norman Mailer, and it soon was obvious that said director was having some kind of unnatural relationship with his daughter. When Godard tried to stage the first scene in a hotel bedroom, Norman was in a rage and said he was not going to do it. He said he would act in a movie if he had a fictitious name and character, but he would not do the things Godard was suggesting using his own name, with his own daughter. He, Kate, and Guy packed their bags and came straight back to the States. Godard immediately called Menahem Golan to complain.

Golan got on the phone with Norman and Godard. Godard was nearly apoplectic that Norman had dared to oppose him as he directed, and Norman said he couldn't work with a director on *King Lear* who had never read *King Lear.* Golan said, "Is that true, Jean-Luc? That you have not read *King Lear*?" Jean-Luc could have lied and made Norman look bad, but he was too egotistical for that. "I do not HAVE to read *King Lear*!" he said. "I am Jean-Luc Godard!" Menahem threw up his hands. He knew it was hopeless, so the collaboration was over between Mailer and Godard, but Menahem was gentleman enough to allow Norman to direct *Tough Guys Don't Dance* anyhow.

Thirty-seven

Life was busy in the early and mid-eighties. Besides painting and showing, I was still taking a few acting classes and trying to get work as an actress, although I slowly realized that I would never have a big career. The biggest part I got was on the daytime drama *All My Children* playing an aging ex-model named Britt Hemingway, who had sunk to dealing drugs since she was so old she couldn't model anymore (I was thirty-four). The part lasted six months. In the story line, my character got Mark, one of the good guys, hooked on cocaine, but he finally saw the light and went to rehab and back to his wife, and Britt faded away, as those kinds of girls on soap operas usually do. It was great fun, and I got fan mail, some from guys in prison, who were big fans of the dope dealer. I even got a few letters asking if I could get someone cocaine. I replied that I could send them a packet of Epsom salts. That was what we used on the show.

I was also working a lot at the Actors Studio at this time. I had been admitted to the Playwrights/Directors Unit through submitting a screenplay—co-written with my old teacher B. C. Hall in Arkansas, called *Little Miss Little Rock*—to Arthur Penn and Elia Kazan, the two legends who ran the unit. The screenplay had the same title as the novel Norman had read, the one I'd never finished, but B.C. and I took the story in a totally different direction. The screenplay actually got so far as to have someone take an option on it, and we nearly got financing a couple of times, but it always fell through, as most movie projects do.

After I became a member of the unit, I also wrote a couple of plays that were produced at the studio. The first was a two-character one-act called *Go-See* that I wrote for Sally Kirkland but wound up doing myself with Rip Torn (who had long ago made peace with Norman), and the second was a short play called *Double Feature* with Rita Gam and Patrick Sullivan. The Actors Studio made me more confident about my writing abilities, and Norman and I had great fun doing things together there. I directed one of his short plays called *The Notebook*, and he directed me in *Strawhead* and another play or two. If one of us put up something for a session, during the critique afterward we would have great mock fights. Once, when I had criticized something he had done, he pretended to cough up a loogie (an old Brooklyn term for a wad of phlegm) into his hand and launch it at my head. I ducked, and half the audience thought he really had done it and went, "EYEEEEW."

We took various of the kids there, too. They used to say that while other kids went to church, they went to the Actors Studio. John was in plays from the time he was seven or eight; Matt ran lights, did the technical work for plays, and also acted; and Stephen and Kate acted. It was a cozy, safe atmosphere in which to practice the craft, and I realized after a while that, as with modeling, I didn't particularly want a big career. I didn't want to go to Hollywood and work on a TV sitcom or be in a play eight times a week on Broadway. I just wanted to live with Norman and take care of the family, go to Provincetown in the summers, write and paint and do a little work at the Actors Studio once in a while for fun.

We still had an active social life, and "Norman and Norris" became almost one word in the social columns. While we did fight a lot, almost as a sport, Norman was always there, supporting me, encouraging me in whatever I was doing, and I was there for him.

The kids were all going to good schools and making interesting careers for themselves. They each had the dreaded twenty-fifth birthday to pass, because that was the age Dad had been when *The Naked and the Dead* was published, and it hung over all their heads. Rational or not, they felt that they, too, were expected to be famous young, but Norman just wanted them to be happy, and in fact he always said that becoming famous so young was the worst thing that could have happened to him. He wasn't ready, and he didn't know how to handle fame. It was why he'd gotten into so much trouble in his early years. With the exception of Sue, who became a psychoanalyst, all of the kids found careers in the arts one way or another. I used to laugh and say that if one of them had come to us and said they wanted to become a dentist, we would have looked at them in horror and said, "What are you thinking?" Now I wish we had a few doctors and dentists in the family.

IN 1984 WE bought a big brick house on the beach in Provincetown that would be our home for the next twenty-three years. I loved that house. It was big enough for all of us—five bedrooms and four and a half bathrooms, with Norman and me splitting the attic floor for our offices. Granted, he had three-quarters of the space and I had one, but my side was cozy. By now Norman was just that little bit older and couldn't be as active, so every year, we were spending three months or more in Provincetown, and we went up during the year for long weekends or on holidays. Norman loved working there. It was an escape sometimes from New York's energy, and often he would go by himself for weeks if he needed to get a big chunk of work done.

Norman's mother always came for part of the summer, as did his sister, Barbara, and her family. Fanny was aging dramatically. Her mind had started to wander, and she began to imagine things. The first clue I had was when she asked me one day to go with her to the cleaners; they had lost her sheets, she said, and wouldn't give them back. I went in with her, and the man, obviously exasperated, said, "Oh, Mrs. Mailer, we don't have your sheets! Please!" He told me she had never sent them to him, and she was just as adamant that she had and he was lying about it. There was nothing I could do. I couldn't force him to produce sheets he didn't have, but I didn't like to think she was, God forbid, losing her mind. After that we began to notice more and more things of that sort. Once she climbed up on the bed to kill a spider with a broom, fell off, couldn't get up, and lay on the floor all day until I came over to visit late in the afternoon.

After that, we got a girl named Rose to stay with her because we were also concerned about her turning on the stove and then not lighting the gas with a match, or wandering away and leaving food to burn. She immediately started reporting that Rose was stealing her long dresses, or her high heels or her teacups. We apologized to Rose and ignored it like we ignored the sheets, as the long dresses were still hanging in the closet along with the shoes, and the teacups were in the cupboard, but in the end it turned out that Rose had indeed cleaned her out of all her good jewelry and any loose cash lying around. We discovered this after Rose tried to write a hot check on Fanny's bank account and then disappeared. Just because someone is hallucinating doesn't mean they are always wrong.

Fanny was living in some other land in her head much of the time now, and we found a great nurse named Eva to take care of her. Fanny still had lucid moments, and was still feisty. Once, she was uncharacteristically feeling sorry for herself, saying that it would be best if she just went ahead and died, and Eva, kidding (at least I think she was kidding), said, "Would you like me to help you along?" "Go to hell!" Fanny said to her, maybe not so ready to move on after all. After we brought her to Provincetown in the summer of 1985, she took to her bed and couldn't really eat or drink much. Eva, Sue, Betsy, Danielle, Kate, Maggie, Barbara, and I sat beside her bed and talked to one another a lot that summer while we peeled the outer husks off silver dollar plants we found growing in the yard, and made beautiful bouquets of them. It seemed to be just a matter of time until Fanny went. The doctor said there was nothing to do except keep her comfortable.

For his part, Norman was in denial about the situation, and would stick his head into her room every morning with a cheery "Good morning, Mom!" wave and then go about his day, as though oblivious to what was going on. He hated being around sick people, hated being sick himself, and was convinced the mind could overcome the body by an act of will if it was just strong enough. A couple of years previously, when his mother had been in better shape but clearly unable to get around well, he'd decided that if she went hiking in Maine it would do her so much good that she would be able to walk better afterward. Nothing could dissuade him—not her, not us. So we all set out on what was, for most people, an easy stroll on a relatively smooth path, but not if one is ninety-some-odd with a bad heart. She soon tired, and Peter and Michael wound up carrying her to our moored boat. The boat ride back was frightening for her as well, and the whole experience was traumatic. I felt so bad for Norman, as we all meanly said to him, "I told you so." He was like a disappointed little boy who just knew he could fix his mother and make her like she used to be, if only she would do as he said, but it didn't happen.

Occasionally, Fanny would come back through the fog and say to me, "I am so sorry I have to put you through this." Once, she said, "I'm so glad Norman has you." It made me cry, and I knew she really did love me. We had been friends for ten years, not such a long time in her long life, but we had been real friends. She didn't have many others outside the family.

One day near the end of the summer, she began to ask to go home. We kept saying, "It's just a few more weeks, Grandma. We'll all go back to Brooklyn soon. Just hang in." But she insisted and insisted, every day. I had gone into the city for a few days to attend an acting workshop with Ellen Burstyn, and since I had to go back to Ptown anyhow, we decided it would be convenient if Michael and Stephen brought her home, along with Eva, and then I would go back with them and get the rest of the family packed up to come back. I was waiting at her apartment when they arrived, and we got her into bed. I sat beside her for a long time, talking, and her head was relatively clear. She told me she was going to die. She used to say that frequently, and I would joke her out of it and say, "Oh, no, you'll just get on the wrong bus and wind up in Schenectady," but I knew she was serious, and this time I said, "Yes, darling, I think you are. Does that frighten you?"

"Yes," she said. "I'm frightened." I took her hand.

"I don't think you should be scared. You've lived a good life, and I believe that God loves us and that we go on to another life, in a different place from this one. I think your sisters and parents will be waiting for you when you get there, I think we'll know each other, and life will be at least as interesting as it is here, except we won't be sick or old. I think we even get a chance to come back down here and have another life. Maybe a lot of them." She was silent for a minute.

"Do you really believe that?"

"I do," I said, echoing the sentiments James Jones had told Norman all those years ago. "It's the only thing that makes sense to me. It is so miraculous for a baby to be born at all, isn't it? Those two little cells coming together and growing into a whole person. What is more miraculous about it happening more than once? What about a child who is killed in a car wreck when he is two years old? Is that all the life he gets? Or babies who are born dead? Do they never get another chance? I don't think God works that way. I like to think this energy we have that makes us who we are leaves these worn-out bodies and goes somewhere else, like a driver getting out of an old car into a new one, and while we are still us—we're the same drivers—we are so much more." I kept talking to her, and gradually she relaxed.

"I'd like to believe that," she said, finally. I held her hand, and she drifted off to sleep. Then Michael, Stephen, and I got into the car and drove back to Provincetown. Labor Day weekend was coming up and we had to get the house packed up and the kids back to school. After the six-hour trip, as we walked into the house in Provincetown, the phone was ringing. It was Eva. Fanny had died peacefully just a few minutes before.

Myrtle stayed behind with John and Maggie and Matt, and Carol came to keep them company while the older kids and Norman and I went back to New York the following day. The funeral was at Campbell's, the ritzy Upper East Side funeral home, which Fanny would have liked. Several of Norman's exes were there. One of his old girlfriends, Shari, a former stewardess, came wearing a white suit and a huge black and white hat with big white sunglasses, and sat in the front row, just in case someone might miss her. The curse of the old girlfriends followed me everywhere, although I should have gotten used to it.

The burial was in Long Branch, New Jersey, where Norman had been born and all his family was buried. We caravanned out to the grave site in the late summer heat. It was a holiday weekend and the traffic was horrendous. After the rabbi said all the things he was supposed to, they began to lower the coffin into the grave. Except the coffin was way too big for the hole. Of course we had picked out a tank of a coffin, with comfy innerspring mattress and all the chrome doodads, while the Jewish tradition was to bury in a modest plain wooden box that took up much less space. We looked around for the grave diggers, but they had gone off on lunch break. Someone from the cemetery jumped into the car and frantically went searching every McDonald's and Wendy's in the vicinity while we all stood in the sun, waiting for them to come back. After an eternity, they arrived, two men in dirty T-shirts, one fat with his exposed belly hanging over his pants, and one skinny, his pants in danger of falling off his hip bones at any moment. We lined up and watched them work. They dug, then tried to fit the coffin, took it out, and dug some more. At one point, the fat one jumped into the hole and started bouncing up and down on the coffin, trying to pound it in, but we all started yelling at him to stop, so they had to keep digging. I can only imagine what Fanny was saying. "Young man, you stop that! Have a little respect! I'm the mother of a famous man! You can just dig a proper hole, and stop all this foolishness!"

Finally, it was over, and Michael, Stephen, Norman, and I set out to make the long trip back to Provincetown one more time. A bad storm blew up after sunset, and the rain pelted down so hard we could hardly see the road and had to pull over several times. We said the storm was Fanny, railing against the fat man who'd jumped on her coffin, and who's to say it wasn't?

Thirty-eight

In the summer of 1986 preproduction started on *Tough Guys Don't Dance*. This time, I wasn't dying to be in the movie. I frankly didn't like the script, and I couldn't talk to Norman about it. He didn't want to hear any of my criticisms. In fact, he really didn't want me involved at all. He said I was too negative. He ended up asking me to read for one of the parts, I think just to placate me in case I ever complained, or maybe he was curious to see what I would do with the role, but I wasn't right for it and we both knew it. The part eventually went to Isabella Rossellini, who starred with Ryan O'Neal.

In putting on his director's hat, Norman suddenly became someone else, a bit of the old rascal Norman, the one I had never met, a man who would approach a beautiful woman at a cocktail party and say, "Hi there, I'm *Norman Mailer*. I'm directing a movie, and you might be right for one of the roles." I could see how he used to seduce women in ten minutes, as he had bragged. Once, at a party, he was talking to Kathleen Turner, his back nearly touching mine, but he had no idea I was standing there. He told her he was making a movie and asked if she was interested in talking to him about it over lunch. I stood frozen to the spot, waiting to hear what she had to say, which was that she had no interest in his movie or lunch with him, although she said it in a nice way. I turned around and tapped him on the shoulder. The look on his face was almost worth it.

During this time, he was away in L.A. a lot, casting and meeting with the producers, getting the crew assembled, and the rest of the things involved in making a movie. I stayed home with the kids for the most part, although once in a while he would take me with him on a trip to California. I was also going to Arkansas frequently. My father had had a heart attack a few years before, and he was in and out of the hospital for several small procedures, a pacemaker and stents, so Norman's and my lives were at cross-purposes a lot during this time. I realized that somewhere along the line I had ceased to be the exciting girlfriend who would hold his hand and jump across the burning roofs. I had become the wife. I finally stopped pretending to be more athletic than I was, more wicked than I was, more adventurous than I was. The Baptist in me showed through my glamorous veneer whether I wished it to or not, and I became the solid base who held down the household and took care of our life and family, while Norman was out setting fires without me.

He had just come off a yearlong adventure as president of the PEN American Center, the writers' organization, where he had raised a million dollars to host the PEN World Congress in New York. It was a magnificent achievement. He had taken a small, threadbare organization of writers and put it on the New York social map by getting people such as billionaires Saul and Gayfryd Steinberg involved. It was a worthy cause that was also chic, an irresistible combination for many in New York society. (Among other good things, PEN supports freedom to write in countries around the world and helps writers who have been unjustly imprisoned, and the world congress was a chance for writers from every country to come together, discuss ideas, and be part of a vast supportive brotherhood.) Norman stopped work for an entire year to devote all his time to fund-raising. The grand finale of the many fund-raisers was a series of readings at a Broadway theater on Monday nights, with two famous writers reading per night.

Letter from Norman to Gore Vidal

NOVEMBER 20, 1984

Dear Gore,

I was talking about you to Nina [Auchincloss] last night at a party and decided it was time to write a letter. Our feud, whatever its roots for each of us, has become a luxury. It's possible in years to come that we'll both have to be manning the same ~~leaking~~ sinking boat at the same time. Apart from that, I'd still like to make up. An element in me, absolutely immune to weather and tides, runs independently fond of you.

In addition to this: I'd like you to speak at one of the evenings we're going to have in preparation for the PEN World

Congress at the end of 1985, or the beginning of 1986. To raise funds for such a Congress, PEN will present a subscription series ($1000 per patron for the full ten evenings) ~~at~~. One or two writers on each given evening, will do whatever they wish. Altogether we'll have a total of 15 novelists. So far, it's Joan Didion, Susan Sontag, Kurt Vonnegut, Bill Styron, John Updike, Isaac Bashevis Singer, John Irving, Tom Wolfe, William Buckley, Arthur Miller, and myself. The assumption is that some writers will want a full evening to themselves, and others will wish to share it. I know Jason [Epstein, Norman's editor] has already issued this invitation to you, but I repeat, if you like the idea, I'd be happy to introduce you for your evening or half-evening—whichever you choose. Please consider this. We won't have a full roster without you.

If you decide in the negative, that will be disappointing, but has no effect on the first paragraph of this letter.

Cheers,

Norman

Gore chose to share an evening with Norman. It was the first time they had been on the same stage since the Dick Cavett show. The series was a howling success, the million dollars was finally raised, and writers from all over the world poured into New York.

The night before Norman was to give the opening greeting at the world congress, we went to a reading of a play by an old friend, Roger Donoghue. He and his wife, Faye, lived in the National Arts Club, a Victorian building on Gramercy Park, and we always loved visiting them. Faye is a well-known painter of racehorses; her paintings are at racetracks and in collections all around the world. Roger had been a promising welterweight fighter until he accidently killed a man in the ring. (Roger was the one who said the famous line "I coulda been a contender" to Budd Schulberg, who used it in his script of *On the Waterfront*, which helped make Marlon Brando famous.) After killing the boxer, Roger got the collywobbles and quit. No one could blame him. He made a nice living selling beer and doing other things, but he had always secretly loved the theater and wanted to be a playwright. His play was about the unlikely friendship between Guy Lombardo and Louis Armstrong in the forties, when it was still jim crow across much of the country and black performers couldn't even walk through the same doors as white ones, never mind eat in the same restaurants or stay in the same hotels. One problem with the play was that only the Lombardo family had given Roger permission to use the music, so he wasn't able to use any of Louis Armstrong's great songs. Still, it was only a reading, and while it wasn't a masterpiece, we all knew it was a work in progress, and we all loved Roger so we clapped and cheered and told him how great it was. Except for Norman. He could never fudge his feelings about anything. His theory was that anyone should be delighted to get the benefit of his criticism in order to make something better, so he of course told Roger in great detail exactly what, in his opinion, was wrong with the play.

We had gone to dinner at Joe Allen, and as Norman went on critiquing the play, Roger's mood went from euphoric to somber to black. Norman didn't notice. He just kept on, really getting into it. Trying to be the chirpy little wife, I interjected that I thought there were some great moments in the play, and I tried to change the subject, but I was ignored in Norman's onslaught. Faye and I just sat silently, looking at each other in misery.

Finally, we paid the check and were standing by the curb waiting for a taxi when Roger started to mock-box with Norman. It was something they often did. Norman loved boxing and in those days boxed every weekend with a group of friends at the Gramercy Gym. He was in pretty good shape at sixty-two. They pretend-sparred, stopping their punches just short of each other's chins and rib cages, until a taxi pulled up. Then, as I kissed Faye good night and started to get into the car, Roger flipped a nice easy little punch that grazed Norman right between the eyes. It was like the work of a skilled surgeon, his forefinger and little finger were held open so that his nails made a crescent cut underneath each of Norman's eyes. It neatly broke his nose. I didn't see what was going on, but I heard Norman swear, and saw him knock Roger's hand away. Then he got into the cab after me, and I got a look at his face. Blood was running down both cheeks, and he was fumbling for his handkerchief. Of course he wouldn't hear of going to the emergency room, so we went home and I put ice on it until he went to bed.

In the morning, both eyes were black and swollen, he could hardly breathe through his nose, and he was due to speak at the PEN World Congress that evening. I ran out and bought heavy makeup of the kind that is used to cover port-wine birthmarks, and we spent the afternoon trying to cover up the damage. With a pair of sunglasses he explained by saying he had retina problems, which at one time he actually had, he could almost get away with it. At least nobody wrote about it; whether or not they talked, I couldn't say.

The world congress was a contentious gathering. Norman had invited George P. Shultz, the secretary of state, to welcome the attendees, which infuriated a lot of the left-leaning members of PEN, and to our horror Shultz was booed when he rose to speak. The State Department had let every single writer, without question, into the country to attend the congress, and the disrespect for Shultz and the office was embarrassing. Then, while Norman was speaking, Betty Friedan staged a protest about the number of women writers who were there. Ironic, because at the time, PEN was one of the few organizations that had more women running it than men. Six of the eight PEN committees were headed by women. In fact, PEN had invited dozens of leading international women writers, but forty-four had declined. The organization couldn't just go out into the streets and drag women there. I was furious at Friedan's phony rant. But Norman, instead of explaining these facts and figures to the audience, only got exasperated and said, "Oh, come on, Betty. Don't play the numbers game." He might as well have lain down on the railroad track and invited the train to run over him. The congress became a huge controversy. There was a faction of PEN who were unhappy that Norman had gotten the wealthy socialites involved, even though now PEN had the money to do a lot more good, and in fact, PEN became a world force. Articles were written for Norman and against him. There was a movement to have him removed from office, which ultimately failed. After his death in November 2007, PEN honored Norman for his past efforts at their annual fund-raiser, and invited John Buffalo and me. I noticed some of the ones who'd complained the loudest at the time were there at the dinner to recognize Norman's contributions. I just wish Norman had been alive to see it.

—

WITH THE CONGRESS OVER, Norman returned his attentions to the movie. Summer of 1986 was spent in Provincetown with the kids, but Norman was distracted with preproduction. I still went grocery shopping, and cooked dinner every night for as many as a dozen people, and life was more or less normal, but things weren't the same at all in our marriage. I could feel Norman pulling farther away from me. While we still had a good sex life, I began to wonder if there might be someone else. I had a vivid dream about him leaving me for another woman, and when I talked to him about it and asked him point-blank if he was having an affair, he told me I was crazy, that there was no one else but me, there had never been anyone but me since we'd met, and he was just distracted with the movie. He convinced me I was imagining things. He was good at that. But he had been distracted for more than a year, first with the PEN congress and now the movie.

They were going to film in our house, so after the summer, the movie crew swooped in and put everything into storage, and the house was transformed into one belonging to a whipped-cream blonde. Every room was painted a different pastel Easter egg color, and our dark wood floors were sanded and pickled white. I came in one day to find that they had taken a little soft-green wicker table and chair I particularly liked and spray-painted them banana-yellow. They had promised they wouldn't use our things, but when I complained, they said the director had okayed it. I gave up and went home.

Back in New York, I played single mom and still went to social engagements, commandeering Michael as my escort when he was home from Harvard. Occasionally I would go up to Ptown for a weekend and bring Matt and John, who loved hanging around the movie set. Matt was fifteen, John was nine, and they both wanted to be filmmakers. Norman was good about letting them watch everything, and Matt particularly loved special effects and learned a lot from that department. Later, when he was at York Prep, he made a movie called *The Deranged*, in which a severed head, much like the severed heads in *Tough Guys*, figured; it was realistically ghastly. (Matt's workshop was in our basement, and the woman who lived on the first floor once got the bedoodle scared out of her when she went down to fix a fuse or something and climbed up in the dark onto a bench that had a desiccated corpse Matt was making for a film lying on it.)

John used to sit on his father's knee, like a ventriloquist's dummy, while Norman directed a shot, and he learned every scene word for word. He would make us howl with laughter by doing all the dialogue with the perfect accents of the actors, like John Bedford Lloyd, who played Wardley Meeks, a Southern rich boy: "Wheah is mah money? Who HAS mah money?" We knew then that, at the very least, John was going to be an actor. I mostly just hung around the edges and watched, feeling far out of it. I was friendly with, but didn't really know, the crew and cast, who had formed a family bond, as they always do. I was just the wife of the director, always in the way of the shot.

We spent Thanksgiving in Provincetown, with a big turkey dinner for everyone. Farrah Fawcett came to be with Ryan O'Neal, and Ryan's sons Patrick and Griffin were there. Back in May that year, Griffin had tragically caused the death of Gian-Carlo Coppola, Francis Ford Coppola's son, when he'd run a speedboat between two boats, not noticing they were attached by a wire, and the wire had hit Gian-Carlo. Griffin had been on drugs at the time. Griffin had also recently gotten into a fistfight with his father, who had knocked one of his front teeth out. (Ryan was a boxer on a nearly professional level, and he used to do it on the weekends with Norman's little boxing club at the Gramercy Gym. He once broke the jaw of one of the inexperienced guys. Ryan was considered lethal.)

At Thanksgiving, Griffin was a bit of a mess, it seemed; he might have just come out of rehab, I'm not sure. Maggie was with us, and the two of them struck up an unlikely friendship that made us all nervous, but it was fortunately just an innocent flirtation. Maggie at fifteen was beautiful with dark curly hair and big blue eyes, but was unworldly, to say the least. Curious, Norman asked her what she and Griffin talked about, and she answered, "Our families. He's so much like me. He understands me," which made Norman and me stare at each other in bewilderment and dismay.

The movie was done shooting by December 14, and Norman came back to Brooklyn. It was hard for him to come down from the excitement of the movie, but I was glad to be with him again, and the kids were thrilled to have him home. I was hopeful that now that he had finished shooting the movie, we would go back to being as we were before, but there was something wrong, I could feel it. It was a lot of small things a woman can sense, like when a famous photographer came to take his picture and she asked to take one of the two of us, he refused to have his picture taken with me and got annoyed when I protested. He was still going away quite a bit, too, doing postproduction things for the movie, and again I felt like a social widow, going to dinners alone, or with Michael, or staying home. People were beginning to wonder why I was always by myself, was anything wrong, and I would reply to their questions that things were fine, Norman was away working. But in my heart I knew better.

We had a big Christmas, as we always did, then I went to Arkansas to be with my father, who was having open-heart surgery. After his heart attack several years earlier and a few smaller procedures, he had kept on working, teaching heavy equipment operation to underprivileged kids through Job Corps in Cass, Arkansas. But now he'd had another heart attack, and the doctors told us if he didn't have quadruple bypass surgery, he would die. He had no insurance, and he was too young for Medicare, so he went to the veterans' hospital. His surgeon was only a senior resident, which made me a little nervous, but the doctor, I'll call him Benicio, convinced us he made up for his lack of experience with youth, agility, and the latest knowledge, or so we hoped, and the operation was a success. My father got better every day; we brought him good food from home. Benicio had said he could eat anything he wanted until he got his strength back, and what he wanted was pinto beans and corn bread. At any rate, at midnight on New Year's eve, I was in the hospital with my father. My mother and I were spending our nights in the waiting room sleeping on lounge chairs. She was asleep, so I tiptoed out and called Norman at midnight to wish him a happy New Year. He was having a small party at the apartment in Brooklyn. Laughter and merrymaking racketed in the background. We said "Happy New Year" and "I love you," but he felt far away.

Benicio was on the floor checking patients. We had become friends during the week, since he stopped in to see my father frequently, and we sometimes had lunch together. It had been one of those odd occurrences when we'd met, as if we had known each other in a past life. As I hung up the phone from my call with Norman, Benicio could see I was upset, and we went down to the cafeteria for coffee. I began to pour my heart out to him about Norman, how he kept pushing me away and how he didn't really even live in New York anymore. He was staying in Provincetown most of the year. I was afraid he was having an affair, and it felt like my life was coming apart. Of course Benicio was sympathetic. And extremely handsome. Before I quite knew what was happening, I had gone with him back to his place. No mea culpa; it was great. It was so wonderful to have someone who really wanted me, even if it was only for a little while. And if Norman was having an affair, I could tell him I was, too.

My father got better, and after we got him settled at home, I went back to New York. Just as I came back, Norman left again, this time for San Francisco for a month to do postproduction sound for the movie. After a couple of weeks, John and I went out to visit him. We had a great time traveling around San Francisco, just John and me, while Norman worked. We went to Fisherman's Wharf and did all the tourist things like the Ripley's Believe It or Not! museum with its shrunken heads, and we rode the carousel and got our pictures taken in old-fashioned clothing.

Norman and I gave a cocktail party for the movie crew at his rented apartment, which had sweeping views of the bay and Alcatraz, and Norman let John be the bartender, standing on a box behind the kitchen counter. The first drink order he got was for a screwdriver. John knew it was made with orange juice but wasn't sure what the other part was. He didn't want to seem ignorant and ask, heaven forbid, so he just nonchalantly made it with beer. The man sputtered and spit it out onto the floor, and Norman gave John a quick lesson in bartending. How many kids can say their father taught them to bartend at nine? "Really," as Kate once said, "when Norman Mailer is your father, how are you going to rebel?"

But there were clues in San Francisco that things were still wrong. One day I came back to the apartment unexpectedly to find an old girlfriend of Norman's leaving. He swore nothing had happened, and I even believed him, but I found a hair clip in the bathroom, just the kind of thing a woman does who wants the wife to know she has been in her territory. I asked him point-blank if he was having an affair, if not with this woman, then with anybody. He swore he wasn't. I broke down and told him about my little fling with the doctor, thinking it would encourage him to come clean, and while he was hurt, he still adamantly insisted he wasn't having an affair. At least the air was cleared for me. I was never good at lying or hiding things. Of course I told Norman it was over and I would never see Benicio again, that I had just felt so abandoned, so alone. Norman held me and told me he loved me and wanted our marriage to work. I wasn't totally convinced.

The movie was done, and we took it to Cannes in the spring of 1987, where it was screened outside of competition. Norman was also a judge that year, so it was an exciting week for us. At last I felt like I was part of the movie, and met a lot of stars. He seemed proud to be with me, we had a good time, and I thought things might be getting back to normal. Benicio called me from time to time, and while we were fond of each other, we knew there was no way we would ever be together. He had a girlfriend, and I really wanted to make my marriage work.

The movie opened in September in the States, to wildly mixed reviews. Nobody had ever seen anything like it. It was nominated for four awards at the Independent Spirit Awards and seven at the Golden Raspberry Awards (the Razzies). Norman won a Razzie for worst director, tying with Elaine May for *Ishtar. Tough Guys* was beautifully shot, thanks to John Bailey, who got one of the nominations for best cinematography, but nobody could figure out what the movie was trying to do, or even what it was. Was it a comedy or a thriller? People laughed when they should have been scared. They were befuddled when they should have been laughing. There were comments that ranged from *The Washington Post*'s "hard to classify; at times you laugh raucously at what's up on the screen, at others you stare dumbly, in stunned amazement" to the *Chicago Reader*'s somewhat kinder "He translates his macho preoccupations (existential tests of bravado, good orgasms, murderous women, metaphysical cops) into an odd, campy, raunchy, comedy-thriller that remains consistently watchable and unpredictable—as goofy in a way as *Beyond the Valley of the Dolls*."

It closed soon after it opened. Nobody took it seriously, and lines like "Oh man, oh God, oh man, oh God, oh man, oh God, oh shit and shinola," which Ryan O'Neal had to say when he found out his wife was having an affair with the police chief, were repeated with delighted incredulity. Ryan just wanted to pretend he hadn't done the movie. In truth, everyone had tried to get Norman to take the "Oh man, oh God" line out, including me, which I regretted because it seemed that whatever I suggested strengthened his determination to do the exact opposite, so I felt responsible in a way for the line staying in.

There were also inadvertently funny lines, such as, "I just deep-sixed two heads," said by Lawrence Tierney, a grand old B-movie gangster who played Dougy Madden, Ryan O'Neal's character's father, after he took the severed heads out to sea. There was a weird scene where Wings Hauser, who played the chief of police and the bad guy, has a stroke, and then recites long minutes of strange dialogue through a twisted mouth to his wife, Madeleine, played by Isabella Rossellini: "Patty Lareine was big time. Ooh, la, la! I thought you were big time, but you were nothing but small potatoes." Of course, Isabella then shoots and kills him, as anybody would, and Dougy, who was listening outside the door, says to Ryan's character, Tim, "I could've told him. You never call an Italian small potatoes." It was painful to watch.

Still, it hurt me when the reviewers were nasty to Norman, in spite of the fact that I secretly agreed with a lot of what they said. Norman was such a little boy at times. He never gave up his wonder at life, his belief in the essential goodness of the world, nor his expectation that this time they would really like what he had done. *The Naked and the Dead*, after all, was his first foray into public love, and it made him an eternal optimist.

We were invited to take the movie to the Cuban Film Festival in 1989. At that time, there were no scheduled flights to Cuba. Americans weren't supposed to go, and if they somehow did go, they weren't supposed to spend any money. We traveled with Tom Luddy, the producer of *Tough Guys*, and Leonard Michaels, a fine writer who wrote a book called *The Men's Club*. We were greeted at the airport in Havana by a gang of friendly writers and filmmakers who put mojitos into our hands. The Cuban government put us all up in a protocol house, once owned by a rich businessman. Nothing in the house had been changed since 1959, when the guy had left in the middle of the night for Miami. It was made of cool concrete blocks, with gray linoleum floors and louvered doors to catch a breeze. In the back garden, there was a small kidney-shaped swimming pool they made a point of telling us they had filled just for us, and a nice metal-and-glass patio set, all straight out of the fifties. We had an ancient Mercedes and a driver who took us everywhere we wanted to go. We had our own chef, who cooked more food at one meal, I suspect, than the average Cuban had all week, but we ate everything, not to appear ungrateful or wasteful.

Tom had brought a shortwave radio along, and we sat out in the garden and listened to Radio Moscow. Tom said how ironic it was that Radio Moscow now provided real news while Cuba still did not. On the radio they were talking about the death of the physicist Sakharov and saying that Russia had lost one of its great patriots. This was thanks to Gorbachev, whom I admired greatly. Only a few years before, the USSR would have branded Sakharov a dissident or an imperialist agent.

Pablo Armando Fernandez, a well-known poet, became our best friend and guide, and we met several other writers, all of whom lived in shabby but genteel homes, surrounded by books and friends. They seemed to be able to criticize the government in conversation, but I doubt they would have been allowed to write and publish the things they were saying.

Norman, me, and Pablo Armando Fernandez.

Havana was beautiful; the vibrant colors of the buildings had long ago faded to soft rain-washed blues and corals and gold. The sun shone every day; the sea was a choppy indigo blue on the other side of the Malecon, a four-mile-long seawall on Havana Harbor; and the streets were full of people who seemed happy. Or at least people who knew the value of a laugh. Rows of schoolchildren in red-and-white uniforms ambled along, and they all smiled and wanted us to take their picture. There were also children in the tattered uniform of the street urchin—shorts and T-shirts with bare feet—to whom we gave packs of gum and candy and ballpoint pens, and they all wanted us to hire them to be our guides. I struck up a conversation with a man who spent his days selling cotton candy and beachcombing, who had a cotton candy cart covered with the detritus of the United States, naked rubber dolls with blond matted hair, plastic cartoon characters, baby pacifiers, soda bottles, and other exotic junk that had floated the ninety miles across the sea—his treasures.

We went to the bars where Hemingway had drunk, El Floridita and La Bodeguita del Medio, which had the best mojitos. We visited Hemingway's house itself, the Finca, and were allowed to go inside and roam around, a treat that was not allowed to the general public. It was just as though Ernest had stepped out for a moment to take a dip in the pool: he had left his glasses beside a sheet of paper on a tall writing table in his bedroom, where he'd worked standing up. There was his scale and the chart where he recorded his weight every morning. We looked at his bookshelves, but didn't see any of Norman's books.

"When *The Deer Park* came out, I sent it to Hemingway, hoping for twenty good words to use for a blurb, which might have meant the difference in a half success or a breakthrough. But I was also angry at myself for begging, so I put a rude inscription in it."

"Did he read it?" I asked.

"Ten days later it was returned in the same package, never opened. It was stamped 'Address Unknown.' But later I got a letter from him. It seems he went out and bought a copy, and said he liked it and it didn't deserve the shitty reviews."

Norman and Hemingway never met. George Plimpton almost arranged a meeting in New York shortly after *Advertisements for Myself* was published, but after Norman waited around all day by the telephone, with George calling every hour or so with bulletins, Hemingway never saw him. It was a little sad, seeing Norman poking about in Hemingway's house, wondering what they might have said to each other if they had indeed ever met. Kind of like the phantom affair he might have had with Marilyn Monroe, if they had ever met, which they didn't.

Norman in the Hemingway house.

PABLO ARMANDO TOOK Tom, Len, Norman, and me to the country outside Havana, where we joined a throng of three thousand people who were making a pilgrimage to a small church in El Rincon. It was the festival of Saint Lazarus, who was also known as Babalu Aye, the saint of healing in the Santeria religion. The night was dark, but every pilgrim carried a candle, bought from vendors who lined the road also selling statues of saints, plates of fried rice and plantains, or spaghetti. The smell of good cigar smoke wafted through the air. I'd worn the wrong shoes, a pair of woven leather flats that got wet and stretched so much that they flopped up and down on my heels, causing blisters. I fervently wished for a Band-Aid, but my discomfort was nothing compared to the pain of the penitents, who were crawling the three miles alongside us, some with cinder blocks wired to their ankles, to honor Saint Lazarus, so I didn't complain.

Castro had only a year or two earlier built a camp for people with AIDS. They were shipped there as soon as they were diagnosed, in hopes of containing the spread of the disease. We passed by it, a tall fence with dozens of people pressed against the wire, holding candles, shouting out to us. We stopped and touched their outstretched hands, hoping to at least give them a little human contact, as we could offer nothing else. It was so poignant, looking through the fence at the big eyes of people who didn't know what was going to befall them. All of us were crying. But we had to leave them, and on we went, marching toward El Rincon, my shoes flapping, the penitents doggedly crawling beside us.

When we finally got there, I was dismayed to see what a tiny church it was. Double doors stood open and a steady stream of people climbed the steps, inched into the front and out the back. In the middle of the church, priests were up on a platform, flinging holy water out over the crowd. There was no way I was going to go into that swarm of people. I am claustrophobic and don't do well with crowds. But Norman, Len, and Tom wanted to go, so I said I would wait right outside and they should come and find me when they came out. They plunged into the maelstrom, as if diving into a boiling stream, and as they started to climb the concrete steps leading to the doors, Tom suddenly was squirted, it seemed, out of the crowd and fell onto the grass beside the steps. I ran over to him and he was okay, but not up to trying it again. "I saw Norman go in," he said, rubbing his head, "and I don't think his feet were even touching the ground. The crowd was just carrying him along."

I began to really worry. Norman wasn't tall. If he fell, he might not be noticed until the crowd had tromped him underfoot. We watched the back door, and there was no Norman coming out. Len joined us, but hadn't seen him, either. We waited and waited. He was nowhere. I pictured the headlines, "Novelist Stomped to Death in Voodoo Ritual!" Then, just as I was deciding to panic, here he came. "I had to crawl out the window," he said. "I couldn't get to the door." He was exhilarated. It had been a fine adventure.

We packed a lot into that trip. We spent an afternoon with Gabriel García Márquez and his wife at their house; Norman went to the Bay of Pigs and checked it out for the book he was writing, *Harlot's Ghost,* and we went to a club and heard Arturo Sandoval, one of the most famous trumpet players in Cuba, who did a Miles Davis and played with his back to the crowd.

The night after our Saint Lazarus experience, we were invited to a reception for the film festival, where Fidel Castro would be present. Norman had always admired him because of his daring to take over a country with just a few ragged troops, and his success in keeping it. Norman always had the fantasy that if he could just talk to Fidel, he could convince him of the error of his ways with Communism, and history would be changed. Now he had the chance. I was impressed with Castro in spite of myself. He was bigger than I'd realized, handsome in his dress uniform, and blessed with the same magnetism that world leaders all seemed to possess. It appears that kind of charisma is a prerequisite to become a world leader. Without it, you might just as well study to become a CPA or whatever.

We were introduced to Fidel, and then we were led over to four chairs at the side of the room. Fidel sat in one, I was seated across from him, Norman was to his right, and the translator was across from Norman. It was a little odd, as there was no table, just the four of us facing one another, but the conversation began, with Fidel speaking in Spanish, looking directly at me, while the translator looked at Norman and translated. Norman spoke to Fidel, who answered him by looking at me, and I sat there not saying a word. It was enough to be able to keep my seat, with that powerful rhetoric I couldn't understand and those dark eyes looking directly into mine. Fidel brought up the Saint Lazarus ceremony as an example of the religious freedom they had in Cuba, and he was surprised when we told him we had been there.

Norman was trying to convince him to come to America and speak directly to the American people, hoping that relations between our countries would turn around if they could meet him, hear him directly, and know who he really was instead of what the American government wanted them to know. Fidel said he would be happy to come, but no one had invited him, and therefore who was going to pay for the security? That was a problem Norman hadn't thought about. Of course it would cost millions in security alone, not to mention, where would he stay? Who would be responsible for arranging his schedule? I can imagine the look on the secretary's face when someone from Fidel's office called the White House and said, "Norman Mailer has invited President Castro to come to America and talk to the people, so he will be arriving next Thursday. . . ." No. I don't think that would be practical. Still, they had a great, animated discussion, with Fidel doing a lot of the talking. He did speak a small amount of English, and he told me later that the next time we came, he would invite us to his house and cook for us. Of course we never made it back.

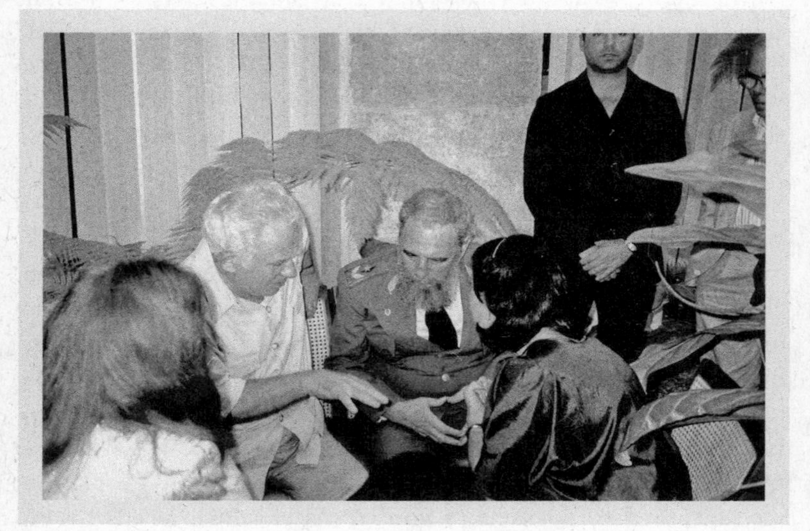

Me, Norman, Fidel Castro, and translator.

The showing of the film at the festival was almost anticlimactic, but it was nice for Norman to once again be the center of attention with his movie. I wish it had been more successful. I wish I had truly liked it, but making that movie was probably one of the best times of Norman's life, and I can't begrudge him that. Even if I was not a real part of it.

When we left, I cleaned out my suitcase of all my hats, scarves, deodorants, lotions, makeup, and toiletries and gave them to the girls who cleaned our house and took care of us. They were so thrilled, even at the half-squeezed-out tube of toothpaste. They never got a chance to buy those things. If I had known the situation, I would have brought over a lot more. It made me so angry to think of how the United States government was starving that poor little island, and forbidding anyone else in the world to do business with them, either, while they were trading like bandits with China and every other Communist country in the world. Somehow, it had to change. The people were courageous, but they were paying a high price for politics that went back fifty years, someone else's politics, started before most of them were even born.

Thirty-nine

We traveled a lot in the late eighties, going to Europe and the Soviet Union several times. The trips were some of the best times for us. We loved walking, poking into little courtyards, and having coffee in small cafés. I didn't speak a foreign language—my horizons in Atkins were somewhat limited—but Norman spoke passable French, and later, when he started working on the book about Lee Harvey Oswald, he went to Berlitz to learn Russian. It was not a huge success. One time, when he returned from a trip, I accidentally washed his passport in his shirt pocket. We put paper towels between the pages to try to dry it out, but it looked like a weird, fluffy blue biscuit. The next time he went back to Russia, the boy at immigration glanced at it and told him it was no good. *"Nyet,"* he said, shoving it back across the desk. Norman tried to explain that the date was perfectly valid, that it had gone through the washer, but he didn't have the words in Russian for "washing machine," so he attempted to tell the officer he'd fallen into a river. I think what he said was that he jumped into a fish, or maybe the passport was a fish, and the boy was so confused he just shook his head and stamped it.

I loved Russia. Maybe it was because Norman had never taken any of his other wives there and each new experience in Russia was our own. In other places, like the south of France, or Paris, I would be aglow with delight about how wonderful everything was, and Norman would say, "Ah, that's nothing. You should have been here in 1948 when I was here with Bea. It was really great then." Or, "It was so much better back in 1956 when I was here with Adele. It's really gone downhill." Finally, at Oxford, I got heartily sick of it. We were looking at the beautiful old buildings, and out behind one was a lovely pasture with brown-and-white cows grazing.

I said, "Oh, how beautiful, just like a John Constable."

He said, "Hm. I do believe this is the same cow pasture I was at with Beverly in 1965, but it was much more beautiful then. The cows were better."

I turned on him. "Do you know *why* it was always better in the old days?" I snarled. "It was because you were *young*!" That shut him up. And it had the added advantage of being true.

But Russia was all my own. I went there the first time in 1984, and then in 1989, Gorbachev invited us to a conference on glasnost. There were several other famous Americans there, such as Gregory Peck and Gore Vidal. We hadn't seen Gore since the night of the PEN reading, when he and Norman had been courteous but stiff, and I was a little nervous about what would happen, but as compatriots often are in a foreign country, we were all quite friendly. Gore and I had always liked each other, and enough time had passed that he and Norman were ready to make an uneasy peace. I don't think either of them ever mentioned the feud again, for which I was grateful.

Norman and Gore Vidal at the Supreme Soviet in Russia.

EDIE VONNEGUT AND I had to give up the painting studio we shared, which saddened me. We'd had a lot of fun together there, and it was the most productive time of my painting life because she was so serious. We would go to the coffee shop on the corner every morning and come back with two cups each and paint like we were in some kind of religious frenzy all day. She did Renaissance-like paintings of angels but in modern-day settings, like an angel riding the subway, or selling her wings on the street. My own style was more realistic. I used old snapshots for reference, making huge pictures of rather sinister children riding tricycles or playing on the beach with their grandparents in old-fashioned bathing suits with skirts and white rubber bathing caps, everyone maniacally smiling for the camera, some shadow of doom over them all. At least that was the way my work was described in one of the reviews. I never consciously put shadows of doom over my protagonists, but I did like to play with shadows. I did commissioned portraits, too, and had a nice list of well-known people as clients, including my friend Pat Lawford, Isaac Bashevis Singer, Roy Cohn, Arthur Schlesinger, and Henry Luce, II.

After Edie and I had to give up the space, Norman and I bought a small studio for me near our apartment in Brooklyn, where I went nearly every day to paint and write. The studio served another purpose as well. Norman paid me long, languid visits there on the occasional afternoon. It felt almost illicit, and those were great times. Afterward, I would go home first, and start to cook dinner, then he would come in, like nothing had happened, but we would share a little secret glance, or he would kiss me on the neck while I stirred the pot.

Those were good years; it seemed like whatever distance Norman had had during the movie filming was in the past. Our date book was full of dinners and theater and lunches and cocktail parties. We entertained at home a lot, too; occasionally, we'd have a big party, but more often we'd have small dinners for the family, or for friends. I would do the cooking, good old Southern/Jewish dishes such as roast chicken, meat loaf, or pot roast, or fried chicken, fried okra, mashed potatoes, and corn bread. But my favorite nights were the ones when I snuggled on the couch with the boys and watched reruns of *Star Trek* and *The Twilight Zone,* and we ordered Fascati pizza and ate Pillsbury slice-and-bake cookies or popcorn.

The kids were growing up, getting married, finding their own careers, and I loved the people they married. Not one of them ever had a drug or alcohol problem, and I'm proud of all of them.

I was happy painting and having a show every year or two, and working at the Actors Studio. I even did a little modeling again. The Elite agency had started an "older" models group. Among other

My portraits of Pat Lawford, Isaac Bashevis Singer, and Norman.

things, I did fur coats (I guess I was destined to be the fur coat girl forever) with my old friend Robert Belott for *Lear's,* a new magazine aimed at the older woman (over forty) that Norman Lear's ex-wife Frances had started with her divorce settlement, and it was a nice ego boost, although I didn't do it for long. There were things I'd rather do than track around New York with my portfolio on go-sees like a young girl and take all that rejection again.

Fur again, in Lear's *magazine.*

I was also working one day a week doing art therapy for Very Special Arts at NYU Hospital, with kids who had cancer or other acute diseases. It was one of the hardest things I've ever done, and one of the best, but after two years, I just couldn't do it anymore. I began to dread going in, with that false cheery attitude, not knowing who would be gone when I got there, who would be too sick to come to the art room. It takes a special person to be able to care for kids who might not be there the following week, and while I'm in awe of the doctors and nurses and therapists who do it, I ultimately didn't have what it takes. But I think it prepared me for when I got cancer myself ten years later, and I like to think I gave some of those kids a little break from the misery of their treatments.

Life was good. Once in a while I would look up at the moon in the night sky and thank God for giving me this life. Then in the late summer of 1991, Norman took a trip to California, I can't remember what for. He traveled a lot in those days. He had to lecture quite a bit to earn extra money to support all the kids in schools, not to mention the alimonies and the expense of having a second house on the beach and two studios. By the late eighties, I had pretty much stopped going with him on speaking engagements. I always had so much to do in New York, and frankly, it was no longer exciting for me to trail around after him. I'd been bumped too many times by photographers and shoved out of the way by adoring fans. But on this trip, things were just a little strange. He called me at two in the morning once, and it was upsetting that he was calling so late. When I questioned him about where he had been, he was vague and defensive and had obviously been drinking. He also told me not to call him, that he was going to be staying with Warren Beatty as his houseguest, which he had done before, and he didn't want me to bother Warren and Annette, so I didn't call.

Still, it was peculiar. I was having those dreams again, the ones where he left me for another woman, and the woman in the dreams was always someone who wasn't a great beauty. In fact, she was always rather plain. When he got back to Provincetown, I asked him some pointed questions about the trip, and somehow he seemed different. Evasive. He didn't want to talk about it and got so angry that I had to let it go. Then the credit card bill came in. I always paid the bills, checking them for odd charges, as anybody does, and this time there were charges in Chicago. A lot of them. From the restaurant amounts, he was obviously paying for dinners for two.

"Sweetie, there were several charges in Chicago this month. I thought you went to Los Angeles."

"Oh, I did, but I didn't tell you I had to make a stop in Chicago to see Saul Bellow about a project we might do."

"Saul Bellow? No, you didn't tell me." He tried to make up some kind of story on the spot, but it became more and more outlandish, then he got stuck in the quicksand and saw I wasn't buying it, so he said, "Okay, I'll confess. I stopped off to see an old girlfriend." (I'll call her April.) I'll spare you the rest of the painful dialogue, but it was all phony anyhow. She had written to him, he said, out of a clear blue sky. He swore it was the first time he had ever done anything like that, it would never happen again, and on and on and on. I was, of course, crushed. I finally discovered why they call it a broken heart. There is actual physical pain in the heart when you are betrayed by someone you trusted. My wonderful life was falling apart. Nothing made sense; his story kept changing. First he said he couldn't perform in bed with April, then he said he did but it was terrible, then he said he did and it was better than he thought it would be, so he felt guilty. He kept adding details and changing details. I was totally confused, and the more I questioned him, the angrier he got.

I became obsessed with finding out the truth. I started going over the phone bills, which listed every long-distance call, and found a lot of calls to Chicago, going back months and months. There were calls to California, too, and other odd calls, to Washington, to Florida. He continued to maintain that this was a onetime thing and it was me he loved and it would never happen again, but I didn't believe him. Small things that had happened over the previous few years came back to me, like the time he helped the daughter of an old girlfriend get into the Actors Studio, and when she hugged him to thank him, right in front of me, she said something about what a nice surprise it had been when she'd seen him in her mother's living room in California the year before. At the time, he explained it away somehow that sort of made sense, and I let it drop. Now I remembered all the comments he had made to actresses about being in his film; his invitation to Kathleen Turner for lunch; all the trips to California he had made without me when he was making the movie; the time he went to Telluride for the film festival with Tom Luddy and said they wouldn't pay for me and we couldn't afford my ticket; the time he went to Paris to see his old friend Jean Malaquais and didn't want me to go because he wanted some alone time with Jean. It all made sense now. I had been a complete and total fool. For years.

We fought and hashed it out for the next two weeks, me crying and getting so angry I physically attacked him a time or two, hitting him with my fists like a child, him promising again and again that it was a onetime thing that was over. It was the end of the summer and I had to go back to Brooklyn to put John, who was thirteen at the time, back in school, and Matt had to start NYU. Norman said he needed a few days alone, so the plan was for the kids and me to go back, and he would stay on for another couple of weeks and write and get his head together. Then he would join us. I saw this as ominous now, too, especially as we were in the middle of such a difficult time. Suddenly all the times he had come to Provincetown by himself to write began to be suspicious. Had he really been alone working? Who could have been with him? Who was this April person? He wouldn't tell me anything about her, but I recognized the name from her picture in a book of photographs we had. If it was the same woman, she was about Norman's age, and not a great beauty, but then in my dreams the woman wasn't, either. Norman refused to talk about her or answer any of my questions. He just wanted it all to go away and for me to "rise above it."

It was extremely hard to go on as if nothing was wrong in front of the kids, but at first they didn't seem to notice anything different. Eventually I had to confide in Danielle, Betsy, and Kate. They were too sensitive to me; they knew something was up. The first time Danielle called and I picked up the phone and said "Hello," she said, "What's wrong?" She could hear it in my voice. They were on my side; they had been through this with their father before—ironically, the last time with me—but they had hoped it would never happen again.

Oddly, when we were packing the car, Norman put a small box of books in the trunk and handed me the keys to his studio. He wanted me to take them over there for him, which was way out of character for him. I *never* went to his studio, ever, not even to clean it. It was in about the same shape our apartment had been in when I'd first seen it. He simply didn't want anyone in his space; even Myrtle didn't go to clean it. I had been there only a handful of times, but I took the keys without question and said I would deliver the box.

I waited a couple of days after we got home, getting up my courage, and then I took the books, walked the long block to his studio, and went in, up the four flights of stairs. The place was filthy, of course, and I marveled again that he could work in such surroundings. Every surface was laden with books and papers and stacks of stuff. Dirty coffee cups and teacups filled the sink. But something else was different as well. Things were missing. He used to keep one of the nude pictures of me I'd given him for Christmas a few years back on his desk, and that was gone, as was a large funny nude drawing I had done of myself for him that used to hang in the bedroom. All traces of me were gone.

I went straight to his desk and opened the drawer, and then sat down. It was crammed full of letters and pictures and notes from other women, small gifts in boxes—not from just one woman but several. Notes that were indisputably love letters. I was shocked at some of them, from women who were supposed to be friends of mine. Other relationships he had explained away by saying the women were old girlfriends and he had wanted to help them out by doing an interview with them, or giving them a reference for a job, or helping out the one in California's daughter at the Actors Studio.

How had I been so blind? He had obviously been cheating on me for a very long time with a small army of women. I remembered women coming up to us at parties and in restaurants and saying hello in overly coy, suggestive ways, which had been odd and certainly annoying. One was an aging porn star I'd had no idea he even knew at all. She was so persistent one night at a restaurant that he had to ask her to leave. Now there was a stack of nude photographs of her in the drawer (obviously not ones taken by him; they were much older than that). He had somehow convinced me he was an innocent bystander who was being pursued by these women because of his celebrity. I'd believed him because we still had an incredible sex life, we had a great home life, and he was so sincere when he told me how much he loved me, that I was the love of his life, that he had never before had what we had, he was so happy with the family, I had given him a life with his children, and so on. And even now I think he was telling the truth, in a way. I know he did love me, I do believe I was the love of his life, and he did love the children and our family life more than anything, but nevertheless he was still able to compartmentalize this other life away from us, and to him, as he said over and over, willing me to understand, it had nothing to do with me. Except, of course, it did.

I was shaken, so sick I had to go to the bathroom. The bathroom was as dirty as the rest of the apartment. As I sat there, trying to get my head together and figure out what I was going to do next, it dawned on me that he must have *wanted* me to find everything. Why else would he have given me the keys to his studio? Why had he been able to cover it up all these years, and for what reason *now* was he leaving clues big enough to drive a truck through?

I got up and flushed. Something in the tank blew up, and water started jetting out of the back of the toilet. Water was beginning to flood the floor and pour into the studio. Soon it would be going down into the floor below. There was nobody in the building except for me. There was no phone. Norman purposely didn't have one so he wouldn't be bothered while he wrote. Soaked from water spurting into my face, I managed to get the lid off the toilet tank and propped the ball thingy up with a book, which I hated to do, but there was nothing else at hand, so the water stopped spouting out, at least, and then I set out to mop the floor and in the process gave the place a good cleaning. I scrubbed for a couple of hours, unleashing my anger—crying and yelling and kicking the furniture with every mop stroke. Then, exhausted, I went back home and wrote Norman a letter. As I've said, the written word was the only way he would understand. We had been trying to talk for the past two weeks and it hadn't worked.

Dear Norman,

Over the years I've often wished for some kind of psychic gift. The few times any inkling of that talent has presented itself has always been in dreams. When you went to Chicago alone that first time, I had a dream that you were leaving me. But you were so adamant about your innocence, I believed you when you swore you were only doing research. The dreams seldom occur, but they're always disturbing, and up to now have always been put aside by your love and assurances. This morning, I woke up in a panic because the dream was so vivid. You know me well enough by now to know that the passion to know is an all consuming passion with me. I really believe I could forgive you anything if I only knew what it is I'm forgiving you for, and if I can believe that it's over. You're asking me to forgive you now, but something is wrong. You are lying about silly insignificant things. You are getting angry when I press you. I don't believe you are really sorry. Even though you swore you'd never see April again, there is still the feeling that you have unfinished business with her. Why else would you tell me different versions of the story? If the scenario was true that it was an uncompleted attempt, then perhaps you believe you have to sleep with her again to save your pride—not unlike the first time you and I made love, is it? Or is the scenario true that it happened and was better than you expected? Are you in a dilemma as to whether or not you will risk our marriage to feed the beast and continue the affair—one obviously just a bit more intense than you pretend?

With the dream sitting on me like a gray wool shawl, I went to your studio to see if I could find a clue as to why I can't seem to get a handle on this. I know it was underhanded, but I feel like I'm fighting for my life, and you did give me the key, knowing full well I would use it. Your studio is such chaos that a systematic search would have been difficult, so I just looked through your desk drawer. Lots of interesting things in that drawer. Actually, I never found the letters from April that I had hoped would enlighten me to the intensity of your relationship, or anything that mentioned April at all, but I did find a Christmas gift, a copy of one of those fat little prehistoric women, with a card from "Your Willendorf Goddess," Rita*, and then a note dated over a year ago from Linda* promising not to ask Norman Mailer for more money until March of 1990, but if you give her a thousand dollars she will love you. Have you been giving her money for sex, or just because she's a "poor kid struggling to make it as a writer in the big tough world" as you once told me when I asked you why you were doing so many interviews with her? There was also a cute card with a row of women showing their butts, and a note thanking you for "One for the road," from somebody in Florida, and a sex poem (one really can't call it a love poem) from Pixie* in Washington. What in the world is THAT? Have I really been such a bad wife these last few years that you have turned away from me searching for a woman who can be all things to you? Or several that can be a little bit each? How have you had the energy? You've hardly lagged in that department with me. Well, maybe a little. At this point I am a very confused woman.

* Not her real name.

After more than sixteen years I feel like I'm living with a stranger. Incredibly, insanely, the sex has been better with you these last two weeks than it has ever been, and I'm remembering the early years. You are all consuming to me now. I only want, more than anything, to go on with you in the life we have. I want us to continue to love our children and have the home life we perhaps have taken for granted all these years. But if you truly are dissatisfied—even a small part of you—and you really need other women in your life to make you complete, then I won't stay with you. I don't want to end up a bitter wife, searching phone bills and Visa receipts for clues of infidelity, dying inside when you take a trip; not believing you when you say in that flat voice, "I love you." I deserve better than that. I've given you my youth, but I'm not yet old, and I can still find happiness elsewhere.

Don't call me right way. Use these next few days to think about what I've said. Sort out your feelings. For the first time, be honest with me. If you decide to go on with me, I want to know the extent of your affairs. Have the courage to tell me. Did you take someone to Paris that time you went to see Jean? Did you arrange to meet women at your lectures? Have you had women to our house in Provincetown all those weeks I thought you were there alone writing? If you can tell me the truth, all of it, I really believe I can come to terms with it, but I have to have the air cleared before I can start over and begin a new life with you—assuming you want to begin a new life with me, and you may not because to me, that means fidelity. For both of us. Talk to me. If in your heart of hearts you don't want to give up other women, then get your balls together and tell me. Trust me. It's not so difficult. My Alpha, at least, is a very understanding soul. And I do love you, it seems. I can't help myself. We can have one of the great loves of this century, or you can finally, truly be free and alone—in Paris—if that's your choice.

I'm not like my mother now. I'm not weeping. I'm dead serious. I won't go on like this, so you have to do some hard thinking and make a decision.

Still your wife,
Norris

I faxed the letter to him in Provincetown, and within ten minutes the phone was ringing.

"Hello."

"That was some letter. You really are a writer."

"Are you trying to flatter me?"

"I'm trying."

"You didn't have to call. I told you to wait and think about it."

"I don't need to. I want to be with you."

"Are you sure?"

"I've never been more sure."

"Then I think you'd better come home."

"I think I had."

HE ARRIVED IN BROOKLYN that night. He kissed the kids and then said we were going out for dinner. Instead, we went over to my studio, where I sat on the couch and he pulled up a chair to face me. Then he started to confess. He had been working on *Harlot's Ghost,* his book about the CIA, for several years and it was due to come out soon. He said his double life started when he began researching that book, and I suppose it could even be true. The timing was about right. All the clandestine talking on pay phones, making secret plans, hiding and sneaking around, were perfect spy maneuvers. He said he needed to live that kind of double life, to know what his characters were going through. (It was an imaginative excuse. I do give him credit for that.)

He said he had been totally true to me, except for one or two tiny one-night stands with old girlfriends when he was on lecture tours, for eight years after we got together, which might even be mostly true. It was his grand experiment in monogamy, and I had believed him. While it could hardly be said the experiment was a total success, it was the longest he had ever been true (more or less) to a woman in his life. His nature was to be a philanderer. Still, if he was (more or less) true for the first eight years of our relationship, that left the last eight years in which he was totally, blindingly, a cheat.

"Why didn't I know?" I said, incredulously. "How could I have been so ignorant all this time?"

"It's not hard to fool someone who loves you and trusts you," he said, with perfect sincerity. No. I guess it's not. I sat there silently and thought about that. "I'm going to tell you everything," he continued, "but there will be no divorce. I don't want this to break us up. You are my life, and I will not let you leave me."

"You tell me everything and then we'll talk about it," I said. "I'm not promising anything now." So he began, and the more he told, the angrier I got. Detail after detail, woman after woman. Once he began, it was like he was vomiting up a bad meal and had to get it all out. At one point, I started screaming at him, then I was on my feet, hitting him and scratching him, trying to really hurt him. He just buttoned up and let me do it, protecting himself as best he could. He never hit me back once. When I was exhausted, I fell back down on the couch and he continued. I couldn't believe how much he had to tell me, how blind and stupid I had been. It went on until I could take no more, and then we went back to the apartment, where we went to bed, totally exhausted, fell into each other's arms, and had wild sex. Go figure.

Great sex aside, my life was in tatters. Now that he had begun, every day brought more revelations, and in the midst of all this Sturm und Drang, our life somehow went on. We accepted social dates, we had family dinners, we became adept at showing one face to everyone and another to ourselves, although I'm sure we weren't fooling anyone. Alone, I was scathing to him. He was brutal to me.

I remember once we were going to have dinner with Jason Epstein, Norman's editor, and his wife, Judy Miller. On the way up in the elevator, Norman said something that made me so angry I reached out and scratched his face, just before I rang the doorbell. I couldn't help it. It was a reflex, like my hand had taken on a life of its own. Three long, red marks appeared on his cheek. As the door opened, I smiled brightly and said, "Jason! How wonderful to see you!" He looked startled as Norman fumbled in his pocket for his handkerchief, and mumbled, "Oh, the cat got me, ha, ha." I swept into the room, Jason following behind me looking confused, and nothing else was said about it.

It wasn't the first time I attacked him. I couldn't control myself, and he couldn't stop confessing, giving me detail after detail, trying to explain why he had done all the things he had, over and over and over again. We might be in the back of a taxi, going to a black-tie dinner, and he would suddenly remember someone else he had slept with that he had forgotten to tell me about. I would dramatically tell the driver to pull over, and I'd get out, either going on to the dinner in another car or making Norman get out and chase after me. It went on for weeks, his confession and my rage.

Then *Harlot's Ghost* came out and publicity started for the book. To my horror, one of the girlfriends, Linda, the author of the note asking for a thousand dollars, a woman he had been giving money to for nine years, came to the book party. She was shockingly brazen, bringing photographers over to take her picture with Norman, standing close to him, looking in my direction as if daring me to come and do something about it. I ignored her. Finally, she came directly up to me, photographer in tow, and taunted me while he took pictures. Norman stood silently a few feet away, drinking, trying to ignore the whole thing. I was about to explode but refused to get into a fight with her, which was exactly what she wanted, a big hair-pulling fight that would land her in the newspapers. So I just told her in a low voice to enjoy the party, that she had gotten the last nickel she was going to get out of Norman, and I walked away. I could feel my insides roiling into a knot. This nightmare was never going to end. How could I continue to live with a man who would have a relationship with such a woman?

But it got worse. I went with him on the publicity tour for *Harlot's Ghost*. He wanted me to. He insisted upon it. One of the first stops was Chicago. As we landed at O'Hare, he told me that the woman who was meeting us, the one who was to be our guide, driving us to the radio shows and appearances, was the woman he had been having the affair with. He had gotten her the job. But her name wasn't April. He had made that up. I'll call her Helen.

I was a wreck as we came off the plane. It was like a scene out of Fellini as she came to meet us at the airport gate. She was his age if not older; she wore a gray wig, was about five feet tall, and must have weighed two hundred and fifty pounds or more. She was nervous, of course. How could she not be? I felt sorry for her; it was awkward in the extreme. Later, when I asked Norman what had attracted him to her, he said that sometimes he needed to be the good-looking one, and that he didn't want to have someone who was competition for me. My head was swimming. It was so cruel to her, as well as to me, and she obviously adored him. I found myself chatting with her, trying to put her at ease, and once when Norman introduced her by the wrong name, I cringed. What was I doing? The world had turned upside down.

We went on to San Francisco and Los Angeles, where there was another old girlfriend in the audience, also around his age. Again, it was awkward; again I was polite to her. I saw a pattern here, and wasn't sure what to make of it. All of the women he had been seeing were older than I was; some were older than he was. But it didn't make me feel any better that they weren't young, nubile beauties. Did he think that made it all right? These women took over my life. I couldn't think of anything else; we couldn't seem to talk about anything else.

At night I prayed. Was I being punished for taking Norman away from his last wife (even though I'd known he wasn't going to stay with her anyhow)? I went over in my head all the things I had done wrong through the years, all the sins that were on the sin list, and there were a lot. I methodically asked God to forgive me. But I didn't feel better. In fact, I felt foolish for being so witless as to believe this was God's punishment for drinking wine or playing cards or having that misbegotten little affair while I was married to Larry, or the few nights I'd spent with Benicio. What kind of a God would punish someone for stuff like that? Still, part of me wondered—would I be better off if I was still married to Larry and trying to play by the rules laid down by the Freewill Baptist Church? And part of me answered, Who was I trying to kid, God or myself? We both knew better. And who had elected *Norman* to punish me for my sins anyhow? According to the sin list, he was waaaay ahead of me in that department. Why wasn't *he* being punished? I began to think I was going crazy.

Sam Donaldson of ABC News came to the apartment with a TV crew to interview Norman, and he wanted to do a little side interview with me on camera. I wasn't anxious to talk about my husband's wonderful book. (Some of our worst fights had been over that book. I—as well as his editor, his assistant Judith, and others—had begged him to continue the exciting spy story with which he had begun the book, but instead he went off on tangents in Uruguay and Cuba that had nothing to do with the story he had started, and then he ended the 1,310-page book with "To Be Continued.") Now that I knew so much from his endless confessions, there were many references in the book that I recognized as being about the other women, and those raised my ire and made me dislike the book even more. But I didn't want to make a big deal of it to Sam Donaldson and take the chance our troubles would come to light on network TV, so I agreed. The soundman clipped the microphone onto my blouse, and Sam and I chatted for a minute. I looked into his eyes, which had the strangest pupils; they were not round but rectangles, like a goat's eyes, and with his rather pointed eyebrows, it gave him a devilish air. But I liked him; we were teasing and having a bit of fun.

I said, "So, what do you want from me? I'll answer any question you have, except for one: 'What's it like to live with Norman Mailer?' Everyone always asks that. It's the kind of question that requires 5 percent from the interviewer and 95 percent from the interviewee, and it's boring. I know you can come up with a better question." He laughed and agreed, and when the camera started rolling, the first thing he asked, with a twinkle in his goat eyes, was "What's it like to live with Norman Mailer?"

I had a twinkle in my own eye as I answered, right off the top of my head, "Well, Sam, it's kind of like living in the zoo. One day Norman is a lion; the next he's a monkey. Occasionally he's a lamb, and a large part of the time he's a jackass." I don't know where that came from. It just sprang out of my mouth. Sam laughed, but I could see he was shocked, as was Norman and the rest of the crew. I had no idea they would leave it in, but they did, and it was picked up and printed everywhere.

After the show aired, one of the calls I got was from Benicio. He said, "I saw you on TV. What's wrong?" I broke down and told him I was thinking of leaving Norman, and he said, "You need to get away. I'll send you an airplane ticket. Come and see me. I just broke up with Laura* [his girlfriend of many years], and it would be good to see you." He had moved a couple of times since he had been in Little Rock, and now he was a surgeon in Atlanta.

While I declined his offer of a ticket, the idea of getting away appealed to me, so I called my parents and Aurora in Little Rock and told them I was coming. I didn't tell my parents about the trouble we were having, just that I wanted to come down by myself, and if they thought

* Not her real name.

it was odd, they were still happy. I told the kids that Aurora and I were taking a road trip to see our old friend Jean in Florida, and Norman decided to take them skiing. I flew to Arkansas and spent a nice restorative few days with my parents. They babied me and cooked all the fried dinners I could eat. We went to Wal-Mart and to Whatta Burger and drove out to the cemetery to visit the ancestors. It was so great to be with the two people in the world, besides my kids, who loved me unconditionally and were good and honest, who would never betray me. But I had never been able to talk to them about my personal problems, and that hadn't changed. I didn't want them to know what Norman and I were going through. They would have just said, "We told you not to marry that old man. You bring the boys and come back down here and live with us." Their way of dealing with things would have been to pray about it, and I'm sure they did that anyhow. They could tell, I know, that something was wrong. Maybe their prayers helped.

Then I went to Little Rock, and Aurora, her husband, Phil, and I got into their car and drove to Florida to visit Jean, the third member of our Three Musketeers. Jean had gotten married for the second time to a handsome younger man named Juan and at age forty had a new baby girl, a sister for her two older sons. Phil and Aurora owned a booth in an antiques mall, so we stopped at every little roadside shop along the way in Tennessee and Mississippi looking for treasures, which I had never in my life done. My father, and then my husbands (both of them), had refused to stop the car for that sort of thing. Aurora had gotten a perm in her straight hair, "to make it easier to deal with on the road," and it became a hilarious running joke as she fought the frizzy mass of hair in the heat and humidity. We stopped for the night in Foley, Alabama, at what we called the Bates Motel. I went out to the pay phone at the side of the road and called Norman, thinking how things had changed, how now I was the one on the road at the phone booth and he was at home holding down the fort. It was a tight, unhappy conversation, as all our calls seemed to be.

Everything on the trip was hilarious. I was on the brink of totally changing my life and was giddy with possibilities. We got to Florida and had a great time with Jean and her new family. On the surface I was strong and determined, but when I was alone at night, I was scared. It was so ironic. Here one of my oldest, best friends was starting out a life of happiness with a baby and new love, and my own life was breaking apart. Of course I told them everything, and as girlfriends do, they circled the wagons around me and made me feel loved and protected.

Aurora, Jean, and me in Florida.

While I was down there, I called Benicio. I couldn't just go back to New York and say, "Okay, I'm back. I will rise above it and forget about all of this and you can go ahead and do what you want to." I had to find myself again. I needed to have someone think I was attractive, someone who wanted me for the woman I was, not for the easy stability I had created, which I thought was the real reason Norman didn't want to leave me. It was a comfortable life I had created for him, and it's not easy to start over when you are nearly seventy.

Benicio met me at the airport, and I soon realized the connection we somehow used to have was gone; we were virtual strangers. But he was newly single, so we commiserated and at least had that in common. He drove a nifty little sports car, and took me to his house, an elegant mansion in a new suburb, and we tried to get reacquainted. I slept with him that night, which was expected, but it felt desperately wrong. He got a call and had to go to the hospital in the middle of the night, so he left me alone, then came back late with a bucket of Kentucky Fried Chicken and woke me up. We ate the chicken and tried to make a little conversation, and he left me to clean up the bones while he went to bed and fell immediately into a sleep as deep as a coma, as only doctors can.

I gingerly got in beside him and hugged the edge of the bed, wondering what I was doing there. In an act of defiance, I had taken off my wedding rings and put them in a dish on the dresser when I'd first arrived, but I crept out of bed, got them, and put them back on. In the morning, he left early for the hospital before I woke up, and I decided to write him a note and call a cab to take me to the airport—until I realized I didn't know what the address was, or even what suburb it was! I didn't know anything, the name of his hospital, his phone number there—nada. It was as if I had just been dropped by parachute into a strange city and wandered into a stranger's house. I had never felt so stupid and alone.

I sat out by the pool for a while and then poked around the house, which was decorated nicely and expensively, but it looked like a show house where nobody lived. There were no photos of friends and family, no knickknacks from vacations. No books, except medical texts and some bound sets of classics that a decorator had put on the shelves. It was the house of someone who worked all the time and just came home occasionally to sleep. I didn't wonder that the girlfriend had left. I was hungry, but the fridge, an expensive Sub-Zero, had only a couple of bottles of white wine and a wedge of Brie. Nothing else. I was even scared to turn on the TV. It was a huge system with surround speakers, a gigantic screen, and a whole row of clickers. So I sat and read a book I had brought, while my stomach growled. I remembered how Benicio had been at the hospital almost around the clock when we'd first met. His beeper was constantly going off. I could never live with someone who worked so much—not that he was asking me to live with him, but I had been there for more than a day and we still hadn't really had a conversation. He'd talked about his practice and his patients, and didn't seem terribly interested in my dismal little tale of woe. As soon as he got back, I had him take me to the airport, saying I had to get back for the kids. I don't think he minded at all.

The visit had been a mistake, but at least it gave me a bit of drama to tell Norman about. That was the real reason I did it, I realized, to tell Norman and hurt him. I wanted him to know that someone else wanted me, that I had other options. Not that I hadn't had chances over the years. There was a long list of men who had come on to me, men who were famous and rich, and I could have had any number of affairs, but I didn't. Now a part of me wished I had said yes to at least some of them. Maybe one of the movie stars. Or the billionaire (although he might have been just a multimillionaire).

Why had I been so consumed by this old, fat, bombastic, lying little dynamo? I obviously wasn't the only one who'd been consumed by him, since I was wife number six. Six! Not to mention the legions of girlfriends. What was I thinking? Didn't I know he was going to do it to me, too? Why did I think I was different than all the rest of them? Why did I think I was the one who was going to "tame the tiger," as reporters were fond of saying in news stories? Nothing would tame that particular tiger except old age, and I strongly suspected that was one of the key elements coming into play with this situation; it was the reason he'd allowed me to find out the details. He could no longer keep up the pace and he wanted Mommy to end it all for him. But would I? Could I stay in this marriage? I had some self-respect left. At least some.

John and Matt were there with Norman when I arrived at the apartment, and we were all happy to see one another. I hugged the boys as if I would never let them go. They were full of stories of the skiing trip, how Dad had taken a pad and pen along in his pocket. "In case you got an idea on the slope?" I asked, incredulously, and he sheepishly nodded. Of course he had taken a hard fall and the pen had jammed into his rib cage, badly bruising or maybe even cracking some ribs. He'd been so disheartened by the deterioration of his skiing abilities and his obvious aging—and I'm sure angry at the fact that I had gone off on a trip, and angry at our whole sorry state of affairs—that he'd been in a foul mood the whole time and had yelled at the boys for every little thing they did. On the way home, when Stephen got lost trying to find the way to Danielle's house, where they were going to spend the night, Norman turned the air blue with invectives against Stephen and John's incompetence, grabbed the map out of their hands, and got out of the car to read it in the glow of the headlights. John said he and Stephen looked at each other and debated whether or not Stephen should let his foot slip off the brake and run Norman over, but they decided not to. It was a merry return on the surface; pictures were taken that night, and I can look at them and tell that both of us were smiling on the outside but devastated inside. It was the hardest thing I'd ever done, but I'd made my decision. I was going to tell Norman I was leaving him. We went out to dinner to talk, and the boys ordered pizza.

Us, just before the big talk.

I really can't reconstruct all the dialogue, but I told him about seeing Benicio, which hurt him just as I'd hoped, although hurting him didn't give me the pleasure I'd thought it would, and then I told him that I was leaving him. Not because of Benicio—I wouldn't be seeing him again—but because I deserved to find someone who would be better to me. I wasn't crying. He hated it when I cried, and it always made him angry, so I tried not to. I was perfectly rational and said we needed to work out arrangements, where we were going to live, who John would live with, all the other details of ending a marriage; he had done it enough times before to know the drill. Then he panicked. "No," he said, slapping the table. "No, no, no, no, no. We are not breaking up!" People in the restaurant were beginning to stare.

"Please keep your voice down," I said. I didn't really want to break up, either. I loved my family, I loved his sister and her family, I loved our apartment in Brooklyn and our house in Ptown and our friends. I loved our life. I even loved him. I just couldn't live anymore with a man who had so little respect for me, and who I couldn't trust. I couldn't live with a man who at nearly seventy needed to have sex with so many other women. My biggest regret was for John. He had been the only child who'd gotten to grow up with Norman, the only one who had lived with him past the age of six, and now that he was a young teenager, it would be the hardest on him, but that was Norman's choice.

Norman began to talk then. He used all his talents and abilities and charm, which were considerable. Somehow—I still don't quite know how—before the dinner was over, he made me believe that he did love me and that he wanted to spend the rest of his life with me. He was ready to give it all up, all the other women, everything. Maybe I was still naïve; maybe it was just that neither one of us wanted to have to go out and find another apartment. No matter; we went home intending to stay together and somehow make it work.

Forty

My favorite quote of Norman's is from *The Deer Park:* "There is that law of life, so cruel and so just—that one must grow, or else pay more for remaining the same." I think we both did a lot of growing in those next years, and it wasn't easy. Things kept popping up that flicked the scab off the healing wound, like the old girlfriend who kept calling and causing trouble, who made sure the story of their affair was printed over and over in newspapers and magazines. Any time something like that appeared, it was painful for me. But miraculously, the kids seemed to be okay with everything and we were continuing our lives. We had family dinners at Barbara's or our house, we saw the grandchildren, went to the kids' plays and art shows. Everyone was just thrilled we had dodged the bullet and had not broken up the family again. But after all the months of confessions and recriminations and anger, I somehow had taken a step away from Norman in my heart, and I thought that was a good thing. It was the only way I could go on living with him, because if I was still so in love with him, so raw and trusting, I would just be hurt again. I had no real faith that he was going to actually give all the women up. I thought he might try, but sooner or later, he would be on a trip and temptation would be too strong. He would just go back to being more careful, and he would have to, now that I knew the signs. I told him if I caught him cheating one more time, that was it, and I meant it. No, it was better to be that little bit less in love and not care quite as much.

Harlot's Ghost made the bestseller list, then dropped out of sight. In spite of the last line in the book, "To Be Continued," and a halfhearted effort to research the next volume, Norman never really wanted to finish that book. His fascination with the CIA had played itself out, and as he said, he didn't know how to end the exciting story he had started.

There were several themes that ran through Norman's life and his work. Now in his seventies, he had written about most of them, but there were still others on the list: President Kennedy's assassination, God and the devil, religion and Hitler, all of which he would end up writing about before his life was over. Now he started working on *Oswald's Tale,* about Lee Harvey Oswald. This necessitated more travel—trips to Moscow and Minsk, and Dallas.

Larry Schiller was back in the picture on this book. He had worked his Schiller magic and gotten the KGB, in the one open moment in its history, to agree to sell him some of the files they had developed on Oswald while he'd lived in Minsk. Norman and Larry had to go to Minsk and Moscow many times, and I don't know all the fine points of the negotiation, but the papers were obtained. The picture they presented was one of a nutty American kid with more guts than brains who had somehow managed to defect to Russia, find a job, and marry a pretty Russian girl. Then, when he realized he wasn't going to be a rock star just because he was an American, that the Russians weren't going to give him some big job in the government and a fancy place to live, he wanted to go back home. He was pretty shrewd, though, in the way he played the establishment, to get them to pay for his travel. Among the papers Larry and Norman received were over two hundred pages of conversations between Lee and his wife, Marina, from a microphone planted in their apartment. Their dialogue could have been between any couple anywhere.

"You never wash the kitchen floor," he complains.

"Yes, I do. I wash it more than you. I have washed the kitchen floor seventeen times and you have washed it none." Marina was not happy with Lee's habit of lying around reading children's comics and "fouling the air with gasses." Lee was not happy with his job in a factory, assembling radios in Minsk. But as banal as some of the dialogue was, it was still rich stuff for a writer because the man who had assassinated the president was speaking the banalities.

Larry and Norman interviewed several high-ranking officers and KGB people who knew Lee, co-workers and friends, and they discovered an interesting phenomenon—everyone seemed to have crystal clear memories of him. It might have been because after President Kennedy's assassination anyone who knew Lee was ordered not to talk about him, even to their families, so the memories hadn't been adulterated by discussion, but the material Larry and Norman were getting was fresh and good. *Oswald's Tale* is, in fact, one of my favorites of Norman's books.

Marina's aunt Valya still lived in Minsk, and Larry hired her to be their cook. Larry gave her money to shop for better food on the black market, and several nights a week they went to Valya's house for dinner. She was a good cook, and an important part of the story as well. Larry was amazing at getting things done. I've always marveled at his ingenuity, and I do to this day. He found Norman an apartment in a workers' building in Minsk—a little two-bedroom in a building made of poured concrete that was five years old but looked fifty—where he stayed for weeks at a time. Then Norman would return to New York and be with us before going back again. I was having a hard time with the separation. I, of course, imagined he was schtupping fat, old, ugly Russian women in babushkas, but tried to go on and live my life as if things were fine. I tried to keep that little step away from him in my heart.

One night at a dinner party, I was seated next to a friend I had known socially for many years, and he began to question me on where Norman was and why I was always alone. He, of course, had seen the stories in the papers about our troubles and had heard the gossip. I found myself confiding in him, and he was a most attentive listener. He gave me a ride home in his car, invited me to dinner the following evening, and I went. That began a brief affair, one that showed me there was a possibility I could have another life if I wanted to. I'm sure he was teasing, but at one point he said, "If you will divorce Norman, I'll marry you." I lightly answered, "You're going to have to stop saying things like that to girls. One of them will take you up on it, and then you'll be in big trouble." We laughed, and nothing was said again about marriage or divorce, but I think we both thought about it. I was terribly fond of him, and still am happy when I see him, but my life was bound up with that crazy wild man who was in Minsk. I wondered what he was up to, and I knew that if I left him I would wonder the rest of my life what he was up to, and be sorry I wasn't with him.

Norman invited me to come spend a couple of weeks with him in Minsk. It was winter, and the city was as dreary as anyplace I had ever been. The yellow mud froze in ruts along the roads, and the snow was piled high, geologically layered in various shades of dirt. The apartment had worn linoleum on the floor, a rug on the wall, and wooden furniture of an angular style that was popular in America in the fifties.

The door to the apartment was padded leather, and the first day I was there, at seven in the morning, someone stood in the hallway pounding on it, yelling in Russian. I had no idea what they were saying, it might have been "The building is on fire" or "Can you help me pull my car out of the mud?" or anything else. Norman didn't know, either, so he just rolled over and went back to sleep. I did, too, figuring if the building was on fire we would soon know all about it.

The kitchen had a stove with four burners and a tiny oven, and a small fridge that smelled of cabbage. Beside the sink was a strange-looking gray cardboard box of dishwashing soap that looked like ashes with bits of bone or something ghastly mixed in it. All the products and foods were fascinating to me—the egg shampoo that was the bright yellow of yolks, and the real, small hard eggs that came in a plastic sack of twenty, eggs squeezed from the butts of sturdy little chickens that continually pecked the frozen ground in search of an insect or worm, scratching out a living like everybody else.

We had a car, an old beat-up Russian Lada, with a driver named Murat who looked like Ratso Rizzo and who protected Norman with his life. I stayed in the apartment and worked on a new play I was writing for the Actors Studio while Norman and Larry went out to do interviews, but after a couple of days I needed to get out, so they got me a driver of my own named Sasha, a young, sweet boy who took me shopping and sightseeing. The stores were poor, indeed, but if there is something to be found in a store, you can trust I will find it. Sasha wanted to take me to the few fancy Western stores that had Revlon cosmetics and more modern-style clothes, but I insisted on going to the real old Russian stores. He couldn't understand why, until I told him I could get Revlon in New York but I couldn't get a good wool coat made in Latvia or a hand-crocheted tablecloth made by a little old lady for twenty dollars.

In one store, I tried on several coats, to the delight of the salesgirls, modeling them like I used to do on the New York runways, and when I bought a purple wool coat, they all clapped and cheered. "Nobody from New York has ever bought anything in here," one of them said, tears practically running down her cheeks. I paid ten dollars cash for it, and they lovingly wrapped it in brown paper and string. It was a nice, warm coat that I wore for many years.

Sasha took me to the market, a huge building that once must have been an airplane hangar, where all the farmers from the countryside came in with their produce and set up little stalls. There was fresh-churned butter, cut into chunks and wrapped in newspaper; chickens that had been killed and plucked that same morning, poor little things that I was embarrassed for, their breasts were so small. I wanted to avert my eyes. It was almost obscene, the way they were lying there, their skinny legs splayed. Little boys rushed around selling lemons, and one came up to me and scratched the yellow skin and stuck it under my nose. I bought it for a dollar, and he presented it to me as though it were a precious jewel. A woman stood with her arms outstretched, a human clothes rack, her knitted scarves and shawls hung up and down her arms. I watched her for several minutes, and she never flinched, never seemed to get tired. I bought a soft brown shawl that felt like a cloud, just to give her a break, I think. It's a comfort blanket. I still wrap my feet in it in bed on cold winter nights. Men in butcher stalls would chop off a piece of meat and roll it in newspapers for you, and women minded baskets of cabbages and beets and carrots, dirt still clinging to them. I didn't want to remember that we were not all that far from Chernobyl, and bought what we needed for dinner.

Norman and I stayed home that night and made borscht. The snow was falling and the room was warm and lit by a bulb hanging from an electric wire in the middle of the kitchen. Neither of us really knew what we were doing, but we sautéed the meat first in its own fat, then threw all the other ingredients into the pot, added some water, and the beets turned the broth a rich deep purple. I chopped more onions fine, sautéed them until they were brown, and mixed them into salty creamed potatoes, and we invited Larry and his translator for dinner. It was one of the best meals we have ever made, and for years we tried without success to reconstruct how we made it, but I think the real secret was the ingredients, grown in the glowing soil of Minsk, the meat grown there, and the sour cream, made from fresh milk by local women and brought to the market in big jars. I still dream about the yogurt and fresh milk, the brown bread and butter, and caviar you could get, five dollars for a big dollop.

The food in the restaurants, however, was another matter. You could get a meal for a dollar and a quarter, and it was worth about seventy cents. The potatoes were burned, greasy, and raw all at the same time. The meat was gristly and fatty. The cabbage salad was limp and warm. There was not enough money to buy a good meal in the whole city, and we tried most of the restaurants.

We went to one place in a nice hotel, and the first thing I noticed was the beautiful girls, all with perfect legs from years of studying ballet, all with long, long hair and short, short skirts. One girl I saw with a certain man was back a while later with a different one. Larry pointed out that they were prostitutes, and I was so upset that these elegant women had to do that.

We went to the ballet to see *The Nutcracker*, and while the theater was a little threadbare, the show was magic. I was wearing my Anna Karenina outfit, as Norman called it, a black shearling coat and a black fox fur hat. When Murat drove us home afterward, there were a dozen or so boys standing outside. Norman knew them. They were teenagers who lived in our building, and they were all drunk. There was not a lot else for teenagers in Minsk to do at night. They stood to one side as we walked to the door, and I was a little uneasy, but Norman said, "They're okay." They were definitely curious about me. Norman said "Good evening" in Russian, and then presented me. "My wife," he said, which sounded something like *"Moy jhene."* The oldest and boldest one of the group, who looked a little like Michael J. Pollard, stepped up with wonder in his eyes. *"Ve jhene?"* he asked. "This is your *wife*?" Then the group broke out in applause, for Norman, for having the good taste to have me for a wife, I guess. I did a little curtsy for them.

We were in a good mood when we went inside, and for the first time since I'd gotten there, maybe for the first time since we had started the marital war, the ice began to melt and we began to come back to each other. We did love each other. We wanted to be together, not just for the family, not just for the apartment and the house, but for us. I knew I was going to be with him the rest of my life, and I think he felt the same way. It wasn't always easy after that. We of course fought, bitterly at times, and once in a while the scab on the old wound would be picked, but this time in Minsk was the beginning of the healing.

When I got back to New York, I went to my friend's apartment and told him I couldn't see him again, that I was going to stay with Norman. He wasn't surprised. "I always knew you were never going to leave Norman," he said. But it was okay. I'm not sorry we had our little fling. It made me see that I really loved Norman, for better or for worse. Maybe it just took a little more for Norman to find this out for himself.

Forty-one

We started spending more time in Provincetown. John went to Andover in the fall of 1994, and there was no reason to stay in New York on the school schedule. Matt was still living at home, but he had graduated from NYU film school and was making a feature version of his award-winning senior thesis film, *The Money Shot*. I was so proud of him. He had worked twice as hard as everyone else to get where he was because he was dyslexic. Reading was harder for him, math was almost impossible, and yet he had gotten to the top of his class and was now working as a movie director.

Norman had always loved working in the Provincetown house. It had a calm ambiance that was conducive to writing. He loved the solitude and being on the sea, and frankly, by then he was ready for a break from our hectic social life. He was also tired and burned out from the last few contentious years. He wanted a quieter life, to refocus on his work. He felt age rounding his shoulders.

The summers in Provincetown were always a madhouse. The five bedrooms were packed for three solid months with kids and friends, sometimes the couches as well, but in the fall things quieted down. The days came down gray and crisp, and smoke from fireplaces scented the east end of town. Ducks and geese and wayward swans stopped and swam in the bay on their trips south, gorging on the schools of minnows. We had few friends who lived there all year, and many evenings were spent alone, watching TV, reading, working late. We rediscovered each other in those years. We became like two old friends who knew everything about each other and liked each other anyhow.

We began to redecorate the house, as it was still decked out in Patty Lareine's Easter egg colors from *Tough Guys Don't Dance*, and those cool pastels didn't go with the cold winters. I had never liked those colors in general, but we'd just never had the time to change it. We both loved wallpaper instead of paint, it was cozy and warm, and the big house could take some warmth, with its wall of windows that stretched along the sea view. Norman enjoyed going to the wallpaper store and poring over sample books as much as I did. The women who worked there were thrilled when he came in, and they scurried around to find things he might like. In fact, he chose most of the papers in the house, but he did it with an eye to the colors I liked, the warm colors of fall. We started out to just do the living room, but as soon as one room was done, the next one seemed to ask for it. John Golden, the meticulous man who did the papering, practically moved in with us for more than a year.

I sold my studio in Brooklyn and we renovated the kitchen with the profits. It was the closest we had been in . . . well, maybe the closest we'd ever been. All alone, just the two of us. No secrets. At least none I knew of. I would never totally trust him again, but I trusted him enough. And I had my own little secret in the bank, so to speak. It was good it was there. It gave me some self-esteem; it made me feel less like a poor sad victim.

I painted and showed in local galleries, we went back and forth to New York, and Norman worked on *Oswald's Tale: An American Mystery*, which came out in May 1995. It was a surprising book to a lot of people, because over the years Norman had been convinced that there had been some kind of conspiracy afloat to kill the president, and during the course of his research he came to the conclusion that the murder had indeed been done by a lone, deranged misfit, Lee Harvey Oswald, as the Warren Commission had ruled. (Well, he said he was 75 percent sure. He didn't want to give up the conspiracy idea altogether.) It was not a conclusion he relished. He would much rather have been the one to uncover some nefarious plot, but the facts just didn't point in that direction.

NORMAN READ A BOOK by a friend of ours, Nat Brandt, called *The Congressman Who Got Away with Murder*, about Congressman Daniel Sickles, who just before the Civil War shot and killed his young wife's lover, Philip Barton Key (son of Francis Scott Key, who wrote "The Star-Spangled Banner"). Norman thought it would make a good movie and asked me if I wanted to work on it with him.

"With you? You mean, you and me sit down and write it side by side?"

"No. I mean you do the research and write a first draft and then I'll work on it."

Hm. That was interesting. "I thought you didn't like my writing that much. You didn't like the novel."

"You've gotten better since then. I attribute it to living with me and learning through osmosis. You sure can write a good letter. If you can write letters like that, you can write anything."

Okay. I admit I was flattered. And I was at an impasse with my painting. My gallery in SoHo had closed, as did a gallery in Washington, D.C., where I'd had a show. I took my slides around to several galleries in New York, but nobody was interested. Some of the galleries were so rude, they wouldn't even look at the slides. One man, looking as though he were smelling something bad, said, "Oh, we don't take *amateurs* here." I never wanted to slap anybody so badly in my life. Art is one of the most heartbreaking businesses there is, along with acting and writing, or anything creative that is judged by someone's personal taste. Which is why nearly everyone in our family has gone into some facet of the arts, I guess. It's the challenge.

So I started researching and began to write the script. I finished a first draft and gave it to Norman to work on. The idea was, he would mark it up and hand it back to me, and I would put in the changes, but unhappily I didn't always agree with his changes. Then we would have a fight. The first one nearly derailed the whole project. I call it the "softly fight." On the first page of the manuscript there is a description of soldiers at an encampment. It is evening, fires are lit, and I say, "one of the soldiers is softly playing a harmonica." Norman hated adjectives and adverbs, so he changed the sentence to: "A soldier is playing a harmonica. Softly." No big deal; I made the change. There were other changes that I was going to have to talk to him about, so the script was riddled with notes, but that was not one of them.

Norman had gotten up early that morning to read the second draft, and I was still in bed. It must have been around six o'clock. I woke up as the bedroom door banged open and Norman thrust the script into my face.

"I can't work with you if you aren't going to put my changes into the script! Why am I wasting my time with this if you won't even do the smallest little change?" He was yelling at the top of his voice, and I was trying to get my eyelids open and find my glasses.

"What are you talking about?"

"Here, on the first page, I changed this word and took out that adverb, and you refused to change it!" He stuck the paper under my nose. I couldn't find my glasses, and I had to go to the bathroom, so I just pushed him aside and stormed into the bathroom. He was still ranting, and I began to think either he had lost his mind or I had. I knew I'd changed that word. I remembered it. It didn't make any difference to me if the word was an adverb in front of the verb or in its own sentence; it was the same thing. I came back out and told him I had changed it; he said I hadn't, and we yelled at each other for a good five minutes. Then I went into the bedroom and slammed the door. That wasn't enough, so I slammed it some more times. Then I sat on the side of the bed and began to cry. After all that effort, it was going to be impossible to work together, after all. Why had I thought we could do it? People were right about him. He was crazy. Then there was a knock on the door. A soft one.

"Honey?"

"What?"

"Can I come in?"

"What for? So you can yell at me some more?"

"To apologize. I was reading the wrong draft."

We laughed about that fight for a long time, and every time we started to disagree, we said, "Remember the softly fight," which was occasionally enough to defuse it.

The script was finished, and our agent sent it to Milos Forman, who loved it and wanted to make it with Jack Nicholson. Columbia Pictures was putting up the money and Francis Ford Coppola and Zoetrope would be producing, so we would work with our old friend Tom Luddy again. Norman was working on another novel, *The Gospel According to the Son*, so I went up to Milos's country house in Connecticut alone to work with him on the script. His house was a former barn, with a big fireplace he kept stoked with wood all day long. Between the fireplace and the cigars he chain-smoked, I smelled like a bratwurst at the end of the day. He had a sweet little guesthouse for me to stay in that had warm flannel sheets and a motherly housekeeper to look after me. It was idyllic country life. The script got better, and we tailored it for Jack. "I can just hear Jack saying that!" Milos would laugh as we wrote some roguish bit of dialogue. Norman came to the country and worked with us for a weekend, and as far as we were concerned, the movie was a done deal.

Then Milos called Jack. Jack didn't reply. Milos waited a few days and called him again. Jack still didn't reply. Milos called Jack's agent, and still Jack didn't get in touch. Jack hadn't read the script, so he couldn't have disliked it. Milos was the director who was responsible for making Jack's career with *One Flew Over the Cuckoo's Nest*. It was the height of bad manners that Jack never got back to him. Finally, Jack's agent called to say that he wasn't interested. Then Milos called Michael Douglas, who at least got back to Milos and told him he wasn't interested, and then after Woody Harrelson turned it down, Milos got disenchanted and went off to make *The People vs. Larry Flynt* with Woody instead. That's Hollywood. At least we got paid.

Norman and I wrote two other scripts together, one for an Austrian producer about Empress Elisabeth of Austria, who was one of the most beautiful monarchs in history, and another for HBO based on a short story Norman wrote in the sixties about the end of the world called "The Last Night." Ironically, in our script, which takes place around 2030, we called the 1990s "the Golden Twilight" because they were the last good years the world had, and after that everything went to hell in a handbasket. We had a young black president in our script who finally left Earth in a spaceship with a group of people bound for another planet, just as the earth was struck by a meteorite and destroyed. None of the movies got made. And finally, we fought too much to have any pleasure in the work. We were just too different in our styles of writing and squabbled over every single line of dialogue, so we never wrote another one.

After all this, I quietly started working on my novel again. Given Norman's reaction to it the first time he'd read it so many years before, I had no intention of letting him read it this time. In fact, I didn't even look at the last version I'd done. I started all over from page one and wrote a whole new book. I think Norman was right. I had somehow learned to write while I was with him, through osmosis, or through reading every draft of every book he had written, or from all those books I had read over the years, but somehow I had improved. I'd written about 150 pages when my oldest friend Susan Gibson from Atkins came to visit us in Ptown and I asked her to read it. She came in from the deck, eyes blazing, and said, "What happens next? You can't leave me hanging there like that!" And I knew it was okay. I then had my stepdaughters, my sister-in-law, and a few more friends read it, and they all loved it.

So one Friday night at a dinner at our house in Ptown, I was sitting next to our friend John Taylor "Ike" Williams, who is a literary agent, and I told him I was writing a book. He of course asked to read it. I was a little nervous, but I gave him the pages and he said he would read it over the weekend and call me on Monday to let me know what he thought. The phone rang at eleven that same night. It was Ike. "Norris. I'm signing you to a contract. Get back to work and finish this book!" I jumped and screamed, and Norman thought I'd lost my mind. I had to tell him then about the book. I think he was a little hurt that I had kept it a secret from him, but he didn't say much.

The two of us worked companionably in our studios in the attic in Provincetown, side by side, and a year or two later the book was done and Ike sold it to Random House in 1998. I was happy to be able to say I sold my book before I turned fifty, which I did the following January. Up until this point, Norman hadn't asked to read it, but when the page proofs arrived, he said, "I think it is about time I read this book." I said, "Okay," thinking that the book was finished and there was nothing he could do about it. I was wrong. He took it upstairs, and about an hour later he called me to come up. "Here," he said, holding out a stack of pages to me, "you start putting in these changes and I'll work ahead of you."

"What? You're *editing* my book?" I couldn't believe it, but there, on the pages, were his marks. "No. You can't edit this book. I have to be able to say that I wrote the whole thing myself. I don't want you to edit it. You know we don't get along, our styles are too different."

"I'm just helping you. I'll make it better. If I can't make marks on the page, I can't read it."

"Fine. Then you'll either read it when it comes out or you won't read it." Without a word he handed me back the rest of the manuscript. I never even looked at what he had done. I know there were a lot of people who would have given three years of their lives if Norman Mailer would have edited their manuscripts, but I was not one of them. I had let him work on the story I'd done for *Cosmopolitan* back in the seventies, and I can still pick out every single word he changed or added. We were just too different.

When the book came out, several people asked me if he had helped me with it. (Anyone who had read any of his work or mine, I might add, never asked that.) I would answer, "No. I did it all by myself." Then they would say, "Are you *sure*?" I guess that is one thing every younger wife of a famous man comes across sooner or later. People somehow think he must have married her for only one reason, and she has nothing to offer except youth, beauty, and sex. Why would an intelligent man marry a woman who was brainless, no matter how good she was in the sack? There are only so many hours in a day you can spend in bed, and then you have to have a conversation sooner or later. Although, come to think of it, Norman used to say we didn't have a fight for the first three years we were together because we didn't understand each other's accents. Maybe there's something to that after all.

Forty-two

Part of my book *Windchill Summer* was set in Vietnam, and in 1997 Norman and I went to Thailand and Vietnam with Jason Epstein and his wife, Judy Miller. Norman had been invited to speak at the South East Asia Writers Conference, so it was a free trip and a chance for me to do a little research. I had stayed away from anything dealing with Vietnam after Larry returned in 1971. I didn't go see *Apocalypse Now* or any of the other movies set there, and I didn't read anything about it if I could help it. It was a frightening place to me, one that had stolen so many kids' lives and hopes, and for no reason at all. It had just been old men posturing and playing politics. Now, beginning my book again, which I'd set in the same period as the first one, 1969, I found myself fascinated by the war and everything connected to it. I had been too close to it in the beginning; it was still happening. Larry was in Vietnam when I'd started to write that book. Now, almost thirty years later, I had some distance from it, but it was still a huge part of my life, my first husband's life, my generation's life, and I wanted to write about it.

Vietnam was a big part of Norman's life, too. He had wanted to go as a journalist during the war, but when he went to see Abe Rosenthal, the editor of *The New York Times*, about doing a series of pieces for them, Abe told him he shouldn't, because he would be killed. By whom Abe didn't specify, but Norman had done his share of protesting, which hadn't endeared him to the hawkish element of America, and he had written *The Armies of the Night*, after all, a book about protesting the war, which had won the Pulitzer Prize. Norman took Abe's advice seriously enough that he didn't go. He had six little kids and didn't need to make them orphans. But he had always somehow felt cowardly about it.

We arrived in Bangkok and stayed at the famous Oriental Hotel. We tried to do a little sightseeing, but the traffic was so terrible that it took us an hour to go three blocks, so we went back to the hotel. Norman's ability to walk had diminished to the point where he could hardly do so at all anymore. He used two canes, and was in constant pain. His vanity usually wouldn't allow him to use a wheelchair at the airport, but this time he asked for one, so I knew he was really hurting. We did take a boat tour down the canals, and went to a few easily accessible places, but he couldn't go to the palace or walk the streets like we used to love to do in a foreign city. He couldn't lift the luggage, either, and I found myself hoisting heavy suitcases up to and down from airplane racks and off baggage trolleys, dragging them when necessary.

The writers conference was a nice dinner, as those things always are. The royal prince was there, and it was a fine perk that the Oriental had named one of their suites after Norman, but it was Vietnam that we had come to see. When we got off the plane, I swear I felt something heavy in the air left over from the spirits of all the Americans who had landed there, a kind of dank miasma. It clung to us like a bad smell, like the thick syrup of the air in the moments before a tornado passes through.

On the ride in from the airport, I tried to shake off the feeling, but as soon as we got to the Hotel Continental and unpacked, we went outside to look around and were swarmed by a pack of children who were professional beggars. One of them was a girl of about ten or eleven holding a dead baby. I wanted to scream, to run away, to get back on the plane and leave again, but the doorman of the hotel just chased them away. There was no escaping the beggars that week. One especially, a coarse little girl who might have been anywhere between six and twelve, was persistent. She was small in stature but as tough as shoe leather, and if one of the other children came over while she was trying to get money out of someone, she would snap, "This one's mine, bitch." They were all afraid of her, and I was, too, a little. I bought copies of Graham Greene's book *The Quiet American*, copied badly and stapled together, or fans and small trinkets, from her and the others, but the more I bought, the more they persisted. I dreaded going out the door. (Norman never passed a beggar without giving him money, and John Buffalo is the same way.)

Once we got into our pedicabs outside the hotel, though, it was thrilling; we were right out in the flow of traffic. Scooters and cars swerved around us, like speedboats around a log drifting downriver.

Girls rode motor scooters in immaculate *ao dais,* the beautiful long silk dresses, and high heels. They wore sunglasses and hats and long gloves; matching scarves covered their noses and mouths to keep out the exhaust fumes. It rained every afternoon, and even in a rainstorm, the girls were clean and spotless; a girl would gracefully lean down and take out a plastic poncho from under her bike seat and put it on as she zoomed down the street. The entire community flowed by on scooters or bicycles. Whole families would perch precariously on a single bicycle, father, mother, and two or three kids. They would haul groceries or building materials or whatever they needed to transport. I once saw a family of four carrying a whole double-hung window on a bicycle. I have no idea how the thing kept its balance. They could have been in the circus.

We went to the war museum, where they had a copy of Robert S. McNamara's book *In Retrospect* in a glass case under a spotlight. It was his attempt at an apology of sorts, and they at least had that small artifact to show that someone in power had recognized how wrong that war was, even though it was too little too late. The photographs on the walls were graphic, showing atrocities committed by American boys, most of whom were not long out of their teens, if they were indeed out of them at all. That was one of the things I tried to address in my book—what kind of circumstance would it take to make a boy who had been drinking milk shakes at a drive-in with his friends kill women and children three months later in a situation like My Lai? It was a sobering museum. Obviously, there were no pictures of what the Vietcong had done to our boys, but you can bet it was just as bad. There were exhibits of booby traps the Vietcong had used, some of which I featured in my book. In cages around the grounds were sad, dusty, live bears.

We went to Cu Chi, the center of the underground tunnels the Vietcong had started building in the fifties when they'd been at war with the French. We saw movies of the tunnels, and then we actually went into one. It was a tunnel made for tourists. It had been dug much bigger, and lights were installed along the way, but it still gave the oppressive feeling of being underground. One of my characters in *Windchill Summer* was named Bean, a tunnel rat, one of those bravest and craziest of American soldiers who crawled through the tunnels in search of the enemy. I got to feel the soil and smell the air in the tunnels, and it made my book better. I think Norman got some kind of peace from it, too, although he couldn't get down and crawl through the tunnel. I have to admit I didn't make it all the way. When I got out of sight of the entrance, I was so claustrophobic I had to turn back. Interestingly, most of the other tourists were Vietnam vets and their families. Our guide was a former Vietcong tunnel fighter himself, and he joked and laughed with the vets like they were old buddies.

We took a boat down the river and stopped at a house to have tea with a family who played a little music for tourists, and we bought a few souvenirs. I got a pointed straw hat for sixty cents that I wound up leaving behind. Jason was a big crossword puzzle fanatic, and I think he missed the entire tour. His nose was firmly stuck the whole time in his crossword puzzle. He even walked down the path through the jungle doing the puzzle. Judy, on the other hand, was a fearless *New York Times* reporter, and she never missed a thing. She would escape from the three of us and go adventuring on her own; we never knew where she was. She was definitely the hare to the three of us tortoises, as Norman could walk only with great difficulty by then.

IN SEPTEMBER 1999, I had a hysterectomy for a prolapsed uterus, which got markedly worse after we came back from Vietnam. (I don't think all that baggage hefting did me any good at all.) The surgery was a weird experience. I loved and trusted my doctor, whom I had been with for more than twenty years (he delivered John Buffalo), but he was in his eighties, and I think I should have given the surgery a little more thought and maybe gotten a second opinion from someone younger. He treated it as though it were going to be no worse than a root canal. The doctor told Norman I'd be in the OR for an hour or an hour and a half, but it was closer to five hours. Norman, out in the waiting room alone, began to panic. But the doctor was casual about it.

"Well, there was a little more there than I'd expected," he told me later. "You had a hernia, and I couldn't get your fallopian tube out, so I left it in." Wait a minute. Why couldn't he get the fallopian tube out? He was vague and said it was no big deal. It was bleeding and I had been under anesthetic too long already. My body would absorb it. I thought that was strange, but if he didn't think it was a big deal, then neither did I. I trusted him that much.

I had more or less recovered from the surgery when I took a nasty fall on the icy brick steps in Provincetown just before Norman was scheduled to have hip replacement surgery, and my back was in real pain. I went and got an X-ray, which the doctor said was fine, no broken bones, but the pain in my back seemed to be getting worse.

Norman had been having more and more trouble walking. He started using a cane in the mid-nineties and moved rapidly to two canes. Two, he said, helped his balance. He tried to walk a half mile a day, but he began doing it on the deck in Provincetown, making laps back and forth, rather than venturing too far from the house, in case he couldn't get back. He needed his knees replaced, but even more, his hip required it, so he checked into Massachusetts General Hospital in Boston to get the procedure. I was going to sleep in the room with him. It was too far to drive every day to Provincetown, and he wanted me with him. They had given us one of the nicer rooms on the "celebrity" floor, which had a pullout couch, but it was desperately uncomfortable, and my back was killing me. I got up in the middle of the night and piled the sofa cushions onto the floor, trying to make a softer bed and find some relief, but there was none.

The next morning, Norman went into surgery. He was semi-awake during the procedure and said it was like lying in a sweet stupor, listening to someone over in the corner sawing and hammering, making a fire cabinet or something. When he was back in the room for a bit, still groggy on Percocet, he announced he was going to the bathroom. I was alone with him and tried to tell him he had a catheter, that he had just had hip replacement and couldn't get out of bed, but he was out of his head and unreasonable. He started to get out of bed, and I tried to hold him down. He was strong and fought me, then pulled back his fist to hit me and I started yelling for the nurse. I couldn't stop him. He got out of bed and walked several steps toward the bathroom on that freshly cut hip. It was a miracle it didn't pull the new hip right out of socket. It took three nurses to get him back into bed, and they had to tie him down.

Dick and Doris Goodwin came to visit that night, and by that time

Norman was awake, but still on the Percocet, and he had never been more garrulous and funny. He told us that if we took the elevator down to the first floor, we would be in Miami, and then if we crossed the courtyard to the right, we would be in London. At one of the tables at the outdoor café, there would be a couple of Nazi agents in uniforms, we'd have no trouble recognizing them. He wanted us to go up to them and explain that Nazism was bad, and what they were doing was a really bad thing. Somehow he had Dan Quayle involved in it, too, and the more we laughed, the more entertaining he thought he was being, so he laughed along with us, having no idea he wasn't making perfect sense, and thinking he was at his most charming. I was almost sorry when he got off the Percocet, he was so much fun.

He went into hip rehab for a couple of weeks, and I went back to Provincetown, where the pain in my back got worse. I went to see my local doctor, Brian O'Malley. He sent me to Hyannis to a specialist who looked like he was about twenty years old, and he was most eager to do an exploratory surgery because he had never seen anything like what I had. I wanted someone who *had* seen what I had. So I got a referral to Doris and Dick Goodwin's doctor at MGH, who examined me and sent me straightaway to see Arlan Fuller, their top man in gynecological cancer surgery.

Arlan was the kind of doctor who inspired confidence in you the minute you met him. He was about fifty, had the most intense blue eyes outside of Norman or Paul Newman, and he radiated kindness and intelligence. He said he thought there was a good possibility it wasn't cancer. It could be that the fallopian tube that was left in was infected, and he told me not to worry about that until he found out for sure. I checked in for a day surgery. Danielle had come up to be with me and drive me home. If I had known what was going to happen, I never would have allowed her to come alone. Of course it was cancer, and she was all by herself when he came out to tell her. It was so upsetting for her. I remember waking up and seeing Arlan's blue eyes looking at me with compassion, and him saying, "It's cancer." I was so out of it I could hardly speak, but I asked, "Is it terminal?" and he said, "No."

It turned out that the fallopian tube the other doctor couldn't remove had a sarcoma in it, and there was another small one as well. Dr. Fuller had just done a laparoscopic biopsy, so we set a date for a larger surgery. There's nothing more boring than having someone recount their surgeries to you, but it was a big deal in my life and I have to go into it a bit. You can skip this part if you want to. The prognosis for the kind of sarcoma I have, GI stromal tumor, was not good. Most people didn't live more than a year or two after being diagnosed. (I don't recommend Googling your illness, by the way.) I don't know why, but for some reason I was never afraid of dying, but the family was certainly distraught. Every one of them came to Boston for my surgery. Barbara; her husband, Al; and her son, Peter; all the kids and in-laws and grandchildren crowded around my bed at five in the morning and walked me down to the elevator as far as they could go with me. I felt like the luckiest woman in the world to have a family like that. They were determined I was going to be all right, and that gave me a lot of courage. I had my first book coming out in a couple of months. I had to go on a book tour. I couldn't have cancer!

Arlan took out the tumors, I began chemo and radiation, and I finished the treatments in June, just in time to go on the book tour for *Windchill Summer*. My hair, of course, fell out, and while I was in the hospital, my friend Diane Fisher found the best wig place in New York (Bitz-n-Pieces on Columbus Circle, ask for Gwen) and she sent me a wig that looked just exactly like my hair, only better. Plus, she wouldn't let me pay for it. How's that for a good friend?

I set out on the tour, twelve cities, in the wig, determined that I was going to be one of those who beat the dismal statistic of this disease. I soon learned that touring for an unknown's first novel is not the same as touring for a Norman Mailer novel. He always had crowds lined up out the door to hear him, and I was lucky if I had four people in the audience. Once, in Kansas City, they booked me into a big church and there was nobody there at all except the people from the bookstore, who were so embarrassed. I sat on the edge of the stage and talked to them and read, and we had a good time anyhow. I looked upon it as practice—I'd discovered I was good at reading. All those years of acting had given me a stage voice, and I was funny. The book was set in Arkansas in 1969, so I got to do all the accents, which I loved.

In Atlanta, I was in the hotel elevator when two cute young girls got on. They were nudging each other and whispering. I thought they were talking about me, which made me uncomfortable, when one of them said, "Excuse me, but we just wanted to tell you how beautiful your hair is. I bet you never had a bad hair day in your life." I grinned. I wanted so badly to grab the wig and whisk it off, but I knew they would faint (I was not a lovely bald woman, although Norman said I looked like a beautiful alien), so I just said, "Oh, I can assure you I've had a few bad hair days. But thank you." Like my home ec teacher, Mrs. Gay, used to tell me, "When you get a compliment, all you have to say is thank you. Otherwise, you insult their taste."

It has been ten years since I had that first surgery, and I'm still here. I beat the odds—up to now, anyhow. I've had seven more major surgeries and too many small procedures to count. I've had 40 percent of my small intestine removed because of radiation damage, I've worn a colostomy bag and a nephrostomy bag, and I still have an internal stent in my kidney. I have lost so much weight that my former model's weight looks chubby, but I'm still here. Three times, a doctor has told me that there is nothing they can do for me and it will be just a matter of time. I don't know why I keep on going, but I'm not questioning it. Maybe it is all the prayers my family and friends have prayed. I don't know how much longer I have to live, but then none of us does. If I go tomorrow, I will still be ahead. I'm living on borrowed time, but borrowed time is sweet. I don't want to go, I'm having too good a life this time out, but I do believe that we get another chance, maybe a lot more chances, to live life here, and the price of our admission is to learn lessons. I think I've learned a few this go-around; I know I've learned a lot from having cancer. I think I'm more compassionate, more patient. ("That's why they call us patients!" I said to someone once when we were being made to wait too long for some procedure.) I've given up on my vanity. I'm just happy if I can get up, get dressed, and throw on some makeup. I don't have to be glamorous anymore. If I'd had only my own cancer to battle, and it is a battle, that would have been quite enough to give me an abundance of lessons, but there was more in store.

I DID PRETTY WELL for a couple of years after the first surgery and the treatments. Norman and I went to Wales for the Hay-on-Wye book fair. I got to read from my book and be on a panel of writers, and for the first time I was part of it all as a writer, not just as Norman's wife. Some of my ancestors are Welsh, and it meant a lot for me to go there. I did feel a kinship with the people and kept seeing my relatives in the faces of the local population. My hair grew back in and was dark—almost black—thick and curly. I had been told it might be totally different from my real hair, and I was sort of hoping it would come in snow-white, like my novel's character, Cherry, but it gradually turned chestnut-auburn again and regained its straighter wave.

In the couple of years before I got cancer, I gained a lot of weight, maybe because of menopause, or inactivity. I'd stopped doing yoga, and then after the first surgery, I didn't do any kind of exercise. I felt really unattractive and bad about myself but couldn't seem to diet. I needed food as a comfort, I guess. I still hate to see pictures of myself during that time. We were living in Provincetown all year by then, so the two of us didn't do much except hang around the house and write or watch TV. We had a few friends in for dinners and went out to eat once or twice a week, but life was definitely in the slow lane.

In order to have something to do in the community, I joined the board of the Provincetown Repertory Theatre, and in 2002 there was a crisis and the director quit. I volunteered to take over and plan a season that year. I thought I could do it for little money, as we used to do at the Actors Studio, and somehow we pulled it off. John Buffalo came up with some of his friends from Wesleyan, one of whom was Tommy Kail, who went on to direct *In the Heights,* which was written by another friend of theirs, Lin-Manuel Miranda, and which won the Tony for best musical in 2008. They did a series of short plays that we once had done at the Actors Studio that were cheap and funny and were a big hit. I called in a couple of my studio friends, too, to do one-person shows, and somehow we put together a season. Which was truly a miracle, because a week after I volunteered to do all this, I got a call that my father had gone to the hospital again and wasn't expected to live.

Everything came crashing down. I turned over the theater business to my assistant, David Fortuna, who single-handedly saved everything, and I went to Arkansas. My father had severe heart damage. Over the years he'd had heart attacks and two bypass surgeries, and he wore a pacemaker and defibrillator. My parents and I spoke on the phone twice a day, a habit we started when I got sick, and when I had spoken to him that morning, he'd been in a great mood. The previous night he had cooked chicken and dumplings and homemade peach pie while my mother worked in the beauty shop. They invited a neighbor for dinner, and I remember him saying, "I haven't felt this good in years. I have so much energy." Then, only an hour or so after he hung up, the defibrillator started going off and it wouldn't stop. He likened it to being kicked in the chest by a horse, and usually once it went off, that was it, the heart went back into rhythm and life went on, but not this time.

They called my aunt Chloe and uncle Ira, who came and picked them up to take them to the hospital in Little Rock, a drive of more than an hour. By the time they got there, my father was in agony, repeatedly being kicked without pause, over and over. They didn't expect him to make it through the night, so I got there as quickly as I could. But the staff at the Arkansas Heart Hospital were heroic. They brought him around, and somehow he got better. I stayed a couple of weeks, sleeping on a lounge chair in his room, my mother on a sleeping bench, or we went back and forth to Atkins, which was a tiring drive. Then we brought him home. He was not able to do much for himself, and my mother, who was eighty-three, wasn't able to take care of him, so we hired a nurse to come in every day to help with his bath, meds, and generally take care of things. I rented a hospital bed, which we set up in the dining room.

Then when I thought they would be okay, I went back to Provincetown and tried to work on the theater stuff and be with Norman, who was not doing so well by himself, either. Not long after I got home, my father had to go back to the hospital. That began five months of going and coming, back and forth, to the hospital and home. John or some of the other kids started coming to stay with Norman while I was away, and Matt came to Arkansas to help me with my father a few times. Or John would come with me to Arkansas and Matt would stay with Norman.

All of this was made even crazier by a project Norman and I had gotten ourselves involved with that George Plimpton had started, a play about the Fitzgeralds and Hemingway called *Zelda, Scott and Ernest*. It started when John Irving's wife, Janet, wrote and asked Norman and me to do a reading of A. R. Gurney's play *Love Letters* as a benefit for a school she and John had founded called the Maple Street School. Norman said that he wasn't the right type to play the role, which was a patrician WASP, but why didn't I do it with George Plimpton? I called George, who was willing, but he said, "I have a play we all three can be in." It was a blast of fresh air in our staid existence at that time. It was written by George and Terry Quinn, all taken from the works of Zelda, Scott, and Ernest, from letters and books, stories and essays. I loved being onstage again, and the two of them were such hams that it was marvelous to watch them. Norman wore his safari jacket, and George wore an orange Princeton tie. I wore some kind of twenties era glamorous garb and did a broad Alabama accent. We had a great time, the audience loved it, and the second time we did it was in Provincetown for a benefit, which raised a lot of money for the theater.

Then somehow, thanks to George, it took wing and we started doing it everywhere. We did it at the Ninety-second Street Y in New York, at the Folger library in Washington, D.C., and at the Fitzgerald Festival in Saint Paul, Minnesota. George was splendid at finding venues for us. He arranged a seven-city tour of Europe, and we did it in London, Paris, Vienna, Moscow (in the presence of the mayor, Yury Luzhkov), Amsterdam, Berlin, and Prague. I began to feel a kinship with Zelda that went beyond an actress's passion for her character. We shared real elements of life. We were both Southern, married to talented well-known writers; I was a painter, as was she; and we both were writers. I was not a dancer, but longed to be one. If dancing hadn't been on the sin list, I would have taken ballet as a little girl, and always was wistful I didn't get to do that.

Norman was a nicer man to me than Scott Fitzgerald was to Zelda, but he didn't especially want me to be a writer. He discouraged me in the beginning and never really took what I did seriously. He liked a few of my paintings, but he preferred abstract impressionism, the favored painting of the fifties, the background of his best young years. It was the same with jazz. He always said he loved jazz, but in fact he didn't really like the music part of it at all. He liked the ambiance of jazz, the language of jazz, the hipness of jazz. If we were in the car on a trip and I put on some Sonny Stitt or Thelonious Monk, he would ask me to turn it off. He preferred silence when we were driving, either silence or conversation or napping. I couldn't listen to audio books on our car trips, either. Those set his teeth on edge worse than music, and he couldn't bear it.

So I felt a true kinship with Zelda and understood her madness and passions. I was never near to madness myself, but I understood it. And a part of me sometimes wished I could just give in and become mad rather than have to be the stable force in everyone's life, the one who was always taking care of people, the one everyone turned to in a crisis. I just wanted to cry and scream sometimes and have someone take care of me, but there was no one who could.

Matt came down to be with my father, who was in the hospital again, while we went on one of our trips with the show, this time to Paris. I worried about my father, but having sat beside his bed for weeks, I needed to get away for a few days.

There was no one more fun to travel with than George. He was always forgetting his tickets or schedule or dirty laundry, which a concierge once ran after me carrying, as George had left it in a bundle in his room. He was constantly rewriting the script, too, and a few times he frantically made changes as we were walking out onto the stage. It was a miracle we ever got the show done, but we did, and everyone seemed to love it.

In Berlin, there was a disturbed girl in the audience who for some reason would yell every time I spoke. She didn't do it when the men spoke, just when I did. I have no idea why Zelda (or I) upset her so much. Everyone around her tried to shush her. They did everything short of throwing her out, which they should have done, but finally, I could take no more. I didn't know if she spoke English or not, but I stopped the show and addressed her directly, still in character as Zelda. "Sweetheart," I drawled, "I know just how you are feeling. I have been a little deranged myself, from time to time, and I surely do understand that once in a while our poor minds just slip off the rails. But I need you to stop yelling while I'm talking, because poor Scott is about to die, and I need to finish this play so we can all go home. Can you keep quiet for me for just a few minutes? Do you think you can do that?" The answer was applause from the audience and more loud abuse from the woman. Somehow we got through the show, and only then did the ushers come and escort her out.

When I got back to Arkansas a week later, my father had not improved. In fact, he was getting worse. He could no longer swallow and was starving to death. He was so thin it was shocking. I couldn't stand the idea of him starving, and I am ashamed to say I forced him to get a feeding tube put in, which he didn't want. But I just knew that if he could get some nutrition he would be stronger, and then maybe he could withstand an operation called an ablation that they had said was the only thing that might save him. I don't know why they didn't just say to me, "He's dying. There is nothing we can do," but they didn't. They held out this carrot of the ablation, even though it was never realistic. I don't think doctors ever want to give up. They look upon death as their own personal failure, and they want the family to have hope as long as they can, even if it's false hope. Which is not good. It's better to know the truth and work with the reality of what is happening.

Getting the feeding tube down his throat was a horrible experience for him, and he couldn't deal with it, so they pegged it directly into his stomach. It only prolonged his suffering. I am so sorry I insisted on it. I hope wherever he is, he has forgiven me for that. Matt and my mother and I stayed with him for several weeks longer, sleeping on the chair or the bench, Matt sleeping on the floor. Occasionally we would go to Atkins to bathe and change clothes, or go to Aurora's house. I was nearing the breaking point.

Then one day I hit it. Matt and I were in a little family room off the waiting room by ourselves, and I began to cry and say that I couldn't take it anymore. I prayed to God, "Why have You let him suffer all this time? It's enough! Whatever he had to learn, whatever we all had to learn from this, it's enough! Just take him and let us all stop suffering!" Matt held me while I ranted to God, and he cried along with me. I have never felt so helpless. It was like we were in hell and couldn't get out. Hell was the waiting room and the recliner and my father lying in a coma on his back, his mouth open and dried out, me constantly rubbing Vaseline on his cracked lips and swabbing his poor dry mouth with a lime-colored sponge dipped in ice water.

That night was the worst. I didn't sleep at all. He would make a noise and I would jump up to see if he was all right. He hadn't been able to speak in weeks, or even open his eyes and look at us, but that night he made whispering noises that I desperately tried to interpret but couldn't. Then I watched the sun come up in a clear blue sky. It was July 21, a Sunday morning, like all the sunny Sunday mornings of my childhood when we would get up early, play Tennessee Ernie Ford gospel songs on the record player, eat breakfast, and then get ready to go to church. I was looking out the window thinking about all this when I heard a noise behind me. It was my father, sitting up in bed. He was wide awake; his blue eyes were clear and shining. His skin was rosy and he looked happy. "Daddy!" I said. "You're awake! Can I get something for you?"

He said, as clearly as if he had been talking to me all morning, "I want you to take your mother and go down to the cafeteria and get her something to eat. She hasn't been eating right and it's going to make her sick." Well, okay! Look at this! He's better!

"Oh, I'm so happy you are talking again! I'll get her some breakfast and then we'll come back and we can talk this afternoon." I got my mother together, and she was happy he was talking again, too, and kept on hugging and kissing him. I lingered behind a minute as she went to the door.

"You just want to get rid of us for a few minutes, don't you? We've been driving you crazy, I know." He nodded. My mother couldn't keep from rubbing him and touching him, and even when he was asleep, he flinched away from the touch. He was too sensitive to be touched; he wanted to be left alone.

"Take your mother up there with you and take care of her," he said. I knew he was talking about Provincetown. I kissed him and promised I would, that he didn't have to worry about her, and I followed my mother to the elevator.

As we were eating breakfast, she shivered. "Did you feel that cold wind blow through here?" she asked, rubbing her arms as if she had a chill.

"No, I didn't feel a breeze at all," I said. There were no windows in the cafeteria; she must have just imagined a wind. We started back to the room, but before we got there, we were met by the nurses. I could see on their faces that he was gone. I guess my talk to God the night before had been taken seriously.

John and Norman flew in the next day for the visitation and funeral.

Small towns really come into their own at a time like that. Women from the church brought food, and our neighbors all came by with a dish of something. We had picked out Daddy's favorite blue suit with a white shirt and a beautiful silk tie I had gotten him one Christmas, and I had it over my arm, ready to go to the funeral home for them to dress him, when our neighbor Euleta, who was in her nineties, came up on the porch. She was carrying a dish of ambrosia and trying to get the screen door open at the same time, and she scraped the back of her hand on the door latch. A whole big piece of skin peeled back, like the skin on an overripe peach. Blood started to go everywhere. I threw the clothes down onto a chair and ran and got a wet rag to wrap around it. But there was nothing I could do. I had to get her to the doctor's.

"I have to take Euleta to the doctor's, Mother. You hold down the fort. I'll be back as soon as I can." Even though she lived only a block away, Euleta had driven over and had parked behind my car in the driveway, so we managed to get her car keys out of her bag, and I was going to take her in her car. Except I couldn't get behind the wheel. She was so tiny that she had the seat pushed up as far as it would go, and with my long legs I couldn't even get in far enough to push the seat back. It was a grim comedy, she with her hand wrapped in a bloody cloth trying to move the seat back, me trying to squeeze in and push it. The clinic was only a few blocks away, but there was no way she could walk it. Finally, after a long struggle, we got the seat back and went to the clinic. There was a waiting room full of people, and by that time, the smile I had pasted on my face was getting a little wobbly. I was learning another lesson in patience.

"Good morning," I said to the girl at the desk. "Euleta here has just cut her hand badly. I know there are a lot of people ahead of us, but I do think she needs some immediate attention." The girl was nice, and went back to talk to the doctor, who let us go right back. I could feel the eyes of the people in the waiting room follow us, all curious to know what had happened, all disappointed they would have to wait yet longer. I knew the doctor from times I had been there with my parents, and he was sympathetic. He glued the skin back in place; there was no way stitches would hold. "Old people's skin gets rotten," he explained, "and stitches would pull right out." Euleta was embarrassed she had done such a thing, and we hurried out of there. So that's what we all had to look forward to. Our skins rotting while we were still living in them.

My father would have had a good time at his visitation, which was held the night before the funeral. He loved visitations and funerals and went to a lot of them. It was the main social activity he had. When I went through the pockets of his suits before I gave them away, I found stacks and stacks of funeral cards.

There was a big turnout; everyone he knew down through his life came. He was one of those people who made you feel happy, just to be around him. He was always helping someone, trying to do some good in the world. Larry was there and had bought Matt a new suit, which was nice of him. He'd always liked and respected my father, even though my parents hadn't wanted us to get married. My mother held up pretty well as we stood beside my father's coffin and greeted everyone. He looked so handsome. He had beautiful high cheekbones and a thin nose, even more so than I did, and he looked like he was peacefully sleeping. I couldn't believe I would never get to hug him or talk to him again. I wished over and over that somehow we had managed to live closer together. But he would never have left Atkins, and if I had it to do over, I still would go to New York. I had stars in my eyes, too many for Atkins, Arkansas, to ever satisfy.

It was a hot sunny day in July as we traveled the backcountry roads up to Shiloh, the cemetery where he was to be buried. It was on the side of Pea Ridge, a hill overlooking the river valley below. The church in the cemetery was formerly the one-room schoolhouse where Daddy had gotten what education he had, up to the eighth grade, and then he'd had to go to work to support his family. He'd had a hard life, but once when I said that, he said, "No, I've had a good life. I've done everything I wanted to do. I was able to work at a job I liked and was good at, I had a wife and a daughter who love me, and I have grandchildren and friends. I've been blessed."

Norman and I, Matt, John, and my mother rode in the limousine following the hearse, and at first Norman was working at making inane comments about everything, the countryside, the weather. No one was responding. Finally, he said, "I guess I don't have to make conversation, do I?"

"No, sweetie. Let's just enjoy the ride through the pretty country."

And we went the rest of the way in silence, which was like a balm. It was soothing to relax into the nice leather seats and watch the green miles slowly roll by, strange to drive up to the cemetery I knew so well, knowing I would be leaving my father there. He loved that place; it was home to him. When I was little, he would bring me out there and we'd cut open a watermelon and eat it beside the graves of his mother and father, my mule skinner grandpa Jeames and his wife, Sallie Pigg, the beauty. When Matt was little, just a baby in arms, my father started taking him up there and showing him the graves of all his relatives. Then John, in his turn. He told them stories of when he was a little boy, how he and his friends would make a flying jenny out of a tree, pulling a small sapling down until they could get on it, then letting it go, which propelled the kid into the air. It's a miracle they all survived. He taught my boys how to drive up on those roads of Pea Ridge when they were eight, way too young to learn to drive, but they were both excellent drivers, just as I was, and I had been the same age when he'd taught me.

Daddy.

We ordered him a big beautiful bluish-gray granite stone, a double one with my mother's name on the other side. I worried over a quote to put on it, and then I picked up his old Bible. He'd worn it out; there were literally Band-Aids holding the front cover together. The book fell open to a page of Proverbs in which he had underlined a passage, the heart of which said, "Love is strong as death." So that was it. He chose his own epitaph, and that was what we put on the stone. I had picked out the biggest, fanciest coffin they had, too, a silver Cadillac of a coffin. He'd always wanted a Cadillac car but felt like it was too show-offy for him, that people would think he was getting above himself. Now he had his big old Cadillac, as close as I could get for him. It was the hardest thing I have ever done, to sit underneath the striped tent and watch as they put my daddy into the ground. I started to hyperventilate, I was crying so hard. Then it was over and we went back to the small house where I grew up, the one where we'd had the excitement of our first bathroom, the one he'd come home to every night, dirty from work, with his little girl running to meet him, crying "Daddy, Daddy, Daddy!" And he'd pick me up and whirl me around. I'd hang off his arm and marvel at the goose egg of his muscle. The house was so much smaller and emptier now that he was gone.

I tried with might and main to get my mother to come back to Provincetown with us and live as I'd promised Daddy, or just to come for a while. Norman backed me up. He was always generous about taking care of her, but she was adamant that she wouldn't do it. I told her Daddy had told me to take her up there and take care of her, but she wouldn't budge. I had no idea how she was going to live alone. She had never been alone. Daddy had done everything for her; he'd given her an insulin shot every day and tested her blood sugar levels. She didn't drive a car. She had never written a check. She was afraid to stay by herself at night. She was afraid of the dark. But nothing any of us said could convince her to leave, so I found a woman who would come and sleep at her house for twenty-five dollars a night, and one who would come three afternoons a week and take her to the store or anyplace else she needed to go. I had a friend who was a nurse who lived on the next block, who agreed to come and help her with her shots and her testing, and while it all added up in costs, it was better than anything else I could do.

We all went back home. Mother and I spoke on the phone twice a day, and she made it pretty well, for the most part, for nearly four months. Then, just before Thanksgiving, I got a call from my aunt

Chloe. Mother had fallen and broken her ankle. Once again, I got on a plane and headed to Arkansas. She was in the hospital, and the doctor there said there was nothing he could do to fix the ankle. Her bones were too fragile and they couldn't be set. She would have to be in a wheelchair the rest of her life.

I blanched. It was unacceptable. She was in good shape for her age. She was still beautiful and looked ten or fifteen years younger than she was. She had all the marbles. She had diabetes, but nothing else was wrong with her. I simply wouldn't accept that she would never walk again. I knew there were better doctors in Massachusetts. I said, "Thank you very much," and Matt and I packed her up and brought her to Provincetown. She didn't want to leave Atkins, but we told her it was just temporary, that she could come back as soon as she got back on her feet. Whether we believed it or not didn't really matter, she came more or less willingly. She didn't want to be in a wheelchair, either.

I took her to a good surgeon, Dr. Paul Benoit, in Hyannis, who examined her and said, "Well, it is a tricky operation. It will be like operating on a paper towel cone, and it will take a genius of a surgeon, but you're in luck because I am one." He was young and charming, and the operation was a success.

But the events of the previous year had worn me down. Besides the trauma of my father's illness and death, after my mother moved in with us I had the total responsibility of taking care of her, pushing her in the wheelchair, heaving the wheelchair in and out of the car trunk, getting up at four in the morning to drive her to Hyannis in the snow for six o'clock appointments, for months taking her to therapy in Orleans, which was forty-five minutes away, twice a week for carpal tunnel syndrome in her wrist, then finally getting surgery on the wrist as well. Then there were endless visits to the eye doctor, and laser surgery on her eyes. Right after that, we noticed an irregular mole on her leg, which was melanoma. That required a skin graft, and more therapy.

I still had to take care of Norman and the house, drive him to his doctors in Boston, drive to my own doctors in Boston, shop, and cook. The stress the previous year had brought had taken my health. My mother was desperately unhappy with us in Provincetown, and with all she had been through, who could blame her? She had a lovely room and bathroom of her own, but she felt it wasn't her home. She and Norman were cordial but had nothing to say to each other. It was like they were from two different planets. She was in a deep depression and did nothing all day except sit and read in a chair tucked into a corner of a small room off the living room, the black ink of her mood seeping out around her. Nothing I could do to amuse her would help. All she wanted to do was go home, back to her old life, which was the one thing I couldn't give her. So we struggled on, trying to carry on our lives as normally as we could, none of us happy.

TEN YEARS EARLIER, in 1993, we were trying to figure out a fund-raiser for the Actors Studio, and Norman came up with the idea to do a reading of *Don Juan in Hell* by George Bernard Shaw, with Gay Talese as Don Juan, Norman as the commodore, Susan Sontag as Doña Ana, and Gore Vidal as the devil, a subtle little dig that Gore wickedly relished. The evening was a big success. It seemed for both Norman and Gore, the feud had faded. Gore and I even exchanged a few letters after Norman and I got back from Moscow. He was terribly claustrophobic, as I was, and we traded claustrophobia stories. Once, in Russia, we walked up several flights of stairs together rather than get into a tiny elevator jammed with too many overstuffed people.

I was still artistic director of the Provincetown Repertory Theatre in 2003, and while it was not easy to put together inexpensive programs, David Fortuna and I were doing the best we could. The reading George Plimpton, Norman, and I had done of *Zelda, Scott and Ernest* had raised so much money that we wanted to try to do it again. So Norman came up with the idea to do *Don Juan in Hell* again. This time, Norman played Don Juan, and Gore delighted us when he came all the way from Ravello, Italy, to play the devil. I played Doña Ana, and our friend Mike Lennon played the commodore. It was beyond kind of Gore to come all that way to help our little theater, given the state of his health. In some way he must have been trying to make it up to Norman for what he had done all those years ago with the "3M" piece.

When I saw him, Gore had aged, as we all had. He had traveled all that way with his only luggage a small duffel bag of the sort cosmetic companies give away with purchases of perfume. His knees were so painful that he could hardly walk. We had booked him into a guesthouse down the street from us called the White Horse, which was run by a lovely couple of friends, Mary and Frank Schaeffer. It was about ten at night when he arrived at our house from the airport, and he and Norman sat in the bar for more than two hours drinking and talking, and then Matt, who was visiting us, and I took Gore to the inn. Mary and Frank had stayed up waiting for him, and offered us a glass of wine, which we accepted. We sat in their living room, which was also the office, and talked for another hour or so. By this time, Gore was pretty far into his cups and could hardly walk the short distance down a gravel path from the office to his room. Matt and Frank practically carried him.

Norman and Gore.

When we finally got him there, he wanted to call his partner, Howard, but there were no phones in the rooms, so we had to walk him all the way back to the office to make the call, another tor-

The cast of Don Juan in Hell *in Ptown.*

turous journey. He picked up the phone to dial, but he couldn't remember his phone number. We spent a frustrating two hours calling information and trying different numbers, none of which worked, while Gore drank more red wine. And more. No amount of pleading or cajoling could get him to go to bed. It was now three o'clock, and Mary, Frank, Matt, and I were turning into zombies. Gore continued to punch in numbers. Finally, by some miracle, he got Howard on the phone. He practically wept, he was so happy to hear his voice. They spoke for a few minutes, and then Gore said he would like to go to bed.

We managed to get him back down the path one more time, and Matt and I waited while he unpacked his little bag. He had brought one change of underwear, one extra shirt, his razor and toothbrush, and a framed photograph of himself and his parents taken when he was about nine. He looked at it for a moment and lovingly set it on the bedside table in a gesture that brought tears to my eyes. Then he got into bed, fully dressed, wearing his jacket, shoes, and socks. He fell asleep and we tiptoed out the door. "At least I can sleep late," I thought. "I'm sure he will be out cold until noon." Before eight the next morning our doorbell rang. Gore had managed to navigate the several blocks in spite of his knees, and wanted breakfast. He asked for bacon, eggs, and an English muffin, which I made. And lots of coffee. Then we began rehearsals.

It was a wild and woolly week, to say the least. Every day was much like the one preceding it—early breakfasts (always scrambled eggs, bacon, and English muffins), rehearsal all day, some kind of lunch, and dinner, ending with a late night of drinking and verbal sparring between Norman and Gore in our bar. I didn't for the life of me see how Gore was making it so well. He had more energy than all of us combined. We were all exhausted. There was still a little friction between Norman and Gore, as Norman was the director and didn't hesitate to direct, but for the most part it was civilized. Norman had masterfully cut an hour-long script from the play, and Don Juan and the devil were delightful adversaries. The night of the performance, town hall was packed to the top balcony, more than a thousand seats. Backstage, before we went on, Gore, who had changed into a red checked shirt for the performance, said, "Norman, when I walk out on that stage, you are going to hear a roar of applause the likes of which you have never heard in your life." I don't know if Norman had ever heard a roar of that magnitude, but when Gore walked onstage, with red lights flashing to announce the devil, it was pretty loud. The audience loved him, and we made enough money to keep the wolf from the theater's door for a few more months.

At the party afterward, he paid me the compliment of saying, "Norris, I'm going to outlive Norman, you know. I have longevity in my genes. When that unhappy event occurs, I will marry you and take care of you." I thanked him but said I didn't think I'd want to get married again after Norman died. He's a hard act to follow. Gore, of course, wasn't serious (I don't think), but my idea of married bliss was *not* drinking until the wee hours every night and then cooking bacon and eggs for Gore Vidal every morning. I didn't have the energy to keep up with him.

Forty-three

Norman had always been fascinated with Adolf Hitler, and had an idea for a novel about him that had been brewing in the back of his head for more than forty years. He called it *The Castle in the Forest*. He wanted to take a trip to Germany and Austria for research, and our Austrian friend Hans Janitschek was delighted to be our guide. We rented a big BMW near the border of France, and I drove it all across Germany, down through the Alps to Vienna. We stopped at every town in which Hitler had lived and tracked down his houses. We went to Wagner's house and to Bayreuth where they performed *The Ring* every year. We visited a huge merry beer hall in Munich, drank gigantic steins of beer that took two hands to lift, and ate delicious sausages and fries from a roadside stand near the stadium in Nuremberg. It was a fun trip, in spite of the somber reason we were there. We went to Dachau, which echoed with spirits, and to Berchtesgarten, Hitler's eagle's nest aerie, high in the mountains, which was breathtaking and chilling.

Hans was Viennese. He had been the ambassador to the UN when we met, back when I was pregnant with John, and he and his pretty wife, Freidl, were our great friends. He sat in the front seat with me and navigated while I drove, but he was more interested in turning around and talking to Norman, who was in the back. I'd be roaring down the autobahn at nearly a hundred miles an hour, which was totally exhilarating, and I'd say, "Hans, aren't we supposed to turn soon?" He would keep talking to Norman. "Hans? We need to focus here. Where do we turn?" He would leisurely finish his sentence, adjust his glasses, fumble with the map, stare out the window for a minute, and then say, in a panic, "Turn right here! NOW!" and I would screech the brakes and try to zip through the traffic to get off the road.

Once, he guided me into an outdoor shopping mall, and I had to navigate between the benches and shops, the trash cans and trees and pedestrians, until I found a place to get out. People were yelling at me, hustling their baby carriages out of my way. I kept calling out the window, "I'm sorry! I'm sorry!" I was mortified, but Hans was unperturbed. He had once missed his plane in Czechoslovakia and chased after it down the runway as it was about to take off. The pilot saw him out the window and stopped the plane and let him on. That was Hans; every day was an adventure with him. Norman got a tremendous amount of research accomplished, and began what would be his last novel.

IT WAS OUR BIRTHDAY, January 31, 2003. It would be Norman's eightieth, my fifty-fourth, so we decided to go to New York and have a party to liven things up a little, but a couple of days before it was to take place, I had a checkup and discovered the cancer had returned. We canceled the party, and on my birthday I was once again getting surgery in Boston.

This time was harder. This time I knew there were no treatments that were going to make this go away. It would in all likelihood come back again, even though they would put me through one of the worst chemo regimes I think exists, intraperitoneal cisplatin, which involved dripping a strong chemo drug directly into my abdominal cavity through a port and then making me roll around on the bed so it could wash over my intestines. The nurse administering it had to wear thick rubber gloves in case a drop got on her skin, it was that toxic.

John drove me home after the surgery and the first treatment. I was climbing gingerly up the stairs to my bedroom when my mother announced that she was going to go back home to Arkansas. She was going to take the bus and I couldn't stop her. It was all I could do to get to my room and into bed. Norman, I think, was happy to have me back, but he was not at his best when I was sick, and until I was able to come back downstairs and function, he pretty much left me to myself. Cancer had always been Norman's metaphor for evil, and now here was his wife, suffused with it. Was it his fault? Had he given it to me? It weighed on him, tormented him, and caused him to stay away from me. He moved into the bedroom down the hall, which hurt me at first, but the luxury of having my own bathroom and my own TV compensated. John and Matt were my mainstays during that time, and then Christina Pabst, my friend from the Actors Studio (we had once done

A Streetcar Named Desire together and forever would call each other Stella and Blanche), came from Wisconsin and cooked and looked after me for a couple of weeks. She played poker with Norman and talked to my mother while I stayed in my room and recovered. She was a godsend.

After a few months of the brutal chemo treatments, I wasn't getting better. Then I stopped having bowel movements and had to be rushed to the hospital. In June, another surgery ensued. Before I went in, Arlan told the family there was a 99 percent chance that I wouldn't survive it. He said afterward that when he cut in, it was so bad he almost just sewed me back up, but he felt like he had to try, and in the end, after an eight-hour surgery, when I woke up, there was a note on my pillow from John that said, "Mom, you're the 1 percent!"

My intestines had become glued together by scar tissue from the radiation and the fiery cisplatin, and only by the grace of God and Arlan Fuller am I here. Arlan worked on me, cutting away the scar tissue and pieces of ruined intestine like he was untangling a fine gold chain, and it worked. I also woke up with a colostomy bag on my belly, which would come off in three months with another surgery to reattach the ends of the small intestine. Living with the bag was not the easiest thing I have ever done—for those of you who have had one, you know—but I knew it was only for a short time, so I tried to take it with a bit of humor. I told my friends I was going to design a "Bag Bag," in all different colors and fabrics, so people could wear them outside their clothing instead of having to find ways to disguise them and stuff them inside. But I was getting scared. Everything I ate went almost immediately into the bag, and not much was being absorbed by my truncated intestines.

It was during this time that I lost a lot of weight, going from a high of 173 down to 103. Suddenly I was a different person. None of my clothes fit. I bought a few smaller-size clothes and they soon became baggy. I decided to wait and just wear what I had, belted. My skin became baggy, and I had wrinkles I had never had before on my arms and body, my face and neck. I watched myself age, day to day, as in time-lapse photography. I had no breasts or hips at all, and my legs were long sticks. Christina came back and stayed another couple of weeks, as did a friend named Elke Rosthal, and Aurora came and spent a week with me, but they eventually had to go back to their lives. Norman tried to help by making his own breakfast and lunch, but he was not in good health himself. He was having chest pains, and of course he wouldn't go to the doctor in Boston. He kept popping nitroglycerine tablets like they were candy, which upset me no end. My mother, who was at least out of the wheelchair and walking with a walker by this time, was more depressed than ever and just continually wanted to go home.

I got to the point where I couldn't cope. The kids all had their lives. They came and helped as much as they could, especially John and Matt, but I couldn't expect them to drop everything and come and take care of us, so we began to talk about getting an assistant in Provincetown. Judith was in New York. She was not about to move to the Cape, and Norman needed someone intelligent who could help him on-site. He had begun writing *The Castle in the Forest,* and there was a tremendous amount of research involved.

Norman and I thought of everyone we knew who might be a possibility as an assistant, and we remembered a waiter at one of the restaurants we went to a lot named Dwayne Raymond, who was an aspiring writer. We always liked having him as our waiter; there was something congenial about him. He was good-looking, personable, smart, and obviously overqualified as a waiter, but then, that is the case with most waiters in Provincetown, and New York, too. Probably most waiters everywhere.

We were trying to remember his last name and get his phone number when Norman decided to go to the grocery store to get a few things, and while he was picking over the bananas, there was Dwayne. They had a little chat, and Norman asked him if he had any interest in working as his assistant, which he did, and then somehow the conversation turned to me and how I had been having so much trouble with the surgeries and couldn't shop and cook like I used to, and Dwayne offered that he was a good cook and could do both jobs. Our lives immediately got easier and more interesting, and I think he could say the same—at least the more interesting part. He was good at both cooking and researching, and gradually he took on more and more of the Mailer duties. He also became my friend and confidant.

Every morning when he came in, he would come upstairs to my

studio and we would talk about what was going on with me and Norman and my mother, and his relationship with Thomas, his partner, who also became a member of the household. Thomas was a carpenter, and we always needed someone to fix something in the house. To my delight, Dwayne got along with my mother and she became somewhat happier. She must have been bored out of her skull with only me for stimulation. She was terribly fond of both Dwayne and Thomas, who was also a good-looking man, with long shiny black hair, and she was enmeshed in their relationship, getting upset when they fought, happy when they were getting along. They both loved to confide in her (to a point), which pleased her.

I had been working on a novel, the sequel to *Windchill Summer*, off and on for years, that I called *Cheap Diamonds*, but circumstances had kept me from finishing it. Now I started it again. It was summer in Ptown, I was alive, and we had someone to help us. Things could have definitely been worse.

I was scheduled for another surgery to remove the bag in October, and Matt and John both came up to help. Then, the day before my surgery, Norman had severe chest pains, and Brian O'Malley, our local doctor, told him to go without delay to Hyannis to the hospital. They did an angiogram, which turned out unspeakably bad because they couldn't get the wound in his groin to stop bleeding. They put a twenty-pound weight on it for hours until Norman was in agony, and it damaged his sciatic nerve, which caused him real pain for quite some time afterward. Then they told him they were going to have to operate immediately. The doctor called the kind of blockage he had a "widow maker," and he didn't want to let it go even one more day. Of course we were all up in the trees, not knowing what to do. I had my bags packed out in the car to continue on to the hospital in Boston for my own surgery, and I wanted Norman to go to MGH as well and have the surgery with the best surgeons there were. Norman decided he wasn't going to let the doctors in Hyannis operate right on the spot, so against their strong advice, John took him home, Matt took me on to Boston to get my surgery, and once again chaos reigned in the house.

My third surgery of the year was the worst of the three, but the bag was gone, thank the Lord. As far as the cancer went, Arlan had heard of a new experimental drug at Dana-Farber, and they got me into that program. The drug worked, the tumors were kept in check for the next four years, and my life slowly got back on track.

Norman did go to Boston, found a good surgeon, and arranged to get the bypass. Unfortunately, they made him get all his teeth pulled beforehand as a precaution against infection. That was the beginning of his decline. An oral surgeon was going to pull the teeth and put in implants at the same time, a relatively new procedure. Stephen took him, and right from the beginning Norman was upset because every ten minutes, each time a bit of work was done, the doctor photographed it using a flash camera. Norman hated flash cameras because he had macular degeneration and the flash was painful to his eyes. He asked the doctor why he was taking so many pictures, and the answer was that he was making a record of it for his students, that it was such a new procedure they didn't have any photos. Norman was enraged. He felt betrayed, and I don't blame him. He may have signed a permission slip, but when you are in a situation like that and the doctor or dentist hands you a paper, you normally just sign it without reading the fine print because it's either sign or go home. The doctor agreed to take fewer pictures, and on they went, for hours, through the hideously painful procedure. They were never able to completely deaden his gums. Then, afterward, the implants got infected and had to be removed. He was left with false teeth that he never got used to. They never fit right, and it was so difficult to eat that he began to lose weight.

The family once again rallied around in the early hours of the morning. This time it was Norman on the gurney and me sitting in the waiting room with them, and again it was a long, brutal surgery. The doctors brought him to the recovery room, then had to rush him back to the OR because he began to bleed through a stitch. He was opened up again, problem fixed, and finally, some hours later, we were able to see him. We were all wrung out, especially me. He was just coming out of anesthesia, and was in one of his crazy-head moods.

"While I was out," he told all twenty-something of us ganged around his bed, "I discovered the plan for the family. We will buy a ranch someplace out west, someplace where land is cheap, and build the Mailer compound. Every family will have their own house. We have enough talent in the family to do anything we want to. We'll make movies, we'll paint, we'll put on plays, we'll write, it will be great. We'll all live together and have dinner together every night, and the beauty of it all is that it will be totally financed by the GFY card." The what? "The GFY card. It will make us millions of dollars. We'll copyright the letters, and print up cards. Can you imagine? It'll sell like hotcakes. If you are in an elevator and someone shoves you, all you have to do is reach into your pocket and hand them a GFY card. You can give them out to anybody, anywhere, rude people in restaurants, people who have barking dogs, book reviewers and reporters." What is GFY? "Go Fuck Yourself! Isn't it a brilliant idea?" We all looked at one another, trying to keep from howling. He was dead serious. He had clearly had an epiphany while he was out, and this was going to be the family's fortune. It was almost as good as the elevator that went to Miami.

John's girlfriend at the time, Gena, made up some cards with a beautiful sunset behind a ship in full sail and the letters GFY in white. She brought a box of them to the hospital, and Norman never had so much fun. He gave them to the nurses, to the doctors, to the cleaning ladies, to everyone he could give one to. People loved it and thought he was the most charming man who ever lived. However, he decided sadly, it was probably not going to work. Copyrighting the letters might be impossible, and it was too easy for someone to rip off the idea, but he got a million dollars' worth of fun out of them.

WITH THE NEW experimental drug, I slowly got better. I got interested in clothes again and spent a lot of time ordering things online in my new size, 2. I tried to take my mother out shopping and for lunch, or for rides, or find anything at all that would interest her, but she preferred to stay in her chair and read. It was getting harder and harder to live with. Norman had completely given up trying to talk to her. After he recovered from his surgery, he spent most of his time up in his studio, working, or in front of the TV.

Finally, it was Mother's Day 2004. John and Matt were there, and Danielle and her husband, Peter, had come up for a few days. I decided to make one giant effort to cheer Mother up. I bought her a new outfit, the boys got her gifts, we all took her out for lunch at a nice restaurant, and I arranged for a pedicurist to come to the house and give us girls all pedicures. She dutifully got through the day, and at the end of it, we were sitting in the living room and she started to cry and said, "I hate it here. I want to go home." Something in me just snapped. I had been through too much, done too much for her when I was too sick to do it. I'd learned my patience quota, and I couldn't learn one more lesson. I had my reading glasses in my hand, and I snapped them in two. "Okay," I said. "You can go back. I'll send you down there, and I don't care how you make it. You are on your own."

Then I went upstairs and started making calls, trying to find someone who would live with her in Atkins, someone who would take care of her. There was no one. I called Susan and said, "I'll give you a thousand dollars if you'll come and take her home and find someone to stay with her. She's going to kill me." Susan, who was usually so understanding said, "You better pull yourself together. I'm not going to take care of your mother. Nobody is going to take care of her. What if she falls and breaks something, like the last time? Who is going to be responsible? You can't hire somebody to be you. You're going to have to figure out something else." And that was that. It was hard to hear, but she was right.

That night, before I went to sleep, I talked to my father, as I sometimes did. I said, "Daddy, you have to come to me in a dream tonight and tell me what to do, because I've run out of options. You are the one who told me to bring her up here and take care of her, but it's not working out. She's going to kill all of us, including herself." And I immediately fell asleep and had a dream. I was standing on the lowest step of a Roman-like arena, with a dusty circle in the middle and tiers of stone bleachers. It was a bright sunny day, and off to the side of the arena was a small stone building. My father stepped out, wearing a gray suit I had seen him wear dozens of times. He was young and handsome, and with him was my aunt Effie, who was a beautiful blonde with big blue eyes when she was a girl, and that's how she looked. She turned to Daddy in surprise and said, "J.A., where are you going?" He looked right into my eyes and said, "Well, she said she wanted to talk to me." And then I woke up.

It was so real. It wasn't a dream; it was a visitation. I had no doubt. But why did he leave so quickly? He didn't tell me anything! Then somehow the idea popped into my head to look online for information on assisted living. I had never thought of that before. I'd been so focused on making her happy living with me, like Daddy had said. I got up, went to the computer, and immediately found a place in Orleans that was not only the closest place to us but the nicest and least expensive. The next morning I took mother and Danielle to look at it.

It was beautiful. There were huge bushes of rhododendrons blooming, cool shade trees, and the building itself was red brick and well kept. We went to the office and a nice older woman showed us a couple of rooms that were occupied, and they were lovely. Each had a view and its own little terrace, and the women who lived there were friendly. She showed us one unit that someone was in the middle of moving into, a two-bedroom, which was really lovely, but unfortunately there was nothing available right then. I told her that we would take anything that became available, a studio, one-bedroom, or two-bedroom. I asked her to just call us the minute she had something. That put us at the top of the list, because most people weren't that flexible. That was on a Sunday. The next morning, the phone rang early. "Mrs. Mailer? I have some news for you. The two-bedroom you saw yesterday is available. I didn't want to say anything yesterday, but the person moving in died the night before, and I didn't feel like I could offer it to you until I had spoken to the family. I'm sure you understand." I was so happy, I nearly jumped for joy.

"Thank you, Daddy. That was quick!" I said to him when I got off the phone. "But you really didn't have to kill somebody off to do it."

My mother became a new woman. I took her to Dr. Brian O'Malley and he put her on Prozac, for starters, which had not occurred to us before, amazingly. And we went to a furniture store and picked out a whole houseful of furniture. She had some money from my father, and she just went through the store and picked out anything she wanted. She didn't once look at the price. She had never in her life done that. She had always scrimped and saved; my father had never wanted to buy anything new. She used to have to buy the cheapest desk or chair and pay it out, and now she was getting anything she wanted! We went to the mall and she picked out sheets and towels and dishes and silverware. It was like she was a girl again and was getting her first apartment. I had never seen her so happy. We had a great time arranging the furniture and fixing things up, like girlfriends, finding art and hanging pictures. We went every week to the Christmas Tree Shop and got flowers and cushions and everything she needed for her new little place. Dwayne and Thomas came and made planters for her to put on her patio, and we got a wicker table and chairs so she could sit outside and watch the birds at the bird feeder and the squirrels. I got bookcases for all her books. She was a different woman, and we were so much

Mother in her new apartment.

happier, too. Norman was getting better, and the tension in the house was gone. If only she had been on Prozac throughout my childhood, it would have been a much different childhood.

Forty-four

The phone rang at seven in the evening; it was Judith. "I'm sending that fax Norman needed," she said. "Look for it to come through any minute." I heard the hum of the fax upstairs as it started to work.

"Oh, Judith, you sent that already this afternoon. I guess it slipped your mind. But thank you so much. It's late. You really ought to take off for the day." Judith worked out of her apartment in Brooklyn, so taking off didn't mean she would go anywhere. For twenty-odd years she had worked down in the little office we'd owned on the floor below our apartment, but Judith was a chain-smoker and nobody in the building except for her smoked. We had tried everything to keep the smell down. We had professional-grade fans and smokeless ashtrays, and we had asked her to smoke outside, which did not work, as her office was three flights up and she couldn't go longer than five minutes without a cigarette. Finally, when one of our neighbors threatened to take us to court, she moved her center of operations two blocks over to her own apartment and Matt took over the office as his room. It was great for him, but to get it in habitable shape, he had to sand and scrape, seal and varnish and paint, getting rid of layers of brown nicotine stains and smoked-in smells.

At nine o'clock, the phone rang again, and again it was Judith, saying she was going to send the fax.

"Are you all right, sweetie? You've sent that fax twice now. Is anything the matter?" It wasn't even a fax that was worth anything, just a small thing that could have been taken care of in a few days.

"I guess it's these antibiotics I'm taking. Levaquin. They seem to be making me a little hazy." Judith had been sick for months with a nasty little cough, a smoker's cough, which, in fact, she had had for years. But it had recently gotten worse. She did not appreciate advice, and if I ever said anything such as "Maybe you should stop smoking until your bronchitis clears up," she would get icy and tell me it was not any of my business, thank you. She even believed that smoking was *good* for her, as the smoke killed germs. I had never in my life seen anyone smoke as much as she did. There were few breaths in her day that did not contain smoke. Still, she was positive she was going to live to be in her nineties, as her father and mother had both done. They'd been smokers, too, after all.

But Judith was increasingly making me nervous. She had begun to do odd things in the previous few months. She had bought a house, sight unseen, in Appalachia, a house that even by Appalachian standards was cheap. It had formerly been a double-wide trailer, but somebody had taken the wheels off and put it on a concrete slab foundation. She was taking driving lessons. She was going to move to a place most people were fleeing from. It was going to be beyond bizarre—Judith, who was a Wiccan priestess, who read charts in the stars and divined spirits, was going to be living in the land of the fundamentalist Christian churches. Would she bring a sweet potato pie to potlucks? Or would she keep to herself and troll the Internet? I couldn't imagine. She fully intended to continue working for Norman, that much we knew. I guess Appalachia was no farther than the keyboard of her computer.

The phone rang at ten o'clock. It was Dwayne. He was out at a restaurant across the street from his house, and his roommate, Tony, had come over carrying a cellphone with Judith on the line. She had told Tony to go get Dwayne and tell him he had to come to the office and receive the fax she was sending, that it was most important. Tony was so used to her precise competence that it didn't occur to him it was a little strange that she had called on his cellphone and told him to walk it over to the restaurant where Dwayne was having dinner. Dwayne assured her that he had gotten the fax at two in the afternoon and not to worry about it. But he was concerned, as was I. The phone didn't ring anymore, but she started to send the fax, over and over, until I finally went upstairs and unplugged it. Sue and Marco were staying in our apartment in Brooklyn for a year—Marco was taking a sabbatical—and as soon as I thought Sue would be up the following morning, I called her.

"Sue, could you go over and see about Judith? She is acting strange and I'm worried about her." Sue went over, and while Judith was obviously not feeling well, she seemed to have her wits about her. She again blamed the antibiotic, Levaquin, and she refused to go to the doctor. Neither of us knew what to do, so we did nothing. Then a few days later, Judith decided on her own to go to the doctor, but she would share precious little information with us. She was fine. There might be some benign polyps on her liver, but she was sure they were nothing. They were going to take an X-ray, but the nurse who was to do it somehow tripped and fell over a cart and hurt herself badly, so it was postponed. Then Judith couldn't get the X-ray because her insurance wouldn't pay for it at the clinic she was going to, and she would have to go across town to another clinic. There was always some reason she couldn't get this X-ray.

Finally, she said she was going in to get a little biopsy, that while she knew it was nothing, they wanted to be really sure. And the next thing we got was an email from a dear friend of hers, Peter Levenda, telling us she was dead. She had died on the table, while they were doing the biopsy. She'd been riddled with cancer from all those years and cases of cigarettes—lungs, liver, and brain. I think nobody was more surprised at her death than Judith herself. She was a master of denial. She even said that cigarette smoke was good for her plants, that was why they were so big and lush. Her cat, though, didn't fare as well. When her friend Noel came and got the cat, it started to go through nicotine withdrawal out in the fresh air and had to be treated at the vet's with nicotine patches for a while. She's fine now. If there ever was a case showing the harmfulness of secondhand smoke, this is it.

Then started a bizarre chain of events, the likes of which I hope never to see again. Judith had no will. She was the only child of elderly only children who were long dead, and she didn't have a cousin or any relative at all. Her friend Peter was the closest person to her, and she had Noel, whom I knew, but they weren't allowed to go near her. She had sent Peter an email saying that when she got out of the hospital she was going to make a proper will and name him the executor, but that never happened. People from the office of the public administrator, Kings County, New York, swooped in and taped off her apartment, then ransacked it looking for anything of value; they took all her jewelry, a coffee can full of change, and a white satin ceremonial robe hanging in her closet. They dumped her family albums into the bathtub and ripped the bed apart looking for—what? Cash? Stocks? I don't know. They threw Norman's papers all over the room and confiscated her computer and all of her work materials that were in fact ours. They took her signed books from Norman.

It was a scandal, the way they treated her possessions. And we couldn't get back our papers or her computer hard drive. A lot of Norman's work was in limbo. It took a lawyer and more than a year to get them back. I'm still not sure if we got everything. In the meantime, no one was allowed to claim her body, or even see the body. No one had permission to bury her next to her parents or do anything at all, so for months she lay in a cold storage locker, and then they quietly buried her in some potter's field, without telling us. We don't even know where. It was a ghastly lesson in the "kindness" of the state and the need to have a will.

The only thing we could do was have a memorial service for her. We had it in Brooklyn, which was nice. She was a private person, as we'd all known, but we then began learning about her secret life, of which we'd had no clue. It seemed she had worked tirelessly for Palestinian causes. She had a website and had apparently spent all her money helping Palestinian people. She'd bought a bread oven for a small village, she'd arranged to have a little girl brought to the United States for surgery, and she'd been the mentor of a young journalist who wrote about Palestinian affairs. We'd had no clue about any of this. Maybe she didn't tell us because Norman was Jewish. Maybe she didn't tell us because she just didn't want us to be a part of her life, but it was the saddest, most hollow feeling when I realized I hadn't known her at all, and during those nearly thirty years she'd thought of us as only employers and not friends, as I had thought we were. I hope she is at peace, wherever she is.

THE MAILERS CONTINUED to grow. Sue and Marco's three children, Valentina, Alejandro, and Antonia, were in school in Chile. Danielle and her husband, Peter McEachern, lived in Connecticut with her daughter, Isabella, and his two children, Colin and Hayley. Betsy and Frank Nastasi lived in the Village with their daughter, Christina Marie. Kate and Guy Lancaster had a little girl, Natasha. Stephen and his wife, Lindsay Marx, had two children, Callan and Teddy. Michael married the talented and gorgeous singer Sasha Lazard at a ceremony in Tulum, Mexico, which I wasn't able to attend because of one of the surgeries, and a couple of years later they had Cyrus, a beautiful little boy with his mother's blond curls, his father's and grandfather's blue eyes, and his grandfather's ears. Barbara's son, Peter Alson, married the writer Alice O'Neill on the beach in Provincetown, and they in time had Eden River, whose second name comes from the poker term, as Eden was conceived at the World Series of Poker. Then Matt and his beautiful girlfriend, Salina Sias, got married on South Padre Island in Texas, and we all went down for that. I wasn't feeling well at all, but I took a lot of pain pills and pasted on a smile.

The wedding was to be on the beach underneath a golden orange canopy. The day dawned bright blue and sunny. Norman and I, like two ancient old ginks, were helped out to the chairs that had been set up on the beach. Then, to everyone's horror, the wind whipped up until the sand was swirling in ferocious blasts. All we could do was sit there and squeeze our eyes shut as the sand scoured our faces and piled up in our hair and on our clothes. Matt and Salina were amazing. They pretended to ignore the sandstorm. They went through the vows, the musicians played, and John gave a beautiful little talk. Others spoke. Salina was heroic. She has a contact lens and a glass eye, which were both filled with sand, and she could hardly see her vows as she read them, it was so painful. But she persevered, and was so gorgeous in her white dress against the Prussian blue sea with its wind-frothed whitecaps and the orange-gold silk blowing in the wind. Finally, we all staggered inside, shook off the sand, and went on to a great party in a restaurant by the beach.

Norman gave a toast that began, "If this marriage works out . . ." He went on to say a lot more, of course, and it was one of his funniest, wildest, best toasts ever. He always did rise to an occasion. I danced and had a good time, but all the while, my kidney was blocked by a tumor and urine was backing up. By the following morning, I was in agony, and all I could do was take as many pain pills as I could until the plane landed in Boston. Then I went directly to the hospital, where I had another surgery. But at least I was at my son's wedding! Now they have two beautiful children, Mattie James and Jackson Kingsley Mailer. Mattie was named after her father, Matthew, and her grandfather James Davis, and Jackson was named after Norman Kingsley Mailer.

John Buffalo was busy writing and acting. He had a novella, *Hello Herman*, published while he was in his sophmore year at Wesleyan, and has been my mainstay throughout these last few difficult years.

Norman began to lose weight. His breathing became more and more labored, and he could hardly walk across the room without sitting down. The doctor was treating him for asthma, which I didn't believe he had. I was afraid it was his heart, but again he refused to go to Boston. He preferred to use an inhaler, take asthma medicine, and do the best he could.

The only bright spot in these days for him was Texas hold 'em poker. He had started watching it on TV, and soon books began arriving. That was the sign he was interested in a new project. He would buy a complete library first and learn everything he could about a subject before he tackled it. We began having poker games at the house after dinner, with Mike and Donna Lennon; Chris Busa; Pat Doyle; Astrid Berg; Hans Janitschek; Norman's sister, Barbara; any of the kids who were there; and any assorted visiting firemen, as Norman used to say. Anyone at all who was willing was dragooned into playing poker.

The person to beat was always Peter Alson, but even pros have bad card nights, and sometimes he would lose. We wagered just enough to make it interesting, twenty dollars to ante. The games were hilarious sometimes. Once, Danielle and her daughter Isabella were playing together because they were just learning the game, and they kept upping the bet until everyone dropped out. It turned out that they had nothing, not even a pair, and had unbeknownst to themselves bluffed the whole table out. Norman won a lot. I pretended with great drama to relish beating him, but I secretly was happy when he won.

He finished his book on Hitler, *The Castle in the Forest*, and we went back to New York for the launch party given by his editor, David Ebershoff, in January 2007. Sue and Marco had gone back to Chile after his year of sabbatical, and our apartment was empty for the first time ever. It was so good to be back home in Brooklyn, so good to have the kids a short subway ride away instead of six long hours. It had been much easier since Dwayne had joined us, and my mother was happy in her own apartment in Orleans, but life on the Cape was still hard on me. I was constantly driving somewhere. My mother lived forty-five minutes away, and my doctors were more than two hours away. I was continually either taking one of the three of us to doctors or visiting Mother, going shopping for her, taking her out to lunch, while trying to write my own book. I was grateful to Dwayne for shopping and cooking and keeping Norman going, but he was there only four hours a day, and there was only so much he could do.

I began to think about moving back to Brooklyn so we would be close to doctors, and finding a place for my mother that would be closer to us so I wouldn't have to travel so far all the time. Not to mention it would be great to have the kids nearby to help us. I discussed it with Norman, but he didn't want to move. He loved Provincetown. He loved his life there and he wasn't going. End of conversation.

We went back to New York in March 2007 when he and Günter Grass did a show with Andrew O'Hagan at the New York Public Library. The kids all came to hear him, and the ones who hadn't seen him in a while were aghast. Kate said, "We shouldn't let Dad do this. We have to take him to the hospital right now!" He had lost so much weight that it was frightening. He couldn't walk more than a few steps, even with his two canes, without resting. He was living on oysters, orange juice mixed with red wine, and Hershey bars. He could hardly breathe. The audience gasped when he walked out on the stage. Still, when he got under the spotlight, all of those problems dropped away and his mind came out, as sharp as ever. He was astounding in his clarity and scope of thought. Andrew was giving Grass a hard time about hiding his youth membership in the Nazi party, and Norman defended him roundly, saying, "How many of us would have the courage at age seventeen to go against the reigning government and fight it alone? Especially one as brutal as the Nazis? Of course he would have gone along with it, and why would he rush to tell about it later? He did no more than any one of us would have done." Günter was grateful to him, and I was so proud of him. No matter what was going on with his body, that powerful mind was still in there, and he was going to say what he thought, no matter if it was popular or not.

But this trip to New York also underscored just how weak he had become. I had to get him and my mother back to the city whether he wanted to go or not. I had to have the help of the kids. I could no longer go on caring for my mother and Norman by myself. I would make the arrangements and he would just have to go along with it.

I researched assisted living places near us in Brooklyn and found a perfect one for Mother, the Prospect Park Residence. Salina and I went and looked at the rooms that were available, and we picked out a sweet one-bedroom with a view of Prospect Park. I went back to Provincetown and told Norman that I was moving my mother to Brooklyn, and I wanted him to come with me. We had to be closer to the kids. I had to have some help. He said he would stay in Provincetown and take care of himself. (I heard the echo of my mother's determination to go back to Arkansas in his voice.) I actually believed that once I moved he would change his mind, I don't know why. I'd certainly known him long enough to know better.

Christina came back to help and we packed up my mother and moved her to Brooklyn. Mother was kind of excited about it. It was an adventure for her. She had changed with the Prozac and her new independence. Thomas came in a truck with her furniture and we spent a couple of days arranging her apartment. It was a lot to learn and get used to for her, but she had her stuff, which means so much to a woman. "Home is where your stuff is." I had gone to Arkansas the previous year and sold her house and had brought up a truckload of her things from there, so she had her old lamps and stereo, her china cabinet, and lots of other things that meant a lot to her. I think she had at last made peace with living out her life in New York. And there was the bonus of being closer to Matt and John and the grandbabies.

The only problem now was Norman. I went back and forth to Ptown every couple of weeks, spending June and July there with him, and then I went on my book tour for two weeks in August 2007 when my second novel, *Cheap Diamonds,* came out. Various of the kids and our friends had been coming to stay with Norman, and of course he had Dwayne, but Norman's breathing was getting so bad that something had to be done. So we took him to Boston, where they drained container after container of fluid from his lung for a week. One lung was covered in scar tissue from the fluid, and the other one was working at only about half strength. The Boston doctors were undecided on what to do about his problems, and Maggie was getting married at the house on the beach. He was determined to come back for that, so we checked him out of the hospital and home we went.

Maggie was a beautiful bride with her startling blue eyes and thick mass of dark curls, and her husband, John Wendling, was Ralph Lauren handsome, a blond, blue-eyed carpenter who had that healthy clean-wood aura about him. Carol, Maggie's mother, came, and we had a happy little reunion. Over the years we had become friends, and we emailed each other nearly every day. It was bizarre, but what the heck. (Maggie and John had a baby boy, Nicholas Maxwell Mailer Wendling, in November 2009, two years later.)

The boys somehow got Norman down the stairs to the chairs on the beach, and Maggie and John were married by Mike Lennon, who had his minister's license, on a clear, sparkling day in September. Then Norman struggled back up the stairs, had a polite glass of champagne, posed for a few pictures, and went to bed. I knew we would have to move soon, and finally, so did he.

Danielle and Peter stayed with him while I went back to New York to get things ready. They drove him to Brooklyn and it was a monumental struggle to get him up the stairs. I could see why he didn't want to come. He would never get to go out at all. The next couple of weeks were tough. His breathing was worse in the city air in spite of the air purifiers I had bought, and before he had been there long, we had to take him to Mount Sinai hospital, where they promptly put him in the ICU.

I wasn't feeling at all well myself. I had a horrible urinary tract infection of some kind, and I could feel the symptoms of the cancer growing again, but I didn't want to believe it. I didn't have time for that now. I had to be in the hospital every day with Norman, and also I had to see that my mother was taken care of, that she had her medicine and everything else she needed.

We tried to keep Norman's whereabouts a secret, but those things leak out, and we had to get a policeman to sit outside the door after a photographer tried to sneak into the ICU and photograph him. Someone in the family was with him all the time. All his friends and everyone he knew came to say goodbye. He was about to publish his last book, a small work he did with Mike Lennon called *On God*. In fact, it came out while he was in the hospital, in his last days, and his picture was on the cover of *New York* magazine, a picture of him with artwork behind it as if he were at the gates of heaven. I read him an excerpt from the book that was printed in *Playboy* magazine. Not the worst way to go out.

At first, he was able to talk, and we had a few conversations. He knew his time was up, and so did I. I was sitting beside his bed crying one day when he said, "You're crying. You must really love me."

"Of course I love you, you silly old coot! Why else do you think I've stuck around all this time?" After all we had been through, he still wasn't sure I loved him? I didn't love every single last thing about him, nor did he about me, and there were a few things I am sure we definitely disliked about the other, but all in all, we had found someone whose quirks we could live with, and we had done all right. We'd made a great son together, and we'd had some fun. There are people who have less. I don't think I ever did take that step back toward him in my heart, but I didn't take another one away, either. I didn't know what my life was going to be like without him, and I didn't know how long I would live after he went.

"I'll be right behind you," I told him. "So have all the fun you can before I get there."

He smiled and took my hand. "Remember the Taxicab Kiss?" he said.

"Like it was yesterday."

"It's gone by fast, hasn't it?"

"Yes, it has." It surely had. I know everyone realizes that when they get older, but it is always a shock, how fast it goes.

Forty-five

"What is that noise?" the nurse whispered, looking alarmed. "Is the ventilator malfunctioning?" I was dozing, and jerked awake at her abrupt entry.

"No," I croaked, and cleared my throat. My voice felt like it had lain out in the rain and rusted. "It's the iPod. We recorded the sound of the ocean for him. It soothes him."

"Oh. Sorry." She looked at the iPod, checked a few dials on the various machines, and went back out. It was morning on the ninth of November, 2007. I was alone with Norman in the ICU, but the rest of the family were on the way. Sue and Marco had come in from Chile, Danielle and Peter from Connecticut. It was Peter McEachern, our beloved son-in-law, who had driven the six hours to Provincetown to put his recorder under Norman's bedroom window and record the waves washing the beach. He'd taped a half hour of it, which was now on a loop, so the sound was heard around the clock, the occasional faint wail of a foghorn punctuating the rhythm like a note from a tenor sax.

Maggie and her husband, John, had come from the Berkshires. The rest of the kids—Betsy, Kate, Michael, Matthew, and John Buffalo—were in New York already, along with their spouses and their children, as well as Norman's sister, Barbara, her son, Peter, and his wife, Alice. Our cousin Sam Radin and his wife, Pam, were there. Everyone was there except for Stephen, who was trying to get back from Arizona, where he was performing in a play. Today was the day we were all gathering to decide whether or not to turn off the ventilator.

Norman had been steadily going downhill since he'd gotten to Mount Sinai, and had been in the ICU for five weeks. He was lying there now, unable to speak, with his leg laid open from an emergency surgery to remove infection that had set in from so many IV needles. He had been good about it all, never complaining—at least not overly much—but we were all worn out. I had a fever of 102 from an infection that would send me to the hospital myself soon, and I felt like crawling up into the bed with him. Before the tube took away his voice, we had spent our days talking about everything that needed to be talked about, and now all I could do was hold his hand, kiss his fingers from time to time, and talk in a one-sided monologue that was most unsatisfactory. We had begun talking nearly thirty-three years before, and had never not had something to say to each other. He slept on, hovering somewhere above his body, I imagined, watching with interest.

The kids started arriving, and soon there were so many of us that they sent us to the biggest conference room. We patched Stephen in on the phone and started going over all the reasons to turn off the machines. Dad hadn't wanted them in the first place, had in fact left a living will to that effect, but when a doctor tells you that it is temporary, that the breathing machine will be on for only a few days and then he will be better, the choice is either to do it or in effect say "Don't do it. Kill him." So a few days went by, then a few weeks; it proved to be impossible to take the ventilator out. His powerful brain was still in there, working furiously, but he was mute and couldn't breathe on his own. He tried at first to write on a pad, but frustratingly, no one could decipher his scrawl, which had never been an easy task. For the first time in his life, Norman Mailer was silent. Still, his eyes were the clear blue that rivaled Paul Newman's, and he could say a lot with those eyes. He wanted to go.

He and I had had endless conversations about death over the years. We both believed that there is another life after this one, and we believed in reincarnation. He loved to tell a joke about dying and going in front of the angel in command, who asked him what he wanted to be his next time on earth. "I'd like to be a black athlete, Your Honor," Norman said, humbly. "I don't care what poor circumstances I'd be born into, and I don't care which sport, I just want to be a successful black athlete, like Muhammad Ali—maybe not as grand, but of that order." The angel flipped through the book. "Well, Mr. Mailer, unfortunately, that is a popular category. Everyone wants to be a successful black athlete. It's already way oversubscribed. And it says here that we have you down for . . . Oh, my . . . a cockroach. But don't worry. I can guarantee you'll be the fastest cockroach on the block!" He laughed and laughed, but I think down inside he was laughing because he was afraid it might be the true scenario.

In the conference room that morning, the family hashed over all the various ways to take him back to Provincetown to die, but the logistics were insurmountable. He couldn't be moved. Finally, after exhausting every possibility with the doctors, we decided to turn off the ventilator the following morning, when Stephen would be there, and put an end to his suffering. Heartsick, we all went back to his cubicle to spend a little time with him. To our surprise, he was sitting up in the bed, eyes wide open, as clear as an October sky. He grinned when he saw us all, and by now several of his close friends such as Ivan Fisher, Hans Janitschek, and Larry Schiller had arrived. People were coming in and going out of the ICU like it was a train station. Rick Stratton was there, and our old friend Christina Pabst arrived again from Wisconsin. Diane Fisher and her twins, Kitty and Clay, came in. The room was crammed. Everyone was trying to talk to him at once. He was nodding and trying to respond as best he could.

"It doesn't seem like he's dying," I said to Michael. "He seems better." His doctor overheard me, came over, and said, "Don't let it fool you. It happens sometimes, when a person is dying. They get a little gift at the end, a jump of energy, a few hours of clarity, but all it means is that the end is near. Just enjoy him for now. Let him know you all love him." I remembered my father and his last few moments, when he spoke so clearly and told me to take my mother down for breakfast. It was true, it was a last little gift. So we had a party in the ICU, much to the consternation of the other patients and their nurses, I'm sure. Norman thumb wrestled with the guys, hugged the girls; he gave Christina a big wet kiss right on the mouth, which popped my eyes, to everyone's amusement.

Then someone—Michael, maybe—said, "It's too bad we don't have any booze." Norman's eyes lit up like a pinball machine and he started pantomiming a drink. Michael or Peter or someone went out to get some orange juice and rum, his favorite drink, and mixed a real drink. All we had was plastic glasses, which were anathema to Norman, and he turned up his nose at them, so one of the nurses found a clean real glass. The next problem was that he couldn't drink, with the tube in his throat. It could choke him. So we got one of those lime-green sponge sticks that are used to moisten a dry mouth, and dipped it in the drink. He made a face and spat it out. Then he grabbed the glass and started taking real sips, one, two, three, four, five . . . I had to laugh because he'd always had a habit of taking seven little sips of a new drink, and he actually made it to five this time. He didn't choke.

He pointed to the drink and then to all of us, wanting us to each have a sip. We passed it around, everyone taking a tiny sip, and then it came back to him, seasoned with the germs and the love of everyone in the room. He finished the drink; I still don't know how he did it. All day, people drifted in and out, others coming to take their place, to touch him, to say goodbye. He glowed in the attention. Late afternoon set in, Norman's least favorite time of the day. It seemed the harsh afternoon light would never fade into cool twilight, but finally it did. He began to tire. The doctor said he was getting weary and needed to rest. Most of the friends left.

The hospital was giving us, for the night, one of the expensive private suites on the eleventh floor that rival the best hotel rooms. We could stay with him up there as long as we wanted. There was even a chef on the floor who would make us all dinner. So we, all of us who were left—his family and a few dear friends—trooped beside his bed as they moved him into the elevator, up to the fancy room, and got him settled into his comfy bed with the blinking lights and the monitors. He closed his eyes and fell asleep then, exhausted from his last triumphant party. We were still having a party ourselves. Nobody wanted to go home. Then ten o'clock came. And then eleven. Only the family were left. We decided to come back early the next day, to all be there together when the machines were turned off for the last time. I was feeling awful at that point, so sick; my fever was raging and my infection was hurting. But I didn't want to go. I didn't want to leave him. "He's asleep," the kids said. "You need to go get some rest. You are going to have a big day tomorrow and you'll really be sick if you don't go home." So I let them talk me into it, and I went, tears running down my face as I said goodbye.

Stephen arrived on a late night flight and came to the hospital room sometime after midnight. He was sleeping on a fold-out cot when the machines started going off around four. He jumped up and called for the nurse, afraid they were malfunctioning. Then Norman sat up in the bed. He looked over at Stephen, as Stephen later said, his eyes wide open, and then he looked away, toward the distance. His mouth spread in a huge smile, and his eyes were alive with excitement, as if he were seeing something amazing. Then he was gone.

DWAYNE HAD COME to stay with me and say goodbye, and he helped me bring Norman's clothes to the funeral home. Norman was going to be wearing his L.L.Bean sweatpants, his rust-colored suede cloth shirt, and his black fleece vest that Russell Crowe had given him on the set of *Cinderella Man,* a movie on which he had been a boxing expert a few years before. He and Russell had gotten along, and Norman loved the vest. In fact, he'd seldom taken it off, just long enough for me to wash it, and then he'd put it back on again, warm and toasty from the dryer. He would also be wearing his UGGs, the boots that he had worn summer and winter for the previous few years. He could no longer tie his shoes, and he could slip the UGGs easily on and off without the need for socks. They kept his feet an even temperature all the time. I wanted him to be comfortable. He'd be wearing them a long time.

We went out to get into the car and a *New York Post* reporter was hanging around outside. Dwayne went over to talk to him and asked him not to bother me, and he didn't. I think he discreetly took a few pictures, but he didn't get in my face, which I appreciated.

We all met at Campbell's, where his mother had had her service, and we picked out a coffin that was not the most expensive, but certainly not the bottom, either. Even the bottom was expensive, I thought. Much more than in Arkansas, that's for sure. The one we chose had inlaid wood, like a table we had in the living room, and I thought he would like it. After we signed the papers and I wrote the check, Maggie wandered into the next room and discovered a whole roomful of less expensive caskets that they had not shown us. I suppose they thought we wouldn't want anything but the best, and what the heck—you only get one.

We all caravanned to Provincetown for the funeral, and met at McHoul Funeral Home there. It was a big room, with nice flowers, and they set him up at one end of the room where we had a visitation that night. Everyone in Provincetown dropped by to say goodbye. His hair had been slicked down too much, and I fluffed it up a little. It was so thin now. When I'd met him, it had been like sheep's wool. I started cutting his hair when we first met, and he had never been to a barber since. In the beginning, I was as besotted as a teenager and used to save his hair and put it into a white satin heart-shaped pillow. By the time the pillow was full, I was over it. It would have been silly to fill more of them. I wondered how many pillows there would have been over the years.

I hated to leave him there alone, but we were coming back the following morning for the funeral. I hoped my health could hold out until this was all over. I'd been taking antibiotics, which weren't doing their duty, and I knew it was more than a bladder infection.

The day of the funeral was beautiful and sunny and cold. As we were getting ready to go to the funeral home, a girl came up onto our deck and knocked on the door. Danielle was standing in the living room and let her in. She was a bleached blonde wearing an outfit that can only be described as L.A. beach, with high platform sandals, a too-short skirt, and a too-low-cut top. She had on a skimpy cardigan sweater, but the outfit was much too cold for a November day on the Cape.

"Hi," she said to Danielle, "I'm a friend of Michael's from L.A. Can I use your bathroom?" Of course Danielle said yes and showed her the small guest bathroom off the living room. She was a little strange, but we didn't question that she knew Michael. He was a movie producer and knew all kinds of weird people. She didn't come out of the bathroom for a long time, and finally Danielle and I looked at each other and knocked on the door.

"Are you all right?"

The girl came out with a dreamy look on her face and said, "Yes, thanks," and walked out the door. At the funeral home, we were organizing everyone to go to the cemetery when she came in the door. She ambled over to the coffin and knelt down on the bench beside it. She was making me nervous, as she was several other people. She rubbed Norman's hands and touched him, and just as Larry Schiller made a move to go over to her, she got up, taking a huge piece from the flower arrangement on the casket, and started walking toward the door with it. Larry stopped her and took it away from her, and she wandered on out. I was appalled, but had other things on my mind.

We lined up, and the hearse led the way to the cemetery. I told them to drag the town instead of taking the fast way there. We used to do that every time we went out to dinner. "Want to drag the town?" Norman would ask, and we'd go from one end of town to the other, just looking at the shops and lights, and then at the farthest end, Norman would always tell his story of the landing of the Pilgrims, how they had stolen the Indians' cache of winter corn and killed a couple of them and then had had to flee to Plymouth, which then, unfairly, got all the credit for the landing. "And on your left is the fabulous motel they put up in memory of that event," he'd say, and he'd point to the Provincetown Inn, a perfectly nice motel right at the end of the Cape where the Mayflower had indeed made its landing. It was something he never tired of. We led the string of cars through town, and people on both sides of the street stopped, and some took off their hats; some put their hands on their hearts. They were all saluting a man who'd been one of them, a man who'd loved that place and wanted to spend eternity there.

THE CEMETERY WAS set up with chairs under a green awning, and as many of us as could sat down. The rest had to stand. There were several great speakers that day—his close friends, some of his children. Mike Lennon, who had always been there for us no matter what, had passed a kidney stone that morning. I don't know how he did it, but through an act of sheer will he was there, standing during the service, speaking, and taking care of everyone. He must have been in pure agony, even with pain pills. I'll never forget it. Stephen got up and sang "Your Song," by Elton John, and his children went up there with him, dancing and helping him. Then Michael got up and began his speech by saying, "Dad would have been appalled by that song, Stephen, but you did it well."

Doris Kearns Goodwin told a funny story about the last time we'd spent the night at their house. Norman had had a terrible time with the toilet in our room, because the water level had been too high, and in the morning he'd told Doris that she needed to get a new toilet if she was going to have him come back, because every time he sat down, his balls dipped into the water. To hear sweet, proper Doris tell that story was hilarious.

Some of the speakers brought tears to our eyes, some were funny. All loved Norman, and it was a good and proper goodbye.

Over to the side was some kind of small commotion, but I couldn't see what was going on. I noticed Michael get up, but I didn't think much about it. Later they told me that the blond girl from L.A.—who was not a friend of Michael's, although he said she had once auditioned for one of his movies—had started to do a little dance and had begun to take off her clothes. She had kicked off the sandals and the skirt and was starting on the top when he reached her and grabbed her and got her out of there. We never knew if she was stoned or just crazy. Maybe a bit of both. She disappeared, and we never saw her again.

It was such a *Norman Mailer* funeral. How could it be otherwise? I'm sure he loved it.

Epilogue

I went to the hospital five times the year after Norman died. But I'm still here. Somehow, it doesn't worry me. I've been told three times to get my affairs in order, and I think by this time they all are. I'm living in Brooklyn, in the apartment Norman brought me to the first time I came to New York. It is home to me, more than any other place in the world. My mother still lives in Park Slope, John and Matt live near me with their families, and I see the rest of the family all the time. We had an incredible memorial at Carnegie Hall for Norman in April 2008, one he also would have loved, and his spirit is definitely hanging around. We've all felt it. So life goes on. As long as there are Mailers, there will be stories of Dad—funny stories, sweet stories, stories of his misbehavior, his exploits, his achievements. Norman changed my life, that's for sure, and the ripples from that first meeting in Arkansas have spread through many lives. I am not in a hurry to leave this life, but I won't be greedy, either. I've had so much more than most. I wouldn't trade with anybody in the world. And who knows what Norman is doing on the other side? I'm curious to catch up with him and find out.

BROOKLYN, NOVEMBER 2009

Acknowledgments

I want to acknowledge my wonderful family, who have given me such joy over the years, and who keep growing! I love you all so much:

My mother, Gaynell Davis
Susan Mailer and Marco Colodro; Valentina, Alejandro, and Antonia Colodro
Danielle Leslie Mailer and Peter McEachern; Isabella Mailer Moschen and Hayley and Colin McEachern
Elizabeth Anne Mailer and Frank Nastasi; Christina Marie Mailer Nastasi
Kate Caliean Mailer and Guy Lancaster; Natasha Annabelle Lancaster
Michael Burks Mailer and Sasha Lazard; Cyrus Force Mailer
Stephen McLeod Mailer and his fiancée, Elizabeth Rainer; Callan Marx Mailer and Theodore Marx Mailer
Maggie Alexandra Mailer and John Wendling; Nicholas Maxwell Mailer Wendling
Matthew Davis Norris Mailer and Salina Sias Mailer; Mattie James Mailer and Jackson Kingsley Mailer
John Buffalo Mailer and his fiancée, Peri Lyons
Barbara Mailer Wasserman (Norman's sister)
Peter Harper Alson (Barbara Wasserman's son) and Alice O'Neill; Eden River Alson
Sam and Pam Radin, our cousins.

I have been blessed all my life with dear friends, and I can't list everyone here who has been important to me—I would leave someone out—but I've tried to be a good friend, and I would hope you all already know who you are and how much you mean to me.

I offer a special thanks to Larry Schiller for his ingenuity and his hard work in forming the Norman Mailer Writers Colony and for being a friend and colleague over the years. Sam Radin, also, was instrumental in the founding of the colony, and is invaluable to me with his sound advice.

A big thank-you and much love to Mike Lennon, Norman's dear friend and authorized biographer, who is responsible for putting together the vast Mailer archive now housed in the Ransom Center in Texas, and his wife, Donna, who is his partner in all things.

I send special thanks to my agent, Ike Williams, who is always there for me, and a heartfelt thank-you to Random House; its publisher, Gina Centrello; my editor, David Ebershoff, who is a fine writer in his own right, and who guided me with an easy hand; Jynne Martin and Carol Schneider, friends and publicists extraordinaire; Janet Wygal, copy editor; Laura Goldin, lawyer; and the wonderful designers, Kimberly Glyder, Paolo Pepe, and Barbara Bachman, who made the book such a pleasure to look at.

Index

Page locators in *italics* signify photographs. NCM is short for Norris Church Mailer. NM is short for Norman Mailer.

PHOTO CREDITS

Title page	*Francis Delia*
41	*Lee Rogers*
46 (top)	*Bill Ward*
46 (bottom)	*Bill Ward*
69	*Jean Jewell Moreno*
70	*Jean Jewell Moreno*
84	*Andy Anders*
130	*Norman Mailer*
146	*Francis Delia*
154	*Lee Rogers*
173	*Milton H. Greene © 2010 Joshua Greene, www.legendslicensing.com*
180	*Lisette Lenzi*
209	*Robert Belott*
220	*Marco Colodro*
226	*Robert Belott*

230	*Photograph © by Jill Krementz, used by permission of the photographer; all rights reserved*
235	*Photograph © by Jill Krementz, used by permission of the photographer; all rights reserved*
245	*Photograph © by Jill Krementz, used by permission of the photographer; all rights reserved*
247	*Photograph © by Jill Krementz, used by permission of the photographer; all rights reserved*
254	*Joel Meyerowitz © 2009 courtesy Edwynn Houk Gallery*
255	*Dotson Rader*
278	*Getty Images/Carl Mydan*
303	*Tom Luddy*
308	*Tom Luddy*
314	*Robert Belott*
328	*Juan Moreno*

A TICKET TO THE CIRCUS

Norris Church Mailer

A READER'S GUIDE

A Conversation Between Norris Church Mailer and Her Editor, David Ebershoff

OCTOBER 17, 2010

David Ebershoff: You say in the beginning of the book that you told Norman you'd never write about him. How do you think he would have responded to *A Ticket to the Circus*?

Norris Church Mailer: Of course he would dislike certain parts of it and insist that I got them wrong—such is the nature of memory—but at the same time, I think he would be proud of me and say, as he did with my other two books, that if he had edited the book it would have been 5 percent better! Naturally, I wouldn't have let him read it until it was safely in print. I also think he might have been a little torn about the reviews, feeling both slight jealousy and pride.

DE: As many reviewers have noted, you are a natural storyteller. Where does this come from?

NCM: No big writers in my family, but my father taught himself to type and wrote a delightful little memoir after he retired from working for the government program Job Corps, teaching disadvantaged boys how to run heavy equipment. But by that time, it was too late for him to have a career as a writer. There had been no time when he was growing up for things like school or writing; life during the Depression and Second World War was too hard for a fatherless boy with a mother and little sister to support, so he did the best he could, learning to operate heavy construction equipment in the Navy Seabees and continuing it for most of his working life, but he always secretly wanted to be a writer, a secret he kept well from my mother and me.

DE: What are some of your earliest memories of books?

NCM: I learned to read by memorizing Little Golden Books, and one day when I was about five, I realized I wasn't just remembering the words, I could actually read them! I was a huge fan of Laura Ingalls Wilder and Lois Lenski, reading their books over and over. I wrote to them, not realizing that Laura was dead, but I got a nice letter from her estate, and Lois sent me a note she signed herself when I wrote to her about my love for *Strawberry Girl*.

DE: Writing a memoir takes a great deal of courage. What did you most fear while writing this book?

NCM: For a while, I was afraid of what people were going to say about me, and then I realized that I didn't have to show the book to anyone unless I wanted to, but that I had to write the truth as I saw it, if for no other reason than to sort it all out in my own head. Then as I got deeper into it, I realized that I really wanted to publish it, I needed to exorcise the bad parts, and relive the joy of the good parts, because there were so many good parts; I wanted to set the record straight from all the falsehoods that had been printed over the years. People could take me as I really was or not like me at all because, finally, it didn't really matter, and I'm glad I did it.

DE: You are also an artist, and before you met Norman you were an art teacher. How has this affected your writing?

NCM: One of the nicest reviews I ever had called my work "painterly," which meant to me that people saw pictures when they read my words. I have always believed all creativity comes from the same well in us, and each medium is just another way of expressing it.

DE: What did you learn most from your marriage to Norman? And what do you think he learned most from you?

NCM: I learned that forgiveness and retribution aren't mutually exclusive, and I think he learned that actions have consequences. I learned to be a professional in writing, to set hours and work when they are set, and not to overuse adjectives and adverbs. Perhaps he learned that sometimes simplicity is more powerful than embroidery.

DE: Can you tell us one anecdote that didn't make the book?

NCM: Most of the actions of my life didn't make the book, there could never be enough pages between two covers to put it all in, but the first one that just now popped into my mind involves expanding on a trip I briefly mentioned to Plains, Georgia, when Jimmy Carter had just received the Democratic nomination for president and Norman was sent by *The New York Times* to do an article on him. We went with him and Rosalynn to their church on Sunday morning (after going parking in the middle of a peanut patch under a dusty blue moon the night before; I was trying to show him the joys of small-town southern life). Sunday was another boiling-hot summer day, the kind where you are soaked in sweat by the time you walk from the air-conditioned house to the air-conditioned car to the air-conditioned church. I wore an ice-cream suit and straw hat with a wide green ribbon, and I knew all the words to the hymns. As I sang in a big, loud voice, I thought maybe Jimmy looked at me with a little lust in his heart, as he had just admitted he did from time to time with other women in his *Playboy* interview, which had caused a bit of controversy; Norman, jealous as he was of every man in those days, was convinced of it. (Maybe he was just looking at me because I was singing off-key, who knows?) Later, Norman and Jimmy did the first half of their interview, and for some reason the first question Norman asked was about Nietzsche, (or maybe it was Kierkegaard), whom Jimmy had quoted somewhere, and, as Jimmy sat and smiled at him in slight bewilderment, Norman began to talk, and as he talked, he somehow got caught up doing all the talking—about philosophy. Jimmy said nothing, just kept smiling, the edges of his mouth slightly quivering with tension. I became more and more nervous that Norman wasn't going to get one question out. Finally, little Amy saved the day by riding in on her red tricycle and announcing that they had to go to Grandma's now for lunch, and so Jimmy gratefully stood up, shook our hands, and we left. The next day was much better, of course, and the article was printed in *The New York Times Magazine*. I always believed that Norman was a big factor in convincing New York to back Carter, and that that's what won him the election, and it made me love him all the more while tenderly becoming more aware that he had a flaw or two.

DE: What has been the most surprising response to your memoir?

NCM: I have been surprised and gratified by the good reviews, I suppose. Most writers are afraid when that time comes, and I was more than a little worried. Then I was surprised by the fact that there are still people in this sex-obsessed culture who were shocked at the sexuality. Of course it was sexual—that's what makes the world spin, and why people are attracted to each other in the first place! Then there were unbelievable moments on the book tour, such as when a radio interviewer asked me to explain the "hierarchy" of the wives, as though we all lived together right then in some Mormon compound and one wife peeled the potatoes while another one washed the clothes. I told him in the simplest terms I could that I was the only wife and that the others were all exes. Not sure what he did with that one. Then there was the boy who started his radio interview off by saying, "Now this book is about adultery—" and I interrupted him and said, "No, this book is my life story, it is not a book about adultery. My life is not adultery." Unbelievable.

DE: You've also written two wonderful novels, each with a protagonist who is somewhat autobiographical. What's the biggest difference between writing fiction and memoir?

NCM: Memoir is much easier because you have the story laid out for you and don't have to struggle to find a believable tale. That said, it is also harder, because it is *you* and real people you care about or love—or real people that you don't care about or love, which is worse—who you are writing about, and you want to get it right and are afraid you might not. You want to be honest and forthright without hurting anybody's feelings, which you soon find is impossible, and so, finally, you just say, "I have to write my story, and if someone doesn't like it, they can write their own version of events." And then try not to worry about it—something I have never been too good at. One thing I do want to emphasize, though, is that my protagonist in my two novels, Cherry, is not me, although we may have shared a version of some adventures. Of course there are parts of me in her, but there are parts of me in all my characters; they were all created by me, through my sensibilities. The moment the reader assumes the person on the page is the writer, that is perhaps when the author is the farthest away from being that character.

DE: Why do you think Norman never wrote his autobiography? If he had written an autobiography, what is the one memory you know he would have included?

NCM: I think for years he might have intended to do it, but there was always another book that took his fancy, and, finally, he was surprised to realize that he had run out of time and that he really hadn't wanted to do it at all. As he said more than once, he was sick of himself and didn't want to analyze himself anymore—he had done too much of it. Even narcissists have limits, it seems.

The taxicab kiss.

QUESTIONS AND TOPICS FOR DISCUSSION

1. One reviewer described Norris's life as a series of emancipations. From what or whom do you think she was liberated? Was she really able to leave her childhood and life in Arkansas, or was her life there too much a part of who she was?

2. How did you relate to Norris's childhood with regard to her religious upbringing? Did you see it as harsh or as loving? How far should you go in allowing religion to dictate how you live your life?

3. Upon beginning life with Norman, Norris realized that public perception of him was often greatly at odds with the man she knew. How should she have handled ugly comments about the man she loved?

4. Being with someone who is so successful in his field can be intimidating, especially if you have aspirations in the same field. Did Norris do the right thing in putting her novel away when Norman was less than enthusiastic about it? Or should she have ignored him and continued writing?

5. *A Ticket to the Circus* shows us how being married to a famous man is a double-edged sword at best. As the wife of a controversi celebrity, did Norris have an easier or harder time succeeding th had she not been linked with Norman?

6. Their age difference didn't seem to be an issue between Norman and Norris for quite a long time, but it made their life hard in later years. In what ways did their age gap bolster their relationship and in what ways did it put a strain on it? What roles do age and life experience play in relationships, especially marriage?

7. Knowing Norman's history and reputation as a womanizer, should Norris have been more guarded? Why or why not?

8. The role of a stepparent is difficult, for many reasons. Why do you think Norris had such a good relationship with the children? How does the definition of what it means to be a mother or father extend beyond shared DNA?

9. At one point, after Norris discovered the extent of Norman's infidelities, she describes herself as having taken a step away from him in her heart. Is it necessary to do that if you want to protect yourself? Can you ever take that step back again and have a relationship as close as it was? If not, what kind of relationship is possible? How do you move on?

10. Discuss how you viewed Norman Mailer before reading *A Ticket to the Circus,* as well as after reading it. Did Norris's intimate, private account of life with a very public man change your opinion of him? Are we ultimately better defined not by what we do but by the people we love—or more important, those who love us back?

PHOTO: © CHRISTINA PABST

NORRIS CHURCH MAILER was the author of two novels, *Windchill Summer* and *Cheap Diamonds*. She also was the mother of two sons, two stepsons, and five stepdaughters, as well as grandmother to two and stepgrandmother to nine. Mailer died in 2010 at the age of sixty-one.